STAND UP!

How to Get Involved, Speak Out, and Win in a World on Fire

Gordon Whitman

BK

Berrett–Koehler Publishers, Inc.
www.bkconnection.com

Berrett-Koehler Publishers, Inc.
1333 Broadway, Suite 1000
Oakland, CA 94612-1921
Tel: (510) 817-2277   Fax: (510) 817-2278   www.bkconnection.com

Ordering Information
Quantity sales. Special discounts are available on quantity purchases by corporations, associations, and others. For details, contact the "Special Sales Department" at the Berrett-Koehler address above.

Individual sales. Berrett-Koehler publications are available through most bookstores. They can also be ordered directly from Berrett-Koehler: Tel: (800) 929-2929; Fax: (802) 864-7626; www.bkconnection.com

Orders for college textbook/course adoption use. Please contact Berrett-Koehler: Tel: (800) 929-2929; Fax: (802) 864-7626.

Distributed to the U.S. trade and internationally by Penguin Random House Publisher Services.

Berrett-Koehler and the BK logo are registered trademarks of Berrett-Koehler Publishers, Inc.

Printed in the United States of America

Berrett-Koehler books are printed on long-lasting acid-free paper. When it is available, we choose paper that has been manufactured by environmentally responsible processes. These may include using trees grown in sustainable forests, incorporating recycled paper, minimizing chlorine in bleaching, or recycling the energy produced at the paper mill.

Library of Congress Cataloging-in-Publication Data
Names: Whitman, Gordon, author.
Title: Stand up! : how to get involved, speak out, and win in a world on fire / Gordon Whitman.
Description: First Edition. | Oakland : Berrett-Koehler Publishers, 2018.
Identifiers: LCCN 2017042701 | ISBN 9781523094165 (paperback)
Subjects: LCSH: Social justice. | Social action--Handbooks, manuals, etc.|
BISAC: POLITICAL SCIENCE / Political Process / Political Advocacy. |
SELF-HELP / Motivational & Inspirational. | POLITICAL SCIENCE / Civics & Citizenship.
Classification: LCC HM671 .W485 2018 | DDC 303.48/4—dc23
LC record available at https://lccn.loc.gov/2017042701

Book design & composition: Beverly Butterfield, Girl of the West Productions
Book editor: PeopleSpeak
Book cover designer: The Book Designers
Book cover photo: Heather Wilson

FIRST EDITION
23 22 21 20 19 18   10 9 8 7 6 5 4 3 2 1

Praise for *Stand Up!*

"*Stand Up!* is full of good sense about how people with the most on the line can use their leverage to create change."
—**Carlos Saavedra Diaz, cofounder of Movimiento Cosecha and Lead Trainer, Ayni Institute**

"Gordon Whitman has done what organizers almost never do: turned his years of practice into a valuable resource for engagement, learning, and action."
—**Marshall Ganz, Senior Lecturer in Public Policy, Kennedy School of Government**

"'Who belongs?' is the most important question of our time. Adopting this as a challenge, *Stand Up!* charts a way toward a more inclusive society through five necessary conversations. Part organizing strategy, part research, part biography, and part history lesson, *Stand Up!* is an important guide for our troubled times."
—**Professor john a. powell, University of California, Berkeley, Director, Haas Institute for a Fair and Inclusive Society**

"*Stand Up!* presents a framework for change that is both practical and inspiring. Group-based, grassroots organizing is the most powerful way you can effect change, and Whitman provides a clear description and explanation of the organizing tools you need to stand up with others in your community."
—**Ezra Levin, Co-Executive Director, Indivisible**

"*Stand Up!* is a terrific guide for those who want to make this a more just world."
—**Heather Booth, organizer and founder of Midwest Academy**

"Upset about the state of the world? Unsure what you can do about it? Read this book! You will be a changed person and more prepared than ever to help change the world."
—**George Goehl, Codirector, People's Action**

"Whitman's book is a must-read antidote for anyone who is struggling to understand how to live a life of purpose or anyone who feels the calling but is not sure what to do."
—**Professor Hahrie Han, University of California, Santa Barbara**

"We need to bring everything we know about people-led social change to the table—that's why *Stand Up!* is such an important book for this moment. It is a must-read for organizers working to develop leaders, build multiracial teams, and win campaigns."

—Saru Jayaraman, cofounder of Restaurant Opportunities Centers United and Director, Food Labor Research Center, University of California, Berkeley

"If you believe now is the time to resist, then this book about organizing and building lasting power is for you. *Stand Up!* links our work across the issues of racism, economic inequality, and climate change. It gives me hope and the tools to build a society in which everyone belongs and can thrive."

—Lindsey Allen, Executive Director, Rainforest Action Network

"Equal parts how-to and inspiration, *Stand Up!* shows how to build democratic multiracial organizations that are both humane and effective."

—Scott Reed, Executive Director, Faith in Action

"Gordon Whitman has given a gift to all of us who yearn to bring people together across lines of difference to redeem the soul of our nation. *Stand Up!* offers both a sacred call to action and a path forward."

—Rabbi Jonah Dov Pesner, Director, Religious Action Center of Reform Judaism

"For those interested in fighting for the social justice so desperately needed in our world today, *Stand Up!* teaches how to build power to make impactful change, combining examples of successful organizing efforts, specific steps to developing power, and a compassionate reflection on the real challenges to social change work."

—Professor Paul Speer, Vanderbilt University

CONTENTS

PREFACE

I started writing *Stand Up!* before the fateful 2016 election. I wanted to boil down what I've learned about social change from working as a community organizer for over twenty-five years. I wanted to explain *how to* make a difference in a system that seems to be stacked against us and *why to* dedicate your life to social change. This preface explains why I wrote the book and some of the experience on which it's based.

Opening Our Hearts

Chances are, we don't know each other. I don't know how you've decided to live your life, your hopes and dreams, or the suffering you've experienced. But we're in the same boat. I have a stake in whether you decide to get involved and speak out. Whether we're awake to it or not, we're facing off together against the same wealthy families and large corporations that have too much influence over our lives. Too often, their interests are to remove as much oil and gas from the ground, automate as much work to reduce labor costs, and divide us as much as necessary to hold on to their power. We cannot trust good intentions or our democratic institutions to protect us. All we have to fall back on is each other and our capacity to work together to create a better society. That rests not on technology or brainpower but on our ability to see each other as brothers and sisters, even if we've never met: to love others as we love ourselves.

I felt this sense of human kinship and interdependence on February 6, 2017, as I stood with 150 people gathered in Phoenix to pray for Guadalupe Garcia de Rayos as she said good-bye to her two children and entered a federal immigration building. The next day she was deported to a country she had left twenty-one years before at age fourteen. The photo of Guadalupe's distraught face as she looked through the grated window of a van taking her away was haunting. It reminded me of how I felt watching Tajai Rice being handcuffed and locked in the back of a squad car while her brother bled to death in a Cleveland park where he'd gone to play and hearing Sandra Bland being told by a White Texas State Trooper that he'd "light her up" for asking why she'd been stopped.

Whether we see this pain in person or on social media, it can break our hearts—if we crack them open wide enough. We're programmed to resist oppression—our own and that of those we love. It makes us angry to see another person treated as less than human. We know that our humanity doesn't flow from the lightness or darkness of our skin, the ID in our pocket, or the money in our paycheck. When we feel injustice, it provokes an instinct to fight back, to resist. Still, we wonder whether anything can be done. After we react to a Facebook post or repeat a hashtag, what comes next? How do we convert our anger and frustration into action that makes a difference, especially if the system seems rigged?

We know that our humanity doesn't flow from the lightness or darkness of our skin, the ID in our pocket, or the money in our paycheck.

For the past two decades, I've had a job teaching and agitating people to come together to improve their communities and the country. I've helped build some of the most effective grassroots organizations in the United States. The organization I work for—Faith in Action (formerly PICO National Network)—equips tens of thousands of people every year with tools to fight racial and economic injustice. We teach the art and science of community organizing—the steps a person can take to become a leader for change. We show people how to put the values they care most about into action. The multiracial, people-led organizations in our network have won hundreds of victories, including raising wages, expanding access to high-quality affordable health care, reforming sentencing laws, and reducing gun violence—creating better lives for millions of people.

Since 2008 (in the shadow of the financial crisis), we've seen more people showing up at meetings wanting to tackle bigger issues and take greater risks. In August 2013, fifteen men and women spent twenty-one days walking through the blazing heat of the Central Valley in California to build support for immigration reform. Their pilgrimage for citizenship began with a Catholic mass in Sacramento. It ended 285 miles later with a three-thousand-person rally in Bakersfield (from which the cover image is taken). It followed (in reverse) the route Cesar Chavez took on the historic 1965 farmworkers' march. More than eighteen thousand people participated in the events along the way. Thousands more walked in pilgrimages in other states. The willingness of people to walk for weeks and the scale of the response surprised some people. But I see it as a sign that people are growing more committed to fighting for social justice.

We're all impacted by the overlapping crises facing our society, but the shock waves hit some people before others. Those who experience injustice most directly are often acting first and taking the greatest risks. They're putting their bodies on the line to show that there is a better path forward. This is what a small group of young people did when they took to the streets of Ferguson to protest Michael Brown's killing, chanting "We're young, we're strong, we're marching all night long." Many met for the first time watching as Michael lay bleeding in the street. They faced down military weapons, tanks, and tear gas and relentlessly told the Ferguson story through social media. Their courage created a moral crisis—a moment of truth—that has rippled through every community in the United States.

Since the 2016 election, people from all walks of life have come together to resist Trump administration policies targeting and scapegoating immigrants, Muslims, people of color, the LGBTQ community, and women. Black Lives Matter activists and faith leaders have ramped up efforts to end cash bail and elect responsible prosecutors who will stop trying children as adults and reduce the number of people behind bars. Low-wage workers have continued to press for higher wages and a union through Fight for $15. Dreamers have been organizing to keep their legal status and protect their parents from deportation. These, and hundreds of other grassroots campaigns that have gotten less notice, give us a glimpse of what's possible when people organize.

But even when you combine all the social justice organizing taking place across different networks, issues, and movements in the United States, it doesn't match the forces we're up against. Our opponents are on the wrong side of history and humanity. But they have enormous resources. They have a web of institutions that stretches from think tanks, super PACs, and lobbyists in Washington, DC, to radio and television stations and activist groups in every state. The richest families in America have made government more responsive to money than people. To counterbalance their influence, *we the people* need to create a level of sustained mobilization, disruption, and grassroots political influence not seen on the side of social justice in the country since the 1960s. That's why I wrote *Stand Up!*

My Story

I learned the most important lessons about organizing from women and men who'd spent their lives fighting the dictatorship of Augusto Pinochet in Chile. In 1990, during the transition from the dictatorship to an elected government in Chile,

I lived with my wife, Julia Paley, in a neighborhood with dirt streets and hand-built houses on the outskirts of Santiago, the country's capital. I spent my days working with a grassroots health collective that had been organizing for years to resist and defeat Pinochet. It was sobering to realize that during those years, the decision to go to a meeting meant risking being tortured or killed. You might not know people's real names at these meetings (many used pseudonyms to protect themselves and others), but you'd better know them well enough to trust them with your life. The last thing you wanted was to rely on good intentions or go into battle alongside people without having deep relationships with them. I watched how seasoned leaders brought new people in by valuing their knowledge and experience, and how they worked with people under intense stress to form groups that took concrete action in the community. I learned how clarifying it is to know exactly who your opponent is and understand that you're in a life-and-death struggle. I came back to the United States clear about how important it is for all of us to have organizations that we control and can use both to protect ourselves and our families and to reshape society.

My path into a life of social change had been shaped by two ideas that my parents taught me when I was young. The first was a Holocaust lesson that you needed power to survive. If you were powerless, then people who hated you could kill you and your family and destroy your culture. The second was that each of us is created in God's image, so you treat people with respect whatever their race, religion, gender, or background.

My mother told me stories about growing up in Mattapan, a neighborhood in Boston. I was struck by the idea that you could walk to the grocery store, see neighbors along the way, and if you didn't have enough money, get what you needed on credit. It may have been an idealized view; still, it seemed so different from the anonymous suburban life we had. I could feel my mother's sadness at losing that sense of community.

She and my father explained what happened to her neighborhood in a way that pointed toward actions taken by powerful institutions. They said that Brahmin (White Protestant elite) bankers held deposits from Irish families who didn't want Black people living in their neighborhoods. So the bankers drew a red line on a map around Mattapan and other neighborhoods where Jews and Blacks lived. They said that these were the only neighborhoods in which Black families could borrow money to buy homes in. This redlining kept White ethnic neighborhoods and suburbs White. Jewish homeowners were not allowed to sell their homes directly to Black families. They had to go through middlemen. Banks and real estate speculators were able to profit off this scheme through blockbusting. They would scare Jewish families into selling at firesale prices and then resell the same homes over and over—at inflated prices. The loans were federally insured, so bankers and real estate agents made more money when homes were foreclosed and then resold.

The story my parents told me about Mattapan fed into the larger narrative of what could happen if you didn't have power or were despised. When I moved to Philadelphia in 1982 for college, I didn't fully understand redlining and blockbusting in Mattapan or the fires in Boston and fights over school busing that I'd watched on the news growing up. But I had an orientation toward the world.

In Philadelphia, during the deep Reagan recession, I saw a lot of people living on the streets and thousands of abandoned houses. That contradiction conflicted with what I'd been taught about valuing people and about problems being solvable. As a freshman, I led my first organizing campaign (Students for a Sensible Calendar) to persuade the university to change the school calendar so that the first day of classes wouldn't fall on the Jewish high holiday of Rosh Hashanah. Later, Desmond Tutu visited campus, and a good friend and I started Jewish Students

Against Apartheid. We joined a twenty-day sleep-in outside the college president's office to press the university to sell stock in companies doing business with South Africa. From the mundane to the global, these experiences helped me overcome shyness, which had made me want to hide in the back of classrooms in high school. Campus organizing gave me a taste of what it felt like to operate with other people in the world. But it also left me wondering how it was that we could fight small wrongs against my own community and great ones a world away but do nothing about the apartheid that defined the city I lived in.

After college, I worked for a network of community organizations that developed housing and employment in Philadelphia neighborhoods. During my job interview, I heard the word *organizer* connected to paid work for the first time. I learned to analyze data showing mortgage lending discrimination and organize community groups into antiredlining coalitions. We won lending agreements with banks worth millions of dollars. At the time, I didn't connect the work I was doing to the stories I'd grown up with. But looking back, I can see that I found purpose in doing something about the redlining and blockbusting that had destroyed my mother's neighborhood. It was the first time I had a glimpse of what being powerful felt like.

When I was first learning to be an organizer, one of the people I worked for, who was African American, helped me see how much privilege I had walking into a room as a White man, how my race and gender shaped people's willingness to respect what I had to say. But I was also told by others that if you were bringing people together across racial lines to make changes on issues that affected their families and communities—like affordable housing, better schools, and safer streets—you didn't need to spend a lot of time talking explicitly about race. Other organizations could focus on intergroup dialogue. We were uniting people from different races to make changes that they could see in their lives.

The underlying anxiety about focusing on race and racism was that it would make it harder to hold multiracial groups together. Then, as now, many White-led organizations that see themselves as progressive emphasize class over race. They believe that this will keep working-class Whites in the fold. But, something else is going on in this thinking. Looking back, I'm sure that I felt emotional satisfaction in being a White person who was able to bring people together across race to make changes in the community, without having to talk about race or my own privilege. And that made me miss something larger and more important that was happening in my own identity and in the groups and communities I was working with.

For several years, I worked as an organizer with a trilingual Catholic parish in a working-class Philadelphia neighborhood that had been devastated by the collapse of the textile industry. When we started organizing, White, Latino, and Vietnamese leaders in the church met separately to talk about community issues. The Spanish-language meetings attracted the most people, and while the neighborhood problems that people raised in them were similar to those raised by White and Vietnamese parishioners, we also heard many stories of people having felt like second-class citizens when they first began attending church. In the White meetings, people expressed thinly veiled racial anxiety and anger about losing control of their neighborhood. In the Vietnamese meetings, parents worried about losing their children to what they saw as an American urban culture of drugs and gangs. The separate meetings created space for people to talk honestly and find their voice. But when we brought people together, we skipped over the racial subtext in each set of meetings and went straight to the neighborhood issues that people shared in common.

At the first big public meeting we held with city officials— focused on abandoned homes on one of the streets facing the church and car break-ins during services—we translated what was being said in English into Vietnamese and Spanish. Near the beginning of the meeting, a man sitting in the pew in front of me shouted, "My brother died in Vietnam; I'm not going to put up with this crap" and then walked out. Ideas about race were on everyone's minds. But I wasn't equipped to go beyond the edges of a real discussion about how race was playing out in the parish and neighborhood—and in people's hearts. And I wasn't sure that was my job.

In hindsight, I can see that our inability to create space for a direct conversation about racism and racial anxiety—felt but not always spoken—made it harder to unify the parish. It limited what we were able to accomplish. We had a tactical alliance among Anglo, Latino, and some Vietnamese members focused on vacant houses and drug corners. But we weren't able to directly confront how city officials were pitting neighborhoods and racial groups against one another for scarce resources. We focused on symptoms, not causes. Not having the language and space to talk frankly about race and racism held us back from confronting how the neighborhood was being abandoned—so that it could eventually be redeveloped for the benefit of an entirely different set of White people, who had money and time to burn.

My ability to choose whether or not to talk about race and racism was part of the privilege attached to being White in American society. This privilege is toxic to making progress on social justice. Talking explicitly about people's experience with racism and privilege may mean harder conversations. But it increases the chances that people will show up fully. It makes racism the responsibility of everyone, not just people of color. If we see how racism is being used to divide us and set us against each other, if we talk honestly about how it lives in our hearts, then we have a chance to build the trust needed for people to work together to create a more just and humane society.

In *Stand Up!* I discuss many of the most pressing issues facing American society and the world. Underlying all of them is a question of who belongs and whose voice counts. As Pope Francis has said, "The only future worth building includes everyone."[1] Yet every day we see more attempts to pin social problems caused by the concentration of wealth and power onto ordinary people who are trying to make their way in the world—targeting our brothers and sisters for blame simply because of their race, religion, and gender. To build a better world we need to construct a movement that makes space for everyone's suffering and hopes, regardless of background, while also acknowledging the specific trauma and pain caused by racial, gender, and other forms of discrimination and exclusion that plague our society.

The underlying message of this book is that each of us matters. Our opinions need to be heard—and can be heard, but only if we stop watching from the sidelines, open our hearts wider, stand up, come together, and get organized. I hope that *Stand Up!* can serve as a useful tool for people (and ideally, groups of people) to reflect on their place in the process of social change. As chapter 5 argues, reading and reflecting on books, articles, and other writings can be a useful part of a process of collective action. At the same time, it is important to underline that the ideas and advice in this book are a shadow of the actual experience of fighting for justice in the world. We learn organizing by doing it, and everything we know about organizing is the fruit of those who've had the courage to stand up and wrestle a better world into existence.

INTRODUCTION

A Survival Guide

Each of us faces a moment of truth when we have a chance to take a risk for something larger than ourselves. Sometimes the knock at our door asking us to stand up, get involved, speak out, take leadership, do *something* is so faint we miss it. Other times we hear the knock but aren't sure how to respond. Is it really for me? Am I the right person? Won't someone else step forward?

Stand Up! is a guide to answering the knock at your door asking you to join other people to change the world. It's about finding your life's purpose in social change. The principles and practices in the book will help you solve local problems in your community and participate in confronting the greatest challenges facing our society. *Stand Up!* explains what each of us needs to know—and be able to do—to survive and thrive in a world that feels like it's spinning out of control. This introduction condenses the main points of the book, beginning with a story that illustrates the connection between standing up and survival.

The knock at Mario Sepulveda's door was unmistakable. It came as a deafening explosion of falling rocks. On August 5, 2010, Mario was operating a front-end loader, deep in a one-hundred-year-old copper mine in Northern Chile. After years of neglect—which had led to scores of workers losing limbs and lives—the mine finally collapsed, trapping Mario and thirty-two other miners two thousand feet underground.

In the minutes that followed the collapse, some men ran to a small reinforced shelter near the bottom of the mine. Without thinking ahead, they broke into an emergency food supply cabinet and began eating the meager supply of food meant to keep two dozen miners fed for just two days. Other miners went searching for their comrades. Once the mine settled, a small group, including Mario, explored narrow passageways looking fruitlessly for a way out. The shift supervisor took off his white hard hat and told the others that he was no longer their boss. Now they were all in charge.

Amid the fear and confusion, Mario began organizing the other miners. He'd seen the massive slab of rock blocking their escape. Later, he told Héctor Tobar, author of *Deep Down Dark: The Untold Stories of 33 Men Buried in a Chilean Mine, and the Miracle That Set Them Free*, "At that moment I put death in my head and decided I would live with it."[1] Mario told the men (women weren't allowed to work in the mine) that they might be underground for weeks. They needed to ration their cookies and condensed milk. Once they accounted for all thirty-three miners, he reminded them that that number was the age at which Jesus was crucified, a sign that they were meant to live. He encouraged them to organize daily prayer meetings, which brought the men closer and helped them overcome the frictions of being buried alive with little hope of rescue.

Mario was not alone in taking leadership. One of the most important actions that he and the shift supervisor took was to give every man a role—from setting up lighting to mimic day and night, to carting water and caring for the sick. The men organized daily meetings where they debated and voted on life-and-death decisions about rationing their food and organizing their living space. Above ground, their mothers, sisters and wives organized to put pressure on the Chilean government, which dragged its feet before mounting a full-scale rescue. The miners' survival was a team effort.

Yet Mario's decision to stand up on the first day likely saved his own and the other men's lives. By carefully rationing their meager supply of food, they were able to survive for weeks on daily crumbs. As important, by organizing themselves, they preserved their humanity. They sustained the belief that they would ultimately escape their underground tomb. When some men gave up hope, others pushed them to keep fighting to stay alive.

Few of us will experience the extreme deprivation faced by the Chilean miners during their sixty-nine days underground. Yet the challenges they overcame—finding a way to share scarce resources, keeping hope alive despite repeated setbacks, not lashing out at the people around them—are similar to those we grapple with in our own lives. And, like the miners, we all ultimately depend on one another for our survival.

Humans can be shortsighted and cruel. Like the men who ripped open packets of cookies they'd need for weeks, we act without thinking through the consequences. We put the mighty dollar above the value of human life—allowing people to work in a death trap to keep profits flowing. We allow problems to fester, prejudice to divide us from people whose fate we share. Yet at our best we're social beings wired to work together to solve problems. We feel in our bones the need to look out for one another. As Pope Francis has said, "For all our limitations, gestures of generosity, solidarity and care cannot but well up within us, since we were made for love."[2]

Martin Luther King, Jr. captured this tension in our humanity in his sermon on Luke 11:5–13. A man knocks at his neighbor's door at midnight asking for three loaves of bread. The man wants the bread to feed a hungry traveler who's arrived at his home. The neighbor with the bread says, "The door is already locked, and my children and I are in bed. I can't get up and give you anything (Luke 11:7)." When it's clear that the man seeking the bread won't stop knocking, the neighbor relents. King says that midnight is a time of despair. The traveler is seeking not just the sustenance of bread but the hope that dawn will come.[3] Like us, the characters in the parable are interdependent. But they must still choose whether to respond or to retreat. The hungry traveler brings to the surface a battle between selfishness and solidarity, which simmers inside all our hearts and comes to a boil at moments of crisis.

A Guide to Surviving a World on Fire

Today, in one way or another, our lives are being made less secure by three interconnected crises—growing economic inequality, hardening racism, and accelerating climate change. These are the equivalent of the falling rocks and darkness that put the Chilean miners to the test. Like the mine collapse, the changes that are pulling our society and planet apart are not simply the result of unfortunate accidents. They flow from decades of disinvestment from people and communities. They are the result of intentional political decisions that have pitted us against each other and concentrated wealth and power in the hands of a small number of people at the expense of our safety and well-being.

Just as the miners had to face the reality that there was no simple way out of the mine (one of the many safety violations found was the lack of ladders for miners to climb up ventilation shafts), we need to recognize that conditions are not going to get better by themselves. No one is coming to save us. There'll be no hero on a white horse. There is no app, no high-tech solution. All we have to fall back on is one another, our human capacity to organize

All we have to fall back on is one another, our human capacity to organize ourselves to create a better society.

ourselves to create a better society. As with Mario Sepulveda and the three men in the parable, the first choice that each of us must make at this moment of truth is whether to engage in the world or retreat into our private lives. On this question hinges the quality of our lives and the future of humanity.

In their book *Hillbilly Nationalists, Urban Race Rebels, and Black Power: Community Organizing in Radical Times*, Amy Sonnie and James Tracy tell a story about Jean Tepperman, who at eighteen years old attended the famous 1963 March on Washington for Jobs and Freedom. Years later—after a lifetime spent organizing—Jean remembered that she hesitated for a moment when a speaker asked people to take a step forward if they were willing to commit their lives to the struggle for racial justice. "Could she really make that promise? She recall[ed] the color and texture of the pavement under her feet as she paused, then stepped forward."[4]

Stepping into social change—for a moment or a lifetime—is never simple. It's hard to give up on the idea that we can take care of things by ourselves, without making waves or being vulnerable to other people. Many of us, especially men, have been taught that living a good life means being self-sufficient, that we should aim for control and accept our fate. But if we're smart, we learn to depend on other people—not just family and friends but strangers. We grow as humans by trusting others and feeling the love that follows. We're like a driver stuck on the median as cars whiz by. We must put our life in other people's hands to make our way forward in the world. That's why Mario had to face his own mortality and dependence on his brother miners before he could lead.

Once we decide to stand up and speak out, we're entering a world of wolves, of powerful forces that want us to keep quiet or disappear. They will not give up their privilege without a fight. We need to bring all the wisdom we have about how to make change. We cannot rely on good intentions or use Band-Aids to

We cannot rely on good intentions or use Band-Aids to treat the symptoms but not the sickness.

treat the symptoms but not the sickness. We need to bring people who are on the sidelines into public life so we have enough people power to win. We need organizations and movements with leverage to negotiate changes in the laws and policies that shape our lives. We need to be able to govern the communities, states, and countries in which we live. That political work can be aided by technology. But it succeeds only if it's rooted in the kind of face-to-face relationships that have sustained every social movement in history.

The primary point of this book is that we have all the power we need to create a just and fair society. People who profit off misery tell us to suck it up: *"This is just the way it is. You can't fight city hall. Your voice is irrelevant."* What those in power are telling us is a lie, no truer than the idea that some people are worth more than others. There is almost nothing we cannot change—*if* we choose to get involved, if we open our hearts to others, if we see that this isn't about helping another person but about our own liberation, if we don't try to do it alone, if we learn from those who've risked their lives to fight oppression, if we have the courage to confront people in power even when we're uncertain or scared.

Beyond Cynicism

To shift the balance of power in our society, many more people need to let go of the idea that nothing can be done or that they have nothing to offer. When we hesitate to engage in politics as more than dissatisfied voters, we end up handing our power to those who are already powerful. We live in a society that tells us that we're on our own, even as a small number of corporate executives exercise outsized control over our lives. Over the past forty years, the people who run the largest companies in the world have succeeded in depressing wages for most workers, increasing profits, and shrinking government as a safety net in hard times. These changes have caused great suffering and shorter life spans.[5] They've also cut us adrift from each other. We distrust not only big institutions but also one another and ourselves. We seek community but doubt it exists. We want our voices to be heard but question if anything can change. We hear how money has corrupted politics, but that just reinforces our disgust with the system.

I wrote this book as a tool to help interrupt this cycle of cynicism. I want to demystify social change so that we see it as something that we're all meant to do as humans. We have to view our engagement with the world—with all its problems—as how we live out our purpose in life. When we organize, we act as our best selves. We experience being an agent of change rather than an object of someone else's imagination. We overcome division and despair. We solve problems that need not exist. This is about more than just being good people. It's about our survival. In a society where wealth is ever more concentrated and the planet is at risk, opting out is not an option. If we don't act now, our lives and those of our children and their children will be immeasurably diminished. It will become increasingly hard to afford higher education, find stable work, and walk the streets without fear of violence.

Ella Baker—the organizing conscience of the civil rights movement—said about her work. "My basic sense of it has always been to get people to understand that in the long run they themselves are the only protection they have against violence and injustice." That means nurturing people's capacity to lead their own organizations. As she said, "Strong people do not need strong leaders."[6]

Stand Up! offers a tested step-by-step framework for becoming an effective social-change leader and building better organizations. It's designed to motivate more people to dive in and take greater risks. It's a call to experience the power and purpose that comes from joining other people to create a world in which we can all belong and thrive. If you are already involved in social change, the book is meant to help deepen your commitment—to answer the question, How do I make a life out of this justice work and bring others with me?

Five Conversations That Can Change the World— and Our Lives

Stand Up! is structured around five conversations that can help people build and lead powerful organizations. Our capacity to talk with one another is the most reliable tool we have for changing the world. We all know the

> Our capacity to talk with one another is the most reliable tool we have for changing the world.

difference between a lecture and a conversation. When we talk *at* people rather than *with* them, most people will take a pass. Some may show up again or respond to the action we asked them to take, but their commitment is unlikely to grow. Any results will probably be short-lived. We need to engage in dialogue with people if we want to see them develop into leaders or to build organizations that can persist against powerful foes.

Conversations take time and can be difficult. They're powerful because they create a "pool of shared meaning" that makes it possible for people to think together.[7] The choices we make about strategy and tactics are better when they stem from dialogue. People feel a sense of ownership and responsibility for them. Social change boils down to building durable human relationships that make it possible for large numbers of people to act with power and purpose—which is why *Stand Up!* is structured around conversations.

First Conversation: Purpose—Preparing Emotionally for the Fight of Your Life

The first conversation is with our own hearts to reflect on our *purpose* in the world. Why am I here on this earth? And what will I leave behind? For many of us, this is a conversation we have with God: What do you ask of me? What lessons should I take from the suffering and grace that I've experienced in my life? For others, this conversation is about wrestling with the meaning of our lives and the difference we want to make in the world.

The starting place for all social change is internal transformation. The process of opening our life up to the world—of finding our place in a larger movement for change—is mysterious. It requires shedding layers of stories we were told growing up about how we're supposed to behave and what our proper place is in society based on our gender, skin color, religion, sexual orientation, or nationality. We realize the truth of what is happening in the world and what is expected of us in fits and starts. We have an experience that causes us pain or embarrassment. We feel a sense of personal power that we don't want to go away. We hear something from someone we love or respect that captures our imagination. Someone pushes us to stand up for something. We react emotionally to a situation and find ourselves involved in a fight that we thought had nothing to do with us.

Oppression persists because people who benefit from it are willing to fight so hard to keep their privileged position in an unjust order. Organizing against injustice requires emotional strength to steel us for a long road filled with disappointment and delay. We need to be clear about what we value enough to struggle for. Commitment that comes from clarity of purpose is the most powerful resource we have against determined enemies. Nelson Mandela brought tears to our eyes when he walked out of prison in 1990 after twenty-seven years, on his own two feet. We witnessed a man who had the fortitude to never give in and never give up. When we're clear about our purpose, and who stands behind us, there is almost nothing we cannot accomplish. We're ready to build a movement.

Second Conversation: Story—Building Relationships That Move People to Action

The next step, the second conversation, is sharing our *story* with another person and hearing his or hers. Stories are the basic building block of social change. Our stories capture the unique set of experiences, people, and beliefs that have shaped our lives. They're how we explain our values and emotional commitments to other people—and how we connect our lives to theirs and to history. When I hear your story, I see you. When we find something in common in our stories—which we always do, no matter how different we may seem—it creates the emotional connection we need to begin walking together on a path to justice.

Because stories are how we make sense of the world, they're the best way to persuade people to look at things differently. We read a book or hear a speech, and years later the one thing we remember is the nugget of a story. People who take time to reflect on the experiences that have shaped their lives and crystalize those experiences into emotionally powerful stories are able to persuade and motivate people to do almost anything. Fr. Jesus Nieto, a Catholic priest in Oakland and a clergy leader in Faith in Action, tells of coming from Mexico to the United States packed tightly with two other people in the trunk of a car. He emigrated in order to reunite with his father. That image of a boy, who would grow up to be a parish priest, struggling to breathe in a car trunk is powerful. It puts us in an emotional space, and tells us what we need to know, to engage in a serious conversation about making US immigration policy more humane.

Third Conversation: Team—Finding a Home Base in a Movement for Change

The third conversation is with a *team* of sisters and brothers we can work with to change the world. Social change is a team sport, carried out alongside people whom we trust with our lives. The best way to stay on the wagon of justice is to be part of a group that meets regularly. What we can get done in the world, and the personal transformation we experience along the way, hinges on the quality of the conversations we have with people we're working with daily to create change. Small groups that build trust and a shared focus have driven social change through history. They make it possible for people to sit down at segregated lunch counters and occupy policed streets with impunity and refuse to be moved. In contrast, large organizations without smaller spaces tend to treat people as cogs working in a larger wheel rather than agents of social change.

It takes hard work and honesty to make social justice teams work. Small groups succeed when they create shared norms, build trust through frank conversations, adopt ambitious goals, create clear roles for people, and make important decisions together. With these ingredients, it's possible to organize large numbers of teams that can function effectively without depending on lots of paid staff. Within groups, people can follow a process of sharing stories, reflecting on text, and acting together that helps teams both get things done and be transformative for their members.

Fourth Conversation: Base—Recruiting a Following You Need to Lead

The fourth conversation is with a *base* of people—in schools, neighborhoods, congregations, workplaces, and social networks—who make us leaders and hold us accountable.

Millions of people are waiting to be invited to create a better world. I began this book by saying that each of us has to make a deeply personal decision about whether, and how, to engage in the world. I used the image of a knock at our door as a metaphor for that choice of whether to stand up or pull back in a crisis. If you're this far into *Stand Up!* I want to be clear that it's not enough to answer the door; you need to go out and knock on another person's door. When we decide to engage in social change, we're saying yes to the messy work of organizing other people. To go back to King's sermon, the protagonist in Luke 11:5–13 is neither the midnight traveler nor the reluctant neighbor. It's the person courageous enough to knock on another person's door at midnight and ask for social sustenance. It doesn't matter if no one answers or if the door gets slammed in our face. The question is whether we have the fortitude—like Nelson Mandela—to keep going until we find someone willing to join in.

The key variable in the mathematics of social change is the number of people we invite to participate. When people are asked to volunteer or contribute to a cause by a friend or neighbor, they tend to respond at surprisingly high rates. When I hear people explain how they first got involved in an organization, they almost always begin their story with someone they knew, or a person sent by someone they knew, coming to talk to them. It seems too simple, but the surest way to get people off the sidelines and into the fray is to ask them directly, especially if the person doing the asking is known to them. Flyers and Facebook posts don't cut it. People need to hear that someone they trust wants them at the table.

Fifth Conversation: Power—Winning Social Change

The fifth conversation is with the *powers that be* to unmask who is benefiting from the pain we see in the community and in society and who has the ability to relieve it and then to begin negotiating change. This conversation helps us begin to figure out how much power we need to overcome the interests that are holding injustice in place. We're talking about direct, face-to-face contact that engages our senses—allowing us to see, hear, touch, and smell the people who are making the decisions that shape our lives.

This visceral contact is not always easy to make happen (although it is often less difficult than we think), but it's essential. It gives us a taste of power. People realize their influence in the world by experiencing their ability to make change, not by being told they are powerful. Engaging with people who lead institutions and systems helps strip away the layers of deference that lead us to hand over our lives, and those of our loved ones, to people with aims other than our well-being. It also forces us to be brutally honest about how politics works.

Most people—especially those who have long experienced being told by others what to do at work and in their lives—have doubts about their power. Organizing changes that. Faith in Action has years of research showing that the more people participate in face-to-face meetings with mayors, city council members, bank executives, and other decision makers, the more they find their own voices as leaders. They are more likely to attend future meetings, accept bigger roles in organizations, and feel more of a sense of agency.[8] In contrast, when people attend a rally or big meeting, it can help an organization show its strength and get results, but it doesn't necessarily translate into their continuing to participate, chairing a meeting, or feeling like they have the ability to make changes in their community or society.

Local organizing that directly engages powerful institutions in our communities is valuable not only because it addresses some of the most important decisions that shape our lives and gives us experience with politics but also because it creates precedent and momentum for larger-scale victories. We need to build campaigns and movements from the ground up. At the base of the pyramid are local efforts through which people work together for changes that they can see and feel in their lives. At the next level are bigger campaigns to change public policies in cities or states. At the top are large-scale movements that seek to fundamentally reshape the rules and culture of the society, like abolishing slavery, ending child labor, and providing health care for all. These changes reshape the flow of the river. They can take decades and generations to make happen—but they begin with people wading into the water in their own communities.[9]

These five conversations—with yourself, other people, your team, your base, and the powers that be—will help you figure out what a larger movement for change needs from you personally. They show you how to be a leader with a following, engage other people, build and sustain organizations and movements, and take action that turns the impossible into the possible and the possible into the inevitable.

Each conversation has a different purpose. Each takes place with different people at distinct moments in a cycle of building an organization. Each involves a different emotional orientation. Together, they make it possible to spin a web of relationships strong enough to confront the people who are feeding off injustice. The five conversations—and the principles and practices embedded in them—can serve as cornerstones of a lifelong commitment to social justice.

The primary audience for *Stand Up!* is people who are frustrated by what they see happening in the world and want to get more involved in change. The book also has a message for people who lead community, labor, and other social justice organizations. It's an argument that we need to redesign the architecture of social change in the United States. The organizations that should be our tools for building better lives expect too little of us. Too often they act as if we live in a postracial society. They skate on the surface rather than engage in real talk about race, gender, class, and identity that is necessary to build trust so people can work together across differences. They ignore our spirituality and our search for purpose and belonging, mistakenly imagining that wanting more money or the stuff it buys is the only thing that motivates us. Too many organizations assume that taking "action" online or making a small donation is the most that can be asked of people facing disaster. That leaves too many of us clapping or booing from the sidelines. We need organizations that ask us to bring our whole selves to the table; that see us as ends, not means; that are organized around members searching for meaning rather than issues searching for support. With that in mind, here's how the book is organized.

Structure of the Book

Chapter 1 tells a short story that summarizes how the five-conversation framework in *Stand Up!* can be used to protect the people and things we care most about. Chapter 2 explains how inequality works; who's profiting from it; why the crises of hyperinequality, racial exclusion, and climate change matter to all our lives; and what we can do about them. This is the context of a world on fire, which makes answering the knock at the door for social change and organizing so important at this moment. Chapter 3 shows why wrestling with our purpose is a first step to becoming effective leaders for change. This chapter is designed both to help us deepen our personal commitment to social change and to build organizations around which people can build their lives. Chapter 4 is about story, how we get clear about our unique story, use storytelling to build organizations rooted in strong relationships, and organize to tell new stories that pave the way for greater racial and economic justice.

Chapter 5 focuses on finding and sustaining a team that we can work with to change the world. Chapter 6 explains the conversations we can use to build a base of people to whom we're accountable, which is the fundamental work of bringing more and more people into social change. Chapter 7 is about engaging the powers that be. It's a guide to winning fights, big and small, and building a movement to reverse the inequality and racism in American society. It includes a discussion of organizing strategy and tactics and examples of (mostly successful) campaigns. The conclusion discusses ways to apply the ideas and practices in the book to your life and work.

1
Pulling It All Together

This short chapter offers an example of how the five conversations can fit together in a tangible way to help us win change that matters for our lives.

My son has special needs. Parenting him has felt like a full-time organizing job for me and my wife, Julia. It's been a driving purpose in our lives. When Isaiah was young, we struggled to have the kind of back-and-forth conversations with him that came naturally with his twin sister. When he was eighteen months old—after being told by one of the best children's hospitals that his hearing was fine—we finally got him the right test, which showed that he was hearing impaired. Then, at age three, he was diagnosed with pervasive developmental disorder—not otherwise specified. That means being on the autism spectrum. To get him the help he needed to learn to communicate and connect, we had an endless set of fights with insurance companies, schools, and hospitals. At one point, we held a family sit-in outside of the office of the director of special education in Ann Arbor, Michigan. It's taken everything I've learned as a legal service lawyer and community organizer to raise my son.

We got a lot of help along the way. The Pennsylvania Medicaid program helped him get his first hearing aids. The Philadelphia Early Intervention system made it possible for him to attend a school for the deaf to learn to understand language and speak. Doctors and therapists taught us how to raise a child with autism. By the time Isaiah had finished elementary school and gone through many hours of therapy, he'd become a social being. He was still awkward, but he'd learned to engage with other people and show his brilliant mind and caring heart to the world. Still, we'd dreaded middle school.

What made the difference and helped him have his best school years was a special program at his neighborhood middle school. The program gave intensive support to students with autism, while making it possible for them to participate fully in regular classes. But when Isaiah was in seventh grade, he came home from school one day and told me that he'd overheard his teacher and teaching assistant talking about budget cuts to the autism program. (Despite being hearing impaired, my son has a knack for eavesdropping on other people's conversations.) He told his teacher to talk with me, saying that I was a good organizer and could help. I thanked him for the compliment but did nothing.

Although I earn a living agitating people to stand up and fight for their families and communities, I almost missed this knock at my own door. I had taken for granted that my son would get what he needed. I had tossed the invitations to special education parent meetings. I couldn't tell you who was on the school board.

A week later, another parent sent out an e-mail asking us to attend the next day's school board meeting to speak out against the budget proposal. Taking a distracted break from responding to e-mail at work, I clicked the link to the budget document, which showed the proposal to cut seven of the twelve aides in the program. That triggered the anger I feel when it seems that people who are weak or different are being picked on. But I wouldn't have given the e-mail a second look or signed up to speak if Isaiah hadn't primed me the week before—if he hadn't essentially reminded me to reflect on my purpose in life (first conversation).

The next day, I joined six other parents of children with autism at my first school board meeting in my county. Most of us met for the first time as we waited to testify. I wrote notes about what I would say and put the folded paper in my pocket. It stayed there. We listened to parents from a preschool program that was facing an increase in tuition. They had on matching T-shirts with their message and told stories about what higher costs would mean for their kids. Then the clerk said that the time for public testimony was over. Not a single one of us autism program parents had a chance to say a word.

In my first job as a community organizer, I'd spent my days talking to parents about what they hoped for their children and thought about the public schools in their neighborhood. I was in my late twenties and knew little about being a parent. Mamie Nichols, a renowned neighborhood leader in Philadelphia, told me that there were two systems you never trust your children to: the school system and the health system. You have to be vigilant with both. I didn't fully understand what she meant until I had my own children, especially one with special needs. And then I knew.

I'd learned as an organizer that it was a recipe for frustration for individual parents to speak at school board meetings. One parent after another would go up to the microphone, tell a heartbreaking story, and then be met with stone silence from the board members. Next. Next. Next. Still, years later, sitting at the school board meeting in my own town, I felt disappointed to not be able to speak about the cuts to my son's program. It felt like we'd let our kids down.

Then I heard the voice in my head that says every problem has a solution. I remembered that I was an organizer. I asked the other parents to join me in the hallway. We circled up and began a round of introductions, which included telling our stories. That story sharing (second conversation) made all the difference. One mother told about how her son had threatened to commit suicide at his old school, where he was essentially being punished for his autism. But now that he was in the autism program, he was finally doing well because of the help of aides and a teacher who understood what it meant to be on the autism spectrum. By the time we'd made it around the circle, we'd experienced emotions that began to bond us. It was clear that we had a lot in common and had a lot at stake in stopping the budget cuts.

> By the time we'd made it around the circle, we'd experienced emotions that began to bond us.

I asked people to do two things: one, come to my house the next week for a parent meeting, and two, go back into the board meeting, wait until it ended, and then ask the school board president for a meeting. During the next six weeks, eight to ten parents met weekly at our house. We became a team (third conversation). We drank together and shared stories about our children that made us cry. We put out a short report on the history of the autism program. We learned that the program existed because parents had demanded it. They'd been upset that their children were being isolated in special education classrooms, a problem that is still all too common.

Before Congress passed the Individuals with Disabilities Education Act (IDEA) in 1975, most children with disabilities were excluded from public education. They were placed in institutions or special schools, where they received little or no instruction. With the IDEA, Congress created a right to a free and appropriate public education for students with disabilities. But it provided only part of the funding. This makes special education programs a constant target of budget cuts by local school districts. Without setting out to, we joined a long history of organizing against the segregation of people with disabilities.

And we were coming up against the structural challenge of how special education is funded in the United States.

The next thing we did was to build a base (fourth conversation). We reached out to other parents, beginning with those who would be directly affected by the proposed budget cuts. Our first public action was to send a letter to the school board signed by more than half of the sixty families with children in the autism program. But we knew we needed a bigger base to win. So we started having conversations with parents of children in other special education programs. We shifted how we talked about what we wanted to make it clear that we were in solidarity with parents whose children needed different kinds of services. Later, when the fight got hotter, we organized a Change.org petition that more than a thousand people signed. Not only did the petition site send e-mails to each of the school board members every time someone signed, but the comments signers left helped us identify people who could testify at hearings. The support from neighbors—many of whom hadn't known that we had a son in special education—was moving.

We began to engage the powers that be (fifth conversation). We met multiple times with each board member and with key school district staff. After the school board president told us that she wouldn't reverse the proposed cuts, we went public. We shifted our message. We'd been making policy arguments about the program being a success that saved the district money it would otherwise have spent sending children with autism to private schools. Now we delivered a blunt message that the board was picking on children with autism. We held a rally on the school district steps. We essentially took over a school board meeting to tell our stories. And we made cuts to the autism program an issue in the school board election that was taking place at the time. We generated a lot of local media coverage, including a story on the evening news on which my son publicly "came out" as having autism.

At one point, a school board member who was on the fence called us to see if we would be open to a compromise. The group was initially split on how to respond to the offer. But the work we'd done to build trust helped us reach a group decision to keep fighting to remove all the cuts from the budget.

Later in the spring, after watching the school board vote four to one to restore the full funding, we stood together outside the school district building for nearly an hour, celebrating and telling stories. It was late, and we all had to get home to put our kids to bed, yet the pull of the community that we'd created together was strong. Six weeks before we'd been strangers; now we cared about one another. For the first time, I felt like I belonged in the place I lived. And I was glad that I was able to answer my own son's knock at the door.

Our fight to save the autism program was a small example of what people can achieve when they organize. I took for granted the education my son was receiving because I didn't understand the history of parents fighting for the program in the first place. Nor did I know about the political dynamics in the school district that put my child's education at risk. We all have fights like this that need to be waged in the communities in which we live. Our capacity to fix problems close to home is a foundation for a functioning democracy. At the same time, we're in, or need to be in, bigger battles with more entrenched and powerful interests. Whether we're trying to stop budget cuts in our communities, save the planet from ruin, or end policies that create financial incentives to put more and more people of color behind bars, we need to be clear-eyed about what we're up against and what it will take to prevail. That is what the next chapter is about.

> Our fight to save the autism program was a small example of what people can achieve when they organize.

2

A World on Fire

Understanding Who's Profiting from Injustice and What Can Be Done about It

To stop an injustice, we have to first understand who is profiting from it. Human suffering, misery, and oppression that fall systematically on people based on their class, race, gender, sexual orientation, religion, or disability are no accidents. Despite what we're often told, and perhaps want to believe, extreme social inequality happens by design. It results from conscious decisions that promote the profits, status, and power of some people over what is good and necessary for the vast majority of us.

When something is by design, it can be changed. The most important question facing any community or society is how much inequality it will tolerate. The answer is in our hands. It results from political struggle. But that struggle is never just about who gets what or who can profit from the labor of others. It comes back to whose humanity is taken for granted and who has to fight to live a dignified life. This is why coming out—asserting your humanity and forcing society to recognize it—has been part of every social struggle in history and why engaging in social change is so important to living out your purpose rather than being a pawn in someone else's imagination.

This chapter explains why racial and economic inequality is increasing, who is benefiting, and what it will take to change course. The first section of the chapter provides a simple framework for how inequality works and how it can be dismantled. The second section provides a brief overview of the historical struggle for racial and economic justice in the United States and the backlash we've experienced over the past four decades. The third section reviews the difficult moment we're in today, with inequality, racism, and climate change fueling one another. The final section discusses how we can break vicious cycles like the one we're in. The chapter provides context for the principles and practices in the rest of the book and a way of thinking that can be used to get to the root causes of injustices in our communities. A main point is that we need to be brutally honest about what we're up against but also clear about our power to create a world in which everyone is included and able to thrive.

How Inequality Works

I've found Doug Massey's book *Categorically Unequal: The American Stratification System* helpful in clarifying how inequality works and why it's so hard to fight against. Massey says that the amount and character of inequality varies across societies and human history but that it always "boils down" to two basic steps. First, societies place people into social groups based on characteristics they're either born with (e.g., skin color or sex assigned at birth) or acquire during their lives (e.g., where they live or what work they do) and rank these groups on a scale of value. These social groups and their ranking are always fundamentally arbitrary. Second, societies distribute resources, opportunities, and authority based on social categories. This process of dividing and distributing works only if enough people believe that the social groups into which they and others have been placed and ranked are natural and that inequality is a logical result of human differences.[1]

When we stop and think, we know this is not true. We know that each human is unique. We understand ethically and emotionally that people have intrinsic dignity. But seeing people as precious individuals requires energy, especially when we feel insecure or scared. Our brains are wired to cut corners. We use simple categories and stories to make sense of complex situations. Against all evidence of human variation, we take the mental shortcut of categorizing people into groups. Once we know a person's group marker—race, gender, religion, neighborhood, job—we think we have that person's story.

Our human tendency to categorize makes us easy targets for the false idea that not only are social categories real, but some groups are more worthy than others. They can be ranked. This "hierarchy of human value" is a source of much of the pain and suffering in human societies. Once a group of people's humanity is diminished or obliterated, it's possible to exploit them and deny them what they need to thrive. Genocide and slavery are the most extreme examples. The wealth of the United States was amassed from lands stolen from Native Americans and labor stolen from African slaves and their descendants. To justify this theft, the most distinguished scholars and theologians of their time spread absurd ideas about the inferiority of people based on their skin color. After slavery was abolished, White elites still needed low-wage agricultural workers to sustain their fortunes. They still wanted to keep Black and White workers from allying. They relied on the same false ideas about race to dictate where and under what circumstances African Americans could work, live, travel, and study. They even replicated a new version of slavery through convict leasing programs.

> Once a group of people's humanity is diminished or obliterated, it's possible to exploit them and deny them what they need to thrive.

A small elite gains most of the benefits from racial discrimination. As Ibram X. Kendi explains in *Stamped from the Beginning: The Definitive History of Racist Ideas in America*, racism is not the unfortunate result of backward ideas. The reverse is true. Elites produce racist ideas about human superiority and inferiority to justify racial oppression. Racism is so pernicious because it fuels a vicious cycle. When people are excluded from resources and denied a say, it reinforces the belief that they matter less. As inequality becomes more extreme or people with privilege feel more threatened, the blame on individuals for unequal social outcomes intensifies. That is why White supremacy is spreading today rather than fading away. We cannot make society more fair and equitable without defeating the idea that some people are worth more than others nor eradicate racism without changing the economic and political rules that fuel its existence.

This double work is what we mean by social change. Whether it's climate change, mass incarceration, gun violence, or the dizzying number of other issues competing for our attention, the work is the same. Organizing is always done with two hands: one focused on crushing the lie that some people are more equal than others and the other on changing the rules of society (government and corporate policies, collective bargaining agreements, legislation, and constitutions) to more equitably distribute resources and opportunities. One of the best examples we have of this kind of struggle that fused demands for dignity and economic equity was the 1968 Memphis Sanitation Strike.

I Am a Man—The Memphis Sanitation Strike

On February 1, 1968, Echol Cole and Robert Walker had finished hauling trash out of the yards of White families in East Memphis. It was raining hard, and they were riding in the back of a decrepit garbage truck when its compactor malfunctioned, crushing them to death. Ten days later, their coworkers—thirteen hundred Black sanitation workers—walked off the job to demand safe working conditions, living wages, and union recognition. While they had many grievances, their underlying demand was to be treated as human beings.[2]

The city's power structure rejected the idea that Black men, who did the dirtiest, worst-paid work, could have a union. Memphis mayor Henry Loeb refused to negotiate. The city's main newspaper stood with Mayor Loeb. It published a torrent of hateful, racist cartoons and articles against the strike. The police attacked the sanitation workers and their supporters as they marched through downtown Memphis. The police went on to lash out at the entire Black community, rampaging through Black neighborhoods, breaking into homes, and beating up anyone they caught on the streets.

The police violence turned a labor dispute into a mass movement to end White supremacy in Memphis. The sanitation workers began carrying large "I *AM* A MAN" signs. Like the message of Black Lives Matter, the signs crystalized a rebellion of the heart and feet against a lifetime of dehumanization. Clergy stepped forward to support the workers. Black women organized a boycott of downtown businesses that brought Memphis to its knees. Martin Luther King, Jr., came. The strike became a symbol of his quest to eradicate America's sin of poverty in a land of plenty.

Dr. King was murdered on day fifty-four of the strike, on his second trip to Memphis to support the strikers. The night before, he'd told the sanitation workers and their supporters, "Like anybody, I would like to live a long life. Longevity has its place. But I'm not concerned about that now. I just want to do God's will. And He's allowed me to go up to the mountain. And I've looked over. And I've seen the Promised Land. I may not get there with you. But I want you to know tonight, that we, as a people, will get to the Promised Land. And I'm happy, tonight. I'm not worried about anything. I'm not fearing any man. Mine eyes have seen the glory of the coming of the Lord."[3] Yet, even with King's blood on the hands of the city, Mayor Loeb refused to relent. It took another two weeks—and the pressure from a grief-stricken Coretta Scott King—before Memphis finally recognized the right of Black workers to have a union.

It was no accident that the sanitation workers began their strike to renegotiate their employment contract with the City of Memphis and ended up marching with I *AM* A MAN signs. Whites in Memphis referred to Black sanitation workers as buzzards. The experience of being treated as less than human was inseparable from poverty wages and life-threatening working conditions. The Memphis workers rebelled against a caste system—a false hierarchy of human value—expressly designed to maintain a large pool of low-wage Black and White workers in the South.

White Southern landowners had put in place the harshest elements of Jim Crow to keep wages low by crushing interracial organizing between White and Black farmers. As Martin Luther King, Jr., explained in his "How Long, Not Long" speech at the conclusion at the march from Selma to Montgomery in 1965, "To meet this threat, the southern aristocracy began immediately to engineer this development of a segregated society . . . direct[ing] the placement on the books of the South of laws that made it a crime for Negroes and whites to come together as equals at any level. And that did it. That crippled and eventually destroyed the Populist Movement of the nineteenth century."[4]

Ideas about the inferiority and superiority of people don't need to be written into the law to facilitate oppression. Before the sanitation strike, the City of Memphis categorized workers who hauled trash "unclassified" hourly employees without civil service protections. Unlike "classified" employees—drivers and supervisors—unclassified workers could be fired at will and weren't paid if rain prevented trash collection. Nothing in Memphis law said that Black workers had no rights, but the system was designed that way.

Today, undocumented immigrants face similar exploitation. Supposedly racially neutral laws deny immigrants—who are primarily dark-skinned men and women from Mexico and Central America, as well as Africa and Asia—legal status and employment rights. Businesses are able to extract extra profit from these workers' labor by paying them less and providing no benefits. We can see another version of exploitation in the increasing practice of police departments overarresting Blacks and Latinos for petty infractions and then sucking money out of their pockets to fund local government. This was a key grievance that fueled the uprising in Ferguson, Missouri. And it flowed directly from the successful efforts of Rex Sinquefield, a Saint Louis billionaire, to limit the ability of local governments in the state to raise funds through property taxes. We need to look beyond the official rules to the actual results. If opportunity and oppression are distributed along a color line, then we're living in a caste society—in which everyone is somewhere in a hierarchy.

White Privilege

One privilege of being White in American society is the ability to imagine that you live outside a racial hierarchy. People who are White can fall into the trap of acting as if race is just about people who are marginalized. Yet all of us are located somewhere on the scale of human value that structures society. It applies to everyone, whether you're at the bottom, middle, or top. It's important to acknowledge where you fit, especially if you're on the winning end of an uneven field. People who are able to walk into a room and be seen and respected because of what they look like carry a valuable unstated and unearned privilege with them. It takes hard, persistent work to reveal and eliminate this privilege in our organizations and society. Erroneous ideas about human value, about makers and takers, about who is lazy and who works hard, are deeply embedded not just in our culture but in our minds and relationships with one another. They create invisible walls that some people crash into while others walk through.

None of this takes away from the importance of cultural identity to our lives. The problem comes when we rank groups or imagine that social categories are immutable. Ideas about human value are fluid and shifting and can be countered. But this is some of the hardest social change work. People will fight to the death to hold on to their place within a social order, even if it is near the very bottom. Elites have long used race to divide and control working people. They've gifted poor Whites small privileges and the idea that whatever troubles they face, they can know that at least they sit higher in the pecking order than people of color. This is also why people who challenge the hierarchy, by complaining about their assigned place or by living their lives as they see fit, are so often met by violence.

How We Got Here

Opportunity Structures

When we say that people have the power to reshape society, we have plenty of historical evidence. One of the best examples is the fifty-year period that followed World War I. During these decades, labor organizing, a revolution in federal policy, economic growth, and the civil rights movement reinforced one another to drive down inequality in the United States to historic lows. This social progress flowed directly from organizing led by women and men who were fighting for their own freedom.

In *Capital in the 21st Century*, Thomas Piketty explains that the decline in economic inequality in the United States and Western Europe during this time was unprecedented. Inequality had increased steadily throughout the eighteenth and nineteenth centuries. But it shrank dramatically after World War I. Piketty says that this reversal resulted from a combination of (1) shocks caused by the two world wars and the Great Depression, which wiped out the inheritances of many wealthy families, and (2) policies that the United States and other developed countries adopted to reduce inequality. These policies were the fruit of relentless labor and civil rights organizing. They included progressive taxation, social welfare programs, collective bargaining, and massive investments in education.[5]

Yet many federal programs that helped working people raise their living standards and build wealth shortchanged African Americans. Southern states won provisions in Social Security and wage and hour laws that excluded domestic and agricultural workers, who were predominantly people of color. Federal housing programs subsidized homeownership but allowed real estate agents to keep Black families out of growing suburbs, locking them into overpriced rental housing in segregated cities. As Ta-Nehisi Coates shows in his article "The Case for Reparations," these policies haven't just disadvantaged African Americans. They've enabled White elites to generate enormous economic benefit from redlining, blockbusting, and access to low-wage labor.[6]

My family benefited from the two-tier opportunity structures created during the years before and after World War II. My grandparents came to the United States in the 1910s fleeing religious oppression in Eastern Europe. Like many Jews who immigrated during these years, they had little education and few resources. They settled near the East Coast ports through which they'd entered, happy to be safe. They had the good fortune of arriving just before anti-immigrant forces succeeded in closing the doors to America in an effort to keep the country Anglo Saxon. In the years after WWII, white-skinned Jews, Italians, and Irish were allowed to "become" White. Federal housing, highway, and education policies made it possible for them to buy homes in the suburbs, attend college, and enjoy the economic and social privileges of White identity in American society and pass into the middle class.

I first experienced the intersection of history, social class, and race while trying to make sense of the differences in how people acted in my father's family. My father was one of six children, five boys and one girl. His family ran a hat store and lost their home to foreclosure during the depression. His three oldest brothers fought in WWII and came back to working-class jobs. His sister, who was disabled, worked at the checkout counter at a bargain store late into her life. My father and his younger brother were too young to fight in WWII but the perfect age to benefit from the postwar opportunity structure. They went to college and graduate school. My father became a judge, and his brother a banker.

My parents' path into a secure middle-class life, and the doors it opened for me and my brothers, were aided by their white skin and policies that made it possible for people who came of age during this period in US history to achieve a measure of prosperity. My parents saw themselves as living in the shadow of the Holocaust. They taught my brothers and me the catastrophic consequences of not having power. They were proud when their rabbi went south to march with Dr. King. Their lived experience and the hope that they had seen in the civil rights movement gave them a belief that things would continue to get better. Racial and gender barriers would continue to fall.

But that belief in progress turned out to be wrong. For very specific historical reasons, social mobility and racial progress ground to a halt in the early 1970s. The civil rights movement dismantled the legal architecture of segregation. It seared a commitment to racial justice into the hearts of millions of people of all races. It gave us models of collective action that we still rely on today. But it left in place the economic and human consequences of centuries of exploitation and discrimination—not just the great gap in family wealth but also a series of racial fault lines running through the nation's imagination and institutions: political parties, labor unions, government agencies, advocacy organizations, and media. Those divisions opened the door for a sustained effort to roll back the social welfare, labor, and civil rights victories that had made it possible for so many Americans to achieve economic security.

Reconcentrating Wealth and Power

Seven months after the Memphis strike ended, Richard Nixon was elected president and the backlash against the civil rights movement began in earnest. Nixon, followed by Reagan and a generation of political operatives, used coded "dog-whistle" language, such as "forced busing," "tough on crime," "war on drugs," and "welfare queens" to speak to the racial anxieties of White voters.[7] They didn't just mobilize Whites to oppose racial equity. They associated most government action, from welfare to spending on education to taxes, as benefiting Blacks and Latinos over Whites. Rather than pushing back on these efforts to divide people by race, many Democratic politicians followed suit. For example, Bill Clinton used coded appeals around welfare and crime to try to hold on to White working-class voters.

The rightward shift in American politics wasn't the result of only manipulation by presidential candidates and political operatives. As Lisa McGirr shows in her book *Suburban Warriors: The Origins of the New American Right*, it was also powered by a conservative grassroots movement. This movement gained strength in booming suburbs and exurbs in the

South and West in places like Orange County, California (where McGirr's book is based). These areas had ironically grown prosperous from federal spending on highways, housing, and the Cold War defense industry. White middle-class residents found community and purpose in right-wing organizations and evangelical churches. Some people who became politically active were motivated by resentment of the growing influence of the federal government in local affairs, others by their concerns over abortion and homosexuality, and many by racial anxiety about law and order. What they coalesced around was a shared disgust toward liberalism as a threat to their way of life—a reminder that for good and bad, the most powerful movements provide not only an outlet for anger but a way of making sense of the world that gives shape to our lives.[8]

The impact that McGirr's suburban warriors had on American society was magnified by a handful of the wealthiest families and largest corporations in the United States. In 1971, Lewis Powell (whom Nixon later appointed to the Supreme Court) wrote a memo to the US Chamber of Commerce. He urged CEOs to get off the sidelines and invest their money and time in building institutions to defend the free enterprise system—which is what they did. In the years following the Powell memo, a small group of billionaires—including David and Charles Koch (oil, gas, and chemicals), Richard Mellon Scaife (banking and oil), and Joseph Coors (beer)—built a network of think tanks, policy organizations, and lobbyists, along with radio and television stations. These institutions linked grassroots activists together and connected them to ideas that would shape how millions of Americans saw the world.

The institutions created in the wake of the Powell memo advanced a generation of public policies that concentrated wealth and influence in the hands of a small number of rich people and large corporations. They cut federal tax rates for the wealthiest Americans and shrank the revenue available to government at all levels. They removed usury caps on interest rates, paving the way for an explosion in payday and other predatory lending. This sucked investments out of manufacturing and other productive activities. Trade laws, supported by both parties, allowed multinational corporations to ship investment and jobs overseas. This left a legacy of vacant factories and hollowed-out main streets across the Midwest and South.

The corporate leaders who dreamed of unlimited wealth and power played a long game. They understood that holding labor and regulatory costs down and spreading their production across the globe was sustainable only if they tilted the democratic playing field in the United States. They used the courts to eliminate almost all restrictions on spending money to influence elections. They used racial gerrymandering to pack African Americans into the smallest possible number of voting districts and voter ID laws to create a modern-day poll tax to decrease voting among people with the least resources. They gutted laws that made it possible for workers to organize, driving private-sector labor unions to the brink of extinction, and then mounted a sustained campaign to destroy public-sector unions. By 2015, the percentage of US workers able to bargain collectively—a right that Dr. King died trying to advance—had fallen from 28 percent in 1968 to just 11 percent.[9]

In 2016, the Koch brothers alone had 1,200 staff in 107 offices nationwide. They spent nearly a billion dollars yearly to advocate for low-tax, low-regulatory, antidemocracy policies that support their oil and gas investments and financial speculation.[10] Art Pope, one of the wealthiest men in North Carolina, spent tens of millions of dollars on a decade-long effort to take control of the state's legislature and governor's mansion.[11] Wealthy families and national corporate-funded political organizations have followed the same playbook in state after state. They've spent massive amounts of money on politics and created new organizations designed to shape public opinion and win elections.

They've won policy changes that limit voting, shrink taxes, and cut spending on social services and education.

Much of what we experience as unsettling in our lives— job insecurity, deeper recessions, more debt, racial tension, extreme disinvestment in some areas and rapid gentrification in others, and polarized entertainment-style politics—flows from changes won by the conservative movement over the past forty years. These changes were made to benefit a small number of extremely wealthy people. They were accomplished by making our political institutions less democratic and by changing our culture and how we see and relate to one another. As a result, today we find ourselves in a vicious cycle of rising inequality, racism, and climate change that will take extraordinary effort to reverse.

A Vicious Cycle

Economic Inequality

The United States is now the most unequal developed country in the world. Inequality is back to levels not seen in a hundred years. The top 10 percent of earners now capture more than half the income produced each year. Senior executives in US companies consume an increasingly big piece of the total salaries and wages paid by their firms. CEOs at the country's largest corporations now earn three hundred times more than their average-paid workers ($16 million compared to $53,000). The gap was just twenty to one in 1965.[12] It takes a typical CEO less than two hours to earn what his or her minimum-wage employees earn working full time for a year, less than two weeks to exceed a lifetime of work at low wages. Thomas Piketty says that as CEOs continue to amass huge fortunes, we'll soon return to a time when most of the wealthy owe their privileged place in society to having inherited fortunes.[13]

But staggering inequality has not changed things just for the rich. We now have the lowest level of social mobility of any developed country. "Parents' income has become an almost perfect predictor of university access" in the United States, according to Piketty.[14] And social mobility is likely to decline even further as higher education costs are increasingly shifted from the government onto students and families. Today, young people in the United States have less of a chance of doing better economically than their parents than any previous generation or their peers in any other developed country. The implications of Piketty's analysis for our future are sobering. He says that unless we're willing to tax capital and make massive investments in education and training, inequality will continue to escalate—and our society will become increasingly unstable.[15]

> Today, young people in the United States have less of a chance of doing better economically than their parents than any previous generation or their peers in any other developed country.

Hardening of Racial Hierarchy

America is being pulled apart not just from the hollowing out of the middle class and the growing gulf between the increasingly idle rich and multiple-job-working poor. Yes, working people of all races—including older White people living at or near poverty—are experiencing deteriorating health and declining life expectancy. But at the same time, the racial divide is growing. This dynamic is creating confusion and anxiety that are easily exploited by demagogues. The tendency to pit people of different races against one another cannot be overcome without acknowledging both falling living standards for most people and growing racial disparities. African Americans and Latinos started with less and have been subjected to more exploitation. The financial crisis destroyed trillions of dollars of wealth held by American families. But the greatest damage was done to communities of color. In 2010, the *New York Times* published an article with the headline "Blacks in Memphis Lose Decades of Economic Gains." Black families in the city were disproportionately losing their homes and life savings and being driven into poverty by the Great Recession.[16] Foreclosure rates in Memphis were seven times higher in Black than White neighborhoods. In 2014, the poverty rate in Shelby County, where Memphis is located, exceeded the level at the time of the sanitation strike in 1968. Nationally, in 2013, more than half of all Black households in the United States had less than $11,000 in net assets; for Latinos, it was $13,700; for Whites, it was $141,900—with the racial gap in wealth at record highs.[17]

Underneath disparities in wealth are disparities in the value placed on lives. In 2015, the *Guardian,* a British newspaper, created the Counted, a website that tracks all police killings in the United States. The number of killings in 2016 hit 1,093. The site points out that "U.S. police kill more people in days than other countries do in years."[18] Reading through the stories attached to each person killed is sad. There are stories of hundreds of young African American and Latino men shot by the police but also many Whites, a reminder of our shared fate when we tolerate injustice. No US government agency has ever made the effort to collect this data—a sign of the impunity attached to police violence. So we don't know whether racially motivated police killings have increased or decreased. We do know that the pattern of racial disparities in police killings is as old as the country. If the number is increasing, we should not be surprised. As our country pulls apart economically and socially, people of all races feel greater insecurity. We can anticipate a rise in racism and violence associated with policing where, when, and how people of color can move in the world.

What we do have precise and chilling data about is the massive criminalization of African Americans and Latinos in the United States over the past forty years. Law-and-order messaging used to mobilize White voters was not just symbolic. It helped shift the role of government from one of providing economic security to working people to one of supposedly keeping us safe from crime and terrorism.[19] With a decline in spending on education came prison building. After holding steady for many decades, the rate of Americans behind bars began skyrocketing in the mid-1970s. In her book, *The New Jim Crow: Mass Incarceration in the Age of Colorblindness,* Michelle Alexander shows how mass incarceration replaced Jim Crow as a way to control and exploit African Americans. Between 1980 and 2015, the number of people under the control of the criminal justice system (jail, prison, parole, and probation) increased from 1.8 million to more than 7 million.[20] That's a fourfold increase, with African Americans and Latinos arrested and jailed at far greater rates than Whites for similar crimes. This unprecedented criminalization entangled a generation of youth of color in the criminal justice system. One in three Americans now have criminal records.[21] Even after people complete their sentences, they are likely to face a host of barriers that make it difficult to obtain work and reintegrate into the community.

One of the tragedies in America today is the mistaken belief that racial inequality is a sad but inevitable condition of our society. This myth manifests itself in the tone of pity that runs through media coverage of racial issues. Despite what the media news may suggest, we have the power to create a society in which race doesn't determine destiny. Ending racial exploitation means overcoming powerful interests that benefit from the hypersegregation of our metropolitan areas and our low-wage, low-tax economy. Change will come from the leadership of people who most directly experience injustice, as it did in Memphis and through the civil rights years. Then and now, the choice for White Americans is whether to look away

> One of the tragedies in America today is the mistaken belief that racial inequality is a sad but inevitable condition of our society.

with indifference or pity or to be part of a shared movement to build a society that is not based on racial oppression.

It is important to recognize that what we're experiencing as a society is not only a matter of excluding some people from the American Dream. Dehumanization begins with those most marginalized but inevitably extends to almost all of us. We walk into stores and see rows of machines that have replaced people. We find ourselves on the phone in autobot mazes trying desperately to press the right button to get to a human being. Our lives and agency in the world get devalued. And we become more distrustful, not just of institutions, but of one another. It's not just our public institutions that have been privatized but also our pain.

If we avoid challenging the implicit idea that some people are worth more than others—and the exploitation that feeds it— we have little chance of addressing the other challenges facing our society and planet. It's too easy for those who grip tightly to the status quo to use ideas about race to divide and conquer. And if we allow inequality to grow on the trajectory it is on, we can expect that the rationalizations that blame people for their situations will only become more virulent. That is what makes this a vicious cycle that we all have a stake in interrupting. And it's all the more difficult because of how economic inequality and racism are fueling and being fueled by climate change.

Climate Change

Bill McKibben has inspired a generation of people to organize against climate change. People often ask him, "How can I prepare myself for climate change?" His answer: "Live anyplace with a strong community." The follow-on question is often "Where do we find those communities?" McKibben's response: "You make them."[22] There are many technical strategies for responding to climate change, but they all hinge on our capacity to organize. Many grassroots organizations today are creating models and momentum for a broader response. People are coming together to press their local and state governments to be honest about the current impact and future threat of climate change and take steps to mitigate the potential damage. They're demanding that cities require buildings to be retrofitted for greater energy efficiency, set deadlines for ending their reliance on dirty energy, and switch to clean municipal-run power companies. And they're running corporate campaigns to force utility companies to transition faster to solar and wind energy.

Climate change is not rocket science. The main reason the US and global response has fallen so short is that many investors and CEOs are amassing huge fortunes by extracting carbon. If the companies that are burning gas, oil, and coal had to pay for the damage they do to the atmosphere, much of these substances would stay in the ground. Instead, energy companies receive nearly a trillion dollars a year in subsidies.[23] We have options—including a tax on carbon—that would interrupt the vicious cycle of climate change. But any solution requires fundamentally restructuring our economy. As Naomi Klein argues in *This Changes Everything: Capitalism vs. the Climate*, a people-driven response to climate change is the best opportunity we have to shift power away from the billionaires and create a new economy based on good, well-paying jobs.[24]

The hitch is that the people, corporations, and nations that currently believe they possess the right to extract fossil fuels regardless of the consequences would lose trillions of dollars in wealth. They are not going to give that up without a massive fight. So what we have is a question of power. Do we have the courage and political power to restructure our economy in a way that saves lives and communities and perhaps the planet, even if it causes some people to lose their dreams of infinite wealth? These are similar foes and the same challenge we face in confronting racism and creating a more economically equal society. Which brings us back to organizing and what we know about how to replace vicious cycles with virtuous ones.

Coming Out

We can interrupt vicious cycles of inequality. Humans may tend toward snap judgments, but we're also programmed to resist our own and other people's oppression. When we see one another's humanity and recognize that we're part of the same human family, we bend toward justice. This is why "coming out"—making yourself seen as "fully human"—is so important to social justice struggles. This is what the LGBTQ community did to win marriage equality and reshape American attitudes about sexual orientation and what Memphis workers did when they went from being "buzzards" to Black men on strike.

We see this demand for dignity among immigrant youth, who've come out as "undocumented and unafraid." They've created an identity as Dreamers. They've risked deportation to make people see immigrants as human. They've put their future on the line to protest the hypocrisy of relying on other people's labor yet denying their existence. Carlos Saavedra, who founded United We Dream and now leads Cosecha, tells the story of immigrant youth donating blood together during a blood shortage in Boston. They created a moral crisis over whether the Red Cross would reject their blood simply because they didn't have legal status. They forced people to see the humanity of immigrants and showed the absurdity of a system that turns its back on people who want to contribute to society.

Formerly incarcerated men and women are walking a similar path. They're establishing a public identity as returning citizens. They're stepping forward to challenge policies that lock people with criminal records out of jobs, homes, and voting booths. Like Dreamers, LGBTQ activists, and the sanitation workers, they're embracing an identity used to justify discrimination against them to undermine the stigma and build a movement to change unjust rules.

People need to be courageous to stand up to institutions and ways of thinking that have pushed them down. In one of the best turnabouts in the Bible, Joseph—who's been thrown into a pit to die by his brothers and then twice imprisoned—is hauled out of jail to interpret Pharaoh's dreams. Figuring out what dreams about seven fat cows followed by seven emaciated cows and seven plump stalks of grain followed by seven that are blighted mean in an agricultural society seems easy. Joseph's real challenge is emotional. He is a person whose life has been destroyed by others, who has seen firsthand how people can be crushed for speaking their minds. He sits, to quote Pope Francis, at the "bottom of the pile"[25]—an incarcerated criminal alien. How could he summon the courage to instruct Pharaoh to take the steps to save society from ruin? And yet, that is what Joseph does. He doesn't stop at analysis. He tells Pharaoh that the only path to survival is to completely restructure Egyptian society. He lays out the blueprint—including a massive new tax system. And for good measure, Joseph takes responsibility to lead the whole operation.

Faced with our own crises, we could use a dose of Joseph's courage. In *Laudato Sí*, Pope Francis says, "As often occurs in periods of deep crisis, which require bold decisions, we are tempted to think that what is happening is not entirely clear."[26] Joseph does none of that. At least on the outside, he has pure confidence that it's possible to change everything. Like Joseph, we need to resist the caution that serves as a green light for the powerful to plunder. We need to have the courage to see a different world and bring it into existence.

Joseph is a reminder that those who—like the Memphis sanitation workers—society most tries to toss aside hold the keys to our collective survival. Joseph tells Pharaoh that he is acting as an instrument of God, who has given him the ability to interpret dreams. And because Pharaoh sees God acting through Joseph, he entrusts this man of low social status with the kingdom. This is an example of how faith can mediate change not only by making it possible for people to speak truth to power but by providing the confidence to believe that change is possible. Martin Luther King, Jr., and the clergy in Memphis played this indispensable role in the sanitation strike, and Pope Francis is doing this in our time.

The silver lining in this moment is that everywhere people are searching for meaning and connection. People are waking up. They're willing to act with courage. Joseph did not just save Egypt from famine and lift himself from prison to riches. He used his power to heal, to protect his family from starvation and bring them to live in his new country. His greatest courage was not in standing before Pharaoh but in choosing to forgive his brothers for trying to kill him.[27] Just as inequality is never only about who gets what but always about who counts, we amass the political power to change the course of history only if we change how we see and relate to one another. We must act as our brothers' and sisters' keepers. That is the only path to freedom. But, like Moses and the Memphis workers, we have to be willing to keep the pressure on against all opposition. This takes commitment and clarity of purpose (the focus of chapter 3).

3

Purpose
Preparing Emotionally for the Fight of Your Life

Why dedicate our lives to social change? Surely there's an easier path to a good life?

People get involved in social change for many reasons. We see problems in our community that need to be addressed. We care about an issue that affects our life. We want to help others. We want to feel a connection to people. But deciding to get more deeply involved, take on leadership, or make a lifetime commitment to fighting for justice takes a different level of motivation. This choice is more about emotion than logic. The payoff for deepening our commitment is less about a specific issue than the opportunity to feel included and respected, to know that we matter and that our lives have meaning. It's less about helping other people than about our own freedom.

The *first conversation* that helps us clarify our purpose is important because it makes it possible for us to join others to take on the most entrenched forces of injustice. If we know that this is how we're meant to be living our lives, then we can persist against opposition. We can motivate those around us. We can build the deep, trusting relationships people need to go into a fight together. That's why the first conversation in social change needs to be with ourselves about the purpose of our lives. One of the biggest mistakes people make when working for justice is to skip over their own internal revolution. Personal commitment is what helps us work through the obstacles that beset even the best organizing strategies, campaigns, and tactics.

This chapter on purpose has three sections. The first looks at the emotional and spiritual work that can help clarify our purpose in life and deepen our commitment. The second section provides practical advice for applying what we've learned about managing our emotions to lead meetings, trainings, and events that deepen other people's commitment and bring the most out of them. The third section lays out a framework for using these facilitation tools and ideas about emotional commitment to build purpose-driven organizations and movements around which people can make sense of the world and create meaningful lives.

Clarifying What's on the Line

When I was learning to be a community organizer in Philadelphia, I met a woman named Rosie Mateo. She worked as a crossing guard in a neighborhood where people drove to buy drugs, day and night. The dealers owned every corner—but not hers. It was across from an elementary school, where I was working with parents to fight for better education for their children. Rosie knew everyone. She didn't just stop traffic—she hugged children and their parents as they crossed from one side of the street to the other. She was a human connector—the kind of person I was taught as an organizer to get close to. In a neighborhood where drug dealing made people afraid to leave their homes—let alone go to meetings—parents whose trust I needed trusted her.

But as much as I tried to get her to participate, and as often as she told me that all the boys and girls at the school were her children, she hung back. Dressed in her crossing guard uniform, she'd stop by meetings and sit at the edge of the room. Most parents saw the school as a haven in a neighborhood that had spun out of control. They wanted to work together to make the streets safer for their children. Rosie had young grandchildren living in the neighborhood, which seemed like plenty of self-interest to me. It frustrated me that she wouldn't join the circle. When I asked her why, she'd say that she would do anything for her (450) children who attended the school, but these meetings were for the parents, not for her.

At one point, without planning to, I asked Rosie whether she was afraid out there on the corner. Her first response was "No, no." But as we continued to talk, she told me how it scared her to spend hours out on the street, watching all the drug dealing and the shootings. She explained how no other crossing guards would agree to take the other corners. She cried, and her fear shook me.

Rosie's willingness to be honest about her own fear broke the wall she'd put up between herself and the parents at the school. Once she could participate for her own sake, Rosie pulled her chair up at the next meeting and she never looked back. She kept talking about all her children—but now began acting like her own life was on the line. Her fierceness and devotion helped set the parent group in motion. It was amazing to see the energy released when Rosie realized she was in the room for her own well-being and not just to help others.

I didn't have the clarity then to share how I was feeling. I felt out of place—shunned by the teachers at the school and confused in the neighborhood. I walked past mothers pushing strollers, young men selling drugs, cops, and burnt-out houses. I'd constantly look down at the index cards I carried to make sure I was knocking on the right door. I was ignorant about the social codes, unsure how to dress, overwhelmed by the stimuli, and barely aware of the privilege that allowed me to float in and out of the neighborhood. But something drove me to be there, to hit my goal of twenty face-to-face one-on-one meetings every week. I wanted this organization to succeed more than anything. The conversation I had with Rosie, and what it unlocked for her and did for the group, helped me begin to see that organizing required something different and more difficult from me. I wasn't there to help other people. My work wasn't just, or even primarily, about finding and connecting people or using my brain to teach them how to change policies. I started to understand that this work of repairing the world began in confronting the emotional stuff in our hearts. And at the time, my heart was the part of me that I least knew how to use.

Rosie's breakthrough illustrates the role that emotion plays in clarifying our purpose and preparing us to act. Rosie had to feel and express her fear before she could lead. Our path into social change doesn't always start with facts. It begins with regret, rage, anger, fear, despair, sadness, love, compassion, and all the other emotions that make us human. As Mario Sepulveda said about his decision to stand up and lead in the collapsed Chilean mine, "At that moment I put death in my head and decided I would live with it."[1]

One of the classic stories of social change in the Bible is Nehemiah's effort to rebuild Jerusalem. Nehemiah learns that the people who remain in the city are "in great trouble and shame. The wall of Jerusalem is broken down, and its gates are destroyed by fire" (Neh. 1:3). Before he approaches the king for materials to restore the city, Nehemiah says, "As soon as I heard these words I sat down and wept and mourned for days and I continued fasting and praying before the God of heaven" (Neh. 1:4). Feeling the pain of a city in ruins gives Nehemiah, and ultimately the whole community, the courage to face what will end up being violent opposition. Like Rosie, rather than bottling up pain and shame, Nehemiah turns these emotions into the primary resources out of which he rebuilds the city.

The experience of acknowledging our fear, sadness, and other emotions clarifies what we have at stake. Even when the knock at midnight seems like a plea to help another person, it's always about our own freedom. We clarify our purpose in life, and the commitment that flows from that clarity, by reflecting on what we personally have at stake in changing unjust systems.

> Even when the knock at midnight seems like a plea to help another person, it's always about our own freedom.

Michael Walzer writes in *Exodus and Revolution* that the biblical story of Exodus teaches us three lessons about freedom: "[F]irst, that wherever you live, it is probably Egypt [i.e., a place where you are not free]; second, that there is a better place, a world more attractive, a promised land; and third, that 'the way to the land is through the wilderness.' There is no way to get from here to there except by joining together and marching."[2] We don't get to a better world by trying to help other people. We do it by walking together.

Yet many of us first come into social change through doors labeled "service" or "advocacy." We see people in pain, children who need tutoring, vacant lots to be cleaned. We say, "Yes, here I am." I had first visited Rosie's neighborhood ten years before I met her. As a freshman in college, I went to work at a soup kitchen run by lay Catholic volunteers. I returned as a legal service lawyer to represent people who were being drained of what little they had by debt collectors, who turned $30 debts into $300 legal demands. One day, I went to a client's home to have her sign a legal document. After she signed, she took me to her backyard to show me the garbage from the abandoned house next door. It had piled up to her fence and brought rats into her home. She told me that she'd been trying for months to get the city to do something. The smell was overwhelming. At that moment I knew that I needed to leave my legal aid job to stand alongside people at fences like this, not sit across a desk trying to solve people's problems. What mattered most wouldn't walk into my cramped legal office. I wanted to build organizations with people, to do what I'd been taught during the year I spent living and working in Chile at the end of the Pinochet dictatorship. That's when I decided to figure out how to become a community organizer.

My client's house was a block from Rosie's corner. When I came back the next time, it was as an organizer. Yet, as my experience with Rosie showed, I still had a long way to go. I had been brought up to believe that it was important to be active in the community and to be helpful to those in need. Too often, though, I've seen people make the mistake of expecting that service alone can cure the underlying illness. And sometimes when we're engaged in trying to tear out the roots of injustice, the urge to help solve another person's problem (rather than walking alongside the person as a coconspirator) trips us up. It keeps us from bringing our full selves—and our own liberation—into the fight.

Henry David Thoreau—who cherished solitude but was nonetheless socially active in the Underground Railroad—said, "If I knew for a certainty that a man was coming to my house with the conscious design of doing me good, I should run for my life."[3] Those are strong words for those of us who knock on people's doors. There is a difference between trying to save another person from oppression versus challenging a person to stand up and walk toward freedom. But the line is not always easy to grasp. As is often the case when things get murky, the answer usually lies in connecting honestly with people. We can follow Michael Walzer's point about the relevance of Exodus for our own lives by asking ourselves, How am I experiencing Egypt in my own life? What would the promised land really look like for me? *Whom can I walk with to get there?*

Practical Exercise

There is no magic recipe for clarifying your purpose and what you have at stake in a fight, but there are ways of getting closer. Try this: Put aside for a moment your opinions, however strongly you feel them, about what is wrong in the world and what needs to change. Put aside the people whom you want to help, however noble that urge may be. Write down what you personally need from the change you want to bring about. What would it mean for your life? Without judging your own response, ask and answer this question three times in a row. Be as honest as possible, even if you think the answer isn't something you're supposed to say. You're aiming at the kind of shift that Rosie experienced. You should get clearer each time.

Our values are shaped by our experiences and the stories we tell about them. Often what we most need is to be included, to find a sense of connection with other people, to know that our lives matter. When we find our purpose in life, we have the commitment to act in the face of uncertainty and explain to others why they should trust us with their lives. Rosie's resolve to stay on the corner despite the danger was tied to a deep religious belief. Her willingness to take the next step—to join others to attack the underlying problems facing her community—depended on seeing organizing as part of her purpose. For Rosie, that flowed from her understanding of what God wanted for her. That's true for many people. For others, our purpose flows from the difference we want to make in the world, what we want to leave behind when we're gone. Our commitment hinges on how aligned the work we're doing is with our understanding of our purpose. If we know this is what we're meant to be and do, it's hard to knock us off course.

> When we find our purpose in life, we have the commitment to act in the face of uncertainty and explain to others why they should trust us with their lives.

That's why creating space in our organizations for conversation about purpose is so important. For some people, the moment when we know we're called to a lifetime commitment to social justice falls like a ton of stone on our heads. For most of us, the breakthrough moments aren't that clear. Figuring out our purpose can be like looking for a lost object that can be found only by searching in our minds. I once filled up my gas tank and drove ten or fifteen blocks before someone leaned out his window and shouted that my gas cap was missing. In the dark, I drove back to the exact spot where it had fallen off the roof of my car. My mind knew just where it was, but I needed someone to tell me to go back and look for it. People who ask us to reflect on our purpose and agitate us to wake up are invaluable because they help us fit all the pieces of our experience together to find the larger pattern. The knock at our door may be so soft that we risk missing it. We may need someone to help us hear that we're being called. Then we have everything we need to make a difference.

Emotional clarity is important because it makes us magnetic to other people. When we're aware of our emotions and clear about our purpose, we're able to forge virtually unbreakable relationships with one another. This trust built from honesty is the collective "endurance" that the abolitionist leader Frederick Douglass described as the one thing that can set "the limits of tyrants."[4] Organizers like to quote Margaret Mead, who famously said, "Never doubt that a small group of thoughtful, committed citizens can change the world; indeed, it's the only thing that ever has."[5] But the trusting relationships that make change possible don't just happen. They take work. And they flourish best when we build organizations and movements around human purpose and transformation.

During the six weeks after Rosie had her breakthrough, the parent group talked to hundreds of people in the community to hear their concerns. The group met with public officials to figure out what could be done to make the neighborhood safer and improve the school. The parents leading the effort were still afraid of getting on the wrong side of the drug dealers who ran the corners, but the work they'd done to clarify what they had at stake and build trust together kept them moving forward. They decided to go ahead with a big public meeting—the first one in many years in the neighborhood. The night of the meeting, more than five hundred people showed up. Parents, children, and neighbors crammed into the school's small auditorium, filled the main hallway, and stood in the schoolyard. People testified about the shootings that had taken place around the school. The main demand was for the local police captain to assign an officer to be at the school at the start and end of the school day. The goal was to create a truce that stopped sellers from dealing drugs during the times when children were walking to and from school.

I remember watching the captain respond to the demand and my not being sure whether we had won or lost. Had he said yes or no? But then I looked at Rosie and the other parents leading the meeting, and I knew from their faces that we'd won. The feeling after the meeting was electric. The next day, a sad-looking cop walked around the school in the morning and afternoon with his head down. His presence was cold comfort, given everything happening in the neighborhood, and did nothing to get at the root causes of the problems. Still, it was a start: a tiny down payment on the idea that collective action could create a reaction in the world.

In the years that followed, the parent group went on to win a new roof for the school, full-day kindergarten, and the first Spanish-speaking teachers (one per grade). When parents began organizing around reading levels and the fact that even children who were receiving good grades weren't adequately prepared for middle school, the principal kicked the parent group out of the school. For six months, we held meetings on

Rosie's corner. Eventually, the parent group pushed the school district to hire a new principal. He was a Latino man who did a lot to reconnect the school to the community, including having ten years' worth of graffiti removed from the building's exterior. Along with an umbrella organization of schools and churches, the parents helped anchor a major campaign to get the city to renovate, and in other cases tear down, hundreds of vacant homes.

None of these changes altered the underlying inequality that still makes Philadelphia one of the poorest big cities in the United States. But they created virtuous cycles in the community and in people's lives. In 2012, eighteen years after Rosie and the other parents first stood up, parents and teachers at the school defeated a plan to close their school. They won that fight by showing that even though the building was old, the school was doing a better job of preparing its students for middle school than other nearby schools. In the news coverage, I noticed that the building (which I hadn't seen in years) was still completely clean of graffiti. Over time, the parents who had had the courage to step forward into uncertainty and danger helped transform their community into a better place to raise children. Along the way, they changed their own lives.

This personal transformation is inseparable from the struggle for social justice. Our growth is both the greatest resource we have and the purpose for the changes we seek in the world. After the first big meeting organized by the parent association, someone made a video about their work. What struck me was how much people lit up when they talked about what had happened to their own lives. People would mention the issues in the neighborhood and the changes they were making. But what they wanted to talk about was how they'd changed. They shared how amazing it was to stand up and speak their minds, to tell officials what to do—and how they'd never imagined doing such a thing.

Angelina Rivera, a parent of five young children, often expressed the white-hot anger of the group. She would bring
people to tears at public meetings about improving the quality of education at the school. ("Just because we're poor doesn't
mean our children don't deserve a good education.") One day
she said to me, "I'm going back to school." I said that was great
and asked where she was going to get her GED. She said, "No,
I'm going back to finish high school in the same school and
the same grade where I left off ten years ago." And she did.
Angelina, like Rosie, taught me that what leads people to stand
up is almost always deeper and more personal than the problem
that they said needed to be solved.

In *Between the World and Me*, Ta-Nehisi Coates tells his
son, "History is not solely in our hands. And still you are called
to struggle, not because it assures you victory but because it
assures you an honorable and sane life."[6] Jerry Wurf marched
with the Memphis sanitation workers as the head of the American Federation of State, County and Municipal Employees. He
said that union organizers "think they're peddling better wages
and working conditions, but essentially
they're offering dignity. And sometimes
the worker who doesn't articulate this very
easily has more awareness than the professional organizer. The civil rights struggle,
the equality struggle or whatever you want
to call it, is just one part of this continuing struggle for dignity."[7]
Ultimately, the work that seems to be about fixing the world
ends up being about finding our purpose and place within it.

That's why it's important to come into social change work
with some idea about how you want to grow personally. The
problems facing our society and planet are enormous. But, like
Angelina, each of us has permission to make our own development a priority. In Faith in Action, community organizers work with volunteer grassroots leaders to write leadership

development plans that spell out what the leaders want to learn and get better at doing. Given that fear of speaking in public is so common, it's not surprising that people often say that they want to learn how to talk in front of a room. But plans can include anything from running successful meetings or advocating for your child at school to trusting people more or deepening your faith. Some people gain the skills and relationships to run for office. A good leadership development plan sets goals that are ambitious but achievable and can be measured. It identifies specific activities that will help you achieve these personal goals, such as speaking at the next meeting or attending a weeklong leadership seminar. We all need coaches to keep us on track. And we need to be in environments that take our growth seriously, which is the focus of the next section.

Using Our Emotions to Bring the Most Out in People

One social-change superpower that we all need to nurture is the ability to channel our emotions. We can use this power not only to shape how we're feeling ourselves but also to shift the emotional state in a room or in a relationship. We can create human environments that make people more open to reflect on their purpose, learn, grow, and develop strong and trusting relationships with one another. This makes it possible for people to take risks together. Our emotional power is the main tool we have to lead people, organize events that engage and energize people, and construct effective organizations.

Two facts about how we're wired as human beings make this possible. One has to do with the inherent way our brains default to mimicking one another. If you and I are talking across the table, we are exchanging thousands of tiny bits of information (which makes being face-to-face so powerful, compared to communicating by phone or e-mail). If I rub my forehead for a moment, chances are that you'll do the same. If I lean forward slightly, you will too. Within a few minutes, without either of us noticing it consciously, we may synchronize our breathing. Indeed, the word *conspire* comes from the root words meaning "breathing together." We're subconsciously influenced by and adopt each other's emotions. If people are dejected from losing a fight, and I walk into a room with a sense of resolve, my emotional state can shift the feeling in the room.

You cannot make someone stop or start feeling a certain way. Nor can you argue with an emotion. Telling people that they don't feel sad—or worse, that they shouldn't feel sad—is never a good idea. It always backfires. And we cannot override the pain or anger that people experience by telling them to be happy or think positively. But we can use our emotional state to shift and channel how people around us are feeling—if we're intentional about it.

Psychologists call this "priming." This is the second brain-related concept that facilitates leadership and collective action. Given how our brains work, we can be primed to feel certain ways. This happens when we are exposed to images, words, and thoughts that our memory associates with a feeling we've had in the past. Simple experiments involving colors and words demonstrate this. For example, people who are shown a yellow card and then asked what they'd like to eat are more likely to choose a banana from among other options.[8] This is how advertising works: it can get us to buy a product by associating it with a memory that made us happy in the past. You can use language as a priming tool to encourage a mind-set in others that disposes them to work cooperatively to build power. A simple example is asking someone to share what she or he feels grateful about. Just saying the word *grateful* and having to articulate that emotion can help take the edge off stress or a feeling of being overwhelmed in the face of so much injustice.

The same basic idea applies to reading the emotional state of a room. If you're facilitating a meeting and running into a lot of conflict and confusion, you can stop and ask people how they're feeling. What people say will shape how others are feeling and influence what the group can get done. But if there is underlying tension, it's almost always best to get it out on the table, so people can figure out together how to move forward. This may take a lot of effort, since part of the reason for the tension is that people are uncomfortable giving voice to challenging subjects (as Rosie's example illustrated). Similarly, at times of stress or crisis, having an agenda with more structure is better. It gives people a sense of where things are going, increasing trust levels.

My friend Carlos Saavedra, who told the story recounted in chapter 2 about undocumented immigrants donating blood, is a great teacher of organizing. He says, "state before story," which means that you have to start by establishing the right emotional state in the room. Then you can go forward with sharing your story, taking the other steps to get organized, and creating change in the world. Part of what makes Carlos an effective organizer is his ability, like an actor, to bring strong emotions to the surface by tapping into a reservoir of powerful memories.

These ideas have practical applications for the choices we make in facilitating meetings and organizing events. What we do to shift the state of a room can be as simple as moving the chairs around. An iron rule of organizing is that if it is physically possible to arrange a room so that everyone can see one another's eyes, you ought to take the time to do this. Even if the chairs are arranged in rows when you arrive, rearrange them into a circle. That way, we don't just *say* everyone needs to be seen and heard, we make it possible.

If you have hundreds of people in the room, put them at round tables so they can spend some time working together in small groups. People need to not only consume what's being said upfront but also process what they're learning and share what they know with others. And try this: ask people to stand up and put their hands underneath the edge of the table. Count to three, and then ask everyone to lift at the same time. Boom! We just had a physical experience of acting together. And we felt how light the tables were when we acted in unison.

The tactile experiences are often the most powerful. When I was in Chile, almost every meeting or training would begin with a *dinámica* (a game of one sort or another) that got people moving and working together in a playful way. Activities included seeing how long a group of people keep a few beach balls up in the air and seeing if people could pass an orange or small ball from one to another without using their hands. These kinds of games shift the state of the room by triggering all sorts of feelings and memories—mostly positive. They're not just activities—they give an experiential taste of a different way of being in the world.

Sometimes what makes all the difference for a group is to go for a walk. I was once in Flint, Michigan, in a church hall, where people were debating what to do with an abandoned apartment complex nearby. Should the church buy it to redevelop into affordable housing (the pastor's idea)? Or push the city to tear it down? Or demand that the owners renovate it? We decided what to do only when we left the church, and walked over broken glass, to see, feel, and smell the state of the buildings.

Sharing a powerful story works as well (something we'll talk more about in the next chapter). But sometimes the simplest step that you can take is to ask a question: What are you feeling grateful for this morning? What was a moment in your life when you felt included? Or excluded? One breakthrough for the marriage-equality movement was shifting from telling people about the right to marry to asking people when they first fell in love. Another simple but powerful state-shifting tool is to ask people to share what they appreciate most about the other people in the room. These "appreciation circles" can be especially helpful when groups have experienced tension. The questions can feel a bit corny when you ask them, but they almost always work.

My colleague Alvin Herring uses a Wall of Truth to prime people for honesty and compassion in trainings about race and racism. He gives people sticky notes and asks them to write down things about race that they think but don't say out loud and then put them up on a wall. What people write is often mind-blowingly honest. Afterward, people walk up and read the notes, and then the group can discuss some of the most challenging or perceptive truths. Effective multiracial racial-justice organizations develop out of hard and honest conversations. These can happen only when we intentionally create spaces where people can say not just what they think but what they feel.

Activities like the Wall of Truth and appreciation circles make us better teachers, trainers, facilitators, chairpeople, and all-around good people to have on teams. When we repeat them, they become rituals. Those rituals shape the culture of our organizations. People come to expect that participation will involve being challenged to think differently—even if it is uncomfortable. At Faith in Action, we begin most meetings with prayers or reflections and sometimes song. I've worked with other organizations that use readings, music, spoken word, and chants to center people and connect them to a larger purpose. We know how central music was to the civil rights movement and to so many other struggles. All these approaches and activities come back to inviting people to bring their whole selves to the table, which is what organizations that follow the framework in the next section do.

Building Organizations That Treat People as Ends, Not Means

We want the small group, larger organization, or mass movement to which we're dedicating our time and energy to treat us as ends, not means. We want it to be a small version of the kind of society we are trying to bring into existence. The work may be difficult and uncomfortable at times. But it always needs to come back to our well-being, learning, and growth. Building this orientation toward people into organizational culture can be done in many ways. One approach is to think about purposeful organizations as four-dimensional: they *teach*, *trust*, *reflect*, and *face outward*.

Teach

Organizations develop their members into leaders when they dedicate time and resources to *teach* people the knowledge and skills necessary for leadership. A lot of research has been done on education reform that highlights the importance of designing schools as places where teachers are constantly learning.[9] If the teachers aren't learning, then students aren't either. The same applies to our organizations. If organizations aren't places where people are learning and growing, they're less likely to be able to make change in the world. Yet people in our organizations often tell us that we rush them into action. We don't adequately explain the context or teach them the skills they need to succeed.

Here are three practices that nurture learning in organizations: (1) explicitly describe what skills and knowledge are being taught and why (don't make people guess why they're attending a training); (2) before teaching adults something, ask them what they already know about the subject; and (3) regularly ask people what they are learning and what difference it's made in their lives. If we don't *tell* people why, they won't know where we're going. If we don't *validate* what they know, they won't feel that we respect them. If we don't *ask* whether it's working, they won't know we care about their growth.

Trust

Investing in people goes hand in hand with *trusting* them with big responsibilities. This is the difference between telling someone to come to the next activity or do a small task versus laying out a big goal and sitting down together to figure out what that person's role is in achieving it. If we don't invest relentlessly in people's development and trust them to lead, we end up replicating racial and class inequality inside our organizations and movements. Some people—often White men—get to be heads, making decisions and developing strategy. While others—people of color, women, those with less formal education, volunteers—are hands, receiving instructions, showing up, and doing the work. We ask too little of people who are prepared to give so much.

We ask too little of people who are prepared to give so much.

Reflect

The third dimension of a purposeful organization is a commitment to *reflect* on all significant action. Every meeting, training, and event should include some reflection and evaluation. We need to set aside time to figure out what we've learned from taking action together. Too often, people spend time gearing up for a big showdown, and then, win or lose, they go silent or move on to the next task. This is especially true when different organizations come together to work on a larger campaign. They may have been able to coordinate their work, but they don't necessarily have a structure to process it together and figure out what comes next. I once talked to a friend who'd been involved in a successful effort to raise the minimum wage in his city. Months later, he told me that the groups that had led the effort still hadn't set up a meeting to reflect on the campaign. They hadn't made an effort to look honestly at how they'd worked together, what they might do differently, and how they could build on their success. If we're creating people-based organizations, we can't afford to miss a chance to learn and get more real with one another about what we're doing together.

Face Outward

The fourth dimension is *facing outward*—actively reaching out and engaging people through direct contact. People want to belong. But all groups, large and small, have tendencies to become cliques, to slouch into oligarchy. Organizations say that they want more people to be involved but send out the opposite message or allow long periods of radio silence. In college, I wanted to become involved in the movement on campus to end South African apartheid. But I couldn't figure out how. It seemed like the cool kids all knew one another and that there wasn't a clear way in. Later, once I'd figured out how to be part of the group, I was at a meeting where people were complaining about how hard it was to get people involved. Now, whenever I'm in a conversation about how to increase participation or about why more people don't show up, I remember that moment. I remind myself that what's important is not our stated desire for people to join our group but the messages people are actually hearing about whether we want them. People remember how you made them feel. Are we faced inward, talking to one another, feeling special and chosen? Or are we turned outward, communicating the feeling of inclusion, measuring our days by the purposeful conversations we've had with people who've waited so patiently for us to knock at their doors?

When I saw people pouring into the school auditorium on that night of the first public meeting organized by the parent group, it felt like an epiphany. Organizing wasn't so hard. If you could get enough people to show up and ask for something, you'd get it. That was an experience of the Utopian Flaw, an idea I learned from the Jesuits. When we're building something new, we put an almost idealistic hope in it. We convince ourselves that reaching the top will solve all our problems. The truth is that bigger mountains lie beyond the one we've just climbed; the hardest part isn't scaling the first one. It's making it through the valley that follows. That capacity to keep going rests on the strength of the relationships we're able to build with other people. And that starts with sharing our story.

4

Story
Building Relationships That
Move People to Action

Getting started on change isn't hard. If you're frustrated about what you see happening in the world or your community or workplace, go out and talk to another person. Share your story. Hear that person's. Talk about what both of you care about. Explain the source of your anger. Build a relationship. Storytelling may seem like a distraction from the real work of politics, but it grounds all social change because stories are how humans make sense of the world. We use them to communicate our values, what we care enough about to act on and even risk our lives to achieve. Four important results happen in organizing when we start with story.

First, we experience a small taste of the world that we're struggling to bring into existence. When I listen to your story with focus, I communicate that I see you. You matter. You belong. When I tell my own story to another person, or to a thousand people, I assert my humanity. Indeed, this may be the action that is most in my control that gives me dignity.

Second, when we exchange our stories, the empathy we give and receive becomes social trust. This is what makes it possible for people to work together. It can take many conversations, but we cannot expect people to take risks together without trust. Sharing the experiences and emotions that have shaped our commitments builds the bonds we need to go into battle together. It also builds bridges between people from different backgrounds, helping us overcome efforts by elites to divide us from one another.

Third, we draw connections between our experiences that expose the social structures that shape our lives. We tend to overestimate other people's personal responsibility for their successes and failures (while minimizing our own). This makes it easy to blame people for the situations in which they find themselves and miss how political decisions help or hinder people's progress in the world. When we share our stories, we often find historical convergence (say, two people discovering that they were the first ones in their respective families to go to college) or divergence (say my having gone to college at a time when costs were low and lots of grants were available and your having taken on tens of thousands of dollars in debt to finance your education). These similarities and differences help us step outside our own sweat and tears. They give us some shared ingredients, or at least shared points of discussion, for teasing out how social structures beyond our direct control have contributed to who we are and our place in the world.

Finally, storytelling is how we rewrite the underlying story of our society to support more equitable policies. The ability to tell stories makes human beings unique among all animals. Scientists say that around seventy thousand years ago—a blink in the history of the human species—we experienced a "cognitive revolution" in the structure of our brains that made it possible for us to think and communicate about abstract ideas. In *Sapiens: A Brief History of Humankind*, Yuval Noah Harari writes that if we could go back in time before this revolution in human thinking, we'd struggle to understand the people we met. But after that point, "We'd be able to explain to them everything we know—from the adventures of Alice in Wonderland to the paradoxes of quantum physics—and they could teach us how their people view the world."[1] For a species that depends on social interaction for survival, our newfound ability to tell stories about things that we couldn't see or touch allowed us to create social trust and cooperation across vast numbers of people. Once things could be imagined, they could be brought into existence. Storytelling was the supertool humans used to build complex societies. Similarly, today, we cannot make the social changes needed to save lives and live better without telling new, more inclusive and equitable stories. Just as stories rationalize the worst actions of human beings, they also fuel the movements that make us live up to our potential.

This chapter is organized into four parts. The first section discusses research on what keeps people engaged in social change and increases their participation. (Hint: the opportunity to share your story with another person is key.) The second shows how we can get better at telling our personal stories to give them greater emotional punch. The third section is about using one-to-one story sharing as a tool to build stronger organizations. The fourth focuses on the role of narrative in the communications work we need to do to win on the issues we're working on and transform our communities and country.

What Keeps People Involved in Social Change?

Too often, activists and social justice organizations lecture people rather than listen to them. We mistakenly think that people need to be persuaded to think a certain way before they take action. Or that you move people by telling them what is wrong. We end up spending too much time communicating *to* people, too little talking *with* them. That's why we teach community organizers that they have two ears and one mouth so they can spend twice as much time listening as talking.

Faith in Action has collaborated with Vanderbilt University professor Paul Speer on research to understand what motivates people to get involved in social change and what keeps them coming back. For five years, Paul and his team studied grassroots organizations affiliated with Faith in Action in different parts of the country. The organizations varied in size, but they shared a basic approach to organizing people of faith (from many different traditions) through their religious institutions. Paul's team collected sign-in sheets from meetings and lists of people who'd met with each other face-to-face as part of the organizations. The researchers also surveyed people who had participated and those who hadn't.

They found that two things keep people engaged: "(1) relationships with other participants and, (2) the opportunity to play a role that is meaningful and challenging."[2] Two specific activities were especially "sticky" (in the sense that they held people and deepened their involvement). The first was a short one-on-one meeting with another person where you shared your story and heard the other person's. The second was a "research action," a small meeting with public officials or someone else with power over what is happening in the community. (Research actions are discussed in more detail in chapter 7 on power.) People who participated in these two (fairly intimate) activities were more likely to keep coming back and take on greater leadership than people who didn't. They also came to see themselves as having more power and agency in their lives. Attending a large meeting or protest may help an organizing campaign achieve its goals, but it had little effect on an individual's likelihood to get more involved in the organization. And interestingly, nothing about people's demographics or the attitudes they had before they arrived predicted whether they would show up once and then walk away or end up chairing meetings. What mattered was whether they had an opportunity to share their story and engage decision makers alongside other people.

This finding has important implications for how we think about building organizations and social movements. It suggests that millions of people could be involved in fighting for social justice if they were asked directly and were invited into activities that gave them a chance to take leadership alongside other people. The one-on-one isn't only a good way for people to get to know each other at the start of a meeting. It's a perpetual-motion machine that we have at our fingertips to pull more and more people onto the playing field of justice.

The Vanderbilt research is consistent with other studies showing that people often come into organizations seeking social connection. For example, one study surprisingly found that half the people active in the pro-life movement first showed up either being supportive of abortion rights or without having strong opinions.[3] They joined because other people in their communities and congregations were involved, and their involvement shaped their views. The power of organizations to influence how people see the world runs counter to the tendency of activists to spend lots of energy trying to find likely supporters to engage. When we're fighting for causes that already have a lot of support, like raising wages or providing a path to legal status and citizenship for immigrants, we don't need to search for true believers. We're often better off inviting a lot of people in and exposing them to meaningful activities that put them into relationship and leadership—beginning with sharing their story with other people.

Getting Clear about Your Story

The story of your life is as unique as you are. But compelling stories have a common structure. And our personal stories follow patterns shaped by history. We know from experience that people can get better at telling their stories through practice and by understanding the elements of a good story and reflecting on how their own lives have been shaped by history. Our brains are wired to make sense of the world more easily through stories than through facts and figures. So when we build up our storytelling muscles—individually and as organizations—we become more persuasive to the people we're trying to motivate and to people in positions of power whose decisions we're trying to influence.

Marshall Ganz, who worked with Cesar Chavez as the organizing director of the United Farm Workers, has taught thousands of people to tell their stories more powerfully. He says that "a good public story is drawn from the series of choice points that have structured the 'plot' of your life—the challenges you faced, choices you made, and outcomes you experienced." Your story needs to answer the question of what motivates you. As Marshall says, people need to "understand the values that move you to act, because it might move them to act as well."[4]

Often, the stories that grip us emotionally revolve around a time of great pain or loss. My friend Desmond Meade, a leader in the movement of formerly incarcerated returning citizens in Florida, describes how, after he had left prison and was homeless, he was about to lie down on a train track and kill himself. At that moment, he had a vision of a different future. That led him to put his life back together and become a lawyer. His choice was similar to the one made by the Chilean miners who looked death in the face and vowed to survive. These stories of rebirth are fundamental to our shared history and religious traditions. Whether or not we've personally faced down death, they remind us of low points in our own lives and how we rebounded, of the trauma we've experienced, the support we've received from those who love us, and our strength and resilience as humans.

The key to powerful stories is not always the dramatic moments of external conflict, although these experiences can help focus people's attention, but rather the emotional drama playing out inside our hearts. We know this from the movies we've seen and books we've read. What first appears to be a physical conflict with an obstacle (usually a villain) is really about the hero struggling with a choice that brings to the surface an internal contradiction in his or her character. The challenge can be self-doubt, overconfidence, wrestling with meeting expectations set by others, and so many other difficulties that bedevil us as we try to make our way in a complicated world. That is why the moral of the story usually comes back to what the main character learns about himself or herself and what we learn about ourselves. Often it's the helper (the "impact character") who forces the protagonist to make a different choice. The "help" doesn't solve our problem but rather helps us see our choices more clearly. This is why coaching is so important to social change and why compelling public stories often include someone who helped us look at the world differently.

We don't need to have had a near-death experience or lived on the streets to explain the source of our motivation. But a compelling story needs to be more than simply recounting our life story. We need to dig into not only what happened to us but also the conflict we faced and the choices we made. In the end, our story is an argument for what we think needs to happen in the world based on our experience. Getting there requires reflecting honestly on the turning points that shaped our lives (there can be many, and we can share different pieces of our story at different times, depending on the impact we're looking to have and what group we're with). Since our motivation is shaped by what has happened to us in our lives, as Marshall Ganz says, we all have "within [our] experience what [we] need to be able to make an impact in the world."[5] We just have to take the time to explain that experience clearly.

Sometimes we have the luxury of sitting down with someone to share our story. Often, we have less time and a less explicit invitation to tell our story. Practice helps us tell a condensed version of our story in a short conversation that might take place when you bump into someone on the street ("I watched my parents lose their home when I was fifteen and decided I'd never let myself be pushed around"). We need to be able to share a snippet of our story that explains our motivation when we introduce ourselves at a meeting, make a phone call, or knock on a door ("I've lived in this neighborhood my entire life, and I'm not going to be forced out now"). Like a precious metal that goes through a refining process, we have to boil our story down to its essence through repetition.

Using Stories to Build Organization

The real power in storytelling comes not from telling our story but from eliciting the stories of other people. When you're working to create social change, you want to think of yourself as an architect of human relationships. The best way to get people into relationships is to ask them to share their stories. One of the lessons we teach in organizing is that while meetings are important to make decisions and to get people marching together, most of the work happens through one-on-one relationships. The best way to make a meeting successful, especially when the stakes are high, is to talk individually with key people beforehand.

Use your power to create community wherever you are and whatever your role is in the organization.

But even if you're in a big meeting, before getting to the tasks, ask people to break up into pairs and share their stories. Use your power to create community wherever you are and whatever your role is in the organization. The deeper the relationships, the easier the work will be. One practice that creates a culture of respect is to ask people to sit across from each other and take turns telling their story for a few minutes while the other person listens without comment. When each person is done speaking, she or he concludes by saying "I've spoken." The other person responds, "I hear you" or "I see you." The same ritual can be done when people tell their story in front of a group. It connects the act of speaking your truth with the experience of being seen as fully human.

With an orientation to relationship building through story, organizations can build stronger bonds between people who already share a lot in common and also bridge people who come from different backgrounds. Caucuses organized by race, gender, sexual orientation, and other identities create space for people to support one another, connect their stories to a larger historical struggle, and build collective power.

When people come together from different backgrounds, starting with story can break down social barriers. You don't need to know whether you agree with someone to hear his or her story. And that experience of being seen and heard by another person is the best tool we have for combatting the false hierarchies that diminish people and separate them from each other.

If you want people to look at the world differently, share a story that opens their heart. Even better, give them the space to explain their experience and thinking. We so badly want people to think the way we do. But without listening to their stories, our wish to convince or influence can end up pushing people into their corners—all the more so now that social media has fractured our communities, making it possible for us to be exposed only to those stories that reinforce our outlook on the world.

Stories are especially important when we are trying to get people to see the underlying structures that shape our lives, the intentional political decisions that we get socialized into thinking are normal and natural. A good way to begin to reveal these decisions is to ask people to explicitly reflect on the structures of opportunity and oppression that have shaped their lives and their families. As I explained in chapter 2, getting involved in organizing helped me see how my family's history was shaped by very specific structural decisions (my grandparents' coming to the United States during a brief window when the doors were open to Eastern European Jews and my parents' coming of age during the post-WWII period at a time when Jews were able to take advantage of the privileges of being White and when education, housing, and labor policies were lifting millions of White working-class families into the middle class). Reflecting on my family history has helped me be more conscious of my privilege, more connected to my heritage of social justice, and clearer about how inequality works.

Focusing on both structures that create barriers and those that provide advantages helps avoid the tendency to look only at the deficit. We have plenty of examples in our family stories of public policies that facilitate social advancement for some people but not others. From federal housing policies that enabled some families to build up wealth in their homes to university admissions policies that privilege the children of alumni and donors, we know that structures shape opportunities. The story that inequality is unfortunate but unavoidable is a myth. When government is accountable to working people, it can create opportunity and make society more racially and economically equitable. We have the capacity to drive that change. Indeed, what makes organizing powerful is that it not only gives us the ability to improve our lives and communities but makes it possible to tell a new collective story about what is right and how change happens. Organizations that run successful campaigns build a reservoir of stories that give people the lived experience that change is possible. This helps us dispute the stories we get told by elites about staying in our place and accepting what is.

Winning the Battle over Narrative

Challenging the Dominant Story

Paul Medellin, an organizer with PICO in the 1980s and '90s, used to lead a workshop on power, in which he drew a sketch of a city with a bubble over it. The media on one side and corporate interests on the other held the bubble in place. Some ideas were allowed in, while others bounced off. At the time that I saw this training, I was working as a community organizer in Philadelphia, and Ed Rendell was mayor. Rendell was a deal maker. He invested hundreds of millions of dollars of public funds in big development projects, including fifteen new hotels, a Disney-Quest entertainment center, the National Constitution Center, and a new home for the city's symphony orchestra. All these projects were located in Center City Philadelphia. His push to revitalize the central business district defined his administration. It established his reputation, outside Philadelphia, as a savior of the city.

Many of us in the city saw Rendell's wheeling and dealing as sucking up the city's resources and political will, making it difficult to get the powers that be to focus on the neighborhoods where most people lived. The investment in Center City was gentrifying nearby residential areas while pushing blight deeper into many communities that were experiencing a vicious cycle of disinvestment. The number of abandoned homes and buildings was skyrocketing. Half of the young people at many neighborhood high schools were leaving school without graduating. Jobs had disappeared. People were seeing their neighborhoods turned into open-air drug markets, and the police department was rocked by corruption investigations. Very little of this "data" about what was happening in the city's neighborhoods was included in the dominant narrative of Philadelphia as a city on the rise, led by a tough, charismatic mayor. And proposals for renovating blighted housing and linking Center City development to neighborhood revitalization through development fees bounced off the magic bubble hovering over the city.

As Rendell was touting a narrative about Philadelphia and what it needed, he was operating in concert with real estate development interests in the region. These men donated millions of dollars to Rendell's election and re-election campaigns, often in checks that exceeded $100,000. Throughout his term as mayor, Rendell worked hand-in-glove with the city's dominant power broker, State Senator Vince Fumo. Fumo controlled so many city institutions, from the port authority to the school board, that he was once depicted in the *Philadelphia Daily News* as an octopus with twenty arms. Together, Rendell, Fumo, and City Council President John Street channeled money into development projects and contracts controlled by well-connected law firms and developers. The building trade unions, which used a combination of political influence and violence to keep Black and Latino workers out of the best paying trades, were key allies—as were some of the city's leading politicians (White and Black), who were tied to law firms that had a slice of the bond work connected to development projects.

Rendell's strategy was to turn Philadelphia into the sixth borough of New York, a mini-Manhattan. The story of Rendell's leadership and Philadelphia's bright future was told in the city's two newspapers, one a tabloid for the people and the other for wealthier and more suburban readers, both owned by the same company. Scandals occasionally broke through. But the intricate system of influence and racial and ethnic politics that determined who got what contracts to do what work was largely left out of the narrative. The main story line was grit and renewal, illustrated by *Philadelphia Inquirer* reporter Buzz Bissinger in his best-selling ode to Rendell, *A Prayer for the City*.

Bissinger's book came out in 1997. By the end of Rendell's term in 2000, the US Census showed that Philadelphia had lost 68,000 people, a higher percentage loss of population than any other large US city besides Detroit.[6] Median family income had fallen by 7 percent. Poverty was up 2.6 percent. Latino poverty was the highest in the nation, and Black poverty among the highest.[7] A time-lapse map of housing abandonment showed blight spreading out from Center City into a host of once-stable neighborhoods.[8] During Rendell's tenure, the US economy gained 22 million jobs, one of the most sustained periods of economic growth in a generation, yet by most measures, Philadelphia lost ground compared to other cities while he was mayor.[9] Unfortunately, these facts didn't get in the way of the inspiring story of a White mayor saving an increasingly Black and Brown city.

By the time Rendell left office, real estate developers had locked in hundreds of millions of dollars in tax breaks that would go on for decades. They were making fortunes from gentrifying the neighborhoods that bordered Center City. Rendell was on his way to becoming governor of Pennsylvania based on the reputation he had built as mayor. Large sections of the city had lived through another decade-long vicious cycle of joblessness, violence, and disinvestment. Eventually, both Johnny Dougherty (the head of the racist building trades) and Vince Fumo (Philadelphia's ultimate power broker) went to federal prison on corruption charges. But that was after the damage was done.

After eight years of urban decay under Rendell and lots of organizing by Philadelphia residents, the gaze of city leaders began to shift to the crisis playing out in the neighborhoods. In 2000, during the mayoral election to replace Rendell, the organization I worked for ran a campaign called Neighborhoods First. At the time of the election, more than two hundred thousand abandoned cars were on the streets of Philadelphia, many burnt out and upside down. None were in Center City. We succeeded in making these junked cars a symbol of the neglect of neighborhoods. At one point, we put stickers on thousands of cars saying "The next mayor will decide how long this car sits on your street, but you'll decide who the next mayor is."

The candidates competed to announce their plans to deal with abandoned autos and community revitalization. The city's newspapers—decimated by falling population and declining circulation—shifted from boosting Center City development to urging the candidates to focus on neighborhoods. John Street won the election and made getting abandoned autos off the street his first major policy initiative. He went on to make neighborhood revitalization a focus of his administration.

Organizing in Philadelphia during those years taught me that we cannot advance social change without taking on the dominant stories that are used to hold structures of inequality in place. The difficultly is that these stories are not just out there in the news waiting to be disputed; they are embedded in people's minds as common sense. Even people who stand to lose as a result of a story may still believe it to be true. And this is not just a matter of people being duped. People embrace dominant stories because they help make sense of a confusing and chaotic world. Simple stories create a sense of security.

Of course, most people living in North or West Philadelphia didn't buy into Ed Rendell's vision of shiny buildings or give a damn about being the sixth borough of New York City. The main audience for Rendell's dominant narrative was the suburban voters and elites who controlled the institutions in the region. These voters helped him become governor and later emerge as a key Democratic Party power broker. Rendell and the developers and corporate executives who supported him raised and spent tens of millions of dollars. They used that money to hold together a coalition on the city council and in the city's Democratic Party. They kept dollars flowing into the right projects and pockets. The light playing on the water of a dominant narrative is always a mix of well-resourced arguments that reinforce common sense and money spread around strategically to hold everything together.

Telling a New Story

Exposing the big lies that sustain inequality is an important part of social change and can be energizing. But the harder work often is creating a new narrative. We can be crystal clear about our opponent's story but mushy about our own. Narrative warfare is almost always uneven. Rarely do we have the resources to create a new story line from whole cloth. We don't always have a platform as big as Ed Rendell had in Philadelphia. More often, we're left with finding an existing story line that isn't getting enough attention and trying to fuel it. Other times, we're fighting to co-opt an existing narrative and make it our own.

One key is to find simple metaphors that make sense in people's guts. Frameworks, an organization that researches public opinion, conducted a study on attitudes about criminal justice. This issue tends to bring out people's least generous views about individual responsibility and punishment for bad behavior. Getting people to focus on how structures and policies entangle people in the justice system and how racism can fuel this process can be hard. Frameworks filmed some troubling videos of White people puzzling over racial disparities in drug sentencing. Studies show that Black people use drugs at lower levels than White people but are arrested and jailed for drug possession at much higher rates. In the videos, you can see focus group participants resist undisputable facts about these disparities. Participants come up with many arguments for why their prejudices are right and the data wrong. That's because the stories people have in their minds almost always trump data.

However, Frameworks did find a metaphor (which, in a sense, is a mini story) that was effective in getting people to think about criminal justice in terms of structures: a maze. If you introduce the idea of a maze into a conversation about criminal justice, people begin to talk about what it feels like to be dropped into a system you don't understand. People with money or influence can see the exits, but others can't. You end up circling back to the same place over and over if you don't get help. Getting people to tell their own stories that explain how mazelike structures shape behavior doesn't take much prompting. The power of a collective story rests on whether people can own the narrative and repeat it in their own words.

The power of a collective story rests on whether people can own the narrative and repeat it in their own words.

In 2000, Oakland Community Organizations (OCO) was working with parents in working-class neighborhoods in Oakland, California, where schools were so overcrowded that they ran on two shifts. Student test scores were abysmal. Liz Sullivan, an organizer with OCO, worked with a group of parents to make a simple map of Oakland that noted the sizes, test results, and locations of all schools, showing visually the link between the number of students attending a school and its educational outcomes. The map helped spark what came to be called the Small Autonomous Schools Movement, which went on to transform public education in the city. OCO was clear that "small" meant schools that were developed by parents and teachers around student needs and accountable to the community. Parents persuaded the school district to create a "small school incubator" out of which more than fifty new small autonomous public schools were created, most of which are still outperforming traditional public schools. Almost all are more closely integrated into their communities.

Skeptics and opponents challenged these small schools, saying that small doesn't mean good. But this pushback helped advance, rather than end, the conversation. A good metaphor gives us something to work with. Parents were able to use the simple and clear idea of small schools to talk about schools in which their children would not fall through the cracks. In doing so, they told a new story about education in their city, a story that was built around the needs of their children, and the controversy it generated only helped.

Of all the social justice stories coursing through our country in recent years, Black Lives Matter has been the most compelling and influential. Alicia Garza, cofounder, describes its origin this way: "I created #BlackLivesMatter with Patrisse Cullors and Opal Tometi, two of my sisters, as a call to action for Black people after 17-year-old Trayvon Martin was posthumously placed on trial for his own murder and the killer, George Zimmerman, was not held accountable for the crime he committed. It was a response to the anti-Black racism that permeates our society and also, unfortunately, our movements."[10] Black Lives Matter went viral because it came out of a common struggle, and so many people saw their own stories in it at a moment of great pain. As Alicia makes clear, the point of these words put together and pushed out into the world by three African American queer women was to radically disrupt the larger society and the social justice movement. The feeble racist response that "all lives matter" can be painful to hear. But it's a sign that Black Lives Matter is powerful and cannot be denied. It's a reminder that good social justice stories don't resolve tension. They force us to go deeper into the truths that dominant narratives try to drown out.

Everyone should read what Alicia wrote directly, but part of what struck me, particularly as a White man, was this: "#Black LivesMatter doesn't mean your life isn't important—it means that Black lives, which are seen as without value within White supremacy, are important to your liberation." The story of Black Lives Matter not only forces a moral choice for every person who hears it to either accept or deny four hundred years of racial oppression, but like the small schools demand, it creates a platform for people whose fates are intertwined to unite around a common struggle—which leads to the next chapter on justice teams in larger movements.

5

Team
Finding a Home Base in a Movement for Change

After college, I lived in a shared house with three other people. One of them was a slug. He didn't clean up, shop, or do any of the other work necessary for four people to live together. For a while, the rest of us tried to compensate. But eventually, we fell into a small-group death spiral. We retreated to our rooms and waited for the lease to end. I know people who've had the opposite experience, who are still best friends with their old housemates. Why do some teams soar, while others crash and burn? And what makes it possible to consistently build social justice teams that bring out the best in their members and are able to drive change in the world?

Having people whom you trust to walk with is indispensable to a life of social justice. All the important changes we make in the world are made alongside other people. Yet finding (or building) a good team of people to conspire with is never easy. The challenge of forming teams—and holding them together—is what organizers spend the most time wrestling with. And it's the Achilles' heel of an American social justice movement in which most so-called members have never met one another—let alone participated in the kind of face-to-face organizing that's been the lifeblood of every social movement in history.

This chapter on building and sustaining social justice teams is organized into three sections. The first looks at the value of small groups—for us as individuals, as well as for organizations and larger movements. The second shares four practices that set teams up for success: trust, shared purpose, clear roles, and a learning culture. The final section offers an example of how large numbers of interconnected small groups that combine personal growth and social action can change history.

Why Small Face-to-Face Groups Are Indispensable for Social Change

Saddleback Church, in Orange County, California, is a large institution built on a foundation of small groups. Led by Rev. Rick Warren, author of *The Purpose Driven Life: What on Earth Am I Here For?*, the church has regular Sunday attendance of over twenty thousand people, making it one of the largest religious congregations in the United States. One key to its growth has been the creation of thousands of small groups that provide a home base for its members. Steve Gladen, the leader of Saddleback's Small Group Ministries, writes that the church has "more people in small groups than attend our weekend services."[1] Through the groups, people pray together, share problems, study, and engage in service and outreach. The church has a structure that provides training and support to group leaders and connects groups to the larger mission and activities of the institution. Gladen says, "We look at the people who are serving as hosts and identify the ones who are natural shepherds. Then we begin to raise these people up through a 'Small Group Leadership Pathway' that helps them understand the ministry, recognize God's call in their lives, and then trains them in head and heart fundamentals so they can be effective in the ministry. We take hosts and turn them into leaders!"[2]

Many of the organizing and leadership-development practices that make Saddleback successful also apply to purpose-driven social change. Small groups give people space to breathe, think, find support, and grow. The larger the institution or movement, the greater the need for small spaces in which people can connect. None of us comes to social justice work fully formed. Becoming a public person who can act with confidence against injustice is hard. We need to be around people who can keep us from retreating back into our comfort zones. We need places where we can test our voices, connect with partners who complement our talents, and find a sense of belonging.

A burning issue might bring us to a first meeting, but what keeps us coming back are the relationships we build. There's a point that successful groups pass—similar to a runner's high—after which people don't need to be persuaded to come to meetings. At that point, the relationships, not the agenda, hold people together and make the work seem easier.

A burning issue might bring us to a first meeting, but what keeps us coming back are the relationships we build.

Being on a team also gives people the ability to negotiate their interests within a larger institution or movement. Even in organizations working in a single city, people without teams can end up becoming cogs in a larger system. If we're not actively engaged with others in making decisions about the social change work we're doing, we can end up being hands, not heads—being given small discrete tasks, such as signing petitions or attending rallies. To be agents of our own destiny rather than objects of other people's plans, we need teammates.

That's why face-to-face chapters, small groups, and teams are the building blocks of mass social movements. An early example in US history is the antislavery movement. Until the 1820s, the primary organizations working to end slavery in the United

States were a small number of societies, led mostly by prominent Quakers. These associations "advocated [for the] gradual abolition of slavery" using "tactics of voluntary manumissions, legal aid for blacks, and petitions to state governments."[3] Their tactics and membership were limited. Many other people—including many free Blacks—had energy for more direct and rebellious opposition to slavery, but these potential participants lacked the organizational structures to express that resistance.

Then something changed. Abolitionists decided to adopt a different organizing strategy and structure in the early 1830s. They were inspired by slave rebellions, such as the 1831 uprising in Virginia led by Nat Turner, and by the Second Great Awakening, a religious revival that spread a spirit of moral reform in the country. In 1832, leading abolitionists launched the American Antislavery Society—a new organization with a nationwide membership that included Blacks as well as Whites. They chose a "federated structure comprising nested local, state, and national chapters [which] enabled a franchise like expansion . . . providing a template for organizing and a way to link local groups to a nationwide effort."[4]

In their article, "Antislavery in America: The Press, the Pulpit, and the Rise of Antislavery Societies," Marissa King and Heather Haveman show how this change in organizational structure and philosophy made abolition the first large-scale American social movement. "The American Antislavery Society initiated a popular grass-roots campaign to promote immediate abolition. Rather than having prominent citizens sign petitions or bring lawsuits, the [society] sought to build widespread support among the citizenry to end slavery through a moral transformation that would turn the entire populace into abolitionists."[5]

The fervor of the new structure is captured in the organization's 1838 constitution:

We shall organize Antislavery Societies, if possible, in every city, town, and village in our land. We shall send forth agents to lift up the voice of remonstrance, of warning, of entreaty, and rebuke. We shall circulate unsparingly and extensively antislavery tracts. . . . We shall enlist the pulpit and the press in the cause. . . . We shall aim at the purification of the churches from all participation in the guilt of slavery.[6]

Membership exploded. At its height, the American Antislavery Society had more than sixteen hundred local chapters. It engaged tens of thousands of people in face-to-face organizing against slavery. The greatest participation was in states with the largest free Black populations. In 1835 alone, the society distributed more than one million pamphlets and slave narratives. Many participants in local antislavery societies went on to become conductors on the Underground Railroad. The core components of the abolition movement—mass multiracial membership, local societies or chapters, traveling agents, direct action, and an ethic of moral resistance to injustice—shaped every subsequent social movement in US history, from women's suffrage to ending child labor to the civil rights movement.

In her book *Diminished Democracy: From Membership to Management in American Civic Life*, Theda Skocpol explains that, like the abolition movement, the largest and most successful social organizations in the United States have been organized along federated lines, with national, state, and local structures.[7] This approach to building organizations and movements has been powerful precisely because it creates spaces for large numbers of people to be directly involved in face-to-face teams, while connecting them together and coordinating their work across great distances.

Organizations that reach deep into local communities and can bring large-scale pressure on the federal government are especially important in the United States because of the size of the country and how our government was designed to block change. The thirty-nine men who wrote the US Constitution (eleven of whom owned or managed slave plantations) made it extraordinarily difficult to pass policies to rein in elites, eradicate slavery, or benefit working people. From the design of the Senate—where one senator can stop an entire piece of legislation from moving forward—to the separation of powers between the president, Congress, and Supreme Court, they structured the rules of government to protect the status quo and to slow change. We play politics on a tilted field. The deep frustration that Americans feel about the inability of Congress to address the issues that matter most in our lives is extreme today. But the cry against do-nothing politicians is not new nor an accident. It's the product of how a small number of wealthy White men designed the federal government, as well as many of our state governments.

Unfortunately, since the 1970s, social justice organizations that reach deep into communities have been eclipsed by what Skocpol refers to as "staff-led, mailing-list associations, without local or state group affiliates."[8] "If a new cause arises, people think of opening a national office, raising funds through direct mail, and hiring a media consultant."[9] In contrast, the Christian Coalition and other conservative organizations have continued to rely on structures that create space for people to take meaningful local action in their communities, connected to larger moral and political issues. But progressive and especially environmental organizations largely relate to members as individual donors or online activists. In 2000, Robert Putnam wrote, "Virtually all the major American environmental groups (as well as thousands of smaller organizations) are addicted to direct mail as a tool of mobilization and membership retention."[10] Today, national organizations fill our in-boxes with e-mail and claim us as members solely on the basis of our donating a few dollars or signing an online petition.

The inherent weakness of mailing-list organizations can be seen in the spectacular failure of the nation's environmental organizations to secure climate change legislation during the first Obama term. Skocpol shows how "Big Green" organizations went into the fight with hundreds of millions of dollars—from direct-mail donations—to spend on lobbying and large lists of "members." But they lacked a deep, mobilized base of people necessary to create moral and political pressure for action on climate change. This made it possible for the fossil fuel industry to use influential lobbyists, hundreds of millions in campaign contributions, and Senate rules to block action on cap and trade legislation.

Lawrence Goodwyn captures the bind we face today in his book *The Populist Moment: A Short History of the Agrarian Revolt in America*. Populism, which began in the 1870s, was the largest democratic movement in American history and a precursor to our current struggle to restrain corporate power. Goodwyn writes, "[H]istory does not support the notion that mass protest movements develop because of hard times. Depressed economies or exploitive arrangements of power and privilege may produce lean years and even lean lifetimes for millions of people, but . . . they do not produce mass political insurgency."[11] The crises we face in our own time are hollowing out the middle class and making more people poor. But neither this hardship nor widespread awareness of the corrupt influence of moneyed interests is enough to create a social revolution. Rather, as Goodwyn writes, "Democratic movements are initiated by people who have individually managed to attain a high level of personal political self-respect. They are not resigned; they are not intimidated. . . . Their sense of autonomy permits them to dare to try to change things by seeking to influence others."[12]

Like the abolitionists after 1832, the populists sought to fundamentally change the way Americans saw their society. They fielded forty thousand lecturers who, like the antislavery agents, traveled the country speaking to groups of farmers and urban workers. Participants weren't just showing up for speeches; they were directly engaged in day-to-day organizing against the economic structures that were impoverishing their families. They had spent many years "talk[ing] to each other about their troubles. They had read books on economics in an effort to discover what had gone wrong" and had formed local cooperative organizations that they controlled. Goodwyn says that this "cooperative struggle . . . engendered within millions of people what Martin Luther King would later call a 'sense of somebodiness.'" This is what gave people the ability to stand up to the proverbial pharaohs of their times. "Thus armed, the Populists attempted to insulate themselves against being intimidated by the enormous political, economic, and social pressures that accompanied the emergence of corporate America."[13]

Much has changed in our times, from the Internet to globalization. But the forces we're up against are only more entrenched. And people's sense of resignation and intimidation is pervasive. Like the populists and the abolitionists, we need a movement that can wake Americans up, that can reach into every town and city. To get there, we need face-to-face structures that connect us to one another and to a larger movement. The spaces where we can become somebody and test the limits set by conventional wisdom are just as indispensable today. That is what makes building powerful, purposeful, interconnected teams so vital. And we know a lot about how to do this well.

Creating Teams and Setting Them Up for Success

Teams are more than just a structure or technique. Like all the conversations in *Stand Up!*, they are a way of thinking about how people create meaning and solve problems together. Seeing social change through the lens of purposeful teams changes how we design our organizations and movements. It shifts the choices we make in facilitating groups and crafting strategy. It's not enough to schedule a meeting and hope people will show up or be happy that the room is full. As a facilitator, I may try to focus people on their purpose, expose the forces we're up against, or ask people to share their stories. But the main question going through my mind is whether people are already organized into small groups. If not, I'm thinking about how I can make that happen as soon as possible. I want to get people into groups, energize those groups, and set them up for success so they can bring more people to the table.

This section focuses on four elements—trust, shared purpose, clear roles, and a learning culture—that help social change teams thrive and make it possible for large numbers of people to work together to advance justice in an uncertain world. When the stakes are high, these four elements can make or break teams and ultimately social movements.

Trust

Social trust is the starting place for successful teams—all the more so for groups that have the audacity to take on the status quo in a society polarized by race, class, gender, and religion. People need to know that they have each other's backs. This doesn't just mean being confident that if you fall backward your friends will catch you or that if you lose your job trying to organize a union your coworkers will look out for you. It means being willing to be vulnerable. In *The Five Dysfunctions of a Team: A Leadership Fable*, Patrick Lencioni defines this kind of trust as "the confidence among team members that their peers' intentions are good, and that there is no reason to be protective or careful around the group."[14] To make teams work, we need to open our hearts and expect the same of others. When teams aren't emotionally truthful places, people skate on the surface. They don't hold one another accountable. One or two people can take the group off the rails. The whole isn't greater than the sum of the parts, defeating the purpose of being a team.

People must learn to be honest about how they experience race and gender differently. We need to fight the tendency to replicate society's oppressive and hierarchical patterns in our own groups and organizations. Everyone needs to be conscious about whose voices dominate discussions in meetings and how someone's race and gender influence how his or her ideas are received. To function effectively in a multiracial movement, we need to master a knowledge base—discussed in chapter 2—about White privilege, racial anxiety and the way societies are structured around false hierarchies of human value. We need to be able to talk about racism and patriarchy explicitly and recognize how they shape our individual behavior, interpersonal relationships, and group dynamics. The capacity to both tell the truth as we experience it and hear things about ourselves that we may not know—without flinching—makes us emotionally intelligent and racially conscious. And if taken as a primary responsibility, not an add-on, these skills can help a team forge itself into a tool for dismantling racism, sexism, and other forms of discrimination.

Of course, it's easier to *aspire* to emotional intelligence and self-awareness than *practice* them, especially when you believe your personal efforts can change the world. One truism about politics is that you can get almost anything done if you're willing not to take credit for it. When I was working on a campaign to get abandoned cars off Philadelphia's streets, our organization got all the local and state officials involved to agree on a solution. But it took another six months to iron out who would get to announce that they'd solved the problem. Most of us want desperately to make a difference. And we also want to get some credit. A necessary conceit of social change is that each of us feels that we added the straw that broke the camel's back. The belief that our contribution matters is part of what keeps us from sitting back and letting others do the work. But there is always tension between what my ego needs to be happy and what I must do as one of many to support a healthy group that can get things done.

Organizers like to quote Rabbi Hillel, who asked, "If I am not for myself, who will be for me? But if I am only for myself, who am I? If not now, when?"[15] In real life, it isn't easy to figure out how to be for yourself and also be for others. Strong teams live at the point where these three questions meet. Strong teams are places where people can be emotionally honest about what they need from the group and the group can be crystal clear about what it needs from each person.

To help groups that we're part of or we coach go deeper, we need to return to the discussion in chapter 3 about using our emotional state to signal gratitude and abundance and to build purpose-driven organizations. People need to know one another's stories and motivations. They need to feel that they belong and matter. They need to hear the group tell them why they're valued. In *The Five Dysfunctions of a Team*, Lencioni pushes further. He outlines a team effectiveness exercise that "requires team members to identify the single most important contribution that each of their peers makes to the team, as well as the one area that they must either improve upon or eliminate for the good of the team."[16] Lencioni is speaking to workplace teams, but the underlying idea that honesty creates trust, and trust generates the capacity to think and act together, applies even more so to social justice teams facing off against powerful opponents.

Shared Purpose

Team members need to work together to achieve an important shared goal that they all understand and own. This seems obvious, but this understanding is often missing from both small groups and large organizations. In a small group, it's good to ask the following questions: If you took each member of the team into a room separately and asked what the team was trying to accomplish, would you get the same clear response from everyone? When you look at how the members of the team spend their time outside meetings, can you see evidence that they are actively working together to achieve the same goal?

When a team has a shared purpose, its members are consumed with trying to accomplish a single important result. They're not just connected by a set of values, an outlook on the world, work that is closely related, or a regular meeting time. They're able to describe clearly what would be different if and when the team is successful. They know what success would mean for their lives, rather than being able to simply give a laundry list of activities that the group is engaged in. All team members can explain not only what they are doing to make the outcome a reality but also the roles that other team members are playing and why each is important to the result.

For electoral campaigns, union organizing drives, or efforts to pass ballot measures, where there are hard deadlines and win/lose outcomes, the shared purpose can often seem clear. But even in these situations, teams must be organized around goals, not tasks. People need to understand clearly how their team's goals are related to the larger campaign's success.

This focus on team goals was a key principle used by the 2008 Obama presidential campaign. The campaign relied on volunteer teams to drive their field program and meet voter registration, persuasion, and turnout goals that most campaigns leave to paid staff. Each volunteer team had meaningful goals that helped people feel ownership over their team's piece of the puzzle and understand what they needed to do and why. As Elizabeth McKenna and Hahrie Han explain in *Groundbreakers: How Obama's 2.2 Million Volunteers Transformed Campaigning in America*, the goals shifted as the campaign progressed. Metrics changed from recruiting volunteers and creating new teams in the early stages to contacting voters closer to Election Day. But the underlying idea that teams needed to have autonomy and agency remained constant—reflected in the campaign's mantra, "Respect, empower, include." [17]

When there isn't a hard Election Day deadline or when teams have a broader mission, focusing everyone on a single measure of success takes more work. The group needs to both define the goal and figure out how to achieve it. When a team is part of a larger movement, it needs to negotiate its own goals with other teams. As with the Obama campaign teams, it's important to define the job in as big a chunk as possible and then shift the responsibility for figuring out how to be successful to each team.

For example, a team working to put a proposition on the state ballot to raise the minimum wage might be responsible for collecting the specific number of valid signatures needed from their county to qualify the measure as part of a larger statewide signature-collection goal. This is different from saying to the group, "Here are the days on which we want you to gather signatures at these locations." The former instills purpose. The latter is about how to execute. The team should figure out the best way to achieve the goal, adjust its strategy, and see the goal to the finish. They need to take into account that some signatures will be tossed out. So the mission is to reach the goal of valid signatures and to go back out onto the streets if the goal isn't met.

Or let's say we're trying to pass an ordinance to require employers in our city to provide paid sick time to their employees. Ideally, we have teams that take responsibility for delivering the vote of the councilperson who represents their district. One way to approach the campaign would be to say, "Let's hold a public meeting in each council district to build support for the ordinance." Then the job of each team would be to organize that event. Nothing is wrong with that approach. But what if we had all the teams meet together and say, "Okay, we're each committing to deliver a specific outcome from our council-person." (Depending on where the councilperson starts out in his or her support, the options might be to cosponsor the bill, vote yes, abstain, or in the worst case, be less vocally opposed.) Each team is responsible for achieving a concrete measurable outcome. How groups meet their commitments will vary. Some might decide to hold a big public meeting with their councilperson. Others might organize a prayer vigil outside the councilperson's office or a meeting with small-business people who support the campaign. Now the discussion in the team has gone from figuring out how to plan a good meeting to how to deliver a yes vote (or neutralize an opponent). This shift might seem subtle, but for a team to have agency, it has to own the strategy. A plan informed by people closest to the problem is likely to be better. And collectively wrestling with how to win is how teams grow and gain confidence. By inspiring teams and then trusting them to figure things out, we help people find their purpose together.

Of course, group purpose can change. People bring different perspectives and interests to the table, and what matters most to them shifts over time. When our parent organization was fighting to protect the autism program in our school district, we started with a very clear goal to stop $171,000 in cuts in the final school district budget. However, once we began to nego-tiate with the school board, parents on our team reacted differ-ently to offers of a compromise. We hadn't done enough work to talk through together what success would look like. This became even clearer when a parent whose school did not have an autism program, but needed it, began to take leadership in the group. Were we fighting to protect one program or to make this effective approach available to all students in the school district? We had to take a step back to hammer out exactly what Concerned Parents of Arlington Students with Autism was trying to achieve—and how we would know if we were successful. That conversation ended up inspiring us because we realized that we had a larger purpose.

Clear goals owned by the whole team need to come with a sense of urgency. The best teams meet weekly, talk daily, and text and e-mail constantly. There is no magic recipe, and many successful teams meet less often. But as money floods our political system, we have to raise the bar on what we expect from one another. When I was organizing with parents in Philadelphia, we worked with a sister organization called Youth United for Change (still one of the most successful youth organizing groups in the United States) that organized students in the same high schools where we were organizing parents. The students met weekly, and that rhythm—combined with being inside the school—gave them energy and enabled them to organize circles around the parents, who met only every few weeks. Of course, many of us have complicated lives, between work and family commitments. But sometimes the events that happen every week, like clockwork, are easier to build into our lives. Even if meetings are short, the more regularly we meet, the more intense heat we can generate.

During the financial crisis, a group of people from Contra Costa County, California (one of the areas of the United States hardest hit by mass foreclosures), cornered Adam Kruggel, a talented organizer with whom they were working. They pressed him to help them charter a bus to drive across the country, to Washington, DC, to raise awareness about the need to keep families in their homes. The result was the *Recovery Express*, which carried families facing foreclosure from California to Capitol

Hill. They stopped for rallies in eight cities, spending two weeks on the road telling their stories and learning together. Their message reached millions of Americans through national media coverage. Their commitment—like the dedication shown by those who fasted for weeks to support immigration reform in 2013 or the Ferguson activists, who marched all night long for Michael Brown—show the kind of change that small groups of people can bring about if they share a consuming purpose. We need to try to match this intensity in all the teams we're building if we expect to keep pace with the forces we're up against.

Clear Roles

Having a shared purpose and a sense of urgency doesn't mean that we all have to do the same work. The third key to successful groups is that they differentiate roles, based on talents and interests. And they're rigorous about making sure that people are in the *right* roles. This is also an area where we can learn from the 2008 Obama campaign. The core unit of the campaign's field program was the Neighborhood Team. Each team (sometimes referred to as a Snowflake) had a Neighborhood Team leader—a volunteer who was responsible for coordinating the activities of the group. Paid field organizers would typically be responsible for coaching the volunteer team leaders from three to five Neighborhood Teams. Each member of the Neighborhood Team had a specific role (e.g., phone bank captain or canvas captain) with defined goals (e.g., talking to X number of voters). The key was that everyone had both a role and clear goals and there were straightforward measures to figure out if the role was right for that person. This commitment to roles and goals led volunteers to take their responsibilities seriously and allowed people to rely on one another. Ultimately, it made it possible to coordinate the work of 2.2 million volunteers, through ten thousand teams, led by thirty thousand leaders.[18]

When I was first taught organizing, I was warned to beware that some people would take positions of authority because they spoke well or had dominant personalities—but end up not doing the work. To avoid this pitfall, I was told to build organizations based on "relational" rather than "positional" power. Under this thinking, the people who lead should be the ones who've demonstrated the willingness to do the work. This often meant putting off the question of who would fill which roles, such as chairperson or team captain. Instead, people would take on specific tasks. Besides being crucial for each person's own development, this gave everyone a sense of who was really willing to work. But people's roles on the team were undifferentiated—each person's role was to show up for meetings when possible.

One downside of this approach was that the organizer (the paid staff person who initially built relationships with people and brought them together) would often remain at the center of the team rather than fading back. In the absence of elected leaders, and without people having clear roles, the organizer became the de facto chairperson. The organizer might be doing important work in helping create trust on the team and keeping work moving ahead. But this came at the expense of leaders owning their team and driving its work forward. At worst, people would wait for the organizer to give them their assignments or tell them the date of the next meeting. When organizers were honest, they'd admit that they continued to attend the meetings of their strongest teams because that was where the action was, not because they needed to be there. And when organizers spent time with existing teams, they had less time to build new ones.

The team-role-goal approach is an important corrective that brings organizers and grassroots volunteer leaders back to their original mission of developing people's leadership skills. The job of the person setting up a team, whether a paid organizer or volunteer leader, is not to chair the team or even to attend most meetings. It's to have a coaching relationship with the team's coordinator or chairperson. The role of the person leading the team is to make sure that all members have the right role and are clear about what goals they're trying to achieve and how they fit into the team's larger purpose. This isn't always easy. It takes figuring out what people are good at, making big asks of people, and regularly assessing whether people are delivering in the role they've taken on.

Trusting teams to get the work done requires investing in more systematic training and development for people who take on roles. Organizations that have shifted to this approach have been able to build more teams and organize more people. But to do this, they've had to change how their organizers spend their time (more coaching, challenging, and training of team leads; less hands-on facilitating of meetings). They've blurred the line between paid organizers and volunteer leaders—making it everyone's business to wake people up and organize them into teams. And they've created more structured and predictable training programs so people don't have to wait for a paid organizer to tell them what comes next. Faith in New York—a grassroots organizing group in New York City—has held ten-week leadership schools in each borough in the city. During the two and a half months that people are "in school," they're expected to build teams at their congregations. Some teams may crash and burn. Some people may take on roles that aren't a good fit and then not let go. Other teams won't have enough internal trust for people to hold each other accountable. But not all teams need to succeed if we have enough of them to build a movement.

A Learning Culture

Teams bond through action. But to grow and thrive, they also need to set aside time to learn together and reflect on what they're doing. Teams need to be places where people feel that their development matters as much as any other task. Creating a learning culture is the fourth key to setting up teams for success. What made the anti-slavery movement societies and populist cooperatives powerful was that they created conditions for people to develop an independent analysis of what was happening in the world and what it would take to bring about change. Engaging successfully in social change requires stripping away myths we're taught about how society and politics work. Small groups are an ideal place for this kind of learning because they give people a chance to test out new ideas and try on new roles.

> Teams need to be places where people feel that their development matters as much as any other task.

You can foster a learning culture on a team by getting people to regularly reflect on powerful experiences, including what's happened to them in the past and what they've done together as a team. People learn best from experiences that bring forth strong emotions. We remember what we feel. Through our hearts, we rethink our values, connect the dots between stories that seem unrelated, see our lives in a new light, and reimagine what's possible. This is especially true for adults, whose minds are already wired by everything they've gone through. Without setting aside time for intentional reflection, people can engage in a lot of activity without learning much or keep powerful experiences buried. As with building trust, promoting an orientation to learning and personal development on teams can be done by engaging in regular practices of reflection—for example, by asking each person to share how he or she felt after significant activities undertaken by the group. These practices set an expectation that participation will lead people to greater wisdom.

If your team is anchored in an institution—like a school or religious congregation—dedicated to people's spiritual and emotional development, you may have a head start in creating a learning culture. People may arrive primed to expect that their personal growth is valued. If you don't have an organizational culture to draw on, the risk is higher that a small group will fall into a string of unprocessed tasks and activities. You can correct for this by being more rigorous about setting group norms upfront and by incorporating reflection into the life of the team. You have to take the time to intentionally create the team's culture— for example, by starting every meeting with a discussion of a reading and how it relates to people's lives or by asking people to share the norms they want the group to abide by. The less well people know one another, the more untethered a group is from a larger structure, or the greater the crisis, the more structured activity you should build into the agenda. Practices that ask people to go around a circle responding to a question may seem awkward at first, but they signal that everyone's voice matters and that the work is both about making changes in the world and about developing the skills and thinking of the participants.

One popular framework that teams can use to structure reflection comes from Catholic social teaching in Latin America. It has four steps—*see, judge, act,* and *revise*—that can serve as the agenda for a single meeting or the elements of a cycle of work unfolding over months.

See refers to people talking about the pain and pressure they experience in their lives. The goal is to develop a shared understanding of the social reality that the group is trying to change. This is the principle of beginning with people's lived experience and emotion, rather than running directly into issues and tasks. This step can be as simple as asking people what pressures they are facing or problems in their lives they are trying to solve. These are also good questions that a team can use when it's building a larger base in the community, which is discussed in the next chapter.

The next step, *judge*, is not about judging people but about comparing the current reality to our values. This step can involve reading a text or watching a video and then talking about the gap between the world as it is and as it should be and about who is benefiting from the gap. It's meant to build the group's social and political analysis so people understand clearly the forces they're up against and the significance of their work.

Act means taking action to bring about concrete changes in people's lives. Teams aren't just study groups. A group's energy and growth come from acting together (such as meeting with a mayor or bank president to talk about evictions, holding a vigil at an immigration detention center, or walking fast-food workers back to their jobs after a strike). The action a group takes can involve both reaching out to other people (chapter 6) and directly engaging the powers that be (chapter 7). This external work is the oxygen that keeps groups healthy. It's especially powerful when the team designs and leads action directly, rather than just participating in events organized by others. Acting together not only builds trust but also gives people shared experiences to reflect on.

Revise is the point at which people reflect on what was learned from acting together. Reflection and evaluation go hand in hand and are both essential, but they're slightly different activities that shouldn't be confused. Good debriefs begin with reflection, which is about how people feel. This is the emotional stuff people need to say and hear from others. It cannot be argued with: I feel what I feel. Next comes evaluation, which is about comparing what the group set out to do with what was accomplished: what worked, where people fell short, and what lessons were learned. A sign of good organizing is that people know instinctively to circle up after whatever they did together, rather than dribble off—which is the usual tendency—and that before rushing into what mistakes were made, everyone has a chance to say how he or she felt about the experience.

The see-judge-act-revise process is one of many that teams can use to develop their members into leaders. Regardless of what processes and activities you choose, the starting place for creating a culture of learning is to convey to people that they are ends, not means—that their experiences, emotions, learning, and growth matter to the group's success. And then set aside enough time to stop and think, to hash out all the different ways in which people make sense of the world, to learn together. The payoff for an organizing team comes when it turns its collective experiences fighting for justice into powerful new stories that can be recounted over and over and that provide people with confidence and clarity to take on bigger fights.

Ultimately, for small, self-directed teams to thrive and serve as the fuel cells for social movements, they need to be connected to one another and supported by larger systems and structures. People on teams need training and coaching to carry out their roles successfully. They need ways to communicate with one another and coordinate their work to achieve bigger goals. Without support and coordination, teams can float off, wither, or simply become tools for getting people to do things. If we're serious about acting through many distributed teams, we need to make their health and well-being a primary focus of our organizations. The American Antislavery Society and the populists grew so large because they had agents, lecturers, and organizers who traveled around the country knitting face-to-face groups into a larger movement. A similar dynamic energized the Brazilian Base Communities discussed in the next section.

Pulling the Pieces Together into a Movement

Sometimes, we might feel like we have to choose between small groups that are inwardly focused on the needs of their members and groups that are externally focused on changing the world. But this doesn't need to be an either/or choice. Teams can combine the burning purpose of an antislavery society with the commitment to mutual support and growth that is a hallmark of small-group ministries at churches like Saddleback. And by integrating personal and social transformation, small groups can be more attractive to people and easier to spread.

One example of the contagiousness of groups that nourish souls while acting politically comes from Brazil. In the early 1960s, Catholic priests and nuns in Brazil began to experiment with small informal groups that brought together laypeople— mostly in poor rural and urban areas—to read the Bible and reflect on its relevance to their lives. The groups typically had fifteen to twenty-five people. Many used the see-judge-act-revise process discussed in the previous section. They would gather weekly for meetings that included prayer, discussion of the political and social dimensions of Christian faith, and sharing of concrete problems faced by members. Often these discussions would lead the group to take action together to resolve a community issue or join larger organizing efforts in their area. Group members saw this participation in the community as "every bit as religious as prayer."[19]

Over time, these groups came to be known as Basic Ecclesial Communities, or Base Communities. People in countries across Latin America were forming Base Communities during the 1960s and '70s, but the Brazilian Catholic Church was unique in the degree to which church leadership embraced this new model of religious action as a primary strategy for growing their institution. While each Base Community was self-governing and led by its members, "pastoral agents" (mostly priests and nuns) would visit on a regular basis. Catholic dioceses developed materials and brought members of Base Communities together for larger regional, and ultimately national, gatherings. Brazil's most prominent theologians wrote extensively about Base Communities.[20] They viewed the ways in which the groups linked popular prayer and social action as God's will at work in the world.

The priests and nuns who first experimented with Base Communities were deeply influenced by liberation theology. They viewed the poor and their struggle for justice as being at the center of history and Christianity. Like Pope Francis today, they made personal encounters with people in poverty a cornerstone of their ministries. Hundreds of men and women—both clergy and laypeople—moved into rural and urban areas to work with people who were most excluded from the Brazilian economy and society. They created organizing structures—small groups grounded in faith, engaged in the world, led by laypeople. These groups spread because they met people's spiritual hunger and material needs and gave them tools to be agents in transforming their communities and, ultimately, Brazilian society. By the 1980s, there were an estimated one hundred thousand Base Communities in Brazil alone, with approximately two million members.[21]

While the leaders of the Brazilian Catholic Church did not *create* the Base Community strategy, they *embraced* the structure and ethic. This institutional support helped the groups grow in the poorest areas of the country. The relationship was symbiotic. Support from the bishops fueled the growth of the Base Communities, making them one of the most dynamic social forces in Brazilian society. At the same time, the Base Communities reinvigorated Catholicism in Brazil. They brought people back to the church. They also gave church leaders a clearer focus on the structural causes of poverty and inequality—at a time when many Catholic churches in Latin America and globally were moving in a more conservative direction.

The rapid growth of Base Communities in Brazil coincided with a brutal military dictatorship, which ruled the country for two decades, from 1964 to 1985. With training and support from the United States and Great Britain, the Brazilian military wiped out peasant and urban social organizations, as well as left-wing political groups. The regime killed and disappeared hundreds of people and tortured more than thirty thousand. Its economic policies halted land reform and undermined labor organizing. The dictatorship made life immensely more difficult for the rural and urban poor.

Base Communities were one of the few spaces in Brazilian society where people could resist the generals and the economic interests that stood behind them. Some historians say that by repressing social action, the military dictatorship unintentionally increased the focus of Base Communities on the political education of their members. At the same time, the Catholic Church was one of the only institutions with enough independent power to stand up to the generals. Ultimately, this made it possible for both the Base Communities and the bishops to play a critical role in the gradual process of ending military rule in the 1980s.

Once Brazil began its long transition to elected government, the Base Communities provided the foundation for Brazil's most important political movements. This included the Workers' Party and the Landless Workers Movement, as well as a host of other grassroots organizations. Many social movement leaders began their organizing lives as members of Base Communities. In many areas, Base Communities constituted a large part of the membership of nominally secular social justice organizations. And the democratic ethic and participatory practices of Base Communities shaped the culture of Brazilian social movements, making them some of the most dynamic and democratic in the world.

In 2003, the Workers' Party went from being a broad-based social movement to being elected to lead Brazil. Over the next thirteen years, the party disappointed many in its base by adopting economic policies that were viewed as too pro-business. It doubled down on oil and gas extraction. And then it became ensnared in a series of corruption scandals. At the same time, the party led one of the world's most successful efforts to reduce

poverty and economic inequality. The Workers' Party imple-
mented a conditional cash transfer program, called Bolsa
Familia, which provides money to families that meet certain
conditions, such as school attendance for children. As a result
of this and other government initiatives, the poverty rate in
Brazil fell from 22 percent in 2003—when the Workers' Party
was elected to lead the country—to 7 percent in 2011. This
moved thirty-five million Brazilians into the working class
and made the country a global model for efforts to eliminate
poverty. Tina Rosenberg described Bolsa Familia as "likely the
most important government anti-poverty program the world
has ever seen."[22]

The relationship between the Catholic Church, Base Communities, social movements, and the Workers' Party is a long
and complex story that merits its own book. For our pur-
poses though, the history of the Brazilian Base Communities provides a window into how teams that nurture spiritual
and social development can become mass movements able to
transform the lives of millions of people, religious institutions,
and society. They show that it's possible to take the nurturing
elements of small-group ministries and fuse them with a passion to change structures that perpetuate racism and poverty.
That spirit makes it possible for people who've been excluded
from decision making to build big enough constituencies to
negotiate their interests—the focus of the next chapter on base
building.

6

Base
Recruiting a Following You Need to Lead

The purpose of social justice teams in larger movements for change is to build a large base of people powerful and unified enough to negotiate their own freedom and well-being. Beware of the team that becomes a clique or a social club or takes whoever shows up and hopes things will work out. We don't win because we're right. As I've said throughout this book, we are up against powerful people who are usually very clear about their interests. They will give up only as much opportunity, resources, and influence as they must. And they will work every day to increase their profits and power. We get only as much justice as we can negotiate. That requires going into negotiation with leverage, which is what building a base makes possible.

If we want a company to change its environmental practices, we need a large enough base of consumers willing to participate in a boycott. If we want our employer to raise wages and benefits, we need a large enough group of workers willing to withdraw their labor by going out on strike. If we want an elected official to do the right thing, we need voters willing to throw the official out of office if he or she refuses. Our leverage comes from having enough of us willing to use our bodies, votes, and dollars to consistently disrupt injustice and discrimination. The strength of our base is what brings the powers that be to the table. Everything else is wishful thinking.

Like the first three conversations about purpose, story, and team, base building is a way of thinking about change that shifts how we act and build organizations. People will ask, "Why do we need to talk to so many people when we already know the problems?" I heard this a lot when I was organizing in Flint, Michigan, which had no shortage of problems. Going out and meeting hundreds of people on their terms to hear their stories and concerns may seem like slow work, especially when you already have a pretty good sense of what people are angry about. But listening helps us find and enroll organic leaders, people who may not be big talkers but whom others look to for guidance. Many people will tell us no when we invite them to come to a meeting. Some will say maybe but mean no. A few will say yes, but even some of those will also flake out. The true yesses are the people who believe in miracles before they happen, are willing to work (not just talk!), and are respected enough to move other people.

Once people do come together, molding individuals with different identities, ideas, and hesitations into a constituency happens in fits and starts. It's a process full of doubt. When will things ever take off? Why so often two steps forward, one step back? Yet we put everything we're fighting for at risk if we skip this careful work of organizing people into a base prepared to act together against opposition, especially if we are building multiracial organizations and movements, without which we face a bleak future. Seeing a group of people stand up and walk together toward freedom is glorious—even if it doesn't happen on schedule.

This chapter has four parts. The first section explains what a base is and why it creates the leverage necessary to negotiate change. The second describes three beliefs that make base building possible. The third shares practices that you can use to build a base. The fourth focuses on how to work with a group of people to clarify their vision and goals so that they can act together with purpose.

Base Building as a Path to Freedom

A classic example of base building is the story of Exodus. When God asks Moses to lead the people of Israel out of Egypt to freedom, Moses denies God's request four times. More than whether Pharaoh will listen (or have him killed!), Moses is afraid his own the people will reject him. He asks God, "Who am I that I should go to Pharaoh and bring the children of Israel out of Egypt?" (Exodus 3:11). Moses worries that the people will not believe that he was sent by God, that they will not listen to him because he is not eloquent. God answers each objection that Moses raises, explaining how to organize the elders to win over their support; showing Moses how he could use what he already had in his hand to persuade Pharaoh; and telling Moses, "I will be with your mouth and teach you what you shall speak" (Exodus 4:12). Yet still Moses begs God to send someone else.

Moses worries that the people will not believe that he was sent by God. Even after Moses relents, he keeps returning to God to complain about his base. The first crisis comes when Moses and Aaron ask Pharaoh to let the Israelites have three days off to pray in the desert. Not only does the king of Egypt dismiss their request; he tells the slaves that since they are making trouble, they will now have to work harder. The Egyptians will no longer give them straw to make the bricks. Moses is clearly on shaky terms with his constituency. The Israelites ignore him and go directly to Pharaoh to complain. Pharaoh taunts them: "You are idle, you are idle; that is why you say, 'Let us go and sacrifice to the Lord.' Go now, and work, No straw will be given you, but you must still deliver the same number of bricks" (Exodus 5:17–18). The Israelite leaders blame Moses for their plight, saying to him, "You have made us stink in the sight of Pharaoh and his servants, and have put a sword in their hands to kill us" (Exodus 5:21). Moses keeps the cycle of blame going, scolding God, "O Lord, why have you done evil to this people? Why did you ever send me?" (Exodus 5:22).

In his book *I've Got the Light of Freedom: The Organizing Tradition and the Mississippi Freedom Struggle*, Charles Payne tells a similar story about the fight for voting rights in the most violent and segregated counties in the Deep South. He describes a moment in Greenville, Mississippi, when the local power structure made a strategic "miscalculation" that boosted the movement to organize the town. Young organizers from the Student Nonviolent Coordinating Committee (SNCC) had done months of slow base building through one-on-one conversations, house meetings, and door-to-door canvassing. Their work was met with beatings and shootings. Most Black people in Greenville were still watching from the sidelines. But some were beginning to quietly provide financial and material support. An increasing number were going to the courthouse to try to register to vote. The county board of supervisors began to see a movement afoot. So they retaliated by "halt[ing] most distribution of surplus commodities from the federal government [which for] 27,000 people in the county, most of them Black . . . were the main source of sustenance during the winter months."[1]

This collective punishment was akin to Pharaoh's forcing the slaves to make bricks without straw or the violence meted out against Black Memphis in response to the sanitation strike. It made some people wish that the waters had not been troubled. But on the whole, it helped fuse the community together. As Charles Payne says, "It put some people in a position where they no longer had anything to lose by trying to register. It made plain a point [that civil rights] workers always want to put across, that there was a connection between exclusion from the political process and poverty."[2] Many people from Green-ville and allies around the country rallied to create a community food distribution program through the churches. This brought to the fore people who hadn't attended citizenship schools or tried to register, who might not have seen themselves as politi-cal. And it began to touch thousands of people directly in their day-to-day lives. Bob Moses, the architect of the Mississippi push, described how "people were standing in line in front of the church waiting for food while their plantation owner was riding by . . . telling them to go back to the plantations . . . and they [the plantation workers] were telling them that they were going to stand there and get their food because their children were hungry."[3]

SNCC's first effort to organize Mississippi in the small city of McComb had failed when the Black community reached a point where they could not take any more of the violent reaction from the White power structure. Community leaders asked the orga-nizers to leave. But in Greenville—as in the story of Exodus—the organizers and the community made it over the bridge. The oppression they faced strengthened them, rather than crushed them. Ultimately, they succeeded in making Greenville an "organized town." That meant that local leaders had built enough of an organized base to continue to fight and win orga-nizing battles long after SNCC had left and the national fervor around the civil rights movement faded. This is akin to what Jane McAlevey describes in her book *No Short Cuts: Organizing for Power in the New Gilded Age* as the muscle that unionized workers develop through repeated strikes showing employers that they have no choice but to negotiate with their employees.[4]

A paradox of Exodus is that if God had decided to liberate the Hebrew people from slavery, why not free them directly? Why choose to work through Moses and an extended confron-tation with Pharaoh? What are the lessons of the story not only about the ethics of slavery but about how change takes place and the role that faith plays? First, faith is not always (re)built overnight—it comes from lived experience—from directly seeing justice happen in the world. Second, people need to become ready for their own liberation. They need to build the fortitude to take the risks needed to break free from oppression. And third, liberation is a collective experience that happens in the context of confrontation. Freedom cannot be granted; it must be taken—together.

And just as the base is being tested, so are the leaders. The self-doubt that Moses feels is no different from what anyone faces who is building a constituency for change under uncertain conditions. At times, God tells Moses to stop overthinking things and just lead. Other times, God says to share power with others. God tells Moses to gather seventy elders and says, "I will take some of the Spirit that is on you and put it on them, and they shall bear the burden of the people with you, so that you may not bear it yourself alone" (Numbers 11:17). This is good organizing advice, but the extended and conflict-filled relationship between Moses and God makes it clear that Moses is struggling with something deeper than organizing mechanics. He cannot build a constituency that he can lead to freedom until he figures out whether he believes in himself and in others.

Three Beliefs That Make Base Building Possible

Before we can get to the practical steps of building a base, we need to bring an understanding about people and power to the table. The first belief that we need to have—or act like we have, despite our doubts—is that enough willing people are out there, waiting to be invited into a movement for freedom and justice. Charles Payne says of Fannie Lou Hamer, who became one of the most important figures in the civil rights movement, that "[l]ike so many of the others, it wasn't so much that she was found by the movement as that she had been searching for it."[5] Hamer had been a sharecropper for years and was working as the time-keeper on a plantation in Sunflower County, Mississippi, when she heard from her pastor and a friend about a voting rights meeting. She'd already been involved in the NAACP and other political activities. After she attended the mass meeting organized by SNCC, she attempted to register to vote. Her boss told her that she had to either withdraw her application or lose her job at the plantation. She decided that standing up for her right to vote was worth losing her job. She left the plantation and hid for a while. She went on to teach citizenship classes and become a field secretary with SNCC. Later, as the vice-chair of the Mississippi Freedom Democratic Party, she spoke at the 1964 Democratic National Convention, leading the effort to break the back of formal racial segregation in American politics.

All evidence shows that if you have enough conversations with enough people, knock on enough doors, make enough phone calls, ask enough people for referrals, and open enough doors for people to walk through, you'll find enough people willing to get involved and speak out. You'll build a base of people who will go on to build their own bases. The question, like the one Moses wrestled with, is whether you have the courage to face the rejection, ill humor, and sometimes violence that come along the way.

The second belief that we need is that people are brilliant. They have the skills and talent to build organizations and lead change. People are the precious resources out of which social movements are built. Charles Payne argues that much of the lasting social and political impact of the civil rights movement flowed from Ella Baker and Septima Clark, who taught the importance of leadership development and organizing "spade work" over flashy events. Baker mentored and challenged at one point or another all the best-known civil rights icons, including Martin Luther King, Jr., and Robert Moses. Clark founded and spread citizenship schools that taught political and organizing skills to thousands of African American working people. Payne writes about the two women: "Part of the legacy of people like Ella Baker and Septima Clark is a faith that ordinary people who learn to believe in themselves are capable of extraordinary acts, or better, of acts that seem extraordinary to us precisely because we have such an impoverished sense of the capabilities of ordinary people."[6]

When I was organizing with parents at public schools in Philadelphia, a woman named Dolores Shaw started to show up at parent meetings at an elementary school that had a student population that was about 40 percent African American and 60 percent Latino. At the beginning, most of the other parents saw Dolores as disruptive. She would egg people on about how Latino kids needed to stop speaking Spanish and learn English. Other parents pushed back on Dolores. But she kept coming to meetings. Over time, she built relationships with Latino parents. People came to rely on her fierceness and self-confidence, the traits that initially drove everyone crazy. At one point, the group demanded that the school hire more teachers who spoke Spanish. Dolores surprised everyone by speaking out in support of the proposal at a public meeting, more strongly than anyone else in the room. By that point, relationships had shifted her understanding of the world and her place in it.

Dolores ended up playing an important role in a series of high-profile campaigns in Philadelphia, including cochairing the negotiating team that reached an agreement with First Union Bank to keep open eleven inner-city bank branches, and make hundreds of millions of dollars in loans available in her and other neighborhoods, as part of the largest bank merger in Philadelphia history. I remember being in her kitchen as she cooked dinner for her family while she was also talking on the phone to a *Philadelphia Inquirer* reporter. When the call was over, she looked at me and said, "Who in the world would have imagined that a news reporter would be calling me up about my opinion about anything?" The truth is that the call made perfect sense. If you strip away the prejudices that conflate where people live, their formal education, and their race with civic virtue and a right to be heard—which is what organizing does—you get Dolores Shaw and Fannie Lou Hamer. And that makes a movement possible—but only if we believe in each other.

The third belief that makes the difference is that our power in the world to create a good life for ourselves and for those we love flows from the relationships we have with other people. What gives us power is having a constituency. Without a base, we have no choice but to rely on good intentions and on systems being fair, neither of which we can count on in times of crisis. Some people appear to be leaders but are not accountable to the people on whose behalf they say they speak. Those are phantom leaders whose power turns on the fickleness of the media and other elites. The ticket to true leadership and power in a world on fire is a following, which is what a base comes down to. Here's how to build one.

> **Without a base, we have no choice but to rely on good intentions and on systems being fair.**

How to Build a Base Powerful Enough to Negotiate Change

Once we embrace base building as necessary for social change, some useful practices can help us organize a large constituency. These practices boil down to careful analysis of our own networks and resources combined with a willingness to go out and patiently listen to and build relationships with lots of people.

Mapping Power Relationships

The first work is to find people who can help us map power relationships. We need to do careful work to understand the power of the people who run the place. But we also need to map out the power of our constituency so that we maximize its influence. One of the most interesting parts of the story that Charles Payne tells in *I've Got the Light of Freedom* is the relationship between Robert Moses and Amzie Moore. Moses was the visionary leader of SNCC. He came south from Harlem with a master's degree in philosophy from Harvard. Moore was the president of the Cleveland, Mississippi, NAACP and a longtime civic leader in the state. Moore grew up on a plantation and had lost his mother at a young age. In the 1930s, Moore was involved in the Black and Tan Party, an organization of Black Republicans. Like many other African American men of the time, he'd come back from WWII motivated both to build a more prosperous life for his family and to take on segregation. Moore knew everyone. "Moore gave Moses an oral history of the state and a political map, analyzing and laying out the whole cast of characters across the state, bringing [him] in on who were the players, how to work with them, what to expect from this one, what this one's orientation was."[7] Together they sketched out what would become the "Mississippi movement of the sixties." Moses, Ella Baker, and other SNCC staff taught this same political curiosity to organizers before they began work in any town or county. SNCC was unique in hiring a staff from different backgrounds, but most of those who worked as organizers grew up in working-class families in the Deep South. Part of SNCC's strength was its ability to surface young people who could organize their own towns, paid or unpaid, and build strong trust relationships with elders like Amzie Moore.

Given time and the right conversations, the social networks and power dynamics that shape life in a community can be made visible. Often the most powerful relationships are hidden, just as the best-networked people are usually the hardest to catch up with. But nothing is impossible with time and curiosity. To reorganize a community, we need to understand its economic base: who owns the capital and the land, who employs the labor and how that is changing. We need to "follow the money" to understand the economic interests that stand behind the politicians.

As we put a community under an x-ray, we're looking for people with both formal and informal authority. Make a list of fifteen to twenty of the most powerful people in your environment (your community, city, or state). Be rigorous. Identify people who have influence over others—because of their formal positions as employers or government officials, through their control of money or institutions, or because people respect and trust them. We need to get close to people who run things— our mayors, councilpeople, and business owners. We don't have to agree with people about everything, or even much at all, to create relationships with them. We give people in positions of authority too much power over us when we don't hold them close enough to know their ins and outs. Your list should also include people who lead civic and religious institutions (visiting these people often gives us useful information and also communicates that what we are building is meant to be open and collaborative to existing organizations and institutions). But don't stop there. Identify more informal leaders, those who don't hold positions but whom people look to when they have problems or questions. Every town and city has young people like those who took to the streets in Ferguson and woke up the nation. They also need to be part of your power map.

Every town and city has young people like those who took to the streets in Ferguson and woke up the nation.

Start with People Closest to the Pain

As we map power relationships and begin to build a base, the most urgent listening we need to do is with people who are closest to the pain of injustice, who've been most pushed around. This includes people who are formerly incarcerated, undocumented, low-wage workers, public school parents, bus riders, and public-housing tenants. They've experienced the trauma of systems out of whack. They know how things work. In Faith in Action, we focus on the combustion that is possible when you bring people who have the most on the line together with religious institutions and people of faith, who can frame issues in moral terms (they're often the same people).

For example, IndyCAN, a faith-based organization affiliated with Faith in Action in Indiana, partnered with the local chamber of commerce to win more than $1 billion in financing for an equitable public transit system for their region. As part of this campaign, grassroots leaders from IndyCAN went to bus stops to listen to the concerns of bus riders. They'd invite people they talked with to participate in organizing meetings, lobby days, and public events in support of mass transit. The combination of bus riders, business leaders, and the faith community successfully lobbied the Republican-controlled Indiana legislature and Governor Mike Pence to approve legislation to enable a regional ballot measure to raise taxes to fund a public transit system. Combining a base of people who are directly impacted by policy decisions with a moral message and influential institutions is a powerful recipe for changing unjust systems.

The Fight for $15 is another example of a breakthrough in organizing people who have been most marginalized by society. Contrary to the stereotypes of kids working part-time jobs, fast-food workers are often parents working multiple jobs to sustain their families. They not only receive low wages but also face dangerous working conditions and unpredictable hours. There has been a long history of neighborhood organizers finding low-wage workers who could tell their stories in support of city and state campaigns to raise the minimum wage. But the organizers whose work led to the Fight for $15 wanted to go beyond recruiting spokespeople and build an active base of workers. With support from Service Employees International Union (SEIU), organizers in New York City began to experiment with new strategies for reaching out to fast-food workers directly at their workplaces. They developed "raps" (short scripts) that helped organizers go into restaurants and talk to workers about working conditions. Organizers used Facebook ads to create lists of workers who wanted to make changes in their workplaces. These techniques enabled the Fight for $15 to identify thousands of fast-food workers willing to walk off the job for better wages and a union.[8]

A Constituency Is Not Abstract

You need to be precise about the specific people you're organizing into a constituency. SEIU's membership base includes many low-wage workers, who've won better wages and benefits through collective bargaining. But low-wage workers are not really a constituency. It's a label we give to people who do many different jobs in different places under different circumstances. In the 1980s, SEIU's Justice for Janitors campaign organized women and men who clean large office buildings. SEIU organizers had to figure out what workers they were organizing, at what buildings, in what cities. The same is true for Fight for $15 (which needed to identify what restaurant chains in what cities) or any other successful organizing drive. Until we can make a list of the people we intend to organize and describe them specifically enough to find them in the flesh, we're just organizing ideas, not people.

> Until we can make a list of the people we intend to organize and describe them specifically enough to find them in the flesh, we're just organizing ideas, not people.

The Power of Listening

The process of building a base is as simple as going out and talking to people about what they care about, what they want to see changed, what makes them angry. When W. W. Law returned home from fighting in WWII, he became a leader in the Savannah, Georgia, branch of the NAACP and found work as a postman. He told me that delivering mail accomplished two goals: it gave him a salary that didn't depend on the local power structure, and it put him out on the streets talking to people every day. As Law walked the streets delivering the mail, he built a political base. Through thousands of conversations over many years, he developed a large and loyal constituency that was willing to follow him and the NAACP into battle. That base sustained sit-ins and weekly mass meetings. It showed the Savannah power structure that it was up against a unified community. Law's ability to represent people whom he was in regular conversation with was his ticket to credible leadership and influence.

Base building works because we're social beings. Over time, if you talk to enough people and then bring some of them together, you'll shift the power dynamic in a community. Take ten people in a community who share common views but don't know one another. Now bring them together to get to know one another. Research shows that they will each become more influential and persuasive in their community.[9]

Similarly, the main factor determining whether people vote is whether their friends, family members, coworkers, and neighbors are voting. People give many reasons for why they voted or not, but these are after-the-fact rationalizations. Research shows that what actually leads people to vote is social pressure from the people around them.[10] This is one reason why door-to-door canvassing, especially by people from the same neighborhood, increases voter turnout.[11] If organizing and base building reach a high enough intensity, you can wake up any community. You can create a culture in which political participation is the expected norm.

Hard Asks

The primary skill that drives base building forward is the ability to make hard asks that challenge people to step up and take leadership. We don't do people favors when we talk to them but fail to propose a compelling next step. Giving someone a thoughtful proposition is a gift. Asking is an art form. Propositions should be big enough to be somewhat surprising but not so big that they overwhelm. We're aiming for small steps that are significant. Make the ask and then stop talking. Wait for the answer. Don't step on your ask.

However, the most powerful propositions are not requests for someone to do a piece of work. They're to become a new person. Turning yourself into a public person with the power to shape the world is not easy. Like the Hebrew slaves, we inevitably face harsh opposition that tells us to get back into our passive places in society. We're dismissed as having nothing to offer. We're just making trouble. It's easy to conclude that the struggle to find our voices and our freedom isn't worth the pain. If you're working to build power—whether you're a grassroots community leader working as a volunteer or a paid organizer—your job is to motivate people to keep moving forward despite the resistance they face.

Make Listening a Campaign

Unfortunately, listening and base building often take a backseat to seemingly more exciting organizing activities like protests and rallies. One way to counter that tendency is to treat the work of bringing new people to the table and developing their leadership skills as campaigns, with specific numeric goals, deadlines, a communications plan, and a distribution of roles.

The United Farm Workers used "house meetings" to build their movement. They propositioned people to invite their co-workers, friends, and neighbors to their homes for an hour or hour-and-a-half conversation. At a typical house meeting, the host starts by explaining his or her personal motivation and the goals of the organization that he or she is helping build. People are asked to share their stories and concerns. At the end, participants are propositioned to organize their own meetings. House meetings create a concrete test for hosts, whose leadership potential is demonstrated by their ability to gather people. The meetings surface ideas and potential new leaders. And the people who attend can decide to keep meeting and develop into an organizing team. Thousands of organizations have used house-meeting campaigns to build their memberships and find new leaders. House meetings were a major component of the 2008 Obama campaign's process for recruiting volunteers and organizing neighborhood teams to contact voters.

Listening campaigns can be structured in other ways as well. "Listening Sabbaths" can bring people together after religious services to share their stories and concerns. When I was organizing in schools in Philadelphia, we learned that you could reach more parents through grade meetings— short listening sessions for parents from each grade. More parents would attend a grade meeting than a schoolwide meeting, presumably because the invitation for all third-grade parents is more personal and relevant. That's an example of the power of small groups. "What matters is not that there was a general invitation that I heard about but that a specific person communicated to me that I was wanted at

> "What matters is not that there was a general invitation that I heard about but that a specific person communicated to me that I was wanted at this gathering."

this gathering." That's the key to listening campaigns that reach thousands of people and begin to unlock the social networks within a community.

Imagining a Nationwide Listening Process

In Spain, Podemos (Spanish for "we can") is a populist political party that grew out of the country's antiausterity social movement of *indignados* ("the outraged"). After the party was launched, it held a two-month public discussion process to debate its ethical, political, and organizational structure. More than one hundred thousand people participated. Podemos leaders were trying to build a political party accountable to an organized base of people, unlike any other party in Spain. They were influenced by Latin American indigenous movements, which made nationwide listening processes a key component of their political strategy.

The rapid growth of Podemos flowed from thousands of *circulos* (volunteer groups)—some organized at a neighborhood level, others among people in the same professions—that both debated party decisions and took direct action, such as stopping evictions. In 2014, the Podemos two-month listening campaign culminated in a national congress attended by eleven thousand people. The party membership debated key decisions in public in front of the country. Podemos has also used social networking tools to grow its base. It used crowdfunding to finance its operations and campaigns and two specific social networking tools (Agora Voting and Appgree) to solicit party member preferences on candidates and poll members on policy proposals. It also used Reddit to support discussion within and across *circulos*.[12] This listening and base building has not been easy to sustain over time, but it has helped lead to a shared vision and agenda that fused people together into a movement and has made Podemos the second largest political party in Spain.

Clarifying Vision and Goals

Because each of us is unique, getting people on the same page and moving forward together can be hard. For one thing, there is the "free-rider" problem, the tendency for some people to sit back and get the benefits of the larger group's work without contributing themselves. Luckily, only a small fraction of any community, state, or country is needed to create a social revolution. Theda Skocpol defines organizations with membership density as those representing at least 1 percent of the target population.[13] For example, Maine People's Alliance has 32,000 dues-paying members from 170 towns and every county in the state.[14] That's about 2.5 percent of Maine's population, which means that decision makers in the state need to take the alliance's agenda seriously.

But even with a small slice of the population, it's still hard to harmonize people's needs and dreams and reach agreement on how to best advance change. Many of us come into organizations with a foggy understanding of how structures shape our lives and which people are profiting from the problems we see around us. Moving a group to clarity about what to do together, and how to do it, takes work and patience. Businesses know their bottom line. That helps them figure out pretty quickly whether they should work together collectively and what demands they should make. But groups of individuals have many different bottom lines that need to be negotiated together through what can feel like endless meetings.

The last thing we want is a base either without a live demand or with a live demand that has no clear strategy for victory.

Getting to a big shared demand and the political strategy to win is a key part of building and sustaining a base. The last thing we want is a base either without a live demand or with a live demand that has no clear strategy for victory. The other common tendency to avoid is that of fragmenting your base by splitting its efforts and focus across simultaneous campaigns. It's better to spend enough time hashing out strategy and building solidarity so people can sequence demands, rather than breaking into committees and running off in several different directions at once.

The next chapter looks closely at political strategy and policy demands. At this point, I want to focus on how we align people around a vision and specific goals. Let's say that we've listened to the concerns and ideas of fifteen hundred people through house meetings and other listening sessions. We've done research actions with public officials and other people who can help us think through the issues people have raised. We know the biggest pain points in the community and have identified some possible opportunities for action. We want to take everything we've heard and seen and use it to set priorities. We want an agenda and strategy that can unite people and begin to put us on a path toward structural changes.

The first set of questions to ask are about vision. If we release ourselves from constraints for a moment, what is our dream for how the world would look? Describe your promised land as concretely as possible. What would our city, state, or country look like if it reflected your values? How similar are our visions? Then let's discuss our political analysis of the situation we're in: What is our power? How prepared is our base to take action together? Will we hold together against resistance, or will we fold? Whom are we up against? What are their strengths and vulnerabilities? How hard do we think it will be to get them to negotiate? Who are allies who will stand with us? Who's on the fence? This kind of shared analysis helps people begin to consolidate into a base. And it lays the groundwork for people making hard decisions about their priorities.

That leads to the next question: Given our vision and our analysis, what are some concrete goals that we could achieve together? Good organizing goals are *strategic*:[15] they not only deliver real benefits to our base but also shift power in our direction or set us up for success in future struggles. The SNCC push on voting rights was strategic. It addressed one of the key contradictions keeping Blacks in poverty in the South—a lack of political power to compel investment in education and economic development in Black communities—while forcing the hand of the federal government to pass a national Voting Rights Act.

We also want our goals to be *measurable*. That way, we know if we succeeded or failed and can learn from the experience. A good way to make goals measurable is to ask people to describe what exactly would be different for themselves and people they know if we were successful. In other words, what does success look like? A lot of times when we talk about the changes we want to bring about, we refer to abstract or lofty ideas, such as our children would get a better education or immigrant families would not feel fear of deportation. These fit into the vision discussion. With measurable goals, we want to push into the realm of things that, if we came back from the future, we could legitimately say we won or lost. If it's not possible to say "Yes we won that" or "No we fell short," then we haven't identified a useful measure of success. Say, for example, that the state you live in (Pennsylvania, in this case) is one of three without any standard education funding formula. Instead, politicians decide each year how much money goes to which school districts. Poor urban and rural school systems are underfunded, and the higher the Black enrollment, the worse the disparity. In this case, our measurable success goal could be a funding formula that eliminates the racial disparities immediately and puts us on a five-year path to equalize funding, with extra weights in the funding formula for students with disabilities, English as a second language, and other special needs.

If demands are too small, people lose interest and won't see the necessary effort as worth it. If demands are too large or not chunked into pieces, people cannot reach the next step. In 2006, organizations in the PICO network decided to work together and with other organizations toward the goal of covering all children in the United States with health insurance. Some of our labor and community organizing allies felt that starting with children was "low-hanging fruit" that might take pressure off the urgency for broader health reform. But from a base-building perspective, we felt that state fights over expanding health coverage, and a national children's health fight, were good steps toward creating a broader, people-led movement to guarantee health coverage for everyone. Ultimately, winning the campaign to expand children's coverage was harder and took longer than people expected. But it helped build a bigger organized constituency for national health reform. That contributed to the successful push for passage of the Affordable Care Act, after more than one hundred years of failed attempts to provide near universal health coverage in the United States (a victory despite ongoing efforts to repeal and undermine the law).

Some measurable goals might take years to achieve. Still, the goals need to be very clear and well understood. And there needs to be a plausible strategy for winning, with steps along the way or else the goals are just words on paper. The key is that you can say with a straight face, "We'll be back in six months or two years in this room. Let's see if we can get to a point where we could all agree that this goal was met or not." Of course, the greater the goals, the larger and stronger the base we need to win.

In our fight to protect my son's autism program, one of the most difficult moments was when we realized that our base was too small to win. We'd engaged many of the parents who had children in the program, but that was too few people to influence the school board. So we made a decision to begin reaching out to other families without children in special education. For some of us, that meant talking to people for the first time about our children having autism. We weren't sure what to expect. But hundreds of parents signed our petition, and many came out to board meetings to support us. That response kept us going. I was touched by some of the people I hadn't expected to step forward. And also by those who shared their own stories of struggling with getting the needs of their children met in school. It was a good reminder to not think too small about your constituency. People saw our children as their children. They understood that a web of interdependence tied us together. We don't always see it, yet what we can achieve in the world is tied to our ability to turn that web into a living, breathing movement of people able to confront and negotiate change with those in power.

7

Power
Winning Social Change

In June 2010, as the nation's biggest banks were spending more than $1 million a day lobbying against federal legislation designed to prevent another financial crisis, I took my daughter, Natalia, to New York City for a march on Wall Street. The night before, she'd been in a music program at her elementary school. The chorus sang Black freedom songs and reenacted famous moments in the civil rights struggle. The students (dressed in white shirts and black pants and skirts) captured the moral clarity of that movement. The next day, marching with thousands of people through lower Manhattan, I could feel Natalia's confusion and discomfort. For a time, we were stuck walking alongside people chanting obscenities. But even after we found others to march with, the cacophony of messages and the lack of a clear moral narrative were painful to watch through the eyes of a ten-year-old.

People often associate social movements with large marches and rallies. When strategic and focused, high-profile events can help push demands forward and demonstrate public support. But they can also leave us feeling empty, wondering what we accomplished. For social change to succeed, breakthrough moments need to rest on a foundation of strategic grassroots organizing. My Chilean organizing friends describe this as the work of *hormigas* (ants). It involves patiently recruiting people, developing their leadership skills, aligning them around a common agenda, developing strategy together, making demands, and delivering changes that people can see and feel in their lives.

An essential element of this day-to-day organizing is directly confronting (and negotiating with) people who are in positions of authority—those who, if they made different choices, could relieve the suffering and injustice we see around us. This confrontation, which doesn't always feel like a polite discussion, is the fifth conversation essential to social progress. Directly engaging people in power is important because it helps us realize our own power and makes our organizations smarter and more courageous. And the victories we win as a result lay the groundwork for larger-scale legislative and cultural change.

More of this kind of grassroots organizing is going on in the United States (and around the globe) today than we're led to believe in the media—but not enough. Face-to-face organizing aimed at improving people's daily lives is a muscle that we've allowed to atrophy. In *Bowling Alone: The Collapse and Revival of American Community*, Robert Putnam says that participation levels in protests and civil disobedience did not change significantly from 1960 through 2000 (although public acceptance of these activities increased to the point where they no longer surprised people).[1] On the other hand, people's involvement in local political and civic activity fell dramatically during this same period.[2] That has to change if we have any hope of taking on the threats facing our communities and society.

This chapter has three sections. The first shows how face-to-face confrontation with decision makers helps people become agents of change. It offers examples of how this approach works in practice and shares a tool (a "research action") that can be used to structure conversations with authorities and begin untangling injustice. The second section explains how campaigns working for tangible changes in communities can pave the way for larger state and federal movements. The third section focuses on four principles of strategy that help organizations and movements win change campaigns. The chapter shows how the conversations about purpose, story, team, and base discussed in previous chapters can lead to victories that make people's lives better. It should also help answer the question of how organized people can prevail over wealthy and powerful forces.

Confronting Power

The primary reason for confronting mayors, district attorneys, bank CEOs, and others in positions of authority is to negotiate changes that matter to our families and communities. In doing so we reclaim some of our humanity and agency in the world. Every moment of our waking hours, companies are competing for our attention, trying to sell us products, emotions, and experiences that we may not need or even want. Our political system increasingly follows the same pattern. Candidates, parties, and special interests spend billions of dollars on massive databases and advertising that treat voters as commodities that can be turned out, turned off, or persuaded to vote in certain ways. This "commercialization of politics"[3] can leave many of us feeling alienated from political issues and passive about the decisions that shape our lives.

That begins to change when we sit down face-to-face with decision makers to explain how we're experiencing injustice— whether losing a loved one to gun violence or trying to raise a family on minimum-wage jobs. When we share our pain and probe what can be done about it or demand changes in policies, we go from being objects of someone else's manipulation to agents of our own destiny. The experience can be exciting and intimidating. It's common for people to have physical reactions of anxiety (like sweaty palms) when they meet with officials. Politicians can use our nervousness and discomfort either to insulate themselves from accountability or to get their way. Lyndon Johnson was famous for using his six-foot-five frame to intimidate people into doing what he wanted (in fact, it has even been called "the Johnson Treatment"). He reportedly would have people come in to talk with him while he was sitting on the toilet, or corner senators whose votes he wanted and lean into them within inches, making his demands.

Although it may not have worked with Johnson, one tool for structuring interactions with powerful people on *our* terms is a "research action." This is a small meeting (attended by perhaps eight to ten people) with a decision maker or someone who has insight into the policies and systems that we're trying to change. Typically, first meetings don't include demands. They focus on figuring out the authority and outlook of the person we're meeting with. We ask questions about how decisions get made. We look for contradictions between what the official says should be happening and what we see taking place. We test out solutions. As with most organizing activities, we prepare ahead of time (to brainstorm questions and distribute roles). Research actions can start with introductions and getting to know the person you're meeting with, move into questions, and conclude with a discussion of next steps (for example, asking the official to attend a larger meeting). What's most important (and sometimes surprising to the person you're meeting with) is showing up with a spirit of curiosity. Often organizations will set up large numbers of research actions after listening campaigns. These meetings with officials and people with expertise help the organization better understand and prioritize issues raised during the listening process and identify opportunities for action.

In studying Faith in Action's work, Paul Speer and Brian Christens found that participation in research actions was the best predictor that someone would take on greater leadership in organizations and feel greater agency in their communities.[4] Small meetings with elected officials can be new and unexpected experiences that help people see themselves and the world differently. That's why it's important to move people quickly into face-to-face encounters with decision makers if you want them to stick around and grow.

These experiences help us realize that we're up against other human beings, and human-created rules, rather than fixed truths. Systems that oppress and exclude are more jury-rigged than we think. They're full of contradictions and inconsistencies and especially vulnerable to confrontation by people on whom they've inflicted the greatest pain—like people who've lost their homes to foreclosure or formerly incarcerated men and women working to put their lives back together. That's one reason why social justice campaigns need to be led by people who've had the most direct experience with unjust systems and have the most at stake in change.

The end goal of any system is self-preservation. Survival trumps the loftiest mission statements, which is why people who run systems often violate their stated principles to preserve their privileges. The starting place for transforming a system is understanding that it is governed by a rulebook (a combination of the official policies and the informal ways in which things are usually done). The rules, some of which are usually hidden, lay out who benefits, who is excluded, who can make whom do what, and who makes decisions based on what criteria—who is eligible for health coverage, who can take out student loans at what interest rates, which workers are covered by the minimum wage and which work just for tips. Rulebooks can be rewritten, but we have to understand them first, which is why research actions can be so useful.

For example, early in our campaign to save my son's autism program, we had a series of research meetings with school board members and school district staff. These meetings helped us realize that the superintendent was our biggest problem. The school board president was backing him up, which explained why we weren't making any progress with her. When we finally met with the superintendent, he sat for nearly an hour without saying a word. I was sitting next to him and watched his hands shaking slightly (nervousness can work in both directions). Eventually, one of the parents said, "I'd like to hear what the superintendent has to say!" The first thing the superintendent said was, "I don't have children. So I can't know how you feel." And then he said, "I don't want to say anything about the autism program because you'll use what I say against me."

This was the kind of research action where we didn't learn much directly. But when we debriefed afterward (which is as important as the meeting itself), the consensus was that the superintendent didn't have a good grasp of the program. He was, as one parent said, looking at the issue through the "green eyeshades" of an accountant. Our experience of meeting the top guy face-to-face and seeing that he hadn't engaged with the substance of our concerns motivated us to hold another round of conversations with school board members. Showing them the value of the autism program wasn't enough. We had to convince them that they shouldn't defer decisions about the program to the superintendent. In the end, four out of five board members voted to restore funding, with the school board president voting against it. She then voted against the whole $500 million budget, surprising her colleagues, who told her that it was a betrayal to lead a budget process, only to vote against the end result. It turned out that we were caught in a larger debate about the balance of power between the school board and the superintendent. To win, we needed to understand enough about the school board politics to disrupt them—which was possible because we'd done a dozen research actions.

When we engage public officials on our terms, over time we also become more confident in our power. Here's another example of how engagement can motivate us to keep fighting and help move our agenda forward. On the day after the 2010 midterm elections, I joined two dozen homeowners and clergy who traveled to Washington, DC, to meet with US Treasury Secretary Tim Geithner. The night before, we'd ditched our plan to prep for the meeting. Instead, we went to see *Inside Job*, a movie that recounts the extraordinary measures that Geithner and his predecessor, Henry Paulson, took to protect the country's biggest banks.

The next day, we sat around a large conference table on the top floor of the Treasury Building. Rev. Lucy Kolin, from Oakland Community Organizations, chaired the meeting. She did two things that illustrate the personal power that people develop from engaging in lots of face-to-face interactions with decision makers. When the staff wanted to begin without Geithner, saying he would join us later, Lucy politely said, "No, we're happy to wait here until he's available." I wondered if the staff thought that they might end up with a group of clergy and homeowners occupying the Treasury and refusing to leave, because their cell phones immediately came out and magically Geithner appeared soon thereafter. When Geithner sat down at the head of the table, he began to talk. Lucy politely but firmly stopped him and said, "We prepared an agenda that we shared with your staff ahead of time. We'd like to follow that agenda." Geithner did a double take and then said, "I'm not used to that, but okay." And Lucy led the meeting from start to finish.

During the meeting, people shared stories of losing their homes to foreclosure. They told of whole neighborhoods that were financially underwater and half-vacant as a result of the financial crisis. We presented a set of steps the Obama administration could take without Congress (which after the midterm elections was soon to be in the hands of Republicans) to prevent as many as one million unnecessary foreclosures. We urged Geithner to adopt specific policies that would essentially break the link between homeowners losing their jobs and losing their homes. Geithner listened. He said he sympathized with us and agreed with our analysis but that his hands were tied and he didn't have the power to do what we were asking of him. At that point, one of the pastors lost his temper and asked Geithner how he was able to move heaven and earth to bail out his banker friends but had no power to help families. Geithner didn't have a response.

It was frustrating to see the Treasury secretary's disengagement up close. But sitting down with him helped motivate us to keep fighting. And it clarified our strategy. None of us left believing Geithner's claim that nothing could be done. We saw more clearly the gulf between what the Obama administration said it was doing to stop foreclosures and what it could do. In debriefing after our experience at the Treasury, we recognized that we weren't going to get answers from Geithner. We decided that we needed to focus next door on the White House. So we worked to get a meeting with Gene Sperling, who'd just been appointed to head President Obama's National Economic Council (replacing Larry Summers). Our first meeting with Sperling in the Roosevelt Room was contentious on both sides. We were angry when Sperling left midway. But we'd taken a step forward. We'd been able to put Sperling in a room face-to-face with families who had the most at stake from the decisions he was making—and he'd been willing to argue with us. We knew we were making progress when we began meeting regularly with Sperling upstairs in his cramped West Wing office. But we didn't break through on our demands until Massachusetts Communities Action Network (led by veteran organizer Lew Finfer) was able to get a story about unemployed homeowners facing foreclosure on the front page of the *New York Times* (it took six months of working with the reporter to get the story published).[5]

That news story and growing criticism of the Administration's approach to foreclosure gave us leverage to begin negotiating policy changes that covered many of the recommendations we'd originally presented to Secretary Geithner. These included giving unemployed homeowners twelve months of delayed payments to keep their homes until they found new work. The changes that resulted from our cycle of confrontation with the Treasury Department and the White House came too late for many families. But they helped some who would have otherwise lost their homes.

People say that elected officials work for the voters, not the reverse. But this happens only if *we the people* take the initiative. People are less intimated negotiating with an elected official if they've met with that official while he or she was running for office. And when our confrontation with decision makers results in changes that we and others can benefit from directly—such as stopping evictions, getting parents released from immigrant detention centers, or raising wages to put more money in workers' pockets—we become political actors shaping the world. And we lay the groundwork for bigger fights.

Creating Precedent and Momentum for Bigger Changes

Victories that we win from face-to-face confrontation with authorities not only deliver better lives; they also create energy, lessons, momentum, and precedent for larger-scale changes in society—if we connect the dots between the issues we're working on and bigger systems and decisions. People who run things want us to believe that the initiative rests with them. And even our own social justice organizations sometimes fall into the trap of asking us to take small actions for important causes (say, signing a petition or making a phone call) without giving us ways to engage more deeply. Yet throughout US history, big social change has usually come from collective action that begins in local communities and is led and driven forward by people who have the most at stake in change.

We know from history that large-scale change can take decades of organizing and then come in incredibly short bursts during periods of intense mobilization. The last time that a social movement provoked large-scale structural change in American society was during a brief period in 1964–65. Eight months after becoming president, Lyndon Johnson signed the Civil Rights Act of 1964 into law on July 2, overcoming the longest filibuster in US history. The act outlawed discrimination in public accommodations, education, and federal programs (but did not address voting). Four months later, Johnson was re-elected by the largest majority since 1820. He began his term with the biggest Democratic Party majority in Congress since the 1930s. Democrats held 68 seats in the Senate and a 155-vote advantage in the House. Five tumultuous months after the election—a period that included Bloody Sunday in Selma, Alabama; the successful march from Selma to Montgomery; and the assassination of Malcolm X—Johnson signed the Immigration and Nationality Act, ending four decades of racist immigration quotas that favored Northern and Western European Whites while keeping Asians, Africans, Jews, and Southern Europeans from being able to migrate to the United States. Thirty days later he signed Medicare and Medicaid into law. A week after that, he signed the Voting Rights Act. Each of these laws, plus the Civil Rights Act from the previous summer, fundamentally changed American life. They shifted the racial and ethnic composition of the country, integrated large areas of public life, changed the nature of citizenship, and created a

> Large-scale change can take decades of organizing and then come in incredibly short bursts during periods of intense mobilization.

cradle-to-grave health-care safety net. All four laws were deeply intertwined. They were possible only because of a powerful and disruptive civil rights movement that had been building steam for a decade.

The achievements of 1964–65 built on historic legislation won by the labor movement thirty years earlier during a similar window of opportunity. On July 5, 1935, President Franklin Roosevelt signed the Labor Relations Act, putting the federal government on the side of organized workers and creating the legal conditions for the emergence of an American middle class. A month later, he signed the Social Security Act, which broke the link between aging and poverty. Pressure for these fundamental pillars of social progress came from a surging labor movement. Working people had lost everything in the Depression and were on the move through a host of organizations making clear demands and willing to disrupt a society that had fallen apart. That kind of social mobilization and structural change is what we need today.

My colleague Joy Cushman describes the process of bottom-up change in the United States as a pyramid. At the base are actions that people can take in their communities to win concrete changes. These are the climate change fights that shut down coal-fired power plants and persuade whole cities to stop buying dirty energy, the mass incarceration fights that get police out of high schools, the jobs fights that remove barriers to airport service workers joining unions. In *Power and Powerlessness*, John Gaventa refers to fights as "limit acts" because they help test the limits of what is possible and set up larger, more structural fights.[6] This level of organizing usually focuses on demanding changes that people can experience in the short term in their lives (like immigrants being able to get driver's licenses despite their not having legal status or returning citizens not being required to disclose a criminal record when first applying for a job).

At the middle layer of the pyramid are campaigns to change policy. Sometimes we use the issues we're working on at the local level to create a new blueprint that can be written into state law. Passing legislation and winning ballot measures requires long-term alliances among organizations that have a broad membership base and political relationships with elected officials. Organizations need to plan ahead (two to four years out or more), sequence campaigns, create the capacity to collect signatures to place measures on the ballot every year (in cities and states that allow citizen initiatives), and build legislative coalitions that can consistently introduce and pass community-initiated bills.

At the top of the pyramid are structural changes that create new rights, fundamentally shift how resources and opportunities are distributed in the society, or significantly alter how political decisions are made. Examples of big transformative national changes include the Emancipation Proclamation, Women's Suffrage, Social Security, the 1965 Voting Rights Act, the Clean Air Act, the Affordable Care Act, and marriage equality. These achievements involve large-scale social, cultural, and legal changes that are difficult to reverse.

The key to structural changes is that they deliver tangible benefits to people while also shifting the underlying power dynamics in society. For example, state campaigns that re-enfranchise formerly incarcerated men and women help individuals put their lives back together while also expanding the electorate and bringing us closer to one person, one vote. Policies that make state taxes more progressive or that tax capital may not initially raise enormous amounts of revenue, but they create a pathway to a fairer tax system and lay the groundwork for more equitable investment in education. In 2015, the National Domestic Workers Alliance finally won a campaign to bring domestic workers under federal labor protections after seventy-five years of exclusion. That's a big structural victory.

Some of the most important organizing fights win smaller-scale changes that set up larger battles down the road. For example, campaigns for transparency around police shootings, racial profiling, or mortgage lending disparities have all served as stepping-stones for larger campaigns.

Here is another example of how the bottom-up change process works. In 2010, Contra Costa Interfaith and other community organizations in Richmond, California, organized successfully to bring down youth homicides that were plaguing their city. Clergy and residents held night walks through neighborhoods where shootings were taking place. They worked with city officials to hire and support street workers who connected with gang members to interrupt cycles of revenge-driven violence. And they helped bring a violence-prevention initiative called Ceasefire to Richmond. Rather than flooding neighborhoods with police, Ceasefire refocuses policing on the tiny slice of people who are responsible for most of the violent crime in a community. People at high risk of committing violence are brought in for "call-ins" that include prosecutors, job training and social service providers, and clergy and community leaders. Men and women who are called in are offered a clear choice: either continue what you're doing, and end up going to prison, or decide to exit, and we'll help you build a new life. These different efforts reinforced each other. Ultimately, years of neighborhood organizing, changes in police practices, and unprecedented collaboration among the community, social agencies, and city officials contributed to a 40 percent reduction in the murder rate in the city.

Many of the organizations involved in the movement to reduce gun violence in Richmond went on to work together to reform their county's criminal justice system. An important group driving this change was the Safe Return Project, which was founded by Tamisha Walker and other formerly incarcerated returning citizens. The goal of Safe Return is to break down the barriers people face when reintegrating into their communities and give those most impacted by mass incarceration a public voice in dismantling it. Building on their success in reducing homicides, Safe Return, Contra Costa Interfaith, and other organizations worked to persuade their county board of supervisors to use new state criminal justice funds to support violence prevention and drug treatment rather than build a new, larger jail. The leadership of people who were formerly incarcerated was a key ingredient in the success of this campaign. They had the strongest personal commitment to fighting for change and the clearest vision for a new approach to criminal justice. And fighting for Ceasefire and seeing it save lives made the grassroots leaders and clergy more confident political players in the county. The night of the vote against expanding the county jail, Jonny Perez, a nineteen-year-old who helped lead the fight, said, "If you told me one year ago that I would help stop the expansion of a jail, I would have called you crazy, but here we are today. I went from being locked up behind someone's jail to stopping the construction at a new jail in my city and county."[7]

Local organizing in Contra Costa and other counties across California in turn paved the way for a path-breaking statewide criminal justice ballot measure in 2014. For years, it was hard to imagine voters supporting policies to empty prisons. Yet that is what organizing does: make the impossible possible and the possible inevitable. Proposition 47, which won with 60 percent of the vote in a midterm election year, reclassified seven nonviolent felonies as misdemeanors.[8] It shifted billions of dollars in savings to education and services for crime victims. It also made it possible for more than a million people to have felonies expunged from their criminal records, removing a hurdle to finding work.

Proposition 47 became a model for people fighting to dismantle mass incarceration across the country. It sent a signal that public opinion was shifting against two decades of tough-on-crime rhetoric and policy. A year after it passed, Tamisha Walker led a group of formerly incarcerated women and men from across the country into a White House meeting with Valerie Jarrett, President Obama's closest advisor. It took months to persuade Obama administration officials to even allow returning citizens into the White House. The meeting with Jarrett helped break the logjam on a new federal policy to "ban the box" on federal employment applications to reduce hiring discrimination against people with criminal records.

In *The Economy of Cities*, Jane Jacobs writes that "People who run government activities, the world over, tend to seek sweeping answers to problems; that is, answers capable of being applied wholesale the instant they are adopted. [They] do not . . . bring their minds to bear on a particular and often seemingly small problem in one particular place. And yet that is how innovations of any sort are apt to begin."[9] The kind of grassroots organizing practiced in Richmond paves the way for transformation exactly because it starts with the lived experience of people rather than abstract ideas. Similarly, Charles Payne recounts Robert Moses as saying, "The problems to be attacked by the [civil rights] movement were so intertwined that all you could do was break off a piece of it, work on that and see where it led."[10]

Strategy Matters

When you're in the middle of a campaign, it can be hard to know if you're making progress or spinning your wheels. Organizing introduces a new dynamic that tries to disrupt the status quo, making uncertainty about our impact a constant by-product. And the governments and firms that we're trying to influence have little incentive to even acknowledge our existence. Social struggles are inherently asymmetrical because people-led organizations don't usually have much institutional power or legitimacy. We compensate by thinking together, revisiting our goals, relooking at whom we're really up against (are we talking to the right person or do we need to go further up the chain of command or behind the curtain to where the real power is?), and debating the weaknesses and vulnerabilities of our opponents and ourselves.

If we want to win social change against determined foes, we need to make strategy a constant part of our organizations and movements and include as many people as humanly possible. Strategy, to quote Marshall Ganz, is "how we turn what we have into what we need to get what we want."[11] It's the great counterweight to authority. It's how we prevail even when we think we're out of options and how we translate local fights into bigger movements. Here are four elements of strategy—act and adjust, shape the playing field, change the rules, and maximize your leverage—that can be used to increase our power as we face off against well-resourced opponents and work to rip out the roots of racial and economic injustice.

Act and Adjust

Creating change requires being willing to act despite uncertainty and then adjust your strategy based on how your opponents, allies, and base react. I grew up playing speed chess, which is regular chess using a clock that gives players a fixed (and short) amount of time to make their moves. Like social change, chess involves making the most of your situation in the face of a determined and often-crafty opponent under unpredictable and changing conditions. Experienced chess players usually begin games by choosing from a long list of possible openings that they've memorized based on thousands of previous games. Yet pretty quickly, you leave the pattern of predictable moves and find yourself in uncharted terrain. The most direct way to play is to look at the threats facing you and the opportunities you may have. You reason out what happens if you do X: "What could my opponent do in response? And then what could I do?"

This kind of assessment of actions and reactions is also important to winning social change. As Ganz has said, "strategy is a verb—something you do, not something you have."[12] We need to constantly readjust our strategy based on new information. We learn about our opponents (including whether they are really our opponents or if they're just standing in for someone else whom we'd be better off negotiating with) from how they react to us. Acting in a way that's surprising or unexpected usually helps us. Often our opponents' response, or overresponse, ends up fueling our organizing. That's what happened in the police backlash against the Memphis sanitation workers, in the decision to cut off food assistance in response to the Greenville voting rights campaign, and in Pharaoh's forcing the Israelites to make bricks without straw in the Exodus story.

Like in a chess game, it's useful to think about campaigns as unfolding in phases, chunking campaigns into pieces, setting clear objectives for each phase, and putting aside time between phases to pause and evaluate what we've learned. For example, in a first phase, the goal of our conversation with decision makers might be just to get on the playing field, to introduce our organization as a political actor with an agenda. At the end of this first phase, we need to stop and reflect on what we learned about ourselves, how we worked together under stress, what support we received, and how the power structure responded. A second phase might be to win the support of powerful allies and officials who are willing to champion our proposal. But the content of this phase and those that follow will always flow from the reactions we get to our actions.

In the campaign we ran to save my son's autism program, we spent the first weeks consolidating as a group. We recruited parents from other schools. We figured out how things worked in our county and educated ourselves and the school district about the autism program. We introduced the idea that we were an organized group of parents of children with autism. We tested out who on the school board might support us. The last board member we met with was the president. It was take-your-daughter-to-work day, and my daughter, Natalia, had come with me. She didn't say anything in the meeting beyond introducing herself, but she sat herself at the head of the table opposite the school board president, which added some accountability in the room. Our first campaign phase effectively ended midway through that meeting, when it became clear that the board president wasn't budging. We said that our next step would be to go public and make a big, messy issue out of the cuts, but we weren't a well-known entity, so that threat didn't shift the conversation. So, in what would become phase two of our campaign, we simplified the message. Essentially, we said, "Stop picking on kids with autism." We began generating media stories. We held a rally, with testimony from parents on the front steps of the school district main office. Our decision to go public helped us win in the end, but at the time it generated a lot of tension in the school district and in our own group. We weren't sure that it would work. That is the nature of being in an action-reaction cycle where you have to take risks, adjust, learn from failure, and keep moving forward.

Shape the Playing Field

In chess, even strong players can think through only a small number of (action-reaction) moves ahead. You rarely win simply by playing out the possibilities. The flow of the game is too unpredictable. Too many variables exist. And each side tends to overestimate the strength of its position. People are willing to wait each other out. This is where you need to look over the playing field at a more conceptual level. You need to figure out how to strengthen your position. You cannot know for certain that moving any particular piece will ultimately lead to winning. But you know that you want to control the center of the board. You want to configure your pieces so they aren't hidden away. It helps to build a wall of protection around your king. You want to put pressure on your opponent's weakest points. All these strategic actions—if you carry them out before being overwhelmed by your opponent—put you in a position to take advantage of opportunities that arise as the game proceeds.

Changing the world is a lot different from winning a chess game. But the idea of a divided mind, one part focused on the back and forth and the other on building power, is similar. For example, base building (chapter 6) is one of the most important steps we can take to strengthen our position going into a fight. Another way to increase our chance of winning is to find powerful allies. Often, we ally with organizations that bring together similar people through different channels. But other potential alliances can be farther afield. We may disagree with parts of the business community over the minimum wage or other issues, but on the question of investment in public transit or expanding Medicaid, we may be able to build strong political alliances with employers. Our opposition is never as monolithic as we think, especially when we're also willing to play political hardball to build alliances around shared goals. The questions of whom to pair up with, when to hold your nose, and what kind of strategic alliances and coalitions to build are among the most important questions that people need to wrestle with when they're trying to make change.

The key here is that everyone is on the playing field, whether they or we know it. And everyone is moving and can be moved. We need to map out who's with us, who's on the sidelines, and who's actively opposing the changes we're trying to make. (You can draw a playing field with two sides and show who's on the field and who's on the sidelines.) A good campaign will track the most powerful players in the environment on a week-to-week basis to see how they're moving. Did we get our strongest supporter to double down on the issue by holding a public event? Did someone on the fence say something positive for the first time?[13] Pay close attention to neutralizing powerful opponents. For example, a lot of bipartisan talk is happening about reforming the criminal justice system to reduce incarceration but there is much less progress in making change because of the fierce resistance of prosecutors and sheriffs, who are often the ones leading the fight against reform. So when we run candidates committed to ending mass incarceration in local prosecutor and sheriff races, we're not only contesting for these important positions but also sending a message to sitting officials that there is a cost to lobbying for more police and jails. Again, we're keeping an eye on both delivering change and shaping the terrain on which we're fighting.

Change the Rules

While you cannot change the rules of chess, that's not true in politics. The people who dream of infinite wealth and power— the handful of rich individuals and families who've taken over state after state and reshaped the American political landscape— spend their waking hours tinkering with the rules. They understand that to control the agenda, and the process by which decisions are made, is to control the outcome. White men with the patience and resources literally ran a fifty-year campaign to dismantle the 1965 Voting Rights Act. They put state tax caps in place that tie the hands of state spending (in states such as California and Colorado). They engineered state constitutions that take away the power of local communities to raise wages or regulate businesses. All these are examples of rules that rig the game against working people.

This is why the Koch brothers are such a problem for humanity. Peel back the layers of organizations, rationalizations, and rebrandings and you can see their ambition to amass more wealth than anyone could count in a lifetime by removing as much fossil fuel from the earth with as little interference as possible. Those who extract oil, gas, gold, tin, copper, and other valuable resources from the earth, as well as the politicians who abet them, are the worst. Their logic is to get as much out as fast as they can while leaving society to pick up the tab for damage to humans and the planet. It's no accident that New Mexico has a volunteer legislature or that Nevada's legislature meets for just four months every two years. Mining companies effectively wrote the constitutions in these mineral-rich states. No need for much legislating, writing of rules, taxing, or spending on education if your goal is to get stuff out of the ground as cheaply as possible.

Yet we can always find cracks in the casing surrounding the dreams of the wealthiest and most powerful. The elites rig the system because they're up against the greatest political idea that humans have created—norms about democratic decision making. We owe the ancient Greeks gratitude for their imperfect experimentation with self-governance. They left a lot of people out, but in the face of unrelenting opposition from elites (including people revered in Western thought, such as Plato and Socrates), they created a set of expectations and practices that value people's voices and lives. The Greeks understood that wealthy individuals would do everything they could to take power away from the people. One way the Greeks tried to counterbalance this tendency was through a process called *ostrakophoria* ("ostracism"). If five thousand people voted to hold an *ostrakophoria*, then people would be called together, given small round disks of clay, and asked to scratch the name of the person in the community that they thought should be forced to leave for ten years. The goal was to eliminate threats to the democracy. In Athens, down the hill from the Acropolis in the Museum of the Ancient Agora, one can see the names of ancient equivalents to the Koch brothers scratched onto clay disks. The need to protect democracy from being captured by the wealthy may be extreme today, but it's not new. It comes with the territory.

In our own time, we face an increasingly oligarchic society, where the wealthy set the terms of the debate. In the United States over the past forty years, the conservative movement, funded by the largest corporations in the world, has systematically deregulated political spending, making it possible for rich people and special interests to spend virtually unlimited amounts of money to influence the outcome of elections and legislative debates. Conservatives and corporate interests have manipulated redistricting in states to take control of dozens of state legislative chambers and made voting more difficult for the poor, the disabled, seniors, and people of color through voter ID laws and manipulation of voting procedures.

To win at politics, people-led organizations need to also focus on changing the rules, to make decision making more transparent and inclusive and our communities more powerful. As we fight for higher wages and an end to police brutality, we also need to work to make our democracy more representative. We can do this by eliminating barriers to voting (such as winning same-day voter registration and making Election Day a public holiday) and removing policies that protect the few at the expense of the many, like supermajority requirements for spending measures. We need campaign financing laws that magnify the power of small donors. For example, under a program approved by voters in Seattle, all registered voters receive four $25 vouchers, which they then can donate to political campaigns that agree to abide by spending limits. The rules about the rules are always up for grabs, and our mission needs to include both exposing them and making them more democratic.

A practical way to institutionalize this thinking in our organizations is to include three questions in any strategy meeting:

1. How is what we are fighting for going to deliver tangible benefits to our base?
2. What demands can we make that would increase our power?
3. What is the story we are telling that motivates people to see themselves as part of our work and that builds public support for our agenda?

We need to make demands that both address the greatest pain people are experiencing and make governments more responsive to people than money so we can win bigger changes in the future.

Maximize Your Leverage

In her book *Challenging Authority: How Ordinary People Change America*, Frances Fox Piven argues that social organizations and movements cannot necessarily control or steer politics in the United States, but they can create moments of disruption that force elites to respond.[14] That happens when people withdraw from daily participation in structures of inequality and oppression through boycotts, strikes, and mass protests. They disrupt the status quo and create divisions within the coalitions that political parties depend upon.

The best example of this process in American history was the abolition movement, which helped provoke a civil war that led to the end of slavery, despite the fact that neither major political party at the time had a strong interest in freeing slaves from bondage. Piven shows how both the Democratic and Republican Parties in the years leading up to the Civil War were multi-sectional, that is, they had constituencies in both the South and the North. The abolitionists forced the major religious denominations in the United States to take clear positions on the morality of slavery, polarizing the public, particularly in the North and the West on the issue. Through organizing local antislavery societies and lobbying Congress, they put the issue of slavery at the center of American politics. Slave revolts and the Underground Railroad added more fuel to the fire. Abolitionists created the conditions that led Southerners to leave the Republican Party and Northerners to abandon the Democratic Party. The leaders of both parties would have preferred to remain neutral on slavery to preserve their economic interests and hold together political coalitions that spanned the North and South. But mobilization by Free Blacks, clergy, religious people, and slaves themselves created heat and controversy that made the status quo untenable.

Since Ferguson, we've seen a contemporary example that points to the kind of disruption needed to reshape American politics. The young people who took to the streets in Ferguson did not influence American politics by building a new electoral coalition. They did it by creating enormous discomfort—beginning in Ferguson, then throughout Saint Louis, and spreading across the country. They made it more difficult for Democrats and progressives to take Black voters for granted by publicly pushing elected officials, unions, religious denominations, and social justice organizations to take clearer positions against police abuse and mass incarceration. By putting pressure on

Bernie Sanders and Hillary Clinton, Black Lives Matter activists made it harder for other Democratic Party candidates and elected officials to support tough-on-crime policies. This is similar to what abolitionists did to the Republican Party in the years leading up to the Civil War—using confrontation to bring moral clarity to the policy debate and purify the party. That's how a committed and relentless group of people who may not seem to have great political access or influence uses their leverage to force elites into choices that they would not otherwise make.

Shifting the Balance of Power

These four strategy principles are closely related and reinforce each other. Seeing the reactions to our actions is how we get insight into the power we're facing. Shaping the playing field is how we test and increase our influence. Changing the rules is how we make the game play to our strengths. And maximizing our leverage is how we use the weakness of our opponents (both their dependence on us and their internal divisions) to increase our power. These principles add up to an orientation focused on finding every opportunity possible to shift the balance of power in society toward ordinary people.

There is no simple answer to how we transform a world on fire. It requires building lots of organizations where people directly engage with decision makers and regularly talk about and test strategy. While we have plenty to complain about and more than enough threats to keep us up at night, we have control over the kind of organizations we build, the fights we pick, and the strategies we adopt. We need to shift our gaze away from what other people are doing wrong and toward how we're using the resources and relationships we have to get what we need. We have power if we choose to use it. The institutions and systems that we most need to change depend on our complicity—to buy their products, vote for their candidates, show up for work, and follow the rules. Arrangements of oppression eventually fold to withering moral critique, matched with strategic, creative, and unrelenting people-led direct action. The path to change isn't predictable. It can feel like the system isn't budging and will never change. But, as with a stuck jar lid, what matters is not just how hard we turn but how long we keep the pressure on.

CONCLUSION

What Next?

What will you do when you put this book down? Many readers are already involved in change efforts. The conversations in *Stand Up!* should help you deepen your commitment. In a world on fire, we all need to dig deeper, not necessarily work longer hours, but open our hearts wider, be more honest with others and ourselves, and take greater risks. I especially hope the book will help you find ways to do more to dismantle racism and other forms of human hierarchy as part of any social justice work you're involved in.

Each of the five conversations in the book is meant to make us better leaders—more aware of our emotions (purpose), clearer about the experiences and values that drive our choices (story), able to build closer relationships across differences (team), more powerful in the world (base), and more courageous and effective in confronting oppression (power). These are habits of the heart. They help us become better people with greater awareness and consciousness in the world. The conversations and the practices that flow from them are not magic solutions though; we already *know* them instinctively but don't always *do* them under stress. That's why they need to be practiced and repeated (wash, rinse, repeat) so they become who we are and what other people expect from us.

If you have the ability to influence how the organizations you're part of operate (which we all do, more or less), then I hope that you can turn these conversations into rituals (through repetition) and that these rituals become part of your organizational culture. For example, you can include reflection and evaluation at the end of any important activity you undertake, or you can intentionally create community by regularly asking people to share their stories with each other. We need more organizations that are humane, racially conscious, and outward facing, that recognize people as the most valuable resource for changing society and give their members real decision-making roles. Organizations that do this are more likely to develop the strategic capacity (discussed in chapter 7) to adapt in the face of conflict and uncertainty. And by creating in our organizations a slice of the world that we're working to bring into being, we make participation more attractive and valuable to people. Our organizations become spiritual homes for people seeking to feel and act more human.

If you're part of an organization that treats you as a means to some other end, that asks you to do small tasks without involving you in strategy, that isn't speaking to your soul, then you need to change the culture of the organization or look for or create another home for your social change work. A simple test is whether you are on a real team that meets regularly. Be truthful! Here are other measures: Are you learning something new about yourself? Are you having experiences that tap into strong emotions? Are you bringing new people off the sidelines and building high-trust relationships with them? These questions will help you figure out if you're on track or not.

The sad reality is that most of the organizations involved in social justice work in the United States don't ask much from their members or constituents. And even organizations committed to leadership development can struggle to keep people engaged and growing. Sustaining social change organizations of any kind is hard, especially when they're grappling with difficult entrenched issues and reliant on ordinary people's time and money. Organizations often run out of steam, devolve into cliques, become captured by their staff, or fracture. Organizations need to be renovated regularly. Sometimes they need to be shut down completely so that we can start anew. Never be afraid to say, "Let's rebuild" or "Let's start from scratch" or "Let's shift our focus given how things are changing around us." What results is almost always better.

> Never be afraid to say, "Let's rebuild" or "Let's start from scratch" or "Let's shift our focus given how things are changing around us." What results is almost always better.

If you haven't yet answered the knock at your door (or heard it), if you're looking for a way to plug in, perhaps by getting off the Internet and into face-to-face organizing, then you need to find or build an organization that will ask enough of you to make it worth your while. Too few organizations are structured around regularly meeting small groups, let alone bring people together across race, class, and other differences; engage in strategic campaigns; and invest in the growth and development of their members.

When my son was thirteen, he had to do a community service project. His first choice was to volunteer with an organization fighting climate change. It turned out to be surprisingly hard to find a chapter of an environmental group in Northern Virginia that met regularly. He ended up volunteering at a soup kitchen in Washington, DC. It was a valuable experience. He did useful work and had some good conversations with people. One thing that surprised me was that the soup kitchen had a waiting list for volunteers—a sign that there's more demand among people to contribute than a supply of opportunities to do so.

I think this imbalance between supply and demand is even more the case for chances to be part of organizing designed to get at the root causes of injustice. So be realistic about what may be limited options for joining existing organizations. Set a high bar for how you spend your time, but expect that you'll need to contribute your leadership to influence the culture of any organization you join—if you want to be part of something that both matters and feeds your spirit. And as Bill McKibben said about community, if you cannot find an organization that meets your needs, build one. If you do that, I hope the example of the autism campaign in chapter 1 and the five-conversation framework can be a useful guide.

One of the most promising shifts taking place in community organizing is that more people are taking the plunge into politics. More and more grassroots leaders are deciding to run for school board, city council, mayor, state legislature, and Congress. The push to elect prosecutors and sheriffs committed to ending mass incarceration is especially exciting. People should see running for office as one of many different roles that they can take on as part of the organization they belong to. That way, if they win, they're accountable to an organized base of people and can work with that base to advance policy change together.

> People should see running for office as one of many different roles that they can take on as part of the organization they belong to.

It might be your turn to run. After all, we cannot just complain that the car we're in is being driven over a cliff; we have to be willing to claw our way into the front seat, grab hold of the steering wheel, and drive our communities and country to a better place. If you do choose to run, and have an organized base behind you, then you can use the principles and practices in *Stand Up!* to design your campaign. You can recruit large numbers of volunteers and organize them into teams that have clear goals and roles; you can spend your resources talking to people face-to-face to hear their concerns rather than sending them advertising; you can focus on the voters that other candidates and parties write off as mattering less; and you can speak from your heart to people's hopes and dreams, inviting voters into a shared vision of community and purpose, rather than trying to sell them a laundry list of issues. You could even become president by using this kind of approach!

The hardest part about standing up and getting involved today may be the experience of not knowing whether we're making progress. Like the Chilean miners, whose story we began with, it feels like we're underground for an indeterminate amount of time without certainty that we'll get free. It can take decades of sustained and strategic organizing to create enough pressure for large-scale social change. We don't have that much time given the threats facing the planet and our society. The vicious cycles that we're in and the resources and will of our opponents make it hard to know if matters are just going to keep getting worse or if we'll reach a turning point. And sometimes victories look like big steps forward but turn into mirages. The notion that "the arc of the moral universe is long, but it bends toward justice" (coined by Theodore Parker, a nineteenth-century Unitarian minister, and made famous by Martin Luther King, Jr.) is a statement of faith, not a description of how politics works.[1] Social change has no guarantees. Periods of progress followed by reaction and backtracking can be long and arduous.

What we do have control over, though, is what we do in the meantime. Through organizing, we can make a dent in virtually any problem that we're able to identify as a cause of pain to people in our lives and communities. Organizing works when applied with discipline. And elected offices at all levels can be filled with our members if we focus our energies on those positions and are willing to run people for them over and over.

Small and medium-sized victories don't transform everything, but they build our muscles and give us a taste of our true power. To go back to Lawrence Goodwyn and the populists, organizing victories build in grassroots leaders the "somebodiness," the "high level of personal political self-respect" that makes people willing to challenge arrangements that are said to be natural and unchangeable.[2]

When we do win, we still have to figure out what to do next; and this is often more difficult than it seems. The Utopian Flaw (discussed at the end of chapter 3) is the slip in our consciousness that makes us think that if we can only achieve this change, everything else will be okay. It won't. Our challenge is to find the will to keep going. In his short book *The Dip*, Seth Godin lays out a framework for deciding whether you're on the right track in your work or life. It applies well to social change. He says you should ask yourself if what you are doing now is something that you believe will make you very happy and that you can eventually be the best at. If you're not confident that you can answer yes to both questions, then quit. But if you're certain, then persist, knowing that you'll need to pass through a long and difficult period of doubt and probably failure—the dip— to get to greatness.[3] Organizing for change takes that kind of determination to pay off.

The true value of the conversations and practices in *Stand Up!* may be that they help us stay human amid darkness and uncertainty. They give us courage not only to keep fighting but to care for one another. As the Chilean miners learned, survival under stress depends on our capacity to see each other as brothers and sisters. In times of trouble, we need to resist the temptation to turn on one another. If we can do that in the face of hate, abuse, and confusion, if

In times of trouble, we need to resist the temptation to turn on one another.

we refuse to give up hope and continue to experiment with our resources, then we have a chance to make it through to a promised land. As Ibram Kendi wrote in the epilogue of *Stamped from the Beginning*, "There will come a time when we will love humanity, when we will gain the courage to fight for an equitable society for our beloved humanity, knowing, intelligently, that when we fight for humanity, we are fighting for ourselves. There will come a time. Maybe, just maybe, that time is now."[4]

NOTES

Preface

1. Pope Francis, "Why the Only Future Worth Building Includes Everyone," filmed April 2017, TED Talk, 17:52, posted April 2017, https://www.ted.com/talks/pope_francis_why_the_only_future_worth_building_includes_everyone?language=en.

Introduction

1. Héctor Tobar, *Deep Down Dark: The Untold Stories of 33 Men Buried Alive in a Chilean Mine, and the Miracle That Set Them Free* (New York: Farrar, Straus and Giroux, 2014), 58.

2. Pope Francis, *Laudato Si': On Care for Our Common Home*, encyclical letter, The Holy See, May 24, 2015, http://w2.vatican.va/content/francesco/en/encyclicals/documents/papa-francesco_20150524_enciclica-laudato-si.html, 41.

3. Martin Luther King, Jr., *Strength to Love*, spec. ed. (Minneapolis: Fortress Press, 2010), 58.

4. Amy Sonnie and James Tracy, *Hillbilly Nationalists, Urban Race Rebels, and Black Power: Community Organizing in Radical Times* (New York: Melville House, 2011), 26–27.

5. Olga Khazan, "Why Are So Many Americans Dying Young?" *Atlantic*, December 13, 2016.

6. Charles Payne, *I've Got the Light of Freedom: The Organizing Tradition and the Mississippi Freedom Struggle* (Berkeley: University of California Press, 1995), 93.

7. Patterson et al., *Crucial Conversations: Tools for Talking When Stakes Are High*, 2nd ed. (New York: McGraw-Hill, 2011).

8. Brian D. Christens, "Tips on Building a Broad Base of Engaged and Empowered Volunteers," Center for Nonprofits, University of Wisconsin–Madison, Fall 2011, https://sohe.wisc.edu/wordpress/wp-content/uploads/ChristensBuildingaBaseofEngaged EmpoweredVolunteers.pdf.

9. Thank you to Joy Cushman for this framework.

Chapter 2

1. Douglas S. Massey, *Categorically Unequal: The American Stratification System* (New York: Russell Sage Foundation, 2007), 1.
2. Michael K. Honey, *Going Down Jericho Road: The Memphis Strike, Martin Luther King's Last Campaign* (New York: Norton, 2008).
3. Martin Luther King, Jr., "I've Been to the Mountaintop" (speech, Masonic Temple, Memphis, TN, April 3, 1968), American Rhetoric, http://www.americanrhetoric.com/speeches/mlkivebeentoth emountaintop.htm.
4. Martin Luther King, Jr., "Our God Is Marching On" (speech, Montgomery, AL, March 25, 1965), Martin Luther King, Jr. Research and Education Institute, https://kinginstitute.stanford.edu/our-god -marching.
5. Thomas Piketty, *Capital in the 21st Century* (Cambridge, MA: Belknap Press, 2014).
6. Ta-Nehisi Coates, "The Case for Reparations," *Atlantic*, June 2014.
7. Ian Haney López, *Dog Whistle Politics: How Coded Racial Appeals Have Reinvented Racism and Wrecked the Middle Class* (New York: Oxford University Press, 2015).
8. Lisa McGirr, *Suburban Warriors: The Origins of the New American Right*, 2nd ed. (Princeton, NJ: Princeton University Press, 2015).
9. Gerald Mayer, *Union Membership Trends in the United States*, Congressional Research Service, August 31, 2004, 23; and Bureau of Labor Statistics, "Union Members Summary," news release, January 26, 2017, www.bls.gov/news.release/union2.nr0.htm.
10. Kenneth Vogel, "How the Koch Machine Rivals the GOP," *Politico*, December 30, 2015, http://www.politico.com/story/2015/12koch -brothers-network-gop-david-charles-217124.
11. Jane Mayer, "State for Sale: A Conservative Multimillionaire Has Taken Control in North Carolina, One of 2012's Top Battlegrounds," *New Yorker*, October 10, 2011, http://www.newyorker.com/magazine /2011/10/10/state-for-sale.
12. Paul Hodgson, "Top CEOs Make More Than 300 Times the Average Worker," *Fortune*, June 22, 2015, http://fortune.com/2015/06/22/ceo -vs-worker-pay/.
13. Piketty, *Capital in the 21st Century*, 447.

14. Ibid., 485.
15. Ibid., 747.
16. Michael Powell, "Blacks in Memphis Lose Decades of Economic Gains," *New York Times*, May 30, 2010, http://www.nytimes .com/2010/05/31/business/economy/31memphis.html?_r=0.
17. Rakesh Kochhar and Richard Fry, "Wealth Inequality Has Widened along Racial, Ethnic Lines Since End of the Great Recession," Pew Research Center, December 12, 2014, http://www.pewresearch.org /fact-tank/2014/12/12/racial-wealth-gaps-great-recession/.
18. Jamiles Lartey, "By the Numbers: US Police Kill More in Days Than Other Countries Kill in Years," *Guardian*, June 9, 2015.
19. See Loic Wacquant, *Punishing the Poor: The Neoliberal Government of Social Insecurity* (Durham, NC: Duke University Press, 2009).
20. "Trends in U.S. Corrections," fact sheet, Sentencing Project, updated June 26, 2017, http://www.sentencingproject.org/wp-content/upload s/2016/01/Trends-in-US-Corrections.pdf.
21. Half in Ten, "Americans with Criminal Records," Sentencing Project, http://www.sentencingproject.org/wp-content/uploads/201 5/11 /Americans-with-Criminal-Records-Poverty-and-Opportunity -Profile.pdf.
22. Verlyn Klinkenborg, "The Prophet," *New York Review of Books*, October 24, 2013.
23. "IMF Survey: Counting the Cost of Energy Subsidies," International Monetary Fund, July 17, 2015, https://www.imf.org/external/pubs/ft /survey/so/2015/NEW070215A.htm.
24. Naomi Klein, *This Changes Everything: Capitalism vs. The Climate* (New York: Simon & Schuster, 2014), 25.
25. Pope Francis, *Laudato Si'*, 49.
26. Ibid., 59.
27. Thank you to Simon Greer for this point.

Chapter 3

1. Tobar, *Deep Down Dark*, 58.
2. Michael Walzer, *Exodus and Revolution* (New York: Basic Books, 1986), 149.
3. Henry David Thoreau, *Walden* (Seattle: Amazon Classics, 2017), 62.
4. Frederick Douglass, "West India Emancipation" (speech, Canandaigua, New York, August 3, 1857).

5. Margaret Mead, used by permission of the Institute for Intercultural Studies, http://www.interculturalstudies.org.

6. Ta-Nehisi Coates, *Between the World and Me* (New York: Spiegel & Grau, 2015), 97.

7. Jerry Wurf, quoted in Honey, *Going Down Jericho Road*, 483.

8. "What Is Priming?" *Psychology Today*, accessed September 1, 2017, https://www.psychologytoday.com/basics/priming.

9. Eleanor Drago-Severson, *Helping Teachers Learn: Principal Leadership for Adult Growth and Development* (Thousand Oaks, CA: Corwin, 2004).

Chapter 4

1. Yuval Noah Harari, *Sapiens: A Brief History of Humankind* (New York: HarperCollins, 2011), 21.

2. Christens, "Tips on Building a Broad Base."

3. Ziad W. Munson, *The Making of Pro-life Activists: How Social Movement Mobilization Works* (Chicago: University of Chicago Press, 2008).

4. Marshall Ganz, "Why Stories Matter," *Sojourners* 38, no. 3, March 16, 2009.

5. Paul VanDeCarr, "Interview with Marshall Ganz on 'Public Narrative,'" Working Narratives, November 26, 2014, http://workingnarratives.org/interview-with-marshall-ganz-on-public-narrative/.

6. "Population Change and Distribution, 1990 to 2000," Census 2000 brief, US Census Bureau, April 2001, 7.

7. Brookings Institution Center on Urban and Metropolitan Policy, *Philadelphia in Focus: A Profile from Census 2000* (Washington, DC: Brookings Institution Press, 2000), 59–60.

8. Research for Democracy, *Blight Free Philadelphia: A Public-Private Strategy to Create and Enhance Neighborhood Value* (Philadelphia: Temple University Center for Public Policy, October 2011), 15.

9. "The Clinton Presidency: Historic Economic Growth," The White House, January 2001, https://clintonwhitehouse5.archives.gov/WH/Accomplishments/eightyears-03.html.

10. Alicia Garza, "A Herstory of the #BlackLivesMatter Movement," *Feminist Wire*, October 7, 2014, http://www.thefeministwire.com/2014/10/blacklivesmatter-2/.

Chapter 5

1. Steve Gladen, "The Saddleback Small Group Difference: The Core Philosophy of the Purpose-Driven Small Groups Movement," SmallGroups.com, http://www.smallgroups.com/articles/2008 /saddleback-small-group-difference.html?paging=off.

2. Ibid.

3. Marissa D. King and Heather A. Haveman, "Antislavery in America: The Press, the Pulpit, and the Rise of Antislavery Societies," *Administrative Science Quarterly* 53, no. 3 (2008): 494.

4. Ibid., 495.

5. Ibid.

6. Ibid.

7. Theda Skocpol, *Diminished Democracy: From Membership to Management in American Civic Life* (Norman, OK: University of Oklahoma Press, 2003), 123–124.

8. Theda Skocpol, "The Tocqueville Problem: Civic Engagement in American Democracy," *Social Science History* 21, no. 4 (1997): 473.

9. Ibid., 476.

10. Robert D. Putnam, *Bowling Alone: The Collapse and Revival of American Community* (New York: Simon & Schuster, 2000), 157.

11. Lawrence Goodwyn, *The Populist Moment: A Short History of the Agrarian Revolt in America* (Oxford: Oxford University Press, 1981), x.

12. Ibid., xix.

13. Ibid., xxiv.

14. Patrick Lencioni, *The Five Dysfunctions of a Team: A Leadership Fable* (San Francisco: Jossey-Bass, 2002), 195.

15. Ethics of the Fathers, 1:14.

16. Lencioni, *The Five Dysfunctions*, 198.

17. Elizabeth Perle McKenna and Hahrie Han, *Groundbreakers: How Obama's 2.2 Million Volunteers Transformed Campaigning in America* (New York: Oxford University Press, 2015), 132–135.

18. Ibid., 132–135.

19. Scott Mainwaring, *The Catholic Church and Politics in Brazil: 1964–1985*, Kellogg Institute Working Paper #98, August 1987, 7.

20. Ibid., 11–12.

21. Ibid., 3.

22. Tina Rosenberg, "To Beat Back Poverty, Pay the Poor," *New York Times*, January 3, 2011, http://opinionator.blogs.nytimes.com/2011 /01/03/to-beat-back-poverty-pay-the-poor/?_r=0.

Chapter 6

1. Payne, *I've Got the Light of Freedom*, 158.
2. Ibid.
3. Ibid., 171.
4. Jane F. McAlevey, *No Shortcuts: Organizing for Power in the New Gilded Age* (New York: Oxford University Press, 2016).
5. Payne, *I've Got the Light of Freedom*, 155.
6. Ibid., 5.
7. Ibid., 106.
8. Thank you to Steve Kest for explaining the organizing that helped launch the Fight for $15.
9. Paul W. Speer and Joseph Hughey, "Mechanisms of Empowerment: Psychological Processes for Members of Power-Based Community Organizations," *Journal of Community and Applied Social Psychology* 6 (August 1996): 177–187.
10. Meredith Rolfe, *Voter Turnout: A Social Theory of Political Participation* (Cambridge: Cambridge University Press, 2014).
11. Donald P. Green and Alan S. Gerber, *Get Out the Vote: How to Increase Voter Turnout* (Washington, DC: Brookings Institution Press, 2015).
12. Carola Frediani, "How Tech-Savvy Podemos Became One of Spain's Most Popular Parties in 100 Days," *Tech President*, August 11, 2014, http://techpresident.com/news/wegov/25235/how-tech-savvy -podemos- became-one-spain%E2%80%99s-most-popular-parties -100-days.
13. Skocpol, *Diminished Democracy*, 24.
14. Jesse Graham, Executive Director, Maine People's Alliance, personal communication with the author, March 6, 2017.
15. This framework is adapted from the Management Center's SMART goals; see Allison Green and Jerry Hauser, *Managing to Change the World: The Nonprofit Manager's Guide to Getting Results* (San Francisco: Jossey-Bass, 2012), 39–45.

Chapter 7

1. Putnam, *Bowling Alone*, 165.
2. Ibid., 38–44.
3. Ibid., 38.
4. Brian D. Christens and Paul W. Speer, "Contextual Influences on Participation in Community Organizing: A Multilevel Longitudinal Study," *American Journal of Community Psychology* 47, no. 3–4 (2011): 253–263.
5. Andrew Martin, "For the Jobless, Little U.S. Help on Foreclosure," *New York Times*, June 4, 2011.
6. John Gaventa, *Power and Powerlessness: Quiescence and Rebellion in an Appalachian Valley* (Chicago: University of Illinois Press, 1982), 208–209. Gaventa takes the idea of "limit acts" from Paulo Freire, *Pedagogy of the Oppressed* (New York: Continuum, 2005), 99.
7. "Contra Costa Community Celebrates Massive Investment in Alternatives to Incarceration: CCC to Invest $4.035 Million in Employment, Housing and Services," news release, accessed September 1, 2017, http://archive.constantcontact.com /fs188/1102195177321/archive/1112168302605.html.
8. "California Proposition 47, Reduced Penalties for Some Crimes Initiative (2014)," Ballotpedia, accessed September 1, 2017, https:// ballotpedia.org/California_Proposition_47,_Reduced_Penalties_for _Some_Crimes_Initiative_(2014).
9. Jane Jacobs, *The Economy of Cities* (New York: Vintage Books, 2000), 209–210.
10. Payne, *I've Got the Light of Freedom*, 127 (paraphrasing Robert Moses).
11. Ganz, Marshall. *Why David Sometimes Wins: Leadership, Organization, and Strategy in the California Farm Worker Movement* (New York: Oxford University Press, 2010), 8.
12. Ibid., 10.
13. This is a key framework taught by Joy Cushman and the New Organizing Institute.
14. Frances Fox Piven, *Challenging Authority: How Ordinary People Change America* (Lanham, MD: Rowman & Littlefield, 2008).

Conclusion

1. Tré Goins-Phillips, "Former Obama Staffer: The President Has Been Misusing This MLK Quote," *Blaze*, January 16, 2017, http://www.theblaze.com/news/2017/01/16/former-obama-staffer-the-president-has-been-misusing-this-mlk-quote/.
2. Goodwyn, *The Populist Moment*, x.
3. Seth Godin, *The Dip* (New York: Penguin, 2007), 16.
4. Ibram X. Kendi, *Stamped from the Beginning: The Definitive History of Racist Ideas in America* (New York: Nation Books, 2016), 585.

ACKNOWLEDGMENTS

The five-conversation framework in *Stand Up!* originated in a session I led in 2014 during a six-day PICO National Network (now Faith in Action) leadership training in Los Altos, California. During the first few days of the training, my colleagues took a hundred grassroots leaders from across the country through a set of powerful activities and teachings about race, faith, power, and social change. They challenged participants to see themselves and the world differently. As I watched, I wondered what people would do when they got home. So I asked for a few hours on a Sunday morning to dig deeper into how people could apply what they were learning to transform their lives and communities. That desire to make organizing wisdom as practical and useful as possible was the genesis of the framework in the book and has been my north star.

It shouldn't be a surprise then that so much of what is in *Stand Up!* reflects the ideas and creativity of my colleagues in Faith in Action. For the past twelve years, I've had the blessing of working alongside some of the best community organizers in the United States. Fr. John Baumann founded Faith in Action (originally the Oakland Training Center, then Pacific Institute for Community Organization, and eventually People Improving Communities through Organizing) in 1972. His humility and discipline anchored the network in a commitment to treat people as ends and not means. That focus on people and their development along with a willingness to adapt and collaborate explains Faith in Action's tremendous growth over the past decade. Our network has become a source of strength and hope for many working people and communities across the county. Faith in Action is now the largest faith-organizing network in the United States with forty-five grassroots community organizing groups in two hundred cities and towns in twenty-two states, with a membership of three thousand religious institutions and 2.5 million people, as well as growing work in Rwanda, Central America, and Haiti. In 2017, PICO renamed itself Faith in Action to better reflect its purpose and work.

Many of my Faith in Action colleagues influenced the ideas and practices discussed in *Stand Up!* They include Onleilove Alston, Juard Barnes, Lydia Bean, Risa Brown, Eddie Carmona, Denise Collazo, Jennifer Farmer, Joe Fleming, Rev. Cassandra Gould, Rev. Jane Gould, Stephanie Gut, Rev. Alvin Herring, Phyllis Hill, Deth Im, Rev. Troy Jackson, Jim Keddy, Adam Kruggel, Wes Lathrop, Tim Lilienthal, Rev. Michael-Ray Mathews, Andrea Marta, Lorena Melgarejo, Joseph McKellar, Kirk Noden, Kristee Paschall, Scott Reed, Edwin Robinson, Bishop Dwayne Royster, Daniel Schwartz, Sarah Silva, Ron Snyder, Monica Somerville, Shoshanna Spector, Lauren Spokane, Liz Sullivan, Ron White, Rich Wood, Felicia Yoda, and Alia Zaki Ludwig. Special thanks to Doran Schrantz for her ideas about the process people go through in becoming agents of change and building a base; to Joy Cushman for so many concepts, including the teams-roles-goals framework, the pyramid of social change, and the playing field; and to Rev. Michael McBride for agitating me around race and the need to let go of sacred cows around whom and how we organize. Thank you to Tamisha Walker for her organizing with the Safe Return Project in Richmond, California, described in chapter 7. Thank you, Lise Afoy and all my colleagues, for helping me create the space to write.

I am also happy to be part of a larger community of organizers who are testing out new and creative ways to transform

American society to live up to its stated values. I'm especially grateful to my colleagues at the Advancement Project, Center for Popular Democracy, Center for Responsible Lending, Center on Budget Policy and Priorities, Community Catalyst, Movimiento Cosecha, Demos, Faith in Public Life, National Domestic Workers Alliance, National Employment Law Center, People's Action, Religious Action Center of Reform Judaism, SEIU, Sojourners, United We Dream, Wellstone Action, and Working Families Party for their support and partnership over the years.

Thank you to Jeremy Nowak for finding me my first job in organizing, Jill Michaels for hiring me, Rudy Tolbert for taking me under his wing, and Patrick Bond for teaching me how to take apart banks. As I say in the preface, I learned some of the most important lessons about organizing from my time living in Chile in the 1990s with my wife, Julia. Thank you to our *compañeras y compañeros* in Grupo de Salud Llareta and Educación Popular En Salud (EPES), including Karen Anderson, Valeria Garcia, Sonia Garcia, Ivan Burgos, Monica Janet Perez, Monica Maldonado, and Eladio Recabarran, and to Juan Carrera for teaching me Spanish and instilling in me a lifelong commitment to building new organizations.

Organizers learn organizing from the leaders they work alongside. I'm especially thankful to everyone who walked with me during my years of learning to organize in Philadelphia, including Angelina Rivera, Rosie Mateo, and Marta Aviles, whom I met through the Sheppard Parents Association (the parent organization in Philadelphia described in chapter 3), Ortencia Cortez-Santiago, Linda Haley, Dolores Shaw, and Sam and Phyllis Santiago, as well as my Philadelphia friends and colleagues Rochelle Nichols Solomon, Len Rieser, Debby Freedman, David Wycoff, Vincent Louis, Ann Farnsworth-Alvear, and Rui DaSilva. From my time organizing in Flint, Michigan, I thank Rick Carter, Rev. David Kennedy, Rev. David Carl Olson, Fr. Tom Firestone, Rev. Ira Edwards, Rev. Claudia Hollingsworth,

Fr. Marty Fields, Fr. Phil Gallagher, Dr. Lawrence Reynolds, Jim Rouse, Sister Joanne Fedewa, and Oscar Barnett. The list of leaders and clergy whom I've had the blessing to work with through Faith in Action is long. Special appreciation to Paula Arceneaux, Paty Madueno, Rev. Heyward Wiggins, Rev. Cory Sparks, Dr. George Cummings, Deacon Allen Stevens, Sharon Bridgeforth, Susan Molina, Gloria Cooper, Rev. Jesus Nieto, Howard Lawrence, and Christy Figueroa.

I've had many teachers and mentors in organizing. Although we've gone our separate ways, the lessons Steve Honeyman taught me about organizing are on almost every page of this book and guide me every day—not just the principles and techniques but the rhythm and orientation. I'm thankful to have been able to work for and with Gary Rodwell, a talented organizer with the Industrial Areas Foundation. I appreciate Lew Finfer for his dogged commitment to community organizing and long investment in my development. Thank you to Scott Reed for investing in my leadership and Denise Collazo for being a constant partner. And to Joe Givens for coaching me in building Flint Area Congregations Together and teaching me to be a political consultant to faith communities.

As my friends and colleagues know, I am a Jew with a special place in my heart for the Catholic Church. I thank Peter Cicchino for drawing on his Jesuit training to give me the courage to take my first job as a faith-based organizer; Bishop Edward Deliman and Sister Dolores Egner, SSJ, for patiently teaching me about Catholicism and its commitment to family and community during my years working out of Visitation BVM parish in the Kensington neighborhood of Philadelphia; Fr. John Baumann for exposing me to Jesuit thinking and being; John Carr, Kathie Saile, Ralph McCloud, Randy Keesler, and others who have been great partners in fighting poverty and injustice during their time working at the US Conference of Catholic Bishops; and my colleagues Joe Fleming, Stephanie Gut, Tim Lilienthol, Joseph McKellar, Lorena Melgarejo, Gaby Trejo, and others for letting me ride along on an incredible journey of realizing the promise of Catholic Social Teaching. It's been an honor to get to know and work with Cardinal Peter Turkson, Fr. Michael Czerny, Juan Grabois, and others from the Vatican as part of the World Meeting of Popular Movements process. And of course, thank you to Pope Francis for showing the world a way to live into a different better future that values the inherent dignity of every person.

People who have deeply influenced my thinking and whose ideas are laced through this book include Jeff Brenner, Joy Cusham, Michelle Fine, Michael Katz, Marshall Ganz, Hahrie Han, Charles Payne, john powell, Stephen G. Ray Jr., and Carlos Saavedra Diaz. Thank you to my social-justice-loving rabbis, Aaron Alexander and Lauren Holtzblatt, who've helped deepen my connection to Judaism, and to Rabbi Jonah Pesner for his collaboration and support. I'm grateful to Ksenia Ovsyannikova for her friendship and wisdom.

I found the motivation to write Stand Up!—and first outlined the book—during my participation in a Rockwood Leadership Institute in 2013–14. Thank you to Robert Gass, Yeshi Neumann, and Shiree Teng and to my cohort members, Lindsey Allen, Sulma Arias, Lawrence Benito, Stacy Bohlen, Juan Cartegena, Andrew Friedman, Ben Goldfarb, Steve Hawkins, Rachel Laforest, Valerie Long, Heather McGhee, Andrea Cristina Mercado, Amy Morris, Navin Nayak, Deepak Pateriya, Will Pittz, Justine Sarver, Evelyn Shen, Shauna Thomas, Cristina Tzintzún, Naomi Walker, Dennis Williams, and Luna Yasui for creating a remarkable (and on-going) space for me to breath and evolve.

When I started writing this book, I had very little idea about how the publishing process worked. I appreciate the advice I received from Steve Phillips and Susan Sandler, Jennifer Farmer, Ai Jen Poo, Jim Wallis, Anna El-Eini, and Norton Paley about how to get *Stand Up!* finished and published. Jane Friedman gave me early advice on writing a book proposal. I had the great fortune to find Lisa Adams, who as my agent has guided me through every step in this book creation process with wisdom and integrity. I appreciate her confidence in the book and in me and her success in finding the right press. One silver lining of the 2016 election was Berrett-Koehler's strong interest in publishing a book that spoke into the moment. I can't imagine a better fit than a publisher whose mission is literally "connecting people and ideas to create a world that works for all"—the very mission of *Stand Up!* Neal Maillet, my editor, has provided thoughtful and respectful feedback that guided me as I rewrote the manuscript. I appreciate the energy that all the staff at Berrett-Koehler have put into *Stand Up!* and their commitment to getting the book into the hands of readers.

A surprisingly large number of people read drafts of this book and gave feedback. Thank you to Hahrie Han, Troy Jackson, Denise Collazo, Monica Somerville, Jim Keddy, Jean Ross, Ellyn Kerr, Don Schatz, Rob Ellman, and Robert Gordon for great comments and suggested edits that have made the book much stronger. Many people also participated in helping title the book, thanks to Berrett-Koehler's commitment to collective wisdom and testing assumptions.

I'm grateful to the Skadden Foundation, led by the remarkable Susan Butler Plum, for providing me with a Flom Incubator Grant to support writing this book and to Faith in Action for a 2015 sabbatical that gave me an opportunity to see the world and write my first draft.

As I say in the preface, my parents, Sylvia and Lewis Whitman, started me off on a path of justice. I thank them and my brothers, James and Bradley Whitman, for their values and support.

I cannot thank Julia Paley enough for her fierce commitment to justice, her companionship and love, and for the unwavering support she's provided throughout my life as an organizer over many years. We've shared so many of the stories in the book, and I could not have learned what I have and become the person I am without her. No one has been a better editor, source of good feedback, and provider of constant encouragement. I wrote the first draft of *Stand Up!* while we were living in Cochabamba, Bolivia, with our children, Isaiah and Natalia, who have been a source of both ideas and inspiration for a lot of what I've written in the book and done in the world. I hope the book can be a source of inspiration to you for lives of purpose and joy.

INDEX

ABOUT THE AUTHOR

Gordon Whitman has worked as a community organizer and social change strategist and coach for the past twenty-five years. He first learned organizing in Santiago, Chile, and helped found successful grassroots organizing groups in Philadelphia, Pennsylvania, and Flint, Michigan. As the deputy director of Faith in Action (formerly PICO National Network), the county's largest faith-based community organizing network, he has coached hundreds of organizers, clergy, and grassroots leaders. He's been responsible for Faith in Action's expansion program, helping people of faith and clergy build some of the most effective new multiracial community organizing groups in the United States over the past decade. In 2008, Gordon opened a national policy office for Faith in Action in Washington, DC, and has led national organizing campaigns on children's health coverage, national health reform, and stopping of foreclosures. Before becoming an organizer, he worked as a legal services and civil rights lawyer in Philadelphia. Gordon has also been the associate director of the Temple University Center for Public Policy. He's written dozens of policy reports and articles on social change and regularly blogs on HuffPost. He has a law degree from Harvard Law School and an undergraduate degree from the University of Pennsylvania in history and urban studies. When Gordon's not organizing, you can find him in the wilderness.

Berrett–Koehler
Publishers

Berrett-Koehler is an independent publisher dedicated to an ambitious mission: *Connecting people and ideas to create a world that works for all.*

We believe that the solutions to the world's problems will come from all of us, working at all levels: in our organizations, in our society, and in our own lives. Our BK Business books help people make their organizations more humane, democratic, diverse, and effective (we don't think there's any contradiction there). Our BK Currents books offer pathways to creating a more just, equitable, and sustainable society. Our BK Life books help people create positive change in their lives and align their personal practices with their aspirations for a better world.

All of our books are designed to bring people seeking positive change together around the ideas that empower them to see and shape the world in a new way.

And we strive to practice what we preach. At the core of our approach is Stewardship, a deep sense of responsibility to administer the company for the benefit of all of our stakeholder groups including authors, customers, employees, investors, service providers, and the communities and environment around us. Everything we do is built around this and our other key values of quality, partnership, inclusion, and sustainability.

This is why we are both a B-Corporation and a California Benefit Corporation—a certification and a for-profit legal status that require us to adhere to the highest standards for corporate, social, and environmental performance.

We are grateful to our readers, authors, and other friends of the company who consider themselves to be part of the BK Community. We hope that you, too, will join us in our mission.

A BK Currents Book

BK Currents books bring people together to advance social and economic justice, shared prosperity, sustainability, and new solutions for national and global issues. They advocate for systemic change and provide the ideas and tools to solve social problems at their root. So get to it!

To find out more, visit **www.bkconnection.com**.

Berrett–Koehler
Publishers

Connecting people and ideas
to create a world that works for all

Dear Reader,

Thank you for picking up this book and joining our worldwide community of Berrett-Koehler readers. We share ideas that bring positive change into people's lives, organizations, and society.

To welcome you, we'd like to offer you a free e-book. You can pick from among twelve of our bestselling books by entering the promotional code BKP92E here: http://www.bkconnection.com/welcome.

When you claim your free e-book, we'll also send you a copy of our e-newsletter, the *BK Communiqué*. Although you're free to unsubscribe, there are many benefits to sticking around. In every issue of our newsletter you'll find

- A free e-book
- Tips from famous authors
- Discounts on spotlight titles
- Hilarious insider publishing news
- A chance to win a prize for answering a riddle

Best of all, our readers tell us, "Your newsletter is the only one I actually read." So claim your gift today, and please stay in touch!

Sincerely,

Charlotte Ashlock
Steward of the BK Website

Questions? Comments? Contact me at bkcommunity@bkpub.com.

Certified

Corporation
bcorporation.net

**Praise for *New York Times*
Bestselling Author Catherine Coulter**

"Her plots are like rich desserts—sinfully delicious
and hard to pass up."
—*The Atlanta Journal-Constitution*

"Catherine Coulter romances readers."
—*Colorado Springs Gazette Telegraph*

"Coulter is excellent at portraying the romantic
tension between her heroes and heroines, and
she manages to write explicitly but beautifully
about sex as well as love."
—*Milwaukee Journal Sentinel*

"Delightful . . . witty . . . engaging."
—*Publishers Weekly*

"Coulter's characters quickly come alive and draw
the reader into the story. . . . You can hardly
wait to get back and see what's going on."
—*The Sunday Oklahoman*

"Charm, wit, and intrigue. . . . Sure to keep readers
turning the pages."
—*Naples Daily News*

"Tantalizing."
—*The Knoxville News-Sentinel*

Impulse

—

Catherine Coulter

A SIGNET BOOK

SIGNET
Published by New American Library, a division of
Penguin Putnam Inc., 375 Hudson Street,
New York, New York 10014, U.S.A.
Penguin Books Ltd, 27 Wrights Lane,
London W8 5TZ, England
Penguin Books Australia Ltd, Ringwood,
Victoria, Australia
Penguin Books Canada Ltd, 10 Alcorn Avenue,
Toronto, Ontario, Canada M4V 3B2
Penguin Books (N.Z.) Ltd, 182–190 Wairau Road,
Auckland 10, New Zealand

Penguin Books Ltd, Registered Offices:
Harmondsworth, Middlesex, England

Published by Signet, an imprint of New American Library,
a division of Penguin Putnam Inc. Previously published in an Onyx edition
and an NAL Books edition.

First Signet Printing, June 2000
First Signet Printing (new edition), October 2001
10 9 8 7 6 5

 REGISTERED TRADEMARK—MARCA REGISTRADA

To Beth Zamichow
Trainer, dancer, friend
—CC

Impulse

Prologue

Margaret's Journal
Boston, Massachusetts
26 years ago

He was a wonderful liar. The best. If I'd been thirty rather than just barely turned twenty, I still don't think it would have mattered. He was so good, you see. At the beginning, of course. Not at the end. At the end there'd been no need for lies. Uncle Ralph and Aunt Josie had taken me to the only French restaurant in New Milford and they'd tried to make things normal and fun for me and there'd been a birthday cake and champagne. And I smiled and thanked them because I knew how hard they were trying. I didn't cry because I knew if I did, Aunt Josie would cry too, because my mother had been her only sister. And two nights later on a hot Friday evening in June, I first saw him at the McGills' party.

His name was Dominick Giovanni, a very rich businessman, according to the hostess, Rhonda McGill, and even though he was a full Italian, he didn't really look all that dark, did he? Probably, she whispered to everyone, he was northern Italian. The way Rhonda was looking at him, I guessed he could have been full-blooded anything and it wouldn't have mattered. He was very polite in a cool, aloof way to the men, charming to the women, indeed gracious to everyone, as though he, not Paul McGill, were the host. Then he saw me, and that started it all. He was the most incredibly sensual man I'd ever met.

I've never kept a diary before, or a journal or whatever one calls it. I like the sound of "journal" better. It sounds more thoughtful, somehow, perhaps more profound.

Which is quite silly, of course. My actions have proved to me my own depths. But no matter. Today, the fourteenth of March, you are eleven months old, my darling; and we're living on old and stolid Charles Street near Louisburg Square in my parents' brownstone. Now mine. Ours.

They're dead, killed instantly I was told—some comfort, I suppose—but how does one really know how long it takes someone to die? They were very rich, and their pilot, August, had drunk too much whiskey and plowed the Cessna into a vineyard in the south of France. That happened in May. Dominick happened in June.

It's a good thing there's no law against a very stupid girl writing about her stupidity. But I mustn't forget that I'm writing this for myself, not for you, Rafaella, even though it may appear that way. No, I'm merely writing *at* you. But you will never read this. It seems easier this way, I guess. I'm writing everything down so I don't keep choking on my own fury, my hatred of myself, my hatred of him. I believe it's called catharsis, this getting things out of one and bringing them out in the open.

Perhaps I'm not quite so stupid after all. But I can't, I won't, allow my hatred for him to come between us or to touch you in any way. You're innocent; you don't deserve it. Maybe I don't either.

But then there was Dominick, and I fell in love with him on the spot.

How absurd that sounds—to fall in love, a condition in which a female suspends all rational thought and becomes willingly besotted, a victim, really, with not *much of a separate identity from that perfect man. Actually, in defense of my stupidity, I was more lonely than you can imagine. I was grieving for my parents. I loved them, more dutifully than emotionally perhaps, but when people die so violently and so suddenly, you don't really care exactly how it was that you loved them.*

So I came to New Milford to stay for a while with my Aunt Josie and Uncle Ralph. They're nice people but they have their own interests. Obsession, rather. They'd probably up and fly to Cuba for a bridge tournament if they could. I was lonely, sad, and didn't have any friends in New Milford. These all sound like weak excuses, don't they? But they come so naturally. I can't help it. It was June 14 and I met Dominick Giovanni and fell in love.

Rafaella, I can't tell you how very different he was from all the college boys I'd dated at Wellesley. He was thirty-one years old. He dressed with sophistication and style, he was exquisitely polite, so handsome you just wanted to watch him—nothing more, just to look at him. You have his eyes—pale blue and clear as a cloudless day. And his hair was black as midnight, unlike yours, my darling, which is a lovely titian color from your grandmother Lucy. He admired me, he focused all his attention on me. He wooed me and I would have done anything for him. Anything at all.

And he said he'd marry me. And I was twenty years old and I gave him my virginity, not all that precious a commodity, but I can remember so clearly that first time, how he spoke so sweetly to me and went so slowly because, he said, he didn't want me to be frightened and he didn't want to hurt me. He didn't. It was wonderful. I remember he drove his white Thunderbird convertible north out of New Milford. He pulled me close and draped his hand over my shoulder. Then he slipped his fingers down the bodice of my sundress. Boys had done this before and I'd found it mildly di-

verting but embarrassing. And nothing had happened. But this time, with Dominick, my nipples got hard and it was because of his fingers, because of him. Then he smiled at me as he turned off the road onto a dirt stretch that led into a wooded area. He left me in the car and opened the trunk. He pulled out a blanket and told me to come with him. He spread the blanket out on a bed of daisies—white daisies—and there were shafts of sunlight spearing through the maple trees and I was on my back and he told me to lift my hips and I did and he pulled my panties off. Then he sat back on his heels and I saw he was looking at me. Then he stood up and took off his clothes, all of them. I'd never seen a nude man in real life before. His penis was huge and I thought: No, this is impossible. I'm making a horrible mistake.

But he merely sat beside me and pulled my sundress over my head. Then he lay on his back and pulled me against him. He just talked to me and told me how sweet I was, how dear I was to him, and how he was going to teach me wonderful new things. And he did. It didn't hurt when he came inside me, not really. I took every inch of his penis, and when he was as deep as he could go, he smiled and told me to lift my hips. I didn't come that first time, but I didn't care. But he did. He taught me quite a lot about myself that afternoon. I trusted him completely.

No, I suppose I couldn't have trusted him, not completely, because I didn't ever tell him who I really was and that I was very rich. I was my parents' only child, and upon their deaths I had so much money it was difficult for me to even comprehend it and the lawyer had told me that I should never volunteer who I was, never say I was Margaret Chamberlain Holland of Boston. What he meant too, of course, was that I should never volunteer what I was worth. Uncle Ralph and Aunt Josie had even introduced me using their name— Pennington, not Holland. I guess they were concerned because I was so young. I didn't tell anyone the truth, not even Dominick. I wonder if that would have made a difference. I doubt it. Dominick was many things, but a fortune hunter he wasn't.

And at the close of that magic summer, I was pregnant with you, Rafaella.

I was terrified but Dominick seemed pleased about it. Then he dropped the bomb. He was married, and couldn't marry me—just yet. It turned out that he and his wife had been separated for years and years. And I told him that he didn't have years and years and he laughed and told me how wonderful I was and how understanding and how I was so different from his wife. He left, to attend to business, he said, to get the divorce proceedings in motion, he said. He left me in New Milford, to face my aunt and uncle and the music. But he came back every couple of weeks to see me. He never came to the house. I always met him at a different hotel or motel in and around New Milford. And every time, he'd bring me to an orgasm and I'd forget my worry, my anxiety, until after he'd gone.

All of this sounds so stupid. So boringly stupid and trite, but that's how it happened. And then you were born and he returned again and visited me in the hospital in Hartford. He stood beside my bed and smiled down at me. And I'll never forget his words for as long as I live. But I still want to write them down, just in case, one day, in the distant future, I'm tempted to look back at this and romanticize it.

"You're looking well, Margaret," he said, and took my hand, kissing my fingers.

I swelled with relief even though he'd said nothing important.

"We have a daughter, Dominick."

"Yes, so I was told."

"You haven't seen her?"

"No, there's no need."

"*Perhaps not at this moment. Are you free now?* ·
Can we get married? I want my daughter to know her
wonderful father."

"*That's not possible, Margaret.*" He released my
hand and took two steps away from the bed.

"*You're not divorced yet?*" Odd how I knew what
was coming, despite my ignorance. Oh, yes, I knew.
Perhaps motherhood brings a little insight, a little wisdom with it.

He shook his head and he was still smiling down at
me. "*No,*" he said, "*I'm not divorced and I don't intend to divorce my wife even though she bores me and
tries to spend more money than even I make. You're
very young, Margaret. I've enjoyed you. Perhaps I
would have married you if you'd birthed a boy, but
you didn't. My wife is pregnant now. Isn't that strange
timing? Perhaps she'll give me a boy. I hope so.*"

"*She's your daughter!*"

He shrugged. He did nothing more, just shrugged.
And then he said, that smile still on his mouth,
"*Daughters aren't good for much, Margaret. You need
boys to build dynasties, and that's what I've always
wanted. A girl is good for cementing certain deals and
for leverage, but things have changed and you can't be
certain that you can control your daughters, make them
do what you want them to. Who knows? Twenty years
from now daughters might go against everything their
fathers tell them. No, Margaret, a girl is worth less than
nothing to me.*"

I just stared at him, frozen. "*Who are you? What
kind of man are you?*"

"*A very smart man.*" And he tossed a check for five
thousand dollars on the bed. I watched it float down
until it touched the stiff hospital sheet. "*Good-bye,
Margaret.*" And he was gone.

I didn't cry, not then. I remember so clearly picking
up that check and looking at it and then very slowly
tearing it into tiny, tiny pieces. I was so happy that I

*hadn't told him about my inheritance, so relieved I
hadn't told him who I really was. Perhaps I'd known
all along what he would do. Perhaps I'd instinctively
kept back my only valuable secret. Perhaps . . .*

One

"Look, he told the police he did it because they treated him like . . . What'd he keep saying?"

"They treated him like dirt."

"Yeah, dirt. Well, he's also crazy dirt. Come on, Al, let it go."

"No way, Rafe. There's more to it than that, I can smell it." Al tapped the side of his nose. "I want you to go to the lockup and talk to the guy. You got the talent for it, kiddo. I can trust you to find out what's going on. You're the big talent here, aren't you? Our twenty-five-year-old investigative reporter from Wallingford, Delaware? On the big-city paper for only two years and you've already got star fever? Runaway arrogance?"

Rafaella ignored that gambit. "The TV people have gone into it more ways than Sunday. It stinks. It's just exploitation and sensationalism now."

"Actually, the TV folk have screamed 'psychopath' and dredged up cases from all over the country for a fifty-year period."

"Longer. They also dredged up Lizzie Borden. Al, listen, it's a crummy story. This guy isn't bright. I've seen him on TV and I've read what he's said. It's pathetic but that's all there is. It's been overdone and

I don't want anything to do with any of it." Hands over breasts, legs slightly spread, chin up. The art of intimidation—quite good, actually, but Al wasn't moved. He'd taught Rafe some of his best tricks in the two years she'd been in his kingdom.

"You ain't got a choice, Rafe, so shut your chops and get with it. The man's in jail. He's harmless now. Talk to him, talk to his lawyer—a young squirt who looks like he just lost his pimples—and get the facts on this thing. I'm positive there's something everyone's missed."

"Come on, Al, he murdered, *axed,* three people—his father, mother, and uncle."

"But not his eleven-year-old half-brother. Don't you find that just a bit intriguing? Puzzling?"

"So the kid was lucky and wasn't home. The kid's still missing, right? We've already treated the story responsibly. Now you want sensationalism, and I don't want any part of it. Call that goon over at the *Herald,* Maury Bates, if you want more gore."

"No, Maury'd scare the guy's socks off."

Rafaella played her ace. "There's no way the police would let me in to see Freddy Pithoe. No way his attorney would let me in to see him. No way the D.A. would let me in to see him. You know how touchy everyone is on a case like this, how scared they all are about anything prejudicial happening. Let a member of the press in to see the crazy guy charged? No way at all, Al, and you know the way I work—I'd be knocking on their door, bugging everybody so I could see him maybe a half-dozen times. Well, maybe if I had to, twice. Yes, twice would be enough."

He had her. She'd talked herself into it. But he decided to reel her in slowly. It was more fun that way. "No problem, if it were kept real quiet. Benny Masterson owes me, Rafe. I've already talked to him. You keep it low-key, *real* low-key, and he'll look the other way. He's cleared you."

"Lieutenant Masterson must owe you his life to allow a reporter in to see Freddy Pithoe. He could lose his pension, he could get his tail chewed from here to Florida. He'd be taking a huge risk. Lord, everyone, including Freddy, would have to be sworn to silence."

Al Holbein, managing editor of the Boston *Tribune,* was more stubborn than Rafaella, and she knew it, plus he had twenty-five more years of practice.

He waved his cigar toward the *Tribune*'s metro editor, Clive Oliver, seated in a sea of assistants and reporters in the middle of the huge, noisy newsroom. There was a near-fistfight at one end, between two sports reporters, and a can of Coke was flying through the air from a police reporter to the cooking editor. "I've talked to Clive. He bitched, but I told him I didn't want him to dump any assignments on you until I told him it was okay." Al reached into his desk drawer and pulled out a folded slip of paper. "Here's your new personal password. Only you and I will be able to access anything you write on this story. Don't show it to a soul—"

"Come on, Al, you know I don't."

"Yeah, well, don't this time either. I want this thing kept under wraps. As far under wraps as possible."

"The only thing that will be under wraps is what I write. This assignment is probably all over the newsroom by now, probably even down in classified." She opened the paper and stared, then laughed. " 'Ruffle'? That's my password? Where'd you get that one?"

Al gave her that smile that had seduced Milly Archer, a TV reporter, just six months before. "It's my favorite potato chip. Now look, Rafe, just maybe there's another Pulitzer in it for you. Who knows?"

That made her laugh. "When was the last time a reporter on a big newspaper won a Pulitzer? No, don't tell me. You've got examples all lined up, don't you?"

"Sure thing. Remember the reporters in Chicago

who ran that sting operation with a bar they opened themselves without telling the cops? That was a real beauty, and . . ." He paused, a light of wistfulness in his eyes. "In any case, just maybe you'll find something. Think about how good it'll make you feel. Remember how you felt when you cracked that group of neo-Nazis for the Wallingford *Daily News*?"

It *had* felt good, no doubt about that. "Yeah, I was pleased that I was still alive and the jerks hadn't shoved their swastika armbands down my throat." Then, "All right, Al, you win. I'll go see the guy and talk to him. I'll try to make him promise he won't tell anyone, including his lawyer, about me. Maybe no one will know. I'll even try to keep it from being public knowledge down in classified. Does your infamous nose have any concrete information for me to go on?"

Al always lied cleanly, to his mother, to his women, and to his reporters, so he shook his head promptly, his expression guileless.

Five minutes later, still grumbling, Rafaella Holland stuffed her oversize canvas bag with notebook, sharpened pencils, and umbrella, waved good-bye to Buzz Adams, the *Tribune*'s other investigative reporter, and left for the lockup to interview a twenty-three-year-old man named Freddy Pithoe, who, in a fit of rage—cause unknown—had wiped out nearly his entire family. His very inexperienced lawyer was going to plead temporary insanity—not very bright. Even Rafaella knew that old Freddy had purchased that ax two days before he did his family in. Premeditation, all the way. He wasn't crazy, at least in the sense his lawyer was claiming. Freddy Pithoe was just waiting to get them all together, tell them what he thought of them, and ax them. That's what the cops said, what the D.A. said, what the news media said. It was certainly the take on it that Logan Mansfield, bright and upcoming assistant D.A., shared. He'd made that perfectly clear at great length during a spate of foreplay that had left Rafaella boiling—but not with sexual yearnings.

Al watched Rafaella wind her way through the desks and reporters and assistants to the wide glass doors of the *Trib*'s newsroom. She was nearly stomping, her London Fog raincoat flapping. He pushed himself back in his swivel chair, leaned his head against the ratty brown leather cushion that he'd refused to let Mr. Danforth, owner of the Boston *Tribune*, replace for five years now, and closed his eyes. He knew that if the anonymous tip he'd gotten from that old woman—she'd refused to identify herself— had any merit, Rafaella would discover it. He'd joked about her Pulitzer, but the job she'd done in ferreting out that den of neo-Nazis had been damned impressive and Mr. Danforth had called Al immediately after her Pulitzer had been announced. She'd taken a job with the *Trib* a month later. Imagine that vicious bunch using a candy store in a shopping mall in Delaware as a front. *Heil* Mr. Lazarus Smith. God, what a story that had made, for months. Rafe didn't even have a sweet tooth for all he knew.

Oh, yes, if there was anything to this thing, she'd find out what it was. She was tenacious and, more important, had the talent to adapt her style, her approach, even her look, to each situation, to each person, no matter how disparate, no matter how weird. She'd find out why Freddy had almost decapitated his old man, struck his mother a good three blows in the chest, and very nearly hacked the uncle's two arms off.

Al just had to wait until Rafe made the decision that she *wanted* to know. He'd really gotten her goat, and she'd have to work that through for a couple of hours, most of those hours wanting to punch him out. Then, he guessed, she'd be down at the jail by eleven this morning. She was good, and under his tutelage she'd get better. And she'd keep everything under wraps. No one would get in trouble over a reporter visiting a prisoner. Not this time. Al sniffed things out; she felt things in her gut. This time his nose had had a bit of help from an anonymous tip.

If Rafe came up dry, then he'd give her the lead, for what it was worth, but not before. He guessed his caller was a neighbor. Rafe would find the neighbor; he didn't have to worry.

Al lit a cigar and looked down at the story Gene Mallory, the paper's youngest political analyst, had written on the budget crisis facing the governor. Boring but top-notch. Attached to the article was a hand-printed note with the names of his sources. Careful, careful Gene, a clean-cut preppie. Al couldn't imagine what Rafe saw in him. Gene was a plodder; she was spontaneous combustion. Al couldn't imagine the two of them ever sleeping together. Rafe would probably fall asleep while Gene went through his checklist of foreplay tactics. Al had heard something about a guy in the D.A.'s office. Maybe he was more promising.

Brammerton, Massachusetts
That evening

"Another glass of wine, Gene?"

Gene Mallory shook his head, smiling slightly. "No, I've had enough. Tomorrow's an early day for both of us, Rafaella." He fiddled with the half of his Italian breadstick, then said, "I heard about your assignment to the Pithoe story. All the guys were talking about how you and Mr. Holbein were going at each other. No, don't get upset, Rafaella. No one but me knows what you were yelling about. I—well, I just happened to overhear Mr. Holbein say the guy's name and warn you about secrecy. I won't say a single word, I promise. I'm just surprised Mr. Holbein decided to make you do it and not Buzz Adams. It's a dirty mess, everyone knows the guy's as guilty as heck, and you're—"

"I'm what, Gene?"

"Well, you weren't raised to mix yourself up with that sort of garbage. After all, Rafaella, your stepfather *is* Charles Winston Rutledge III."

Rafaella slugged down the rest of her wine to keep her mouth shut. She felt tight all over, and the bolus of wine didn't help. "And you were?" she asked mildly. "Raised for garbage?"

"Of course not, but it's more a man's story—going to the grungy jail, speaking with all those guards and finally to that maniac. It wasn't part of Mr. Holbein's budget. He didn't even mention the story in the news meeting."

"His name is Al. I've heard him tell you to call him Al. He didn't make the story part of his budget because he wants to keep it under wraps, which is very important, critical, as you very well know. However, Sally, the cleaning woman, knows about it. How, I haven't the faintest idea. She left a note on my desk. *He's got a weak chin. Guilty, I know it.*"

"Mr. Holbein still should have brought the story up in the news meeting, and he shouldn't have assigned it to you."

Rafaella forced herself not to get mad and tear into Gene. She didn't know what his problem was, but he was showing himself to be a royal pain in the butt this evening. She hadn't noticed it so much before. He'd interested her simply because he was so straight. And he was good-looking in a very fair WASP way, and had a body that was worked to its limit every day. He'd been on the *Trib* staff for only two and a half months now.

She chose her words carefully. "I can handle any story that Al dishes out. My sex has nothing to do with anything. Or my background. Do you think you can interview men better than you can women?"

"No, of course not, but I'm not certain about a woman psychopath."

He had a point there. "I'm not so sure about a male psychopath either. But I did it with Herr Lazarus Smith, if you'll recall. Fascinating stuff, Gene—Freddy Pithoe, not old Lazarus." Rafaella forgot her irritation and propped her chin on her folded hands.

"Al was right; he got me so mad I was ready to kill him. Instead I boned up on Freddy, read everything we had in the library, then went to see Mr. Pithoe. He didn't want to talk at first. Sullen and blank-faced. It took me ten minutes just to get five words out of him. Tomorrow I'll try my little-sister approach. That might make him respond better. I sure hope so. I can't count on more than two visits to him."

"I still don't like you dealing with the dregs of humanity."

She poured herself some coffee. It brought patience. "We're both reporters. We deal with all kinds of dregs, including the newsroom coffee. You deal with politicians—can you get more dicey than that?"

"At least they can all read and write."

"Which makes them all the more dangerous."

"What did the man say?"

Aha, he wanted all the dirt, the hypocrite. "I'm keeping it under wraps right now. I have to, even with you. It's the way Al wants it."

Rafaella could tell that Gene was put off by her tonight. She wanted to laugh. He'd winced when she said "damn" earlier. She also realized at that moment that she usually tended to censor herself when she was with him. She looked at him now, saw the expression of dissatisfaction that marred his mouth. She was beginning to think she'd been wrong about him. He wasn't an intellectual, just a bore and a chauvinist.

Thank goodness she hadn't gone to bed with him. He probably would have been mortified in the morning and accused her of having compromised him. That made her smile, and she thought of the message taped on the wall in the *Trib*'s women's room: BE THE VIRGIN OF THE MONTH. STAY HEALTHY.

She was still smiling as she said, "You're right, Gene. Tomorrow's an early day." She rose and walked to the front closet, hoping he'd follow. He did. She helped him on with his fur-lined Burberry and stepped back. He looked at her for a moment, then said good night and left.

No good-night kiss for her. This was probably the end of the line with Gene Mallory. No big loss when you got right down to it, for either of them.

Rafaella methodically locked the door, slid home the dead bolt, and fastened the two chain locks. It was very likely unnecessary having all this paraphernalia in Brammerton, Massachusetts, but she was a single woman living alone. She walked into her living room, furnished with an eclectic collection of Nouveau Goodwill, as her mother fondly referred to her trappings, and went to the large bay window. It was quiet outside; snow covered the street and glistened under the streetlamps.

It was always quiet here in Brammerton. A small town some twenty miles southeast of Boston, near Braintree, Brammerton used to be wildly blue collar. Now it was next to nothing, the paper mill having closed its doors in the late eighties and moved elsewhere. There weren't even companionable drunks out singing at the tops of their lungs on Saturday nights. It wasn't a bit like Boston. There wasn't a single university within Brammerton's city limits, nor had there ever been one. It was a town filling up with retired people and social-security checks.

Rafaella shut off all the lights and went to bed. It was her favorite thinking time, those fifteen or so minutes before falling asleep. If she had a problem, she'd set it up before she went to sleep, fully expecting a solution to appear the following morning. Solutions frequently did appear.

She didn't spare any more time for Gene Mallory.

All her thoughts focused on Freddy Pithoe and what he hadn't said to her that morning. It could be that Al's nose was right again, because now her gut was twisting in that weird way when things weren't actually as they were thought to be. She'd carefully read the police report and the three shrinks' reports. She'd also forced herself to go through the coroner's report and the crime-lab pictures taken of the three dead family members. She thought of those now. Of the information in them, and more important, of the information not in them.

And again and again she found herself coming back to one thing: Why had Freddy axed his family? Rage? Come on, everybody got enraged once in a while. Just working with Al Holbein got her enraged, but it had never occurred to her to take an ax to him. There had to be a reason. Another thing: Where was Joey Pithoe, Freddy's little brother? There had been speculation that the boy had seen the carnage and fled for his life. He would turn up, the police thought, soon enough. Poor kid. What chance would he have? They were trying to find the boy, but they weren't really trying all that hard.

They had their psychopathic killer. Who cared about a kid?

Rafaella did. Because there was more to it than just Freddy buying that ax and doing in his family. Why such mutilation on the mother and the uncle? Sure enough, the near decapitation of the father was gruesome, but it was only one blow. Not multiple cuts like the other two. Rafaella fell asleep at last. Her dreams were quite pleasant but there was a recurrent theme of a boy, lost and frightened and—something else, something vague, something churning in her gut.

Rafaella was at the jail the following morning. Sergeant Haggerty, a hard-nosed old cop who had been on the force for nearly thirty years, just gave her a bored smile and said she could spend the rest of her life talking to the crazy scum, he didn't care. But, yeah, he wouldn't say a word to nobody. She knew he did care, but Lieutenant Masterson had been good to his word—but for just this visit and that would be it.

Rafaella was sitting in the interview room on the other side of the wire cooping. It was not a dirty room, just depressing, with the peeling light green paint and the institutional chairs. There wasn't a phone system here, just the wire screen separating prisoners from their visitors. Freddy Pithoe was gently shoved into the room by a blank-faced young guard who'd already seen too much and wanted to protect himself from seeing any more.

She studied Freddy as she had before. He was the most pathetic young man she'd ever seen in her life. He wasn't scum; he was frightened and nearly over the edge with what was happening to him.

And in ten minutes she got him to talk, at least a bit.

He'd bought the ax at his father's request, he told her. This was familiar ground to him.

"But, Mr. Pithoe, didn't you tell the police that?" she asked, trying to keep her voice calm and pitched low; her eyes never wavering from his face.

"Yes, ma'am, but they said I was a fucking liar and crazy. I told 'em again and again, but it didn't matter. They said I was a crazy fucking liar."

"Did your father tell you why he wanted you to buy the ax?"

Freddy just looked at her, his brow puckering, nearly drawing his thick dark eyebrows together over the bridge of his nose. "I don't know, ma'am. He just told me to buy it. That's all, I swear." Then Freddy Pithoe said something Rafaella hadn't expected in a million years. "He said he'd beat my fucking head in if I didn't buy the ax."

Rafaella felt a tingling along her backbone, and her gut was playing the marimba. She had to tread carefully now. "You know, Mr. Pithoe—do you mind if I call you Freddy?—you can call me Rafaella—you need to see a doctor. Your left eye is red and kind of weepy. Did he ever actually beat you?"

"Who?"

Easy now, Rafe, easy. "Your father. Did he beat you?"

Freddy nodded, his expression stolid. "Since I was a little kid. It weren't just me, though. It was Mama and my little brother. Pa called Joey a bastard and said he was gonna beat the shit out of him. He did, all the time."

"You should have told this to the police."

Freddy gave her a puzzled look. "Why would they want to know about that? Everybody beats everybody. They wouldn't care."

"What about your lawyer, Mr. Dexter?"

"Mr. Dexter just said I was to keep my mouth shut and don't worry because I was crazy—for about ten minutes I was crazy, he said—something like that."

Freddy Pithoe, twenty-three years old, didn't look particularly intelligent with his small dark eyes and the coarse dark hair. Nor did he look particularly crazy. His complexion was unnaturally pale, his shoulders slumped, making him appear much shorter than his six feet. He'd tried to grow a beard to cover his receding chin. It just made it look worse because it was so splotchy. He was a mess, no doubt about that. An abused mess. And he was telling her the truth. He did need to see a doctor about that eye.

"Did you ever go to a doctor, Mr. Pithoe—?"

"You can call me Freddy."

"Thank you. Did you ever see a doctor after your father beat you?"

"Oh, no, ma'am. He said I weren't worth it. Once when Uncle Kipper let me have it, he broke my arm, but Pa just bound it up and told me to shut up. It was just Mama who had to go and—"

"Do you remember which hospital, Freddy? How long ago was it?"

"Yes, ma'am. It were that general place, the emergency room."

Mass General. Excellent. Why had none of this come out before? *Because everyone thinks he's a fucking liar, that's why.*

"Didn't the psychologists ask you about this, Freddy?"

"Yes, ma'am, but I didn't tell 'em that Pa beat any of us."

"But why not?"

"It was just one of their questions on this long sheet of paper. They wanted to know what it really felt like to sink that ax in my pa's neck, and if my mom pleaded with me not to kill her."

Rafaella gagged.

"I didn't like any of 'em. One reminded me of Uncle Kipper."

Rafaella had the vagrant thought that if she vomited in this holding room, no one could tell, it would all blend in. She looked closely at Freddy. Such a mess.

"When did your ma go to the hospital, Freddy?"

He looked blank for about a minute, then said very carefully, "Fourteen months ago, ma'am. She was hurting real bad. Pa told 'em her name was Milly Mooth. He thought that was real funny."

"Did you ax your father to death?"

"Yeah, sure I did, and the others too."

Rafaella leaned close to him. "I think you're a fucking liar now, Freddy."

He stared at her, drawing back. "I ain't no fucking liar, ma'am, I ain't!"

She'd just said the words, not really thinking about

them. They'd just come out, and now there was this
look in his eyes. She said more firmly, "Yes you are.
Tell me the truth, Freddy. All of it."

He refused to say anything else. He screamed for
the guard, nearly tumbling off his chair. And he was
rubbing frantically at his eye. Oh, damn. Had she
blown it?

"I'll see you tomorrow, Freddy," she called after
him. "I'll tell them you need a doctor for that eye."

The words had doubtless come straight from her
marimba-rhythm gut. Of course he'd axed his family.
Hadn't he? She found herself shaking her head. Rafaella rose quickly, wanting only to get out of this miserable room. Gut was one thing; investigation proved it
or disproved it, and grunt work. Lots and lots of grunt
work. And she'd have to see Freddy again. How to
get Lieutenant Masterson to approve one more visit?
She'd have to. She had no choice now.

Her next stop was Mass General Hospital, the records room. The trick about getting to patients' records
was to wear a white coat, hang a stethoscope around
your neck, and act as confident as the chief of staff.
She'd done it before, twice, and it had worked both
times. The clerks were overworked, didn't think to
question someone who looked like he belonged. Rafaella waited until the two records clerks on duty were
dealing with at least half a dozen demands before she
walked in and made her own demand. No problem.

There was only one page of doctor's notes. What
was attached was a Polaroid picture of Mrs. Pithoe,
aka Milly Mooth, looking like a prisoner of war. She
looked old and bent and so weary her obvious pain
wasn't all that obvious. Rafaella quickly read the
notes. *Mrs. Mooth accepted treatment but refused ad-
mittance. Was discharged AMA.* Against medical advice. No apparent internal injuries. Two broken ribs,
one broken arm, multiple contusions, face swollen
with bruises, and cuts requiring twenty-one stitches.

Why had Freddy axed her? And so viciously? She was every bit as much a victim as her son.

Something was missing. A whole lot of something. Was she wrong? Was she putting too much faith in her gut? No, it was Freddy's reaction, his eyes, that tipped her off.

She'd know soon enough. She didn't need to see Freddy's lawyer. That poor guy didn't know a damned thing, for the simple reason that Freddy hadn't talked to him.

She needed to interview neighbors. Something the police had already done, but they hadn't gotten everything. She was sure of it.

Which brought up another question. Al Holbein never gave an assignment like this unless he had a very good reason—or had heard something that made him wonder—or had been told something no one else knew.

He had something. And he hadn't told her what it was.

Rafaella went home and dressed carefully for her trip to the North End. The name Pithoe wasn't remotely Italian, and she wondered why they lived there. An hour later she was walking past Paul Revere's house. She walked three blocks down Hanover Street, wishing she could take time to buy fresh fruit and vegetables sold in the outdoor stalls. Even in February, the food looked more appetizing than her supermarket. She passed the Caffè Pompeii, one of her favorite Italian restaurants. Up another block was Nathan Street. The Pithoe neighborhood was another block west. It was blue-collar, clean, but with that slightly ragged appearance, like a frayed collar on a once nice shirt.

She looked like a bouncy college kid—the Boston University look—in not-too-tight jeans and a blue turtleneck under a western shirt. She wore a down vest and low-heeled black boots. Imp boots, Al called them. She'd perfected her approach on three neighbors by the time she reached 379 Prosper Street, a narrow brownstone with a small square front yard buried in at least a foot of dirty snow. Its backyard backed up to the Pithoes'. The fences between the two backyards was wood and rotting.

And it was from Mrs. Roselli, a tiny wrinkled grandmother who'd been born in Milano and spent most of her time in her second-floor bedroom looking out her window toward the Pithoes', that Rafaella learned some very interesting things.

Two

Marcus Devlin, whose real name was Marcus Ryan O'Sullivan, pulled off his T-shirt, smoothed it on the white sand, and sprawled out onto his back. He crossed his right arm over his eyes against the bright midday sun. It felt blessedly hot but not miserable enough to make him sweat, because there was always a cool breeze off the Caribbean.

Marcus had been back on the island for only a day now, called back from Boston by Dominick because of the Dutchmen. They'd agreed to terms. No more negotiations. They were coming here, to the island, today, a sort of hail-good-fellow, let's-drink-champagne.

He scratched his belly and wondered what he really felt about this deal with the Dutchmen, what he really felt now that things might be coming to an end. But things were never simple; he'd learned that again and again. All he knew was that things were tough. He knew he had to be gritty and hard, and he couldn't let down his guard, and that was tough as well. God, he wanted out of here. Once this was all over, he didn't think he ever wanted to come back to the Caribbean. But that would be in the future, if he managed to buy himself a future.

Now he was here, lying on his back as if he didn't have a care in the world, worrying. The hot sun did feel good after the wretched weather in Boston. The snow, ice, and general grayness got him down. Even though Chicago could be every bit as depressing in February, emotionally it was still home and still in his heart. In Boston he'd dutifully made arrangements to meet with Pearlman in a small hotel in Brookline, but it hadn't come off because Dominick had called him, and he'd taken the first flight back to Antigua, then to the island. Not that he'd known what the hell he was supposed to say to Pearlman—supposedly it was Pearlman who would have given him information.

Of course the deal was smuggling military aircraft parts—perhaps even navigational gyroscopes and TOW missiles—he wasn't at all certain. It could be F-14 Tomcat parts bound for Iran, the only country with the F-14. Or C-130 aircraft bound for Syria. Or somewhere else—Libya perhaps? Malaysia? Going through Singapore or Borneo?

One thing he was sure of: there were no licenses or permits from the U.S. State Department. It was illegal all the way. Dominick was perhaps one of the most powerful arms dealers in the world because no one could find out anything specific about his myriad activities. He was too smart, too well-protected, too buried behind middlemen, and he didn't trust anyone. Including his only son, DeLorio, a whining bully who was afraid of his father. Including Marcus, a man he should have come to trust by now.

But this deal with the Dutchmen—intermediaries, Marcus had been told—they would come and drink champagne and he would discover what was being shipped where. At least he'd find out what the end-user certificate said was the destination, if there was one in this case. Marcus felt his heart begin to pound and a cramp twist in his stomach. This time he'd find out, he knew it. This time he'd know, and then he'd act. He'd get the proof. Then he'd be free. Even as he thought it, he remembered the half-dozen or so deals that had gone through, deals he hadn't been able to discover enough about to make it worth anyone's while, and the familiar frustration crept through him. So very long now, and he was tired of it, tired to his soul of playing a part, of manipulating and lying to gain information, of thinking carefully before he ever uttered an opinion to Dominick, of recognizing that he could die with just one slip. He wanted it to be over, wanted it to the depths of his soul. He wanted to go home and pick up his life again. He thought again of the phone conversation he'd had with his cousin, John Savage, when he'd been in Boston. John was worried. "It's past time for you to get out, Marcus. You've done your duty. It's been more than two years of your life. Forget nailing Giovanni, forget these damned Dutchmen, and come home. We do occasionally need you here, you know."

Marcus begged to differ. Savage was one of the most ruthlessly efficient men he'd ever known. Thank God he was also his best friend as well as his first cousin. He'd hate to have him for an enemy. Marcus said mildly, successfully, he hoped, tamping down on his growing sense of defeat, his growing sense of losing what should be his, without strings—the days and weeks and months of his life—God, now it was years: "We drew straws, John, and I won, or lost, depending on my mood at any given time. I'll come home when I've got enough proof to send Giovanni to federal prison for the rest of his sorry life, and not before. You know I can't. There's Uncle Morty."

John Savage had been silent for several moments and Marcus knew he was remembering the sting operation by the U.S. Customs Service people and how they'd caught Uncle Morty dealing with this beautiful Soviet spy and they'd made a deal. Marcus's cooperation for Uncle Morty's staying out of the slammer. That was the deal. Still, John had said, "Uncle Morty

wouldn't have expected all this sacrifice, Marcus. No
one would."

"Uncle Morty's a naive idiot who doesn't know his
ass from his elbow. He's doing okay, isn't he?"

Marcus sighed now, stretching onto his back, feeling
the sun seep into his very bones. He'd made the deal
with the feds and he had to stick to it. No way around
it. Dominick Giovanni for Uncle Morty, and that
was that.

He sat up abruptly at the sound of an approaching
helicopter. It was on this side of the island, not the
Porto Bianco side, so it wasn't a group of jet-setters
who would in all likelihood drop an average of ten
thousand each at the casino. No, it was the Dutchmen,
and they'd land on the compound helicopter pad. He
had another ten minutes, he guessed, before their visitors would be drinking iced tea with Dominick in the
main house. It would be longer than that before business discussions started. He pulled off his cut-off jeans
and ran into the water. He'd take his time. He'd swim
off his fear, his frustration, his anticipation. The last
thing he wanted was to have Dominick think him
overeager. He'd clam up and send Marcus quickly on
his way back to the resort.

He swam hard for ten minutes. He swam off everything except his bone-deep sense of defeat.

Eddie Merkel watched Marcus swim back through
the breakers, and he thought: *Marcus is a dangerous
man, ruthless but not stupid, and I quite like him.* It
had taken nearly two years, but Merkel had finally
filed him under "To Be Trusted." He was conniving,
ingenuous, his own man, tough as nails, and even
though he deferred to Mr. Giovanni, he was strong
and decisive on his own. Pigheaded, in some people's
book. Hell, look at how well he ran the resort. Little
got by him. He'd made the casino into a gold mine,
kept all the rich members and their guests happy, and

probably made private deals with the businessmen who came, to line his own pockets.

Mr. Giovanni didn't trust him yet, at least not completely, but as far as Merkel knew, he didn't completely trust anyone. He'd said to Merkel after he'd completed Marcus's background check that Marcus was almost too good to be true, his background wonderfully eclectic and rich, preparing him almost too well for what Mr. Giovanni expected of him. Navy intelligence in the early nineties, then CIA, primarily in Europe—that was the bulk of Marcus's adult background. Merkel understood how those experiences would make Marcus tough and conniving. But he didn't understand how that made him such a good resort manager. Merkel thought Mr. Giovanni was crazy to complain when Marcus managed the resort well and made tons of money.

Merkel watched a nude Marcus walk through the waves to the shore. A big man, strong, lean, and some of his perpetual tan lost from the visit to Boston. He was Irish, from his thick black hair to his dark blue eyes, but unlike the Irishmen Merkel had known, he'd never seen Marcus drunk. No, Marcus liked to keep control, both of himself and of those around him.

When Marcus reached him, Merkel said nothing, merely handed Marcus his cut-offs and his T-shirt.

"Mr. Giovanni sent me to find you," Merkel said in a soft voice that sounded ludicrous coming from a two-hundred-and-thirty-pound man with no neck.

"Yeah, I heard the helicopter," Marcus said, trying to sound a bit bored. "It's the Dutchmen?"

"Three of them this time. Two we know—Koerbogh and Van Wessel—and a Dutchwoman we don't know. Her name is Tulp—"

"Last name I hope," Marcus said, his voice muffled through his T-shirt as he pulled it over his head.

Merkel gave a sour smile. "I don't know her first name, but she's tough as nails. Everyone's smiling and nodding and looking like it's the greatest day of their lives. Tulp doesn't say much. Great tits," he added absently.

Marcus nodded as he zipped up his cut-off jeans.

"You're white as a dead whale."

"Give me another three days."

"DeLorio left for Miami an hour ago. Link and Lacy went with him."

Marcus grinned at that. "Well, there must be a God somewhere to rid us of the complaining little bully. I still can't believe he's actually Dominick's son. Flesh of his flesh and all that."

"Mr. Giovanni sent him away. It wasn't DeLorio's idea. Paula wanted to go too, but Mr. Giovanni said no."

"Too bad. Well, maybe DeLorio will open a window in the jet and get sucked out. Maybe he'll attack Margie when she serves him a drink, and she'll shove the glass down his throat."

Merkel didn't say a thing, didn't change expression, although he agreed with Marcus. DeLorio and his wife were royal pains in the ass.

Merkel was wearing his uniform, Marcus saw, a three-piece white suit with a pale blue button-down oxford shirt, a blue-and-white-striped tie, white Italian loafers, and a Rolex on his meaty wrist. He had five white suits and ten shirts, all the same color and material.

"Paula had one of the boys drive her over to her resort. She seemed mad enough to gamble away her wedding ring."

"Since all the money comes back to Dominick, her wedding ring included, no big deal."

Merkel said now, frowning, "The Dutchwoman, Tulp, I don't like her—"

"Even with her big tits?"

"There's something about her that makes you shiver. You know what I mean?"

Marcus started to say yeah, he knew—Frank Lacy made him shiver—when suddenly there was a shout from the direction of the main house, then a shot.

Merkel, built like a linebacker with a massive chest and huge thighs, was off like a forty-year-old Charlie Garner. Marcus passed him, his arm in front of his face to protect him from the thick vegetation that slapped at him as he ran through the dense jungle.

He ran as hard as he'd ever run before, tearing through the damp, heavy foliage that Dominick's servants hacked back every day, and came to a sudden stop at the edge of the jungle. Panic stilled and calm took over. He heard Eddie Merkel puffing behind him, heard him slow down and pull up at his back.

Marcus concentrated on what was in front of him, shut off everything but his brain. The big house, all whitewashed adobe with bright red-tiled roof, with hibiscus, bougainvillea, orchids, and frangipani climbing up its walls and framing its windows—no men hiding there. In front of the house stood Dominick Giovanni, clutching his arm. He was wearing an open-collared white shirt and white pants, and the blood was oozing through his fingers down his arm. The contrast between the stark white of his sleeve and the glutinous red of the blood turned Marcus's stomach.

The Dutchwoman, Tulp, was standing in front of him, a 9-mm automatic in her hand. She was wearing a tailored blue suit, smart-looking, and she did have big tits. The two Dutchmen were beside her. Koerbogh, the short bald one, was staring upward, shading his eyes, looking for the helicopter. Marcus could hear it coming now, only minutes away.

What had happened? What had gone wrong? The deal had been settled on; everything, he'd understood, was set. It had been his chance, his first big chance in a long time.

Yet something had happened. Did the woman intend to kill Dominick? Or just wound him, as she'd done already? Dominick looked calm, his pale blue eyes clear and steady on the woman. If he felt pain from the wound in his arm, he didn't let on.

Marcus whispered, not turning his head, "Give me your automatic, Merkel."

The Kalashnikov automatic rifle, the old standby from Russia, could wipe out a dozen men in under ten seconds. Marcus preferred it to the lightweight RPK machine guns Dominick had procured for his men from a German dealing with a middleman in Russia.

"What are you gonna do?" Merkel whispered, and Marcus could feel the heat of his body nearly touching his back.

"Stay ready," he said, and waited, tense, scared, but controlling it. Damned bloody bastards! If they ruined everything—No, he couldn't accept that. It made him want to spit. What had happened?

The helicopter was circling low overhead now, blowing off several red frangipani blossoms, flattening low bushes. Koerbogh was waving frantically. The other Dutchman, Van Wessel, crouched over, even though the blade wouldn't have touched him because he couldn't be more than five-feet-six. The Dutchwoman still didn't move. Marcus could tell she was talking to Dominick, but he couldn't hear a thing over the whirling rotor blade. He realized that she was the boss, she was the one giving the orders. The two men were frightened and it showed. She was frightened but it didn't show. She was the leader.

Marcus slipped out of the cover of the jungle. He ran, bent low, to the far side of the helicopter. It was white, and painted on its side, just behind the cabin, lettered in bright green, was *Bathsheba*.

Its rotor was whipping wildly around, churning up the bushes and the plants, causing enough of a visual diversion, Marcus hoped. He waited just behind the cabin, out of sight of the pilot. He saw the woman,

Tulp, nod to the Dutchmen, then calmly turn back to Dominick and raise her 9-mm automatic. He heard her then, yelling at Dominick, "You bloody rotten bastard," and just as she raised the 9-mm to fire, Marcus leapt from behind the helicopter, aimed, and pulled the trigger. The bullet barely grazed her right wrist. The sound was like the popping of a toy gun over the noise of the whirling blade. The woman whipped around, and Marcus saw that blood was pouring out of her wrist, but she hadn't dropped the gun and it was now pointed at him. He clamped his jaws together, and within an instant two bullets ripped through her chest. She stood there, her mouth open, surprise in her eyes, and then she fell, slowly, heavily, her legs folding, onto the ground.

The two Dutchmen were running, screaming, but Marcus didn't fire at them. He watched Merkel take both of them down, slamming Koerbogh in the jaw and Van Wessel in his fat stomach. The helicopter pilot, no fool, lifted off. Marcus raised his automatic rifle and carefully aimed. He stopped.

He heard Dominick call out to him, "Bring him down, Marcus."

But he shook his head. Slowly Marcus lowered the rifle. He couldn't do it; he couldn't bring down the helicopter and kill the pilot. It wasn't worth it. He wasn't a dispassionate, cold-blooded killer, not like Dominick Giovanni.

He hurried back to Dominick. He was smiling, his hand still pressing over the wound in his upper arm. Had Marcus imagined his order?

"Thank you, Marcus," Dominick said in his aloof, polite voice. "I wasn't too worried, well, not until the very end there. The bitch was going to kill me," he added, amazement in his voice. "And I don't even know why. You'd think she would have told me, wouldn't you?"

"What the hell happened?" As he spoke, Marcus

pulled Dominick's hand from his arm. He ripped open the sleeve and looked at the wound. "The bullet went through, thank God. I think I can handle this. We don't need to call in Haymes."

Dominick nodded, and Marcus, for the first time, saw the strain on his face. He watched Dominick pull himself together. "The servants are all locked in the cellar. Coco is tied to a chair in the cabana. Our twelve men, every last one of them, are unconscious in the dining room. Koerbogh gassed them. Quite efficiently, I might add—knocked them out within seconds. I'm familiar with the stuff they used. Invented by the Chinese. The men will be coming out of it in about four hours."

"And Paula had already left for the resort?"

"Yes."

"You can tell me more about it later. Come in now and lie down. I'll see to things." He called over to Merkel, who was standing over the two unconscious Dutchmen, "Tie up those hyenas and we'll question them in a little while."

"Right," Merkel called back, and picked up the two men, one under each arm, and half-dragged them toward what was called the tool shed but was in reality a place to store people also.

"Marcus! Watch out!"

Marcus whirled about to see the woman, Tulp, come up on her side, blood streaming out of her chest and mouth, the 9-mm automatic raised in her wounded hand and pointed at him. Everything stopped. He wanted to duck, to leap out of the way, but it was too late.

He heard Dominick yell.

Then he heard a shot and then another.

A cold numbing pain sliced through his shoulder. And he thought: This is damned unfair and I don't want to die.

Brammerton, Massachusetts
February 2001

Rafaella was dreaming about Freddy Pithoe, and then, quite suddenly, she jerked awake, eyes wide and ears fully tuned. It was quiet as a tomb, not a sound, just echoes of the shots she'd heard in her dreams. She started to get out of bed, when she felt a pain in the left side of her body. She rubbed her shoulder and her arm. An odd pain, as if she'd been struck, hard.

It was weird, no doubt about it. Maybe she needed a vacation. She was letting Freddy Pithoe get to her. She stuck her feet into her decade-old Mickey Mouse slippers and pulled on a ratty pink robe. She went into the living room and flicked back the curtain. The street below was quiet, as usual, and the newly fallen snow undisturbed. There were no backfiring cars, no irate old men yelling at each other, and no testy retired ladies twittering at their poodles, nothing to account for the shouts and the gunshots she'd heard so clearly.

Rafaella went into her kitchen, saw it was near dawn, and made some coffee. As she waited, she rubbed her shoulder and her arm. They felt numb now. It was weird.

Those wretched shots. Dreams had to come from something. Rafaella shook her head. Of course, she'd been thinking violent thoughts. She'd simply translated the awful ax murders into gunshots because the other was too horrible for her to handle, even her subconscious.

She poured herself a cup of the fresh Kona coffee and sat at her small pine kitchen table. Forget the stupid dream, she told herself. She thought instead of her run-in with Lieutenant Masterson that afternoon. Sure he owed Al a favor, but it was obvious that he was thinking the favor had been paid, in full. He had a big beefy face, a paunch, and he sweated a lot. He'd stopped Rafaella on her way in, demanding, "You want to see the nut case again?"

"Yes, I would. I sure do appreciate it, Lieutenant."

"You've already seen him twice. Twice! You wanna see me go down? What are you doing? Writing his biography?"

She wondered if he was serious. She had written a biography of the dashing French resistance leader Louis Rameau, DeGaulle's right hand. "No," she said, keeping her voice pitched low, very respectful and deferential. Louis Rameau had also been quite the ladies' man, unlike Benny Masterson here.

"One more time, kid, and that's it. You got it? You tell Al that he's pushed me too much on this one. And you keep your trap shut. No one's to know, no one's to find out."

"I'll tell him, Lieutenant. No one will find out, I swear. Thank you very much for your cooperation."

As he walked away, he turned back, saying, "Oh, yeah, kid, you come up with anything, you tell me, you got that?"

"Certainly, Lieutenant. I'll come to you right away."

He'd given her a sour look, then shrugged. "There's nothing to find, but just in case you think you have something, you call me, or I'll have your head."

But Freddy had refused to see her. The guard told her that he'd vomited up his guts just an hour ago. The food probably, he'd added, the franks and beans had looked sickening enough.

Tomorrow, she'd thought, first thing tomorrow morning. It will be all over.

Rafaella drank the rest of her coffee and took herself to the shower. Today was the day. It was very early, but she didn't care. She was too keyed up now. She bundled up against the twenty-degree weather and reached the Metro station at just after eight in the morning. The dream had faded now, even though her left side still ached a bit.

Thank God Freddy had agreed to see her. Thank God Masterson hadn't told the people not to let her in again.

He looked worse today, his shoulders slumped forward like a hunchback's. His eyes were bloodshot, his skin pasty.

"Good morning, Mr. Pithoe. I hope you're feeling better today?"

He nodded and slipped into the chair opposite her, behind the wire mesh.

"Listen to me, Mr. Pithoe—Freddy. You remember you said it was okay for me to call you Freddy. Well, I spoke to Mrs. Roselli. She's the old lady who lives behind you. Do you know her?"

He looked suddenly very afraid. He wrenched out of his chair.

"Sit down, Freddy," she said, her best nun's voice, kind but implacable. "It's going to come out, you know, all of it. Sit down."

He sat. "She's a lying old bitch."

"Perhaps, but not about this. Where's Joey?"

Silence.

"You do know where he's hiding, don't you, Freddy?"

"Go away, ma'am. I don't wanna see you again. You're just like the rest of them."

"No, I won't leave. And I'm not like the others. You don't belong in here. Mrs. Roselli told me how you always protected your little brother, taking blows for him from both your uncle and your father, but mainly from your father. She told me how she heard your father shout and yell at your mother that he'd found out that Joey wasn't his kid, that he was a damned little bastard, and he was going to kill both of them. He was going to cut them into little pieces."

"No, ma'am, that ain't true. It ain't!"

"Yes, it is. Was your father right? Was Joey his kid or not?"

His face turned even more pasty.

"Please, Freddy, you can't go on like this. You can't go on lying."

"Joey didn't mean to do it!"

Rafaella held herself perfectly still and waited.

It was as if the dam had finally burst. Freddy lowered his face into his hands and wailed with pain and release.

Rafaella waited.

Finally she said, "Your father had you buy the ax so he could kill your mother, didn't he?"

"Yeah, and Uncle Kipper too."

"And he did, didn't he?"

Freddy nodded. He looked incredibly weary.

"And Joey saw him do it. He tried to stop your father—tried to protect your mother?"

"Yeah, the little guy tried. Pa smacked Joey aside the head, then kilt them. He turned to Joey—he was gonna chop him too—but Joey got away from him. He threw a lamp at Pa, and when Pa fell, Joey grabbed the ax and swung it at him. He didn't mean to kill him, ma'am, he didn't, he just wanted to stop him 'cause he'd gone crazy."

"No, I'm sure he didn't do anything on purpose. It's over now, Freddy, all over. Tell me where I can find Joey. He needs some kind people to take care of him, you know. He must be very frightened. He must miss you a whole lot."

"My Uncle Kipper were his father, and that's why Pa decided to kill Ma and his brother."

"And you came home and found them. And you decided to take the blame—and you sent Joey where?"

"Down to that big warehouse on Pier Forty-one."

"Thank you, Freddy. It's over now. I promise you no one will hurt Joey."

Lieutenant Masterson allowed her to come along with him to get Joey. The kid was a wreck. His clothes were covered with dried blood, he was thin as a scarecrow, his eyes were dead, his mind too dull to make him afraid anymore. Lieutenant Masterson said to her as she was leaving to return to the paper, "I don't know how you did that, kid, but I don't like it. Freddy should have spit it out to us."

You wouldn't listen. All you did was call him a fucking liar. It was difficult, but Rafaella kept her mouth shut.

"Just lucky, I guess," she said finally, and got out of the lieutenant's sight as quickly as possible.

The story broke in the *Tribune*'s evening edition, and Rafaella got the byline, lots of congratulations, and Gene Mallory looked as if he'd swallowed a prune. The headline editor had outdone herself. Two-inch letters plastered across the entire width of the paper: BOY AXES FATHER IN SELF-DEFENSE.

Al just smiled when she told him about Mrs. Roselli, and when she accused him of holding out on her, he said, "Well, kiddo, I didn't think you liked things handed to you. Remember, you didn't tell a soul that your stepfather was Charles Winston Rutledge III."

Rafaella told him that he was a pig, she'd read it in the women's room, and kissed his cheek.

And that night, at ten minutes after midnight, Rafaella's phone rang.

Three

Marcus took the bullet in his back, just above his right shoulder blade. The pain was instant and blinding, and he staggered; the pain turned into frozen cold, so cold that it burned him. He was unconscious before he hit the ground.

Merkel spun about and kicked out, his Gucci loafer clipping the 9-mm, sending it flying from Tulp's hand. His next kick smashed cleanly into her nose, sending it into her brain. Dominick Giovanni hadn't moved. He winced at the crunching sound of shattered bone, then walked slowly over and dropped to his knees beside the woman. Her eyes were staring; she was quite dead.

Merkel looked from Dominick to Marcus. Dominick waved him away. Merkel leaned over Marcus. He ripped away the shirt to bare the wound. "He's alive, Mr. Giovanni, but he needs a doctor. The bullet's still in him."

Dominick pursed his lips. "Carry him upstairs and get him into bed. I'll get hold of Dr. Haymes at the resort. Then you'd best lock up these goons. Oh, and, Merkel, have the woman buried."

There was blood all over Merkel's beautiful white suit, and it was the first thing Marcus saw when he opened his eyes. He was lying on his stomach. Merkel was sitting on a cane chair beside the bed, reading *GQ*, his favorite magazine. "Do you know you'd look like Santa Claus if you only had a white beard?"

Merkel folded down the page he was reading and set the magazine facedown on the night table. "Yeah, it's your blood, at least most of it is. You can buy me a new suit. You feel alive?"

"More so than otherwise. It hurts like hell and the drug Haymes shot me up with is making me feel like my brain is cotton candy. What happened? How's Dominick? How are—?"

Merkel held up his hand. "I'll get Mr. Giovanni. He can tell you all he wants to." Merkel rose and nodded down at Marcus. "You know how he is," he added, and Marcus closed his eyes. He knew exactly how Dominick Giovanni was. He probably knew as much about Dominick Giovanni as any other living person. He had a cold, perfect memory of that day in October, two and a half years ago, when he had finally engineered that meeting with Giovanni, under the auspices of the U.S. Customs Service, and his immediate contact, Ross Hurley. He'd never felt so scared in his life, or so determined. Dominick had seemed so human, so civilized, as he'd spoken of the resort Porto Bianco. He'd been a gentleman of wit, of education, which he still was. He was also deadly.

Marcus didn't see Dominick then. As much as he tried to fight it, he dozed off again, not waking until it was dark. He was thirsty and his back thudded with waves of pain. He cursed, but it didn't help. He heard a small clucking sound and realized that Paula was now beside him, holding a glass of water. "Here," she said, "drink this."

He did, gratefully, thinking that perhaps Paula wasn't such a bad sort after all.

He quickly changed his mind when she said after a moment, "Enough now, Marcus. Dr. Haymes told me water was the first thing you'd want. Now I suppose you have to use the urine bottle. He said to keep you in bed or you'd open the wound and start bleeding again."

He watched her, without words, as she handed him the clear bottle that looked for all the world like an empty wine carafe. He stared at it and then back up at her.

Paula merely smiled down at him and pulled back the sheet, and he felt her hand lightly sweep down to his lower back, then smooth over his buttocks.

Marcus closed his eyes for a moment. "Paula, please, don't. I do want to use that bottle. Call Merkel for me. I won't be able to do a thing with you standing there."

Her fingers touched his inner thighs and he heard her draw in her breath. "Perhaps later then," she said, and laughed. "You're nice, Marcus, real nice."

She left the sheet down at his knees and he realized he didn't have the strength to twist over and pull the damned thing back up. He was on the point of shouting, but fell silent as the grave at Merkel's loud guffaw.

"My, my, bare-assed. What did Paula do to you? Both your face and your ass are red. I can't imagine you doing anything close to fun—" He laughed again, a big belly laugh. Marcus sighed. He'd tried for nearly fifteen months now to get a real live, spontaneous laugh out of Merkel. He'd tried every joke, Jackie Gleason gags, practical gags; all had failed. And now he'd done nothing but lie on his stomach with a sheet pulled down to his ankles, and Merkel was nearly in hysterics.

Marcus wasn't amused. His shoulder hurt, his stomach was roiling with nausea, and he felt like a jackass. He also wanted to relieve himself. He tried to push upward, and Merkel shut up, at least for the moment.

A few moments later, Merkel gave the bottle to one of the silent-faced houseboys, who took it away without a word. When Marcus was back on his stomach, the sheet up around his back, Merkel chuckled again.

"You're lucky old DeLorio didn't waltz in when Paula was playing with you. He'd have had a fit. He'd have blamed you, even though any fool would know you couldn't have moved even if that little blond, Joanie Fields, had waltzed in here." He laughed again, enjoying his own mental conjuring scene.

"You could have left my shorts on."

"You weren't wearing any. Don't you remember? Just those cut-offs and a T-shirt. Haymes didn't care. To look in here and see you lying bare-assed." More laughter, and Marcus gritted his teeth, regretting that he'd ever made a vow to get laughter out of the damned big silent stone. Another man he liked, another man who could be deadly.

"Well, my boy, I see you finally got Merkel to crack. Quite an accomplishment, and, I should add, unexpected, considering your current state."

Merkel shut up the moment Dominick walked into the bedroom. He stood respectfully at attention, his expression now carefully blank.

"Unless, of course, Merkel was laughing because he's a closet sadist and is enjoying seeing you felled and wounded."

"Sir, of course not. Why, I—"

"I know, Merkel," Dominick interrupted him. "Let us alone for a bit. Two of our men are still a bit woozy. Check on them, then make sure Lacy's got the others back to their duties. Ah, yes, the Dutchmen. I think we'll let them fester in the tool shed for a while longer. I'd like to wait and have our hero of the hour, Marcus, with me before we question them. Have Dukey feed them, but not much."

"Yes, sir," Merkel said, and left, not looking again at Marcus.

"A fine soldier," Dominick said absently, glancing after Merkel. "Well, my boy, you could be looking better. On the other hand, you could also be looking dead, which wouldn't give me any pleasure whatsoever. Is your head clear now?"

"Yes. Tell me what happened. I thought Koerbogh and Van Wessel were all wrapped up. Who was this woman Tulp? She was the leader—I sensed that immediately when I saw them. What was she saying to you?"

Dominick smiled gently and held up a narrow, quite beautiful hand. "I'll tell you everything, just relax."

Marcus watched Dominick Giovanni ease his aristocratic body into the chair recently vacated by Paula and Merkel. He made it look like a throne. Strange, but it was true. There was something about Dominick, an aura, a communicated feeling that he knew about things and how to fashion them to his liking. His arm was bandaged and he now wore a short-sleeved shirt with a fresh pair of white slacks. He looked urbane and quite cool despite the carnage that had swept over the western side of the island, leaving him shot, his men gassed, and a deal gone sour. He was fifty-seven years old and looked younger. He had fine bones, Marcus thought, studying him. And good muscle tone for a man of any age. Coco insisted in that understated French way of hers that all of Dominick was well toned. Pale blue eyes, starkly deep eyes, that saw everything. His once-black hair was peppered with white that made him look all the more powerful, all the more charismatic. Marcus kept silent now, knowing that Dominick would talk when he chose to do so. He forced himself to be patient, trying to relax and not fight against the waves of pain. He knew well enough that tensing his muscles would only make it worse. He remembered suddenly that first time he'd believed Dominick to be utterly human. He'd been showing Marcus his art collection. He'd been the proud father praising his children, and Marcus had nearly forgotten. Marcus shook away the memory.

"Is DeLorio back?" he asked finally.

Dominick shook his head. "I told him to remain in Miami, to have that meeting with Mario Calpas. He's not needed here. Haymes says you'll be just fine. The bullet tore muscle, but you'll heal if you don't overdo for a couple of weeks. He also said you'd get back all your rotation and your strength. I know it'll be hard, but you've got to heal, Marcus." He absently rubbed his wounded arm. Then, "The deal with the Dutchmen was set. You know that, you went to Boston to wrap up the final details with Pearlman. Their appearance today was primarily one of diplomacy, if you will. A show of our continued goodwill; their continued desire to do business with us. They were, supposedly, the consummate middlemen." He shrugged.

"Who or what is *Bathsheba*?"

"What are you talking about?"

"That word was on the side of the helicopter. It was in green letters—*Bathsheba*."

"I don't know. Painted on the side of the helicopter? Like a company name or logo?"

At Marcus's nod, Dominick said slowly, "Well, there was Queen Bathsheba, a woman I'm sure was nothing like Tulp. It's interesting, though. A name of an organization. We'll find out. I've already got contacts working on Tulp. Pearlman claims, ah, vociferously, that he doesn't understand a thing. As for the phone number in Amsterdam, it's disconnected. The two Dutchmen are in the tool shed, doubtless contemplating their sins." Dominick fell silent a moment, then added, looking bewildered, "It's amazing. They actually believed they'd get away with killing me and getting off this island." He patted Marcus's arm and rose. "You get some rest, my boy. Then, when you're feeling up to it, we'll question our guests and find out what the hell happened. But, you know, Marcus, I'd be very surprised if the two men know anything. A pity, but I hate coercion-forced persuasion, if you will."

"But there's no need to wait, Dominick. Bring them in here, or I can go—"

"No, Marcus." Dominick shrugged. "Perhaps that's why I'm content to wait. They won't know anything. You know I'm right."

"All right, then, but at least tell me how three people managed to knock out all our men."

"It was cleverly done, yet very, very basic. They came in friendship, but Link, you know, is the most suspicious of men. He wanted them searched. I'd already sent Merkel to get you. Before any searching could begin, the woman, Tulp, after shaking my hand, stuck her nasty little automatic in my ribs. I knew, strangely enough, that she was fully prepared to kill me if the men didn't drop their weapons and agree to be herded like donkeys into the dining room. They went, and Koerbogh gassed them. As for DeLorio, he'd already left for Miami. Paula was at the resort, and my poor Coco was locked in a cabana. Merkel would have been gassed too if I hadn't sent him to find you just before they landed. I knew you were my only hope, and you didn't disappoint me, Marcus. My thanks."

He took Marcus's hand and lightly squeezed it. "I'm dining with Coco. She's a bit on edge, as you can imagine. I'll see you later. Merkel will bring your dinner and stay with you." Then Dominick Giovanni was gone.

There were so many more questions, so much more Marcus wanted to know. It was very quiet now. He felt the pain like an inexorable tide, ebbing briefly, only to gather momentum, rushing through him, tearing at his resistance. He had three scars now: one on the inside of his left thigh, a long thin scar over his belly, and now the souvenir on his shoulder. Two were from knives and one from Tulp's bullet. He'd survived

Navy intelligence and the CIA without a scratch. He'd gotten all his scars after he'd joined Dominick and become a criminal.

Well, the pain was better than being dead. He was asleep again shortly after eating a bit of beef broth and homemade bread with Merkel. He suspected that the lemonade was drugged, and so it was. He slept soundly until late the following morning.

It was then that Haymes appeared again and none too gently removed the bandage from his shoulder. Marcus, teeth gritted, heard Haymes grunt, and wondered what it meant.

There was another grunt.

"Think you could manage some words, like in English?"

"Lie still, Devlin, and shut your trap. Your flesh looks pink, the wound is closing nicely, and it's just your black soul that might cause infection and kill you off. Hold still."

Marcus yowled when the needle slammed into his left buttock. He felt Haymes's hand hold him down.

"More antibiotic. Most efficient in your butt." The needle was pulled out, leaving a cold, shocked track, and Haymes rubbed a cool alcohol pad over the spot.

"You sadistic butcher."

"I'll take out the stitches in seven or eight days. Keep the shoulder immobile. You don't have to stay in bed, but don't run any marathons, and that includes up and down the stairs."

"Thanks."

"Have someone massage you to keep your muscles flexible. Oh, yeah, lover boy, no sex for another week at least. You tear that wound open, and I won't send you a bill, I'll bury you. You got that?"

"I haven't got a horny bone or muscle in my body, Haymes."

"I'm not worried about your bones or your muscles.

And that's not what I heard from a very nice girl named Susie Glanby."

Marcus groaned. "She seduced me, I swear it. I was innocent. I didn't know she was married to a boxer, for God's sake. You think I've got a death wish?"

Haymes grinned, showing the wide space between his front teeth. "Old Marty's a piece of work, isn't he? He smacked Susie a couple of times, knocked her silly, got scared, and called me. And that's how I know what happened. Ah, well, young lust. Stay celibate, Devlin."

"I can't believe you were a Polo Lounge society doctor in Beverly Hills."

"Yeah, look how human a guy gets, surrounded by sterling characters like you and Merkel."

"Come on, Haymes, you've got all those rich guys at the resort to pander to."

"For the most part, they're boring as hell. Do you know how prevalent syphilis is still? You'd think the fools would have more brains than to screw around with no protection." He shook his head and rose. He paused a moment and looked down at the young man who now had his eyes closed against the pain.

"Don't be so bloody macho, Devlin. Oh, what the hell."

Then Marcus felt another deep jab in his right buttock and yelled.

"It's for pain," Haymes said, and pulled the sheet back up.

"You're responsible for the pain."

But Haymes only waved at him and slipped out of the room. A redheaded leprechaun who was a sadist, curse him.

But the pain was receding, almost at once, and it was wonderful not to have to concentrate on keeping it to himself. He fell asleep and slept deeply.

Coco and Dominick appeared later that evening. Coco was the quintessence of a rich man's mistress.

She was just a bit older than Marcus, model-thin, with long legs and big breasts and ash-blond hair that hung long and perfectly straight to between her shoulder blades. She looked expensive, which she was, and she deferred to Dominick in the most charming way. She was a smart cookie, Coco was. She'd been a high fashion French model, just peaking in her career five years before when she'd met Dominick in St. Moritz on the slopes, both of them avid skiers. They'd shortly become an item, the French paparazzi going crazy over the power-broking mystery man, twice indicted, once on tax-evasion charges, once on organized-crime corruption, and both times acquitted, and the beautiful model. Then they'd become lovers.

Marcus liked Coco. She was loyal, she was intelligent, and judging from the occasional yells from the fastidious Dominick when he'd chanced to be walking by their suite, Marcus imagined that she was incredible in bed.

She didn't seem to pay much attention when Dominick presented her with fabulous jewels. But his son, DeLorio, did, the greedy whining little jerk.

"Hello, Marcus," she said, her French accent quite absent this evening, as it usually was around the compound. "Dr. Haymes said you needed to be massaged. Paula volunteered. I counter volunteered. Dominick has seconded the motion. Paula is, how do we French say it? Ah, peesed off but trying not to show it because she's not sure when DeLorio will be back. I brought my Keri Lotion." Coco Vivrieux, Marcus knew, was actually just as American as he was. But she did the French routine very well.

Marcus eyed Dominick, who'd sat himself down on the wicker love seat and was reading through a sheaf of papers.

"She won't leave you bare-assed," Dominick said, not looking up. Marcus saw his unholy grin before his face disappeared behind a *Wall Street Journal*.

Marcus moaned when her long fingers smoothed deeply into his back muscles. Her fingers were incredibly strong and she hurt him, but it felt so good he couldn't complain.

"I'll be well enough tomorrow to have a chat with the Dutchmen," he said when Coco moved to his thighs.

"All right," Dominick said, still not looking up from the paper. There was, however, a sudden frown on his forehead. "Merkel tells me they're not very happy with their, er, accommodations. I suspect that they expect the worst. I'm rather enjoying letting them sweat. And I'm more than certain they don't know a damned thing. If they did, they'd be squealing loudly, hoping for a deal. They don't know that I haven't the taste for good old-fashioned torture."

"Ah, that's wonderful, Coco. Who was that woman? Why was she going to kill you?"

"Be quiet, my boy, and enjoy what Coco's doing for you."

"I want to talk to those goons first thing in the morning, Dominick."

"Fine," Dominick said just as Coco probed deep and long and Marcus moaned.

Marcus spent a quiet night, heavily drugged, but he awoke to loud shouts early the following morning. He was struggling to get out of bed when his bedroom door opened and Link stuck his head in.

"Mr. Giovanni told me to make sure you stayed put. The Dutchmen poisoned themselves."

Marcus fell back against the pillows. "They're dead?"

"Deader than week-old mackerel."

*I just kicked Gabe Tetweiler out of our house. God,
I can't believe I could ever be so wrong about a person,
about a man in particular. Which sounds excessively
dumb, doesn't it, after Dominick Giovanni. But he was
so sincere and appeared to be so rich, and that being
the case, of course he wasn't interested in my money.*

Will I be a fool for the rest of my life, Rafaella?

*You can't answer that, of course, my darling. You
won't ever see this. You're ten years old now, a skinny
little kid and so bright it sometimes scares me. I'm no
intellectual giant, God knows, and here you are as
bright as the sun, as your teacher, Miss Cox, likes to
say. It's from him; I guess I'll just have to admit it.
Miss Cox also says you've got a real smart mouth,
which I've mentioned to you. I tried to tell her that
your one-liners are quite astounding for a ten-year-old.
Dominick was amusing too, when he chose to be. His
was a dry wit, I suppose you'd say, unlike yours, which
is straightforward, open, guileless. His was also cruel,
now that I remember it.*

I guess I'd forgotten just how smart Dominick was.

*He was brought before a Senate committee some
weeks ago on an organized-crime probe. Senator Wil-
bur from Oregon spearheaded it. He wasn't very bright.
Dominick made him look like a fool. He looked so
calm and controlled, but I could tell by his eyes that
he was angry. Here I go again on Dominick! But sometimes it's tough not to, because every time I look at
you, Rafaella, I see his pale blue eyes. I'm so glad your
hair isn't dark like his. No, you have such lovely titian
hair, like your grandmother's, not like his or like my
light hair.*

*I digress. I was meaning to sort out my stupidity
with Gabe.*

He was sincere. He was a good talker. He was an even better lover. You hated him. I realized that, but I didn't want to see it, to accept it. And of course you were right.

He wasn't after my money, I was right about that. He was after you, which makes me want to slit his throat. I don't understand why you never said anything. You just turned sullen whenever he was around, and were so rude when you had to speak to him that I wanted to smack you.

But you knew. You felt he wasn't right. Ah, I'm sorry, Rafaella. Please forgive me. I'll never forget this night, never so long as I live. I wonder if you will. You didn't cry, you didn't reproach me at all. I wonder if I will ever understand you properly. There that bastard was, in your bedroom, trying to fondle you, and you were fighting him, so silent you were, not screaming, not making a sound, just fighting that bastard with all your strength.

I realize now why he didn't wait. He knew, guessed, that I was drawing back, and I guess he is so ill that he couldn't help himself.

He's gone now. I've decided to hire a private detective to follow him. I want to know where he goes. I've decided to ruin him. It finally occurred to me that I'm very, very rich. And money can buy lots of things, like revenge. What do you think about that, Rafaella? Revenge tastes sweet. How I wish I had taken my revenge upon Dominick. Maybe that would have put it all to rest. Now he's so far out of my reach. Perhaps he was already far out of my reach ten years ago.

Do you know that he still looked so handsome on TV that I wanted to cry? How about that for a fool of a mother. . . .

Gabe's gone but I'll find him and I'll make him pay for what he tried to do to you. And to me.

And Dominick? I pray he will meet a rotten end, but

I have become a cynic now and I tend to doubt—divine intervention in particular.

I hope you will get over this thing, Rafaella. I've tried to talk to you about it. Please don't freeze up on me, don't repress this thing.

It's been over ten years and still Dominick haunts me. I've not written about him all that much, have I? Not more than perhaps fifteen percent of all my pages? Not more, truly. All right, then, maybe forty percent of my pages. Obsession perhaps? No, it isn't true. It's simply a deep hatred of a man with no moral instincts in his makeup, a man with no compassion, no empathy, a man who is completely and utterly immoral.

No, please, I mustn't still hate him. The whole purpose of this journal was to excoriate him, then to expunge him, to keep his ghost from touching you by cleansing myself of him. Lord, he doesn't even know your name, or mine for that matter. He never cared enough to find out.

I wonder if he ever got his precious son. I wonder if he's got six precious sons. God, am I stupid. Here I've been talking about hiring a detective to get Gabe when I could hire a detective to get me all the information I ever wanted about Dominick Giovanni.

Wait. Is that sick of me? Is it an obsession? I must think about it, truly think about my motives. What should such information mean to me? He's nothing to me save the man who betrayed me, who took my innocence—doesn't that sound Gothic?—the man who made me feel like dirt.

The bitterness is still there, deep and grinding. And now another man has betrayed me. One a man who didn't want you in any manner whatsoever, the other a man who wanted to molest you, a child. I have failed you twice, my darling Rafaella. I promise it will not happen again.

The Bridges
Long Island, New York
February 2001

Rafaella closed the journal, slowly fastening the clasp.
It was a particularly fine Spanish red leather, intri-
cately tooled, and just as finely locked.

And she'd picked the lock. This was the second volume on which she'd picked the lock. She closed her
eyes a moment, leaning back against her mother's
desk chair, the chair Margaret had very probably sat
in to write in her journals since she'd married Charles
Winston Rutledge III some eleven years before.

Rafaella had come into her mother's room several
hours before, looking for some stationery, and searched
through her desk. She'd found the stationery and she'd
also found the small latch that, when manipulated
properly, released two hidden drawers. And in those
two drawers she'd found the journals. She'd never
known they existed. She'd hesitated only briefly, then
begun reading.

Rafaella remembered the phone call that had jerked
her awake at midnight. Her stepfather, Charles,
sounding calm and controlled, but Rafaella could
make out the underlying fear and anxiety.

"Your mother was struck by a drunk driver, Rafaella. You must come right away. The doctors don't
know. She's in a coma. They don't know."

His voice had broken and Rafaella had stared at
the phone.

"No," she whispered.

Charles, drawing in his breath, regained his poise.
"Come right away, my dear. I'll have Larkin meet you
at JFK. Catch the seven-A.M. flight, all right?"

"She's alive?"

"Yes, she's alive. A coma."

Her mother was still in a coma two days later.
Peaceful, her face not older, but strangely youthful,

her lovely pale blond hair combed and fastened with barrettes behind her ears. And all those damnable lines running in and out of her arms.

So quiet. Her mother lay there, so very quiet.

"Rafaella!"

It was Benjamin, her stepbrother, calling from the hallway.

"Just a moment," she called back. She rose stiffly, carefully laid the journal back in the desk drawer, re-locked it, and went to have dinner with the family.

Four

Rafaella sat on one side of her mother's bed, Charles on the other. She was looking at her mother, but her thoughts kept returning to the newspaper clippings that had been stacked in neat piles in one of the secret drawers. So many photos, some grainy, others quite clear. And she couldn't stop telling herself over and over that her real father was a man whose name was Dominick Giovanni, and he was a crook.

Her mother was lying in a private suite in the east wing of the private hospital, Pine Hill. The decor reminded Rafaella of the suite she'd stayed in once at the Plaza—muted colors, and very expensive. Except for the regulation bed, the slender tubes in her mother's nose, and the lines in her arms, her mother could have been sleeping. They'd been here, sitting quietly, for nearly a half-hour now.

Rafaella's stepfather, Charles Winston Rutledge III, was the quintessential WASP, old money, prep school at Bainbridge followed by Yale, a wealthy entrepreneur in his own right. Odd that he had eyes very nearly the color of hers—pale blue—when she now realized that it was also the color of her real father's eyes. Mrs. McGill had been wrong about Dominick

Giovanni being pure Italian. Those pale blue eyes had to have come from a more northern country.

There was only one other similarity between the two men besides the color of their eyes. Dominick Giovanni and Charles Rutledge were nearly the same age. Only a year separated them, Dominick Giovanni being the older.

"You're very quiet, Rafaella."

She jumped at the unexpected sound of Charles's voice. It was pitched low, just above a whisper, so as not to disturb her mother, which was absurd, since her mother was in a deep coma.

I was just thinking about my father, who's a criminal. Rafaella wasn't about to tell Charles of her discovery. It would be needlessly cruel. He loved her mother, and the knowledge of her mother's journals, her seemingly endless obsession with Dominick Giovanni, would give him incalculable pain. No, Rafaella wouldn't tell him a thing. "I was just thinking about things. I'm scared, Charles."

He simply nodded. He understood, too well. "I spoke to Al Holbein. He called yesterday to see how Margaret and you were doing. He told me about you breaking that Pithoe case in Boston. He said it was par for the course—you were bright as hell and tenacious as a pit bull—but a cop, Masterson is his name, is trying to take all the credit, which, Al says, isn't working, but is also par for the course."

"Actually all the credit should go to a little old Italian lady named Mrs. Roselli."

Charles cocked a beautifully arched brow at her. "Tell me about it."

Rafaella smiled. "Al called me in and assigned me to the case. I didn't want it. The press had sensationalized it, and it was particularly gruesome. And nobody really cared anymore, because the crazy who had done it—Freddy Pithoe, the son—had confessed right away. It just gave the media a chance to do another dance

on Lizzie Borden again. But you know Al, he got me
going, made me so mad I wanted to slug him. He
didn't say a word about any anonymous tip he'd gotten, and of course he'd gotten one—from Mrs. Roselli.
When I asked her later why she hadn't told the police
what she'd told Al, she said that the snot-nosed kid
they sent had no manners and treated her like a *strega
stupida*. Why should she say anything to a snot-nosed
kid with no manners who treated her like a stupid
witch? I had no answer for that.

"I then asked her why she'd told Al. She said that
he'd done a series about ten years ago on the Italians
in Boston and he'd mentioned her husband by name
and written what a fine man he'd been. Guido Roselli
had been a fireman killed in a runaway fire in the
South End. She pulled out the yellowed clipping and
read it to me.

"She told me too that she didn't really like Freddy.
She thought he was weird. It was the boy, Joey, she
cared about."

"Yet she cleared Freddy and showed the boy to be
the guilty one. Interesting."

Rafaella nodded.

"Why do you think Freddy Pithoe opened up to
you? Was he another Mrs. Roselli?"

Rafaella gave him a crooked smile. "He told me
over and over, when I asked why he hadn't told the
police about X or about Y, that they'd just called him
a *fucking liar*—excuse the language, Charles—and told
him to shut up. I listened to him and didn't comment
until I realized he wasn't telling me the truth; then I
kept after him until both of us were hoarse." She
raised her eyes to the ceiling. "Thank you, God, for
Mrs. Roselli."

"What will happen to the boy, Rafaella?"

"Hopefully he'll get into a decent foster home and
have a very good shrink."

"And Freddy?"

"I spoke to Al. He promised to find a job for Freddy on the paper. He'll be all right. Freddy's one of the walking wounded, but he's also a survivor."

Charles fell silent. Rafaella watched as he carefully lifted her mother's hand and kissed her fingers. Rafaella wished at that moment that Charles, kind, handsome Charles, was her father. But he wasn't her father. Neither was her father a man named Richard Dorsett, a physician who'd been killed in a freak car accident. *A very brave man, a very good man.* All a lie. She should have realized it was a lie so much sooner—because she didn't carry his name. She carried her mother's. She remembered her mother explaining that to her, and since she hadn't really cared, since that shadowy man had never been real to her, she'd paid little attention.

She wondered if there were a man whose name was Richard Dorsett. If there were, he'd sure be a better father than her real one was.

Her father was a criminal. There were six and a half journals covering twenty-six years. Rafaella had looked to see the last entry. Her mother hadn't written a word since November. Was it possible that Charles knew about the journals? About Dominick Giovanni? She shook her head. No, her mother would protect him from that, just as Rafaella would.

She was nearly halfway through the third journal and she itched to get back to them. She looked down at the five-carat marquise diamond on her mother's left hand, a gift from a man who loved this woman more than he loved himself, more than he loved his own life. She wished she could talk to him, pour out her fear to him, her questions. But she mustn't.

Dominick Giovanni had been her mother's private penance, a demon she'd exorcised again and again, or tried to. Rafaella hoped writing the journals had helped her. She knew that her mother would never have shown the journals to her.

Rafaella had learned in the third journal that her mother had gotten her revenge on Gabe Tetweiler. She'd gotten him; but good. It had cost her ten thousand dollars or thereabouts, but old Gabe was now in prison in Louisiana for attempted child molestation.

Rafaella said, "You're a very fine man, Charles. I wish you were my father."

"I agree with that, my dear."

Rafaella lifted her mother's other hand. So cold and so very limp. "I don't want her to die."

Charles was silent.

"She's not going to die, is she?"

"I don't know, Rafaella. Would you rather she spent the next twenty years hooked up to all this cold equipment, a vegetable? Dead but alive thanks to these machines?"

Rafaella laid her mother's hand down beside her and rose. "Who's the man who hit her?"

"Nobody knows. There was a vague description of the car—a dark sedan, four-door, but that's it. Man, woman—the guy who saw the accident wasn't sure. Whoever it was, the driver was weaving all over the road—a drunk, the cops say."

"So this drunk hits her, guesses things are bad, and takes off?"

"That's what the police are saying. They put out their bulletins on him, but—" Charles shrugged.

"Yeah, I know what you mean. I'm going for a walk. I'll be back soon."

Charles gave her an intent look. "Don't lock all your feelings inside, Rafaella. You don't have to keep all that hurt to yourself. I'm here, you know, and I love you."

Rafaella merely nodded. She walked from the room, closing the door very quietly behind her.

Giovanni's Island
February 2001

Marcus was in pain; he was also confused by what had happened. Why had Van Wessel and Koerbogh poisoned themselves? And why now? If they'd planned to, why not immediately? Why didn't Dominick come and explain it to him?

But Dominick didn't say anything when he visited. Nor did Merkel. The late afternoon of the Dutchmen's demise, Marcus was alone, bored, in some pain, and woozy from the lingering effects of the Demerol. He didn't open his eyes when he heard the door open quietly. It was probably Merkel with an ad to show him from the most recent *GQ*, a suave new suit he wanted to buy. He'd shown Marcus a good half-dozen now, telling him that he owed him for getting blood all over his suit. All the suits were white; they all looked like the ones he already owned. When Marcus had suggested a double-breasted Armani, he thought Merkel was going to expire.

"Hello, baby."

He would have groaned except he decided in that instant to feign sleep.

"It's just as well," he heard her say more to herself than to him. He felt the bed give as she sat beside him. Then he felt her hand slip under the single sheet and stroke over his side.

He didn't need this, he didn't want it. "Paula, stop it, for God's sake! I'm a sick man and you're married."

"DeLorio is still in Miami and I've decided to make you feel better. Think of me as your private nurse. I quite like you, Marcus, even though you act like a jerk toward me sometimes. But then I wonder how many women you've made love to, and it makes me hot." Her hand was on his butt now, and he brought his legs together, but it didn't matter. Her long fingers slid between his thighs and she was touching him.

"Paula, stop it!" He reared up, trying to turn, and the pain stopped him cold. He gasped, frozen.

"Lie down, baby, just lie down. Paula will make you feel better."

"Get out," he said, but his voice was low and indistinct, and he was, incredibly, hard as a stone. Then she helped him onto his side, something he hadn't expected, because it forced her to get her hands off him. Just for a moment. Then she had the sheet down and he was nude and he was hard and she was looking at him and smiling, and holding him on his side against her body.

"Very impressive. A long time, Marcus? I like to see a man appreciate me. Let's see how far the appreciation goes, shall we?"

"Please," he said, wishing he had the strength to push her away. He could have found the strength, he finally admitted to himself, he was just choosing to lie to himself and not use it. He tried to roll back onto his stomach, but she just moved closer, sitting against him, holding him still. He groaned when her hand closed over his cock. She found her rhythm and she talked to him, sex talk, that made him furious and aroused him quickly, too quickly. His breath was heaving and he was shuddering. She released him and he felt her warm mouth close over him and he was shoving into her mouth and she took him, and God, she was good, not giving him a moment's respite, and he jerked in her mouth and as he came she caught him in her hand again. He panted, sucking in deep breaths, the pain in his shoulder momentarily suspended. She was on her knees next to the bed, and strands of her white-blond hair were clinging to his sweating belly.

She looked up him. "That was very nice—for you,

Marcus. Next time, it's for me, okay? I hear someone coming. Probably Merkel. Just keep the sheet up and he won't know what you've done." She giggled as she wiped her hand quickly on the sheet.

Marcus heard her say something to Merkel in the hall.

He pulled the sheet to his nose. He felt raped, furious, and eased. Masturbated by Paula, for God's sake. She was good, and that made him even angrier.

He opened an eye to see Merkel looking down at him.

"Smells like sex in here."

Marcus closed his eyes again.

"DeLorio's coming back tonight. You'll be safe from her then. I think I'll spray some pine-forest air freshener in here."

Then Merkel laughed again. Another spontaneous laugh, at his—Marcus's—expense.

"Go drown yourself."

"You want a washcloth, buddy?"

"I never want to hear your horsey laugh again, you stupid Neanderthal. Yeah, give me a washcloth."

"Hurt my feelings, Marcus, you surely do. I know you've tried to make me laugh for more months than I can count. Now you did it and you're pissed. You're weird."

What Marcus wasn't was weird; what he was, was frantic. He had to get out of here. Paula and her play with him could ruin everything. It could get him killed. He had to get away from here, back to the resort. And that night he did, at least as far as Dominick's downstairs library and meeting room.

He made it, breathing hard, his skin filmed with sweat from the exertion, but he was determined. Dominick hadn't told him a damned thing. He had to find out what was going on. He closed his sweating hand over the doorknob, then paused. He heard De-

Lorio say in a loud voice, "A shame the Irish trash didn't cash it in."

Dominick's voice, mild and calm: "Marcus saved my life. Incidentally, you've got some Irish blood in you."

"He had his reasons, no doubt. Anyway, what do you expect? You treat him like he's more important to you than your own son. My God, if I'd had a go at him, he'd have been in hell before he hit the ground!"

Marcus backed off. He hadn't realized DeLorio hated him so much. He wondered if DeLorio would be a problem, a real problem he'd have to worry about. The good Lord knew he had enough problems, and now this tantrum from a twenty-five-year-old man whose wife of ten months had given him head only four hours before. Marcus made his way back upstairs. His shoulder hurt and he felt dizzy.

He still hadn't found out anything about the Dutchmen. He had to get away from here.

Boston **Tribune** *Newsroom*
Boston, Massachusetts
March 1, 2001

One day back, and the wretched phone hadn't stopped ringing. Rafaella grabbed it on the third ring, scrunched it between her shoulder and her ear, and kept reading the articles she'd found in the *Tribune*'s library on arms smuggling. Not much, but it was a start.

"Rafaella Holland here."

"Hi. It's Logan."

"Airport?"

An old joke between them, not funny anymore, yet she'd said it out of reflex action.

"Yeah. The first-class section. Where have you been? What's going on?"

She found herself blinking. She'd forgotten all about

Logan Mansfield, an assistant D.A. "My mother was hurt in an accident. I flew there last Friday."

"Oh. How is she?"

"Very serious." Her voice cracked. "In a coma."

"Oh. I'm sorry, Rafaella. I want to see you tonight. It's been two weeks, nearly. I need to talk to you."

She was leaving tomorrow. She chewed on her lower lip, staring at the article in her hand about the scandal in Sweden. Bofors illegally sold weapons to Iran and Iraq. Not too good for Nobel Industries, she thought. Logan made an impatient noise and she said quickly, "Sure, Logan. Come on over to my place around eight o'clock. I've got to clean out my fridge. You can help me."

He agreed and rang off.

I shouldn't have invited him over, she thought, then shook her head. She and Logan Mansfield had been together for nearly three years now, lovers occasionally, friends occasionally, adversaries occasionally, neither one wanting commitment. A perfect arrangement for both of them.

She read on about the "Irangate" in Italy, this one about Borletti's northern Italian weapons manufacturer illegally shipping mines and other weapons to Iran. Lord, it was complicated, all the machinations they went through to get the illegal arms from point A to point B. She read about end-user certificates that were all a scam, about different methods of smuggling—mines and arms or whatever, in crates labeled "medical equipment" or "farm equipment"—the list was endless. Criminal ingenuity—and in the U.S. there was only the U.S. Customs Service to stop them.

Besides Borletti, she read about a man named Cummings who said he'd sell to anyone if the government allowed it except Qaddafi. There was Kokin and his Los Angeles arms emporium; and Soghanalian, who had branches in Miami, Beirut, and Madrid. Some did business with the CIA, others didn't. Most claimed they were as honest as the sky was blue. If that were true, Rafaella thought, then how had the war between Iran and Iraq lasted so very long? And the war in Angola?

There were other names mentioned, and among them she found, finally, the name she was looking for—Dominick Giovanni. She read intently now. ". . . Little is known about Giovanni, a U.S. citizen. He is protected by intermediaries, and prizes anonymity. It's rumored that his power and influence base exceed those of Robert Sarem and of Roderick Olivier in the world arms market. He operates solely out of his compound on his own island in the Caribbean . . ."

"You still going, Rafe?"

She looked up at Al Holbein. "I need a vacation, just like I told you. Charles agrees I should go. I'll keep in touch with him every day to see how my mother is doing." It hurt to lie to Al, just as it had hurt to lie, by omission, to Charles.

"*If* it's just a vacation," Al said, moving closer, blocking her from Gene Mallory's view. "Ignore lover boy," he added, "he's just jealous."

"I will. It's a good thing sometimes that you're twenty pounds overweight, boss."

"In your ear, kiddo. Where are you going, Rafaella? And why? You might as well tell me the truth. I can always tell when you're lying to me."

He rarely used her full name. It gave her pause. Had he spoken to her stepfather? It wouldn't have mattered. Charles wasn't all that intuitive at the moment, all his energies focused on her mother; he didn't know what his stepdaughter was up to. She'd been very careful.

"A vacation, a long-overdue rest. In the Caribbean. For two weeks. You jealous? And I don't lie."

He didn't answer, just looked at her closely. He looked down at the pile of articles on her desk. "You'll send a postcard?"

"Count on it. I'll try to find one of those *Men Are Pigs* cards, just for you."

"Your mom's condition still the same?"

Rafaella nodded, tears closing in her throat. Now her frantic machinations over Freddie Pithoe seemed mundane compared to what she planned to do.

Al patted her shoulder. "Get out of here. I've got my hands on Larry Bifford—he'll be taking over your assignments until you get back."

She felt a spurt of paranoia mixed with a good dose of insecurity. "He's pretty good," was what came out of her mouth.

"Yep, the best," Al said cheerfully. "Take your time, kiddo."

She watched him amble away, graceful despite his bulk as he wove his way through the closely placed desks to his office. He seemed oblivious of the continuous noise in the newsroom, oblivious of the young sports reporter who tossed a football to the entertainment editor. It sailed by Al's ear, missing him by two inches.

"You're too smart, Al," she said under her breath. She managed to get out of the *Tribune* office with a minimum of words to Gene. He gave her a stiff goodbye, and she gave him an easy see-you-around.

Brammerton, Massachusetts
March 1, 2001

Logan roamed through Rafaella's living room and followed her into the kitchen, not volunteering to help, just watching her and fidgeting with a can opener.

"All right, Logan, what is it?" she asked finally, slapping down the hot pad and looking away from the warmed-up tuna casserole. "You've been acting strange. I'm tired, not in such a good mood, and I'm worried about my mother. Now, what gives with you?"

That gave him pause. Logan, another ultra-WASP, she realized, studying him. Blond, blue-eyed, tall, lanky, a passable lover, a sense of humor, and now—now she just wished he'd spit out what was bothering him. She was tired, frantic with worry for her mother, and scared of what she knew lay ahead.

"Pithoe," he said, as if that said it all.

Rafaella served the casserole onto paper plates. They had to eat it fast or it would soak through. She set a bottle of white wine on the table and pulled out several day-old bagels. "Sit and let's eat before it gets cold."

They sat and ate. "Pithoe," Logan said again after two bites of casserole.

"What about it? Them? Freddy or Joey?"

"Them. Both of them."

He took another bite. Rafaella looked at him. "You gave me a hello kiss like you wanted to bite my tongue off. What's wrong, Logan? Is it because I'm leaving?" From the look of surprise on his face, she realized it hadn't really clicked with him that she was leaving.

"Where are you going?"

"Away. I need a rest." Their last vacation, they'd gone together, to Athens, then on to Santorini.

"I see," Logan said. "All right, Rafaella, what you did was crummy. It was unprofessional. It wasn't fair to anyone. I hope you never pull anything like that again."

"Do what again? What are you babbling about?"

"Pithoe. You circumvented the police, you didn't say a word to me, to anyone in the D.A.'s office. Nothing. You behaved irresponsibly, unprofessionally. You acted like the little detective of the cosmos, and everyone's quite annoyed. You jeopardized the D.A.'s case, you could have destroyed Pithoe's defense, prejudicing

every possible juror beforehand. You could have ruined everything."

"I see," she said, and she did. She smiled at him.
"I truly do see now, Logan. Forgive me. It's certainly
obvious to me now that the police weren't completely
satisfied with their investigation—oh, no, far from it.
They were just taking a breather after getting Freddy's
confession. Of course they were busting their butts to
find Joey Pithoe. Can you believe all the manpower
they had on the case?

"As for the D.A.'s office, they really *weren't* all that
anxious to toss Freddy in the state hospital for three
lifetimes. They *weren't* all that satisfied that the massa-
cre had been so cut-and-dried, and—"

"Enough sarcasm, Rafaella. You know very well
what you did was wrong and stupid, and you just
wanted the limelight all for yourself. I could have used
a bit of your inside information, you know. You could
have called me, you could have told me what you were
doing, what you'd discovered, and I'd have gone about
getting things taken care of. In the proper way,
through the proper channels, protecting everyone
and—"

Rafaella rose from the table. She said very slowly,
"You and I, Logan, have known each other for over
two years. We've had fun for the most part, we've
respected each other's careers. At least that's what
I've always thought. Now I want to take a shower."

He opened his mouth to argue, but she forestalled
him, her hand raised. "The police dropped the ball on
this one; the D.A.'s office never picked up the ball.
The media were thrilled to have gore for their pathetic
newscasts. But bottom-line, nobody gave a good
damn. Nobody cared if that pitiful Freddy Pithoe
was getting a raw deal. Nobody cared if an eleven-
year-old boy ever turned up. Nobody. You're a prig,
Logan, and a hypocrite, and jealous because you
didn't do what had to be done and I just happened

to be the one who did. Just get out of my apartment and my life."

"You find another guy who appeals to you more?"

The conceit of men, Rafaella thought, marveling at his logic. He hadn't listened, hadn't heard a word she'd said. No, it had to be another man. So be it.

Logan saw her smiling and knew he'd better leave or he'd be tempted to say things that would alienate her irrevocably. He didn't want to make an enemy of her. That wouldn't be good for a man who wanted to be Boston's D.A. But he just couldn't hold it in.

"Bitch," he said, threw his napkin down to the floor, grabbed his coat from the back of a chair, and slammed his way out the front door.

"I do believe," Rafaella said, staring around at the shambles in her kitchen, "that I've just severed the last of my connections."

At eight o'clock the following morning she was on an American flight to Miami.

She was excited and she was afraid.

And she found herself wondering again how it was possible that a man, any man, wouldn't care enough to find out the name of his own child. But he hadn't cared enough to discover that his name, Dominick Giovanni, wasn't listed as the girl-child's father on the birth certificate. He hadn't cared enough to discover that Margaret hadn't used her real name with him.

Well, it just made it easier for her. Lies were difficult. At least she didn't have to worry about using her real name.

Her curiosity about her father had begun to consume her, and that bothered her because she didn't want her hatred for him diluted in any way; she didn't want to lose her focus; she didn't want to lose her edge. He didn't deserve her respect, he didn't deserve anything at all from her, but she had to see him, to really look at him, to study him. To see herself in him? To learn for herself whether he was really corrupt to his soul or if there was something good in him? She had to know.

Five

Marcus worked out steadily, without pause, until Melissa Kay Roanoke, better known as Punk, the weight room's assistant manager, grabbed his arm and said, "Enough, Superman."

He looked up at her baby face, topped by a tangle of pink curls, and grinned painfully. Punk was all of twenty-three years old, tall, fine-boned and big-breasted, and had a karate black belt.

"I've got to get the rotation back in my shoulder, Punk. When did you add that yellow stripe?" He stared up at the half-inch-wide stripe that went from just over her right eye back to the last curl at her neck.

"You don't have to do it all in a week. Give it a rest now. Orders from Dr. Haymes. He warned me you'd probably try to be a stupid macho about this. What happened, anyway? You get a knife in your back? I had Sissy add the yellow stripe. She said it would be bad."

"It is bad, real bad. Just what did Haymes say to you?"

Punk shrugged, her eye roving to a thirtyish affluent banker from Chicago who'd just stretched out on his back to do some bench presses. He wasn't in bad shape. "Just that you'd hurt yourself using some kind of machinery over at Mr. Giovanni's compound and you'd try to kill yourself again getting back in shape. So stop it. I'd better go see to Mr. Scanlan. He's not as yummy as you, boss, but he'll do. Do you think he's got all his rotation?"

"All the rotation you could take," Marcus said, and watched Punk swing over, her very sleek body leotarded all in black, with hot-pink leg warmers, her hips so squeezable-looking that occasionally even Marcus was tempted. The banker didn't have a chance, despite the yellow stripe, unless he was married, which he wasn't, or Punk wouldn't be so blatant about going after him. The guy was going to have a wonderful vacation. Since Punk didn't enjoy gambling, the rich young banker would probably save himself a bundle by staying in bed and away from the casino.

Marcus sighed and slowly worked his shoulder. It was better, but Punk was right: he'd overdone it today. He showered and dressed in his manager's clothes: white slacks, a pale blue Armani shirt, styled to show off his physique, open at the collar to show off the hair on his chest. His orders from Dominick two and a half years ago had been to look expensive, act charming, and be efficient. "You're to look like you're every woman's fantasy lover, act like you're a down-and-dirty macho with all the men; and you're to manage the resort and casino like it's a combination nirvana-crapshoot, the only one on the planet, and you're a five-percent owner," which was true.

Marcus stepped out the back door of the gym into the lush tangle of hibiscus, bougainvillea, frangipani and orchids that blossomed in profusion along each side of the path. Clashing sweet scents filled the heavy air. Although every damned growing thing in the resort grounds was trimmed on a schedule set by Kinobi, and carried through by his two score gardeners, it still seemed that if you didn't pay attention you'd get a good slap in the face by a thick green arm.

He was tired. He'd been back only three days from

the compound, and things were piled up, everyone had a problem, his secretary, Callie, was in a snit for some reason he couldn't fathom, a Mrs. Maynard from Atlanta, Georgia, was due to arrive in her own private Cessna, and expected him to greet her personally. Mrs. Cecily Maynard had tried to get in his pants during her last visit six months before. He devoutly prayed she wouldn't try this time. He thought of Hank, one of the casino guards-studs. Hank would be more than pleased to pick up a few extra bucks.

He'd agreed to manage Porto Bianco just to get close to Dominick Giovanni, to become part of his organization. Nearly two and a half years now of his life: How close was he? He knew Dominick was one of the most powerful international weapons dealers. So did the U.S. Customs Service. He didn't have enough proof yet to convince a grand jury, but neither did any other agent in the U.S. Customs Service. He'd been close a number of times to nailing Giovanni, and the U.S. Customs Service hadn't. Well, he'd saved his life. He'd done it deliberately, knowing that his deal with Hurley and the feds was to get evidence on Giovanni, irrefutable evidence so they could lock him up for the rest of his miserable life. The feds wanted him in prison, not shot dead by an assassin's bullet. Marcus too had wanted justice—most of the time. But the hell of it was that with Dominick dead, the organization would continue with DeLorio at the helm. At least that seemed the likely outcome.

Odd how the two Dutchmen had poisoned themselves. Even more odd was the fact that Dominick had avoided speaking of the consequences of what had happened. He'd spoken about none of it to Marcus and he'd left, finally, frustrated and weak and irritable. He knew no more than he had before. What was the meaning of *Bathsheba*? An organization? A woman from the Bible? He'd left immediately after a breakfast at which Paula had very calmly run her fingers up his thigh and told a joke while she fondled him beneath the table, with her husband, DeLorio, sitting next to her.

"Marcus, hurry, Mrs. Maynard's on the way from the airstrip!"

"All right," he said, and speeded up. "I'm coming, Callie." He'd collar Hank, who was at present recovering from a sexual marathon with Glenn, a very hungry lady from San Antonio.

Six hours later, at ten o'clock in the evening, Marcus fell into his bed. He didn't care if the women thought he was a jerk for leaving them, if the men thought he was a wimp for ignoring the heavyweight fight from Las Vegas on the giant-screen TV. He was so bloody exhausted he could scarcely walk. As for Hank, he imagined that young man was far from sleeping. Cecily had approved of him.

Marcus's sleep wasn't restful. He dreamed the dream that had haunted him for twenty years now, on and off.

The dream had changed over the years. It was still the boy's and yet it was tainted by the man's experiences. The dream unrolled like a film, a nice easy start, scenes really, like soft paintings, flowing in front of him, setting the ambiance, easing him back to Chicago, back to his old neighborhood, in that long-ago summer. A boy, thin, lanky, guileless, and outgoing, who trusted everyone. A nice kid, that's what those soft scenes showed. An only kid with two loving parents, a paper route, good grades, sports, an all-American boy. A naive shithead.

Now the film speeded up, events ran a crazy race, became tangled, lurched out of sequence, but remained bright and urgent and terrifying.

His father, Ryan "Chomper" O'Sullivan, a newspaperman, who was an intellectual, a narrow-shouldered man fanatically devoted to truth. He was visible now, shoving up his glasses that were always slipping down his narrow nose, and his mother, Molly, big-boned, tall, stronger than her husband, laughing as she leaned over her husband to push up his glasses and nip the end of his nose with her white teeth. He was called Chomper because he didn't let up.

Once Chomper was onto something, he rooted around like a damned bulldog, didn't ease off, ever. He'd interview the devil if he had to, to get to the truth, then to print the truth.

The eleven-year-old Marcus had been impatient with his old man. He couldn't throw a football worth a damn. He could help with math, but he was normally too busy. Molly was a loss at anything that had an X or a Y stuck in it. But he loved his pa; his pa knew the history of every pro baseball player in the world.

More scenes, brighter now, the blood redder and deeper, spreading, oozing over everything, in his eyes, flowing into his nose, his mouth, choking him, all the red, so much of it, all of his father's blood—

Marcus moaned, then yelled, jerking up in bed, choking and wheezing. Sweat flowed down his neck, under his armpits. God, would it never ease off? He was having trouble breathing. His shoulder throbbed. Fear clogged his throat. The room was cold, with the air conditioner on high.

He shivered and jerked the covers over him, burrowing beneath them.

Wouldn't it ever stop?

He knew the answer to that; yes, he did. He managed to slow his breathing, telling himself over and over that he wasn't a freaked-out eleven-year-old kid anymore. He was an adult, and thank God he'd gotten up before the dream had continued to its familiar conclusion.

But he was afraid to go back to sleep. He looked at the digital clock on the nightstand. Five A.M. He didn't hesitate, but got up and went into his bathroom.

He stayed under the hot shower spray until his skin tingled.

Then he went running.

It was just past dawn, pinks and pale grays slashing through the morning sky, mixing with the blues of the Caribbean, gleaming off the white sand on the beach. It was a beautiful sight, and so quiet he could hear his heart beating. His pace was steady as he evenly inhaled and exhaled the sweet clean air. He wondered how it had been here several hundred years before, when the hills and central mountains had been covered with sugarcane fields extending from the highest points nearly to the sea, black slaves brought over by the Portuguese bending over the stalks, tending them, sweating under the hot Caribbean sun. The fields had been gone since before the turn of the last century; the four or five owners had left, selling their land until just one man, a rich American Yankee merchant who'd wanted to impress a French aristocratic wife with his wealth, had bought the entire island. Of the few natives that had been born on the island, most had drifted away, making their homes on the other islands, primarily Antigua and St. Kitts. There was little native culture now, hadn't been for years and years; no written lore, no rites or rituals remained. But then again, there was no poverty either, not on Giovanni's Island. All natives who remained were employed and paid well and given housing.

Marcus held his hand under his elbow to keep stress off his injured shoulder. He looked up and saw a woman ahead of him, her pace steady and smooth. He frowned, wishing that for just once he could be alone, just once not have to make inane conversation with a guest. He slowed just a bit. The woman had long legs; he'd let her get far ahead. She disappeared around a curve about a hundred yards ahead.

When he rounded the curve, he looked around instinctively. He didn't see her. Had she speeded up and already run through the jungle paths back to her villa?

He hoped so. He continued, his breathing steady, his heart rate even, sweat soaking his hair. Still he found himself looking for her. Could something have happened? She hadn't been running that fast. Then he stopped short.

The woman was seated between some large rocks near the shoreline, her legs drawn up to her chest, her head buried in her hands. There was some sort of book lying on a rock beside her. She had red hair—no, actually more auburn, with some brown and blond in it—drawn back in a ponytail, a red stretch sweatband around her forehead. She was wearing red shorts and a baggy cotton top.

She was crying. Low, deep sobs that sounded like they came from her gut, like she couldn't bear it. Wrenching sobs—soul sobs his mother, Molly, would have called them.

Well, shit. She hadn't heard him. He considered leaving her be. Then he knew he couldn't. He stopped and approached her quietly.

He dropped to his haunches in front of her.

"Are you all right?"

Her head snapped up and she stared at him, surprise in her eyes.

"I'm sorry to startle you. Don't be afraid."

"I'm not," she said, and he saw it was true. Her eyes were a pale blue with perhaps just a dollop of gray in the early-morning light.

"Excuse me for bothering you, but I saw you here. Are you all right? Is there something I can do?"

She was young—mid-twenties, he guessed. Her face was blotchy from the tears. She was amazingly lovely, even with her nose running, her eyes red and swollen from crying, and her hair sweat-soaked, her face clean of makeup.

"I'm quite all right, thank you. It's very beautiful

here. I thought no one in his or her right mind would be up and out here this early. You just never know, do you?"

"No, you certainly don't. I was pretty surprised to see you too."

She scooted back just a bit, then rose to her feet. She wasn't all that tall, coming only to his chin.

"Forgive me for disturbing you," he said, wondering what the devil was wrong with her. A man, probably. It usually was. There wasn't a ring on her left hand. Yeah, man trouble, for sure.

He nodded and trotted away from her.

Margaret's Journal
Boston, Massachusetts
March 1991

I've met a man who isn't a crumb. Nor is he a liar. I'm sure of it this time. And you like him, my darling girl. His name is Charles Winston Rutledge III. How do you like that for a handle?

He's very rich—older money than even my parents'—very kind, and something I simply can't believe: he appears genuinely to love me.

He's forty-six years old and he's got two kids of his own, the girl married, and his son, Benjamin, at Harvard. He's a widower. His wife evidently died of cancer four years ago, poor woman. He owns newspapers, I don't know how many yet, and he hates the thought of the groups like Remington-Kaufer buying up papers, making them all the same. I tease him and ask him how his are any different. Doesn't he influence policy? Doesn't he tend to have his own political slants, and his papers reflect them? Ah, that gets him going. All this takes place after you've gone to bed, Rafaella.

Then we start kissing and he's good, very good. I'm a thirty-six-year-old-woman, I tell him, and I'm in my prime. I'm concerned, I continue, that he's over the hill and doesn't have any interest anymore in physical things. Ah, Rafaella, it's wonderful!

I met him on the beach at Montauk Point. I had simply driven out there because I'd heard it was interesting and it's at the very end of Long Island. Remember that weekend? We were visiting the Straighers in Sudsberry. Anyway, he was running and he ran into me, literally. Knocked me flat. And when he stretched out his hand to pull me up, something came over me— something crazy. I giggled, took his hand, jerked him off balance, and pulled him down. He was so surprised he didn't say anything for at least three minutes. And I just lay there giggling like a fool.

Then, of all things, he grinned at me, rolled over on top of me, and kissed me.

That was three weeks ago. He's asked me to marry him and I told him I probably would because he barbecues a good steak, stays awake most nights to make love to me, and he doesn't snore too much. I'll talk about it this evening with you. I know you'll be happy for me—this time.

Ah, let me stop a moment with all this true-love gushing. I got him, Rafaella, I finally got Gabe Tetweiler. I finally hired the right detective, a sleazeball named Clancy, and he turned up Gabe in Shreveport, Louisiana. He was still a land developer, of sorts, and he had money. Clancy discovered he'd come into it suddenly, and he figured he'd blackmailed some married woman when he'd been in New Orleans. In any case, Gabe was having a very good time with a local woman, but more particularly, with her eleven-year-old-daughter. Clancy plays no holds barred. He didn't interfere; he just took lots of pictures of Gabe molesting the little girl. Then he went to the mother and the both of them went to the Shreveport police. Gabe's in jail, trial pending.

It makes me feel very good, as if, finally, I've done

*something right in my life. I hope you've forgotten that
experience. You're so bright and happy, even with all
those teenage hormones wreaking havoc in your body.*

April 1991

*I saw him today, in downtown Madrid, coming out of
a boutique, a beautiful sloe-eyed, olive-complexioned
woman on his arm. Here I am on my honeymoon and
I have to see Dominick. It doesn't seem fair.*

*I haven't told Charles a thing about Dominick. He
believes that my first husband, Richard Dorsett, was an
honorable man whose life was cut tragically short. He
accepts the story that I changed my name and yours
back to my maiden name—Holland.*

*And there was Dominick, laughing and taking a
shopping bag from the woman, and then he looked up
and straight at me. His eyes flickered over me, a man's
casual checkout; then he turned back to his companion,
who couldn't have been more than twenty-two. He
didn't recognize me. I was a complete stranger to him.*

*I stood there under the hot Spanish sun, staring after
him, not moving, tears streaming down my face, and
then Charles was beside me, and he was scared something had happened to me.*

*I've become the liar now, a very good one, as a mat-
ter of fact. I told Charles I had this sudden awful cramp
in my left calf and it hurt so bad, and he picked me
up in his arms, sat me down in a chair at a sidewalk
cafe, and rubbed the calf until I told him it was gone.*

*What's wrong with me? I hate the man, I swear it to
you. I hate him, I fear, more than I love Charles. But
not more than I love you, Rafaella.*

*I've got to stop this! Dammit, he's been out of my
life for years upon years. Yet he looked immensely
wonderful. He must be at least Charles's age, but the
years hadn't changed the basic man. He looked like an*

*aristocrat, that long thin nose of his, his long slender
body, those narrow hands with the exquisitely buffed
nails, his immaculate dress, his hair as black as it was
then, except there was white in the sideburns, and it
just added to his magnetism. And his pale blue eyes.
Your pale blue eyes, Rafaella, with just a touch of gray,
maybe, if one looks very carefully.*

He didn't recognize me. He stared right through me.

Giovanni's Island
March 2001

Rafaella watched the man run down the beach. Another guest up at dawn. Well, at least he'd been polite
enough to leave her alone quickly enough. It had also
been kind of him to stop when he realized she was
crying.

She pulled her loose shirt free from her shorts and
rubbed her eyes. Crying, of all the stupid things. Crying for her mother's pain that had now become her
pain. But mixed with that was the other—*her* father,
the man whose blood was in her. Why did it hurt
so much?

Her mother had protected her all these years. Her
mother, who still lay in that hospital bed with all those
obscene tubes in her body, was now helpless. Well,
she—Rafaella—wasn't helpless.

Rafaella jumped to her feet. She became aware of
the beauty surrounding her. It was morning now, the
sun brightening, the air soft as her face-powder brush,
the breeze from the sea salty and light. She drew a
deep breath, picked up the fourth volume of her mother's journals, and began her run back to the resort.

The place was incredible. The airstrip couldn't accommodate jets, so she'd flown to Antigua yesterday
afternoon, then hired a private helicopter to fly her to
Giovanni's Island, otherwise known by its resort

name, Porto Bianco. She'd found out in Antigua that
most people bound for the island had their own private planes. As she ran steadily, she remembered
when she'd dropped in to visit her travel agent to get
reservations to the island. When she'd told Crissie she
wanted to book into Porto Bianco, the agent had
dropped her jaw.

"Porto Bianco? You want to go *there*? Do you
know how much it costs? And there's probably a waiting list a mile long—good grief, Rafaella, did you just
inherit a fortune? Oops, I forgot about that trust fund
of yours. Well, in any case, the club's private, members only."

And Crissie carried on and on about all the gold-
plated faucets in the bathrooms and how even the
Jacuzzis had gold-plated jets. And there were many
security guards so that all the wealthy women could
drip with their diamonds and rubies without fear
they'd be stolen. And the casino was more elegant
and understated than the casinos in Monaco. It was
the most exclusive, most expensive resort in the Caribbean. Did Rafaella know it had been built back in the
thirties by one of the Hollywood movie moguls? Crissie thought it was Louis B. Mayer, or maybe Sam
Goldwyn, she wasn't sure. But she'd heard he'd
bought it from the estate of this American merchant
who'd had this French aristocratic wife who'd left him
for a fisherman on Antigua.

Rafaella had listened to her carry on; she hadn't
bothered to tell her that Dominick Giovanni had
bought the resort, the entire island, back in 1997. She
asked if there were any photos of the place, and was
told that no, there weren't. This wasn't a place that
wanted new business. Their business was mouth-to-
mouth from old money to more old money. It was
exclusive; it was private; it was members and their
guests only.

"Ah," Crissie said, her voice lowered to wickedness,

"I know what it is. You want yourself a handsome playmate, right?"

"I don't think so. I just broke it off with Logan."

"Forget Logan—he's got hang-ups, right? You probably broke off with him because he acted like a jerk, right? I heard that Porto Bianco has gorgeous men and women there for the guests, if you know what I mean."

That was a kicker. A giant pleasure palace, replete with male and female playmates.

"Do you know anything else about the place, like how I can get in?" How difficult it was to keep her voice light, uncaring.

But Crissie had just shaken her head. "Do you know any members? That'd be the only way. What I told you, I've just heard gossiped about by other travel agents. I don't have the foggiest notion of how to get you there, Rafaella, without being a member, sorry. I remember now that it changed hands back in the eighties—it was all run-down then. Then somebody else bought it just a few years ago—a rich Arab or a rich Japanese, something like that, and he poured millions into it and got it back up to what it had been in the thirties. I'd give a year's pay or my virginity to get in there, just for a week."

"You're not a virgin, Crissie."

"You've been in the men's room again, Rafaella."

But it had been so simple, in the end.

Al Holbein wasn't a dummy. He'd found out about Rafaella's access of their information service and her search through the *Trib*'s library. And since all topics were either on private arms dealers, or Dominick Giovanni, or Porto Bianco, he didn't have to strain to come up with some of the answer. He was toying with the idea of demanding what she was up to when she walked into his office.

"What is it, Rafe? You can't handle the heat out there in the newsroom? You'll get used to all the jealousies. Goodness, you'll be jealous yourself before too long."

"It isn't that."

"Logan what's-his-face at the D.A.'s? He giving you a hard time?"

"Logan's history. No, it doesn't have anything to do with work or men. I decided I needed *more* than just a vacation. I want to take a leave of absence, Al."

Al stared at her, nonplussed. "I beg your pardon?"

Rafaella tried to get her act together. What to say?

"Is this about your mother? You want to be with her?"

She started to lie; he'd given her such a fine opportunity. In the end, she just stared at her shoes and shook her head.

"Does it have anything to do with Porto Bianco?"

"So, you know."

"Just about your research. Why the interest in the island? Or in arms dealing? Or is it Dominick Giovanni?"

Rafaella drew a deep breath. "Can you get me in at Porto Bianco? As a guest?"

It was Al's turn to study Rafaella Holland. She could have asked her stepfather, Charles. He could have snapped his fingers and gotten her on the next flight to the Caribbean. But she'd asked him, Al. Slowly he nodded. "Yes, I can get you in. Senator Monroe's a member, and he owes me. It's important?"

Rafaella rose. "It's the most important thing in my life."

Rafaella stopped running. She was on a narrow, winding path, one of a dozen that led from the resort to the beach and back. She walked now to one of the main paths that led to her small villa. There were forty villas in addition to the lavish main facility, and Al had managed to get her one of them.

She was here, so close to him, and it was the beginning for her. She had a plan that she'd thought about and examined and thought about some more. It would work. She simply had to keep her focus, keep her edge, and not let anything distract her. She felt the familiar mingling of fear and anticipation, making her heart pound and her breathing shallow.

Six

Rafaella ate another tart grapefruit slice. Her lips puckered and she quickly downed the remainder of her coffee.

She was seated for breakfast on one of the four outdoor patios, this one latticed overhead by bright red and purple bougainvillea to protect against the sun. She was facing one of the swimming pools shaped like Italy, down to the boot, which was the hot tub.

There were only a half-dozen or so guests breakfasting outside at eight-thirty in the morning. The weather, as usual, was in the low seventies at this hour, the sky perfectly clear, despite the fact that every morning about eleven o'clock there would be a heavy downpour that would last for some twenty-five minutes and then the sun would shine blindingly again and everything would continue as if nothing had happened.

She studied the guests as she ate slowly. The beautiful people did appear different from their mortal counterparts. They were, on the average, more slender, more fit, more evenly tanned, and what was astounding was that even those in their forties and fifties bore no sun wrinkles on their faces. Not a ripple of cellulite on any female thigh. However did they manage it?

The men looked wonderful in their white tennis shorts and knit shirts, and the women—their legs long and sleek—wore Lagerfeld hand-painted silk coverups, Armani trousers, Valentino organza madras, and Tantri sandals: at least those were the designers she recognized from her three-day crash course in the latest hot fashions.

They looked pampered and flawless. She overheard a conversation next to her between a man in his fifties and a young woman who couldn't have been older than Rafaella. Initial impressions had told her father and daughter.

Boy, was she naive. They were lovers, and the young woman, very blatant about it, laid her hand in his lap, turned it downward, and molded his penis with her fingers. Rafaella stared.

"More coffee?"

Rafaella jumped. The waitress was standing beside her, an amused twinkle in her eyes. "Er, yes, thank you."

"They look much sweeter than they really are, don't they?"

"What? Who?"

"Your grapefruit," said the waitress.

"Oh, certainly. I feel very stupid."

"I did too when I first got here. This is a playhouse. Don't think it's sexist, because it isn't. You'll see very mature ladies with hunks you wouldn't believe. Well, I hope you enjoy yourself. You should, you know. This is a wonderful place."

"I hope so too," Rafaella said. The waitress was beautiful enough to be a model. Speaking of which, hopefully today she would finally make contact with Coco Vivrieux, Dominick Giovanni's French mistress and former model.

Rafaella left the lanai and wandered through the lush colorful grounds. The place was almost more than the senses could take. So much color, and foliage and flowers so abundant. She'd counted twenty-one different gardeners. They seemed to blend into the greenery and they worked very quietly. Acres and acres of beautiful gardens, none of them rigidly manicured like Charles Rutledge's English gardens.

There were golf courses, tennis courts, three swimming pools, plus, of course, the beautiful Caribbean splashing up onto white-sand beaches. The island was shaped like the upper northwestern chunk of San Francisco and was only about three square miles. Antigua was to the east and some guests flew into St. John's. The resort took up the east side, the Giovanni compound the west side. It was paradise, no doubt about that, and it was only for very, very rich people—and her father.

Rafaella supposed she fit in well enough. Her trust fund was substantial, her stepfather was one of the richest men on the east coast, and she did recognize a Givenchy dress when she saw one.

She returned to her villa, a miniature Mediterranean, all whitewashed walls, arched doorways, and red-tiled roof. It was surrounded by frangipani and hibiscus, all yellows and pinks. She had complete privacy. The interior furnishings were late baroque, heavily ornamented Louis XVI, the floors hardwood with Kashmir wool and silk carpets as throws.

Almost too much, Rafaella thought as she turned the gold-plated faucet of her washbowl, a hand-painted porcelain bowl from Spain.

She allowed herself another hour of decadent appreciation, then got herself into gear. She went for a workout in the gym.

What a gym, she thought, eyeing the newest of Nautilus equipment. She changed into the designer leotards a friendly young woman gave her, a woman who had pink hair with a wild yellow stripe and said, "Hey, call me Punk! I'll show you everything. You don't look like you need much help, though. You're already there. But any questions, just holler."

The leotard was pale blue with matching tights. Rafaella didn't bother with the leg warmers, which she'd always considered an affectation, particularly if one were in the Caribbean. She'd wondered where the natives were, if indeed there were any on this private island, and finally saw three or four local black women who appeared to be in charge of the guests' dressing rooms. They were handsome women, silent and discreet, and Rafaella wondered what they thought of this outrageous place.

She took herself to the soft-as-butter leather floor mat and began her workout. As she stretched, she checked out every person there—men and women. Most were friendly, particularly the men. She met a half-dozen within thirty minutes.

She was doing leg lifts when she saw him again.

It was the same man who'd stopped early this morning on the beach and been nice to her, a stupid weeping woman. He was speaking to Punk; then he laughed, worked his shoulder a bit, and sauntered off to the men's dressing room.

When he came out, he was wearing shorts, sneakers, and a white T-shirt. She could see an elastic bandage around his chest and over his shoulder beneath the soft white material. She hadn't noticed the bandage earlier.

He was built very well. In his early thirties, she guessed, hair black as sin, and eyes a deep blue. Yes, he was very well-built, with muscular thighs, just what she liked. A man to whom fitness was important and always would be. He had a strong face, a hard face, a face that promised both character and secrets. He was a man who would be noticed and remembered.

He looked around and saw her. Rafaella nodded, then did another leg lift.

Marcus strolled over to her. "Good morning," he

said, and stuck out his hand. "I didn't introduce myself this morning. My name's Marcus Devlin."

His smile was nice too. "My name's Rafaella Holland."

"You just get here?"

"Yes, yesterday afternoon. From Boston. I can't tell you what it's like to wear no clothes and still be warm. The weather back home is—"

"Yes, I know. I was in Boston last month. Sure, and even my toenails were cold."

She grinned. "You're Irish."

"As I tell folk, I'm half Irish and half South Chicagoan."

"I thought South Chicago was primarily black."

"It is. And I'm more Catholic than the pope."

"Then why in the name of the pope are you here?"

"You don't like it? The freedom to do about anything you please? It would seem to me that a lovely young woman could enjoy herself immensely here."

"If my mother knew I was here, she'd probably turn Catholic and pray every hour on the hour for my lost self and soul. Why, just this morning, you wouldn't believe what I saw, and—"

A black eyebrow went up. He looked amused, and was waiting for her to finish, but she didn't.

"Yes? You were saying?"

"Nothing more than two people enjoying their freedom. What an interesting way to phrase it. It was just that one of them was old enough to be the other one's father. Sorry, I must sound like a Victorian spinster, which I'm really not. Excuse me, I've got to do twenty more leg lifts."

Marcus recognized a dismissal when he heard it. It surprised him because he wasn't used to being dismissed, particularly by women, particularly by young women who were very rich and used to getting what they wanted when they wanted it. He almost laughed at his sudden attack of ego, but contented himself by walking away from her with merely a nod to her over his shoulder.

Rafaella wondered at her sudden collapse of restraint. She'd nearly talked the man's ear off, and she didn't have any idea who or what he was. It would be just her luck if he were one of the male playmates.

"Who is that man?" she asked Punk when she came over to help Rafaella reset the weights on the Nautilus.

"Who? Oh, Marcus. Isn't he a hunk? Oh, drat the man, I told him not to overdo it, and there he goes again!"

"You mean—I can see the bandage underneath his T-shirt. What happened to him?"

"I don't know exactly. Dr. Haymes—he's the resort doctor—he said something about Marcus getting hurt on some machinery over at the compound. But now Marcus is trying to get all his strength back in a week. Excuse me, I want to go chew on his ear."

"But who is he?" Rafaella said to herself, watching Punk walk to the man and pull on his arm.

The compound. It had to be Dominick Giovanni's compound.

Was the man a crook? Was he one of her father's men?

"You need some more help?"

Punk again, hovering, her words meant for Rafaella but her eye roving over the men who were grunting with varying degrees of pain through their routines.

"Marcus seems like a nice man."

That got Punk's attention, and she looked Rafaella over closely. "I hate to be the one to tell you this, honey, but you're really not his type. It doesn't matter how rich you are, either. He doesn't play around much, and when he does, it's with petite brunettes. I wonder if he had a wife who was black-haired and little, and—she left him or she died, or something—"

"Dramatic?"

Punk laughed and shrugged. "Yeah. You know, even I've tried, but he just isn't interested. He says a guy should never dip his quill in company ink. He also says I'm too young for him. He says he sees me only as an uncle would. He works much too hard. Pity, I bet I could make him very happy. Look over there— that guy's from Argentina and he's got the yummiest accent, and from what I've heard, he knows just what to do in the sack. Callie—she's Marcus's secretary— well, she told me he has the nicest fingers and—" Punk shuddered.

Rafaella wanted to say something to that, but she kept her mouth shut. Punk was a veritable fount of information and should get past the sex soon.

Unfortunately Rafaella couldn't get Punk off the Argentinian's sexual prowess, so she merely nodded at appropriate intervals. Finally another woman hailed Punk and she left.

Rafaella's workout came to an abrupt halt when an older woman—an incredibly beautiful woman with shoulder-length ash-blond hair—walked into the gym. She saw Marcus and quickened her pace over to him. She touched his shoulder and began speaking to him.

He stopped and spoke to her. He put his hand on her arm as if he were reassuring her about something. Then he turned, spoke briefly to Punk, and disappeared into the men's dressing room.

The older woman—Rafaella mentally deleted the adjective—the woman was mid-thirties, exquisitely fashioned by a very kind set of genes, with high slashing cheekbones, giving her a nearly Tartar look, a wide mouth, and arched eyebrows over the greenest eyes in nature. Rafaella looked more closely. Her heart speeded up.

The woman was Coco Vivrieux, Dominick Giovanni's mistress. She was far more compelling than her photographs, which was odd, because models seemed to make it to the top because they weren't necessarily gorgeous, just very photogenic. Rafaella couldn't believe her luck. Slowly, her mind racing, she strolled over to where the woman was waiting, drumming very long fingernails on the back of an Air-Dyne bike.

"Excuse me. I'm terribly sorry to bother you, but aren't you Coco?"

Coco nodded, distracted, wishing the sweating woman would leave her alone.

"I've admired you forever, it seems. You're the most beautiful woman in the world."

Coco decided on the spot that this sweating woman wasn't to be dismissed so lightly. She seemed quite a good sort. "You're very kind to say so, Miss—"

"Holland. Rafaella Holland." She stuck out her hand, and Coco, after looking at it for the barest instant, shook it.

"I can't believe how lucky I am to finally meet you. Are you a guest here at the resort, Coco?"

"No, I live here, on the western side of the island. You're a guest?"

Rafaella made a decision and shook her head. "Yes and no. I really came here to—"

"Who's this, Coco?"

It was Marcus Devlin. He didn't sound very friendly now. He sounded suspicious.

"This is Miss Holland, Marcus. She's one of your guests."

Marcus looked her over slowly. He'd assumed she was a guest, and here she was bothering Coco. What the hell did she want with Coco? He said, "She and I met at dawn today, as a matter of fact, and again over leg lifts just a minute ago."

"I'm a runner, just like Mr. Devlin." What did these two have to do with each other? Rafaella wondered. She decided to strike first at Devlin, because she'd heard the suspicion in his voice, seen the blatant distrust in his eyes when he'd looked at her again. She'd learned that if you took a man down, he tended to show his true colors very quickly. And she wanted to know who he was now. "Are you the tennis pro? The golf pro? Or just a pro?"

There was challenge and disdain in her voice, and Marcus realized she thought he was one of the resort studs, here to screw her eyes out for a goodly sum of money. In her case, not much money at all, if any. She could have all the men she wanted free of charge. Why the attack? He hadn't really provoked it. He smiled, and, for the moment, said nothing.

Coco, surprised, opened her mouth, but Marcus forestalled her then, saying easily, "I'm *the* pro, I guess you could say, Miss Holland. Or, in addition to going braless, do you also go by Ms.?"

Now it was her turn to be on the receiving end of the contempt. He was better at it than she was, and to give herself time, she sent her chin up.

She flicked a fleck of lint from her leotards. "It's Ms., and braless is very comfortable."

"I thought as much. Now, if you would excuse us, Ms. Holland—"

He was dismissing her. Just as if she didn't exist, he was dismissing her. Rafaella supposed she deserved it, but she didn't like it. Now she had to make her move with him listening. She said quickly, "It was wonderful meeting you, Coco. Could we have lunch perhaps? Tomorrow on the Hibiscus Lanai? I'd appreciate it ever so much, truly. And I do have something specific to speak with you about."

Coco didn't know what to do. She shrugged, then smiled. "Tomorrow, then, Miss Holland. Have a good day—"

"Yeah, with the pro of your choice. Given your age and your looks, it shouldn't cost you all that much."

"You're dead wrong," Rafaella said. "It won't cost me a dime."

That was true enough, Marcus thought again. He

nodded to Ms. Holland, took Coco's arm, and left the gym.

"You were quite horrible to her, Marcus."

He didn't want to talk about Ms. Holland, and said, his voice curt, "She's nothing but a selfish rich—You know the sort, Coco. Both of us have met her type before."

"Perhaps you're right, but still, she is a guest. I've just never seen you act so dismissive and so edgy with a female guest before. I wonder what she wants."

"I do too. I don't like people singling you out like that. It was as if she were just waiting for you to show up." He shrugged then. "Maybe she's just a famous-person groupie."

"She doesn't look it. Oh, Marcus, I'm scared out of my mind. You've got to do something!"

"Keep it down, Coco. Let's go to my office."

Callie was at her desk, and she quickly rose when Marcus came into the executive suite. "I've got a ton of messages, Marcus, and—"

"In a couple of minutes, Callie," he said, raising his hand. "Miss Vivrieux and I will be in my office. No interruptions. Hold all calls."

Callie didn't like Coco, but she managed to keep her feelings to herself. She wondered if the model was going to seduce her boss on his desk. She wouldn't put it past her. Callie, whose roots were Sioux City, Iowa, had nonetheless become a thorough sophisticate in a period of two years. Her last lover, a Señor Alvarez of Madrid, had told her of the island resort and, at her insistence, had gotten her a job here. She loved it. She watched now as Marcus quietly closed his office door.

Marcus didn't like antiques, at least not the three-century-old French sort that abounded in the villas. His office was starkly modern, all glass and chrome and pristine white carpeting and earth-tone leather furniture.

"You want a drink, Coco?"

She shook her head. "No, I don't want anything. It's Dominick. Something's going on, you know that. After the Dutchmen poisoned themselves—I'm just not sure they *did* poison themselves. Are you?"

He looked at her, saying nothing. He didn't think so either, but it didn't make sense. Had Dominick had them poisoned? Had he gotten the information he wanted, then ordered them killed? To look like suicide? To keep someone in the dark? Who? Him? Coco? Every damned one of them? It did make some sense, but it was the crookedest road Marcus had ever walked.

"Why do you think that?" he said easily now, pouring himself a cup of rich black Jamaican coffee.

"I heard him on the private blue phone—you know, the one that only he uses, the one locked in his desk drawer."

"Yeah, I know."

"I—well, I heard him talking to someone about it. He said, 'All right, you cretin, whoever you send to kill me, you'll fail. Look what happened to the Dutchmen and that damned woman.' That was it. Link was coming and I couldn't let him think I was eavesdropping."

"So, it was a different set of Dutchmen who came to the island. Is the deal still on?"

"What deal?"

"Come on, Coco. The arms deal. The Dutchmen were supposed to be the middlemen, here to finalize things."

"Dominick doesn't talk business to me, you know that, Marcus. Nor is he one for pillow talk. He goes to sleep."

"Then there's someone out to kill him. It was planned, and it was just a first attempt. Well, I think—"

A soft buzzing noise came from his top desk drawer.

Quickly he said, "There's my damned beeper. Let me mull it over, Coco." He took her arm and led her toward the office door. "Try not to worry. I'll speak to Dominick, and, yes, I'll protect you. Don't worry."

Once he'd closed the door again, Marcus locked it and quickly walked back to his desk. He unlocked the drawer and quickly pressed two buttons in rapid succession. He then picked up the phone receiver.

"Devlin here."

"It's me, Marcus. Savage. As if it *could* be anyone else. Thank God you're there."

"What's going on? I wasn't expecting a call from you until the end of the week. Is Mom all right? Is—?"

"Molly's just fine. Now, slow down a bit. First of all, Molly sends her love and wonders when you'll get back to Chicago to visit her. Second, the company's fine and we've got no unsolvable problems at present. Now, what happened is this. Hurley called me last night. He was worried, thought you might even be dead. Rumor has it that there was an attempted hit on Giovanni."

"Yes, there was. Dominick was shot in the arm but he's fine. I was shot in the back but I'm all right now. Stop worrying. Yes, there was a hit, but who's behind it, I don't know yet. Dominick still doesn't trust me enough to tell me everything. I was trying to discover something before I called you to report to Hurley. This whole arms deal—Tell Hurley that the Dutchmen were decoys, the woman leading them, an assassin. Her name, supposedly, was Tulp. A big woman, large-boned, mid-thirties, dark brown hair and big breasts, quite at home with a nine-millimeter automatic. A professional all the way. Maybe Hurley can I.D. her. As for the Dutchmen, they were the same ones I'd already told you about. When the real deal goes down, I'll get to you, Savage, then you'll call Hurley. Now

I've got work to do and a puzzle to solve here. Anything else?"

There was a deep sigh. "No, nothing else. You'll take care of yourself, won't you, buddy? We survived that last year in Afghanistan—hell, we even survived college and getting our munitions business off the ground." He gave a mirthless laugh. "We're honest and we don't charge the feds sixteen thousand dollars for a screwdriver. And here you are trying to pin a dishonest arms dealer. Oh, shit. Don't blow it now, O'Sullivan, you've got too much going for you. Oh, yeah, Molly's found a nice little Irish gal for you. I'll call you on Friday, hopefully with an I.D. on the woman." Savage rang off.

Marcus gently replaced the receiver, closed and locked the desk drawer.

There was a knock on his office door. "Marcus? I've got a Mr. Lindale on line three. There's a problem with a shipment of beluga caviar, and—"

"I'll be right there, Callie."

Rafaella didn't want to gamble, but that seemed to be the pastime of choice among the guests in the evenings—that and sex—so she at least had to pretend a passion for blackjack and roulette. She'd gone shopping in Boston, wishing she could call her mother and ask her to help select clothes she would need, but her mother was in a coma in Pine Hill Hospital. She'd ended up at a small exclusive boutique near Louisburg Square. Eight thousand dollars later, she looked dressed to kill, at least she hoped so. The evening gown she was wearing was sleek, black, sleeveless, and was held together at the waist by a single button, decorated with a large red silk hibiscus covering the button. With it she wore high strap black sandals and under it only a pair of black bikini panties. The dress folded softly and demurely nearly to the waist, showing the curve of her breasts quite clearly. "This Carolyne

Roehm is wonderful advertising," the woman had told her. "Men go nuts wanting to slip their hands inside, don't you agree?" Rafaella had indeed agreed. "It's so modest and yet so provocative." Her only jewelry was a pair of large gold hoops. "Nothing more," the woman had told her. "The style is severe and romantic and must be left alone."

Rafaella felt somewhat strange in her new plumage. But the first man she saw gave her such a stunned, lustful look that she immediately felt better. She could carry it off.

She'd managed to get her hair to cooperate, and it was piled high on top of her head with tendrils floating about her face. Did she look sophisticated? Look like she belonged? She sure as hell hoped so.

She spotted Marcus Devlin almost immediately. Talk about beautiful, he could rival the women, in his stark black evening clothes. He was busy charming the socks off two older women, who were hanging on his every word. She'd found out, finally, that he managed Porto Bianco. Of course he knew Dominick Giovanni. But was he a criminal too? Did he work with her father? She'd find out. He and Coco were her best leads.

Marcus looked up at that moment and saw Rafaella Holland, looking good enough to eat and good enough to make love to until the point of exhaustion. His reaction surprised him. That gown was a knockout— at least on her it was. His initial encounters with the woman hadn't given him any sort of sexual punch. He could see her sitting on that rock, her knees drawn up to her chest, her shirt and headband sweated through, her face clean of makeup, crying her eyes out. Hard to reconcile that woman with this one. This one was the woman in the gym, the smart-mouthed woman who'd put the moves on Coco, a woman not to be toyed with or dismissed lightly. He wondered just who she was. He would check her out first thing in the morning. She was probably just some rich groupie.

In some indefinable way she reminded him of Kathleen, his first wife, a petite Irish girl who'd been all of nineteen and caught up in IRA terrorism, and who'd been killed near Belfast six years ago after she ran away from her stodgy young American husband, Marcus O'Sullivan.

He turned to smile at Mrs. Oscar Dallmartin, a Greek heiress who'd married a Texas oilman. She was twenty-eight and her husband of three months was an octogenarian. She immediately began a recital on the benefits of having Portuguese sailors for her yacht crew. Marcus tuned her out while memory flooded through him. Memory and regret and some guilt, still lingering, coming out at odd moments like this. If only he and Savage hadn't been working twenty hours a day with the new company, if only he'd spent just a little more time with Kathleen, asked her what she was studying, and listened, really listened—But he hadn't. He'd been too busy—the business, and graduate school.

He'd kissed her good-bye every morning, made love to her nearly every night, even if he had to wake her up when he got home, and then she'd run away—So long ago. And she'd died, killed by a terrorist bomb set in a Belfast bus.

And he'd gotten the phone call. He'd never told his mom precisely what had happened, just that Kathleen had left him to return to Ireland and she'd died there, by accident. Truths and half-truths. Life was filled with them. Probably Ms. Rafaella Holland, like everyone else, was loaded with half-truths. She was young, but she looked strangely intent, her eyes older than her years would indicate. She looked as if she had to concentrate, had to figure out something, and whatever it was, was very important to her.

Marcus made up his mind at that point that he'd

talk to her, he'd gain her confidence. He'd take her to bed. That vagrant thought—no, now it was a decision, it was something he wanted—surprised him. He told himself it was because in his experience a woman who was well-loved was more open, more spontaneous, more revealing of herself. He had no idea what Rafaella Holland, once pleasured to the best of his abilities, would have to say, but he wanted to find out. This was something new to him—coldly calculating to take a woman to bed. No, he amended to himself. There was nothing cold about his decision at all. And that frightened him because it made his focus blur a bit. No, he wasn't about to allow this woman to sidetrack him even for the pleasure he'd surely get from her in bed. He couldn't afford it. He'd be a fool to allow it. If he lost his edge, his concentration, he could be dead. No, he had to keep himself apart—and he could do it.

"Would you like a glass of special champagne?"

Rafaella turned very slowly, her eyes level with the middle of his white-as-snow dress shirt. She didn't say a thing, just slowly raised her eyes until she was looking at him full-face.

"What's so special about your champagne?"

"It's from California."

She laughed.

"It's also the cheap—rather, the least dear of the champagnes served at Porto Bianco. The owner likes it—that's the only reason we carry it."

"Who's the owner?"

"A Mr. Dominick Giovanni." He watched her, smiling easily, as he spoke. Her expression remained one of polite interest, but her eyes— Something had flickered there, some sort of recognition. Well, now he knew what he was going to do. He was also pleased, as well as vastly relieved, that she was responding to him. As he signaled a waiter, he asked, "Do you know Mr. Giovanni?"

"I would say from his name that he's Italian, that's about all."

"He's really from San Francisco. Born and bred an American."

"Oh? Why ever did he buy this place?"

"You are full of questions, aren't you? If you drink that champagne with me, I just might tell you."

Rafaella shrugged. "Why not?"

"Why not, indeed." He offered her his arm.

Nice breasts, he thought, very nice. No bra. He could just slip his fingers inside and feel—

Marcus frowned at himself. His brain wasn't operating smoothly. He mentally set her aside. He didn't trust her. He wanted to hear it from her own mouth that she was just a celebrity groupie and that that prompted her interest in Coco. But he didn't believe it. No, she'd been too intense in those few minutes she'd spent with Coco. It was as if it were vitally important to her that Coco cooperate with her. He would find out soon enough all about her. More than anything, he realized now, he wanted to know why she'd been out running at dawn, then crying as if her heart were breaking.

Rafaella was enjoying herself. Marcus Devlin was coming onto her and she knew she could handle him quite easily. She didn't know why he'd changed his attitude toward her, but it was a relief. She had to deal with too much to have to worry about fending him off, him and his distrust of her. Even in her fine new plumage, though, she knew she couldn't compete with all the truly gorgeous women around in the casino, and yet he seemed to have chosen her. She remembered what Punk had told her and wondered some more. So he liked only brunettes, did he?

He directed her to a small table just outside the casino on a patio that overlooked the Caribbean. There was a half-moon, immensely beautiful, starkly white. The waves hissed and splashed over the sand

and rocks on the beach some fifty yards away. The casino was set on a slight promontory with frangipani trees everywhere, and their sweet scent filled her nostrils.

"This is wonderful," she said as she sat down.

"Yes," Marcus agreed, and nodded to the waiter, a gorgeous hunk of a man with auburn hair not far from the color of Rafaella's, who'd brought the champagne in Waterford crystal goblets on a silver tray.

The California champagne was more tart than Rafaella was used to, but it was bubbly and cold and she smiled as she sipped it.

She stopped herself just in time. *Tell me about yourself, Marcus.* God, if she said something like that, he'd probably get up and leave.

"How long have you been here on the island?" she asked instead.

"Since it opened in the fall of 1998—rather, since Mr. Giovanni bought it and opened it. A long time, actually. I travel a good deal. One needs to. An island, no matter how beautiful, is still an island, and you tend to go a bit crazy if you stay too long at a time."

Rafaella digested that. "How did you come to be the manager here? Were you the manager of a resort back in the States?"

He just shrugged. "If I give you your twenty questions now, then what will we talk about?"

"Sorry, I'm just interested."

Like a reporter would be interested? Now, that was a possibility.

"My turn now. Would you like to tell me what you do? Or would you like to dance? Or have a late supper? Or play roulette? Or make love with me?"

Rafaella looked him straight in his very dark blue eyes and said, "All of the above, I think. All a matter of time and energy, I suppose."

He gave her a lazy smile and she realized that she'd just made her decision. It astounded her, but she didn't want to back down. She'd also been seriously inaccurate about this man. He was slippery and smooth and dangerous. The thought of trying to manipulate him, to control him, was laughable. If she had a brain, she'd get out of his sight this very minute. She wasn't comfortable with one-night stands, and had had only one, with her journalism professor at Columbia, an older man she'd worshiped. She'd seen him as the most perfect of men, the highest human form, an intellectual, and probably the perfect lover. Well, he'd been lousy in bed.

Marcus wouldn't be lousy in bed. Some handsome men were, because they figured women should do whatever they wanted just to be seen with them. Marcus wouldn't be that way. She told herself she could hold back, could change her mind; she could still settle for sanity. She could say no.

He rose suddenly and smiled down at her. "In the order I mentioned, or would you like to go from the last backward to the first? Or perhaps start in the middle?"

"I thought you only went to bed with petite brunettes."

He raised an eyebrow at that. "I imagine that Punk told you I don't usually go to bed with anyone, Ms. Holland, particularly guests of Porto Bianco."

"Then you expect me to say no? Throw my special champagne in your face?"

"It's just not my practice to sleep with my guests."

"You're gay, then?"

He laughed. "All right, you win. You've challenged my manhood, denigrated my machismo, throttled my ego, cut me to my masculine quick."

"All of that? I hadn't realized I was so good."

"We'll see just how good you are, Ms. Holland. While we walk to my villa, why don't you tell me what you do for a living? Or are you one of the rich and idle?" He paused a moment, and looked down at her profile: It was arrogant, the tilt of her head. He remembered that vulnerable woman crying her eyes out on the beach at dawn. "No, you've never been idle in your life, have you? Careful, watch your step."

"No, I haven't."

"What college did you go to?"

"Columbia."

Marcus stopped in front of his villa. It was set back, the most private of all the villas, surrounded by bushes and trees and overflowing bougainvillea. He slowly turned Rafaella to face him. He lifted her chin with his fingertips and lowered his head. His mouth covered hers.

Her mouth was soft but cold, unresponsive, just as he'd expected. At best, she was uncertain about going to bed with him. Why had she agreed? Or had she? Why the hell did he want her so much? He decided to push her, just a bit.

He very calmly slipped his fingers beneath the silk hibiscus and unfastened the button that held her gown together, and before she could react, he shoved the panels off her shoulders and pulled the top down to her waist, held there only by the red silk flower. Her pale breasts were bare in the moonlight.

"Very nice," he said, bent her back over his arm, and took her nipple in his mouth.

Seven

Marcus raised his head and looked down at her. She was staring up at him, her eyes wide, bewildered. He felt slight quivers going through her. "You're very lovely, Rafaella," he said, and looked down again at his hand cupping her breast.

Rafaella felt sexy, and she wanted him, wanted him more than she had wanted any man in a very long time. What she felt most of all was surprise. She hadn't expected this. She wanted him to do more. She was standing in the moonlight—a more romantic spot on earth she couldn't imagine—letting a man she'd just met and probably didn't like all that much fondle her breasts, and it was wonderful. Her dress was hanging at her waist, held up only by the silk hibiscus.

She suddenly felt very much a fool, standing there half-naked, Marcus completely in control, completely dressed. "I'm cold," she said, and tried to pull away from him.

"In that case—" he said, and pulled her against him. She felt the buttons on his dress shirt press against her naked skin, felt his warm hands stroke up and down her back. "Better?"

What could she say to that? Either *No, it's not better, I want to go home now.* Or *Yes, it's better, but could you please just get on with it?*

Instead she just nodded and raised her face. He smiled and kissed her again, this time deeper, his tongue easing slowly between her lips, touching hers, not pushing, just acquainting himself with the feel of her, her scent. He tasted like the California champagne and he felt hard and very nice indeed beneath her hands. She hadn't realized that she was squeezing his back, feeling him, until that moment.

This was odd, she realized in a moment of dispassionate sensibility. She wasn't the sort to get carried away by the passion of the moment. Most important, she didn't like not being in control. And here she was hanging over his arm like a heroine in a 1920's Valentino movie. It was humiliating and embarrassing. She tried to pull away, but not with all that great an effort.

"Listen, Marcus, when I want to have an orgasm, I'll tell you."

He raised his face, taking in her outburst, and laughed. "You will, will you? Well, Ms. Holland, let's just see, shall we?"

Still he didn't take her inside his villa. Instead he kissed her again, talking into her mouth, telling her how he liked her breasts, the feel of her dark pink nipples, and as he talked he unfastened the silk flower and her gown pooled at her feet, leaving her standing there wearing only her panties and her high heels. "Now, let's see," he said, and his fingers slipped inside her bikinis and splayed over her buttocks, squeezing her flesh, fitting his fingers around her. Then he lifted her a bit, and his fingers rubbed against her wet flesh, and then he rested, hugging upward against her. She'd never had a man do this to her before, and she'd never felt anything like it in her life.

His fingers were just resting there, not moving at all, and she was burning and burning and she wanted him to get on with it, but he seemed content with things just the way they were. She shoved against his chest.

But not very hard. He just pulled her more tightly against him and continued kissing her and telling her what he was going to do with his fingers.

"The first thing is to learn how you're shaped, just to cup around you and see how you feel to me. Nice, Ms. Holland, very nice. You're wet and very warm, and now, let me move just a bit—"

His fingers were sliding over her, pushing downward to touch her and part and find her, and it was the most exciting feeling she could imagine and she couldn't believe it. She held her breath until he was laughing in her mouth and saying, "Now, Ms. Holland, that's quite a reaction from you. I want to see how you feel around my finger, and then I'll try two fingers—"

She jumped and clutched his shoulders when he slowly worked his middle finger into her. "Ah, I could call this home, I think." And she felt him ease another finger into her, then widen them inside her and sigh with pleasure. He started pushing deeper, and she didn't even think about objecting, because then his thumb was rubbing over her and she thought blankly: *My God, I'm going to come and I'm standing here like an idiot, naked, and this damned man is completely clothed and—*

She cried out and he caught her mouth again and then did something that sent her right over the edge. Again. He lifted her, his fingers still working her, and laid her on her back on the sweet grass, her gown spread beneath her. He pulled her legs apart, widened them, and brought them over his shoulders. He fitted his hands under her, lifted her, and then brought his mouth down on her. The instant his tongue touched her, his fingers went back inside her and she yelled and exploded inside.

His mouth covered hers again and he told her to keep crying out, that he loved it, told her to keep jerking her hips against his working fingers, and he kept speaking as he looked down at her face, soft and pale in the moonlight.

"I like this. You're very responsive, Ms. Holland."

And he caressed her until she was limp and exhausted and wanted to just float away into pleasurable oblivion.

"Surprised?"

"An understatement," she said, and touched her fingertips to his cheek. "I've never before felt quite like this—well, that is, you are very—"

"Now, my dear Ms. Holland," he said, interrupting her easily, "let's get you back to your villa."

"What? My villa? But don't you want to—?"

She shut her mouth, stared up at him, and it was then that she knew, she fully realized, what he'd done to her, realized that she'd been too blind to see what he was doing to her. She'd wanted him to the exclusion of all rational thought, she'd even forgotten that earlier in the day she'd been wary of him and as distrustful of him as he had been of her. Only he'd won. He'd kept control; she'd lost hers. He'd used her and controlled her. His victory over her had been complete. She wanted to scream at herself for being such a fool, and she wanted to kill him.

"Get away from me."

"All right," he said, and rose. He simply stood over her, dressed in his formal evening clothes, and watched her get herself together, jerking her gown up over her hips, trying to fasten that stupid button at the waist. The red silk flower looked wilted. Rafaella looked wildly around for her panties but didn't see them. They were actually in the pocket of his jacket, but he knew she was too furious with him, with herself, to ask him if he knew where her underwear was.

He'd never taken off her heels, and he watched her try to straighten the straps that had gotten off-kilter with her frantic movements. "Here," he said, knelt, and shoved the straps into place. She stood there for an instant in mute surprise, then yelled at him, "Go to hell, you bastard!" She ran away, nearly stumbling on the three-inch heels, until she was gone from his view.

He stood there breathing fast, his cock hard and so heavy he hurt. Why the hell had he treated her like that? He'd never done such a thing before. He'd caressed her into oblivion, then humiliated her, and he didn't understand why he'd done it. And then he got a glimmer of why he hadn't allowed her to touch him, to actively love him, to share herself with him. Why he hadn't allowed himself to be free with her. He'd realized on a gut level that the risk was too great.

She was different; she wasn't just a spoiled rich lady here to have fun with the help. No, she was different. She would see him, perhaps guess more than she should about him, and if she did, it would be his fault and it could ruin everything.

The hell of it was that he hadn't learned a thing about her, not a damned thing except that she was beautifully responsive and giving and loving until she realized what he'd done to her. Watching her, feeling her quiver, hearing her cries, knowing all her pleasure was from him, made him swell with triumph and pleasure and need. He tried to tell himself that what he'd wanted to do was teach her a lesson, but it wasn't true.

In the end he'd held himself back, protected himself from any involvement with her. He wasn't certain why he didn't trust her completely, but he didn't, and his instincts about people had sharpened dramatically over the past two and a half years. Her come-on to Coco, her endless questions—She was up to something.

He didn't know now if he was off the mark or not. He could be completely wrong about her. She could be better; she could be much worse. She could even be dangerous. He sighed deeply, went into his villa, downed a brandy, looked at himself with disgust in his bathroom mirror, then changed into running clothes and took off down the beach, his only company the night sounds and a moon to show him the path clearly.

He shouldn't have been surprised when he saw a woman running ahead of him, turning the same bend she'd turned early that same morning. He'd known her for one day—It was incredible. The runner was Rafaella Holland, the woman he'd just brought twice to orgasm.

This time he speeded up. She was really moving, unlike this morning. She was in very good shape, no doubt about that, and he imagined that her anger was making her go faster than was her habit.

Then he rounded a bend another hundred yards up the beach and there she was sitting on that same damned rock, looking out over the sea.

He came up behind her quietly. She didn't hear him. He looked at the back of her head and decided he still couldn't let down his guard, not now, particularly not now. He eased down beside her and said, "A sandy beach isn't my favorite place to have sex, but why not? It's my turn now, don't you think?"

She erupted, and he prepared to learn more about her, and, he admitted to himself, to enjoy himself, because she had a sharp tongue and a sharper wit. Too, in anger people said amazing things, and her barometer, from the looks of her, was fast reaching the fury level.

"You touch me, you cretinous jerk, and I'll kick you so hard you'll sing in the choir."

"Goodness, from that reaction one could think I was a selfish pig and did a wham-bam-thank-you-ma'am on you. When really all—"

Rafaella jumped to her feet. "What do you want, Mr. Devlin? Or is your name really Devlin?"

He smiled easily, controlling his leap of anger at the snide contempt in her voice, and came to his feet to face her. "Is Holland really *your* name? Maybe you could tell me why you wanted to hop in the sack with me after knowing me about fifteen minutes."

She looked at him, then looked out over the Caribbean, then back again, and she said without guile, "I don't know. I guess I'm a first-class idiot. Go away now. I was here first."

"I'd rather make love to you. You're no longer in the mood? I gave you too many orgasms? I wore you out and you're in R.P.?"

"I don't know what R.P. is."

"You seem like a very curious type. Look it up."

Here she was talking to him when all she wanted to do was kill him. Instead, she turned away and began walking down the beach, shouting over her shoulder, "Keep out of my sight!"

He laughed. He hadn't really meant to, but he did, and when she heard it she stopped cold, whipped around, and looked at him like he was about to die. "You moronic jerk," she said, and in the next instant he saw the smooth line of her body as she leapt forward, leg extended, and caught him square on the right shoulder with the side of her foot. He was so surprised he just stared at her as he went reeling backward, his hand clutching his shoulder. His only thought was: *Thank God it isn't the injured one.* Of course, she hadn't gone after him with murderous intent—he knew that, at least intellectually. He marveled aloud at her talent, knowing even as he baited her that she was likely to come after him again. "My God, you could take Punk. Maybe even Merkel."

She let her breath out in a hissing yell, leapt toward him, her side to him, turned like a dancer, and sent the side of her open palm into his belly. But she didn't get off scot-free this time, because he wasn't stupid or slow and he was ready for her. He clutched her arm just above the elbow, quickly gained leverage, and used her own momentum to flip her over, sending her flying onto her back in the sand. "You're good, but not that good, lady. On second thought, maybe Punk could wipe up the floor with you."

Rafaella was up in a flash.

When he said calmly, "Go home. I don't want to hurt you," she saw red. Her hand was open and there was blood in her eye and she was out to let him know that she could hurt him if she wanted to, if she chose to hurt him. Then, suddenly, Marcus heard something, a whizzing sound, and he stood there an instant, listening harder, and then just as suddenly she flew at him, knocking him flat, and pressed herself down on him.

Another hissing sound, and he heard something ricochet off one of the rocks. It was a damned bullet! And she was on top of him, her arms wrapped around his head, protecting him.

In a quick move that sent grinding pain through his healing shoulder, he rolled over on her and pressed his mouth to her temple. "Hold bloody still, do you understand me? Don't you dare move. This isn't fun and games anymore."

He ducked his head just as another bullet hissed about a foot over his head. He had to get her out of here, but they were on the open beach. The shots were coming from the jungle some twenty feet away, and the only cover was the rocks. But what did that matter? The guy with the gun had only to walk out here, look them straight in the eye, and shoot them cold. Where were all the resort security guards when you needed them?

Then Marcus heard the most wonderful sound—the sound of people, drunk people, very drunk and very happy people, and they were singing and coming closer, toward them, down the beach.

"Hey, come on, you guys, let's go swimming!"

"Your cock couldn't shrivel any more, Crowley. It'll disappear in the water."

"What about—? Hey, what's that? That fellow's humping that girl right here on the beach."

Wild drunken giggles and lewd comments.

Marcus found himself grinning. He raised his head and looked down at Rafaella Holland.

"Saved by a roving band of resort drunks. I would have done something heroic, but they came along first. And they are flying high."

"Hey, man, you've got your pants on! How you gonna make her happy with your pants on?"

"Shall I tell him how to do it?—Okay, I won't right now." Marcus turned to look at the man. The guy was naked as a jaybird, waving his finger at him. A woman was giggling behind him, as naked as he was. There were four more drunk stragglers, all in different states of undress, and Marcus would gladly have kissed them all. There was one woman so drunk she'd tangled her bra around her neck and looked in danger of strangling herself.

Marcus raised himself on his elbows and called, "Thanks, guys. The lady and I would join you in the water, but she just started her period—"

"It doesn't matter, it's a big ocean."

"Fool, it's not the ocean, it's the Caribbean!"

"True," Marcus said in a mournful voice, "but she's got cramps too." Rafaella was struggling beneath him. "She wanted to neck but not put out." And he laughed, rolling off her, then coming up and offering her a hand.

He heard comments from the group before one of the women yelled as she dived into a wave, the woman whose bra hung off her neck like a horse's halter.

"Come on," Marcus said, his voice low, "let's get out of here before they decide to toss you in, period or no period." He grabbed her hand and pulled her after him, turning briefly to wave good-bye to their drunk saviors.

Rafaella was in a mild state of shock. She recognized it for what it was and tried to force herself to relax, to calm, to breathe deeply.

"Sorry about that," Marcus said, but she kept looking straight ahead. "You okay?"

"Yeah, just ducky. You're a criminal and someone tried to kill you and I was lucky enough to be on hand to share in the bloodshed."

"No bloodshed. Don't overreact on me now."

Rafaella felt cold to her toes. "I won't. I'm stronger than you are, you ass."

When they reached his villa, she realized suddenly where they were and whirled about on her heel. Marcus grabbed her arm, unlocked the door on the first try, and hauled her inside. "Don't be a fool. You need some brandy and there isn't any in your villa."

"There is brandy in my villa," she said, but followed him inside. Unlike her villa, this one belonged in the twenty-first century. It was all earth tones and glass and brass and leather, and oddly enough, at least in her view, it looked homey and quite comfortable. She watched him pour her a brandy, watched him turn and smile at her and walk toward her. He lifted her fingers and closed them around the snifter.

"I don't like your furnishings. Fake, phony, plastic, and sterile, like you."

"All that? Thank you."

"I hate brass and glass and chrome and dull colors."

"Still on a roll, huh? All right, sometimes I do too. I prefer it, however, to Louis XVI settees." His voice had changed, no more mocking amusement, only a gentle calm. "Drink it down. Then you can go after me again."

He watched her down the brandy. He took the snifter from her fingers and pushed her down onto a rich chocolate leather sofa. He covered her with a geometric afghan, all in shades of brown and cream, punctuated with soft yellow squares. "You get yourself together, then we'll talk."

"I'm not your grandmother, so stop fussing. Leave me alone."

"Okay," he said mildly. She watched him pick up a telephone, punch a couple of buttons, and speak softly

into the receiver. Security? She hoped so. She hoped
they'd find the person firing that gun, but she doubted
they would.

Rafaella closed her eyes, not opening them until
he'd sat down opposite her in an overlarge leather
recliner.

It didn't take long for Rafaella to regain her head
of steam. "Someone tried to kill you. Do you know
who?"

Marcus was scratching his stomach, wondering the
same thing. At her question, he inadvertently rubbed
his shoulder and winced.

"Another attempt? It's a bullet wound, isn't it?"

"What are you, a nosy reporter? Forgive me, I'm
being redundant."

"As a matter of fact, yes, I am. A reporter, that is."
There was no reason to lie about it. He'd find out
quickly enough. She'd decided before she came to Giovanni's Island that there was no way she could cover
her tracks—from the Boston *Tribune*. Keep the lies to
a minimum; that was the key.

So he'd been right about that. He had a horrible
sinking feeling that the attempt on Dominick's life had
leaked to the press and they'd sent her here to get
the scoop.

"I knew I was right not to trust you, not to take
you for face value. What are you doing here?"

"I'm here to write a book, if it's any of your business, which it isn't, because it isn't about you. Who
tried to do away with you?"

"We haven't even started on you yet. A book about
what? About who?"

"*Whom*, and the answer shop is closed. Who was
that? Do you know? A man or a woman? Did you
see anything?"

He looked mildly apoplectic for a moment, then
shrugged. "Thanks for saving my life. When you
slammed down on me, I thought it must be a newly

invented Japanese trick, or maybe a new-age sex move. Odd; I didn't think you'd care one way or another."

"I don't. It was instinct, nothing more."

"No, more an impulse. You're the impulsive type, aren't you? Think of me as the only man who's ever made you feel like singing opera after sex and you—"

"That's really quite enough."

Her hair was hanging loose around her face, smudges of beach sand on her cheeks and chin and sticking to her hair. Her clothes were dirty, one sock scrunched down at her ankle, and he said, "I've always believed women had great instincts. They birth us, nurture us, and save our hides when we're jerks. A book about who? Whom?"

Rafaella just looked at him. "Give it up, John Doe Devlin. I'm sleepy, and for my first full day at one of the most expensive resorts in the world, I can't say much for the restful quality of the experience."

Amusement returned full measure as he rose. "But you should have something nice to say about the restorative powers of our earlier encounter."

"Drop it, buster."

He gave her a small salute. "Sleep well, Ms. Holland. Do you want me to walk you to your villa?"

"No. The nut with the gun might ambush us again. Alone I've got a better chance of making it."

"Rafaella?"

She turned.

"Thanks. About tonight, listen, I—"

He stalled and she gave him a look so hot it could have fried an egg.

Marcus made a second call to security after another shower, this one to get the sand off. As he'd suspected, they'd had no luck locating anyone, but they'd found a couple of shell casings on the beach. From a Glock-17, Hank, his security chief, said. A Glock-17 was a specialized steel-barreled plastic pistol, small, easy to assemble, easy to haul around, easy to dispose of if the need arose.

As for Ms. Holland, Marcus decided he'd find out all about the lady first thing in the morning.

Who had tried to kill him? He realized he was shaking his head. There'd been three shots from that Glock-17, or maybe four. Surely the killer could have gotten him with one of them. Was it a warning? If so, a warning not to do what?

"Ah, that's wonderful. A bit lower, dear."

Coco obligingly smoothed her fingers past Dominick's waist to his buttocks. "Better?" His skin was remarkably youthful, but he was an older man and there was really no way for him to keep aging at bay for much longer.

The phone rang and Coco picked it up.

"Marcus? Can't you tell me? Dominick is stretched out getting a massage. What happened?"

Dominick took the phone from her. "Yes, what is it?" Coco watched him, knowing well the intense look of concentration in his eyes, the set of his mouth as he learned of things that disturbed him. "I want you over here at the compound until we find out who's responsible."

He listened some more.

"If you insist. But I don't like it. It doesn't make sense. You're right. If the guy wanted you dead, it seems to me you'd be dead. A warning, then. But why? About what? Coco told me she's lunching over there today with a young lady she met yesterday. Tell her anything you manage to remember or learn." He listened again, then hung up.

"Strange," Dominick said, and stretched again onto his stomach.

"What is?" Coco said as she rubbed some more coconut oil onto her palms.

"The young lady you're having lunch with—she was

with Marcus on the beach last night and she hurled herself down on him and saved his life."

"Goodness!"

"Yes, goodness—Ah, deeper, Coco."

"I was thinking, Dominick. This *Bathsheba* thing— did you discover anything?"

"Not yet, but don't worry, my dear. My right shoulder. I'm stiff there. What did you do to me last night?"

"Nothing that you didn't want, Dom. I thought you rather enjoyed yourself."

"If only I'm as lucky as Rockefeller," Dominick said, "when my final time comes."

"Don't say that, even joking."

Dominick raised himself on his elbow for a moment and looked closely at Coco. "You all right this morning? You look a bit pale."

"I'm fine," she said quickly, then smiled and stroked her fingertips over his cheek. His skin was surprisingly resilient. "I'm just fine. Worried, but fine."

He clasped her fingers and kissed them, one by one.

There was the sound of a man's and woman's voices coming toward the gym. Coco looked up to see DeLorio standing there, Paula beside him. Dominick released her fingers and resumed lying on his stomach.

"I heard there was trouble at the resort," DeLorio said. "Someone tried to shoot Marcus."

"That's right," Dominick said. "He's okay, saved by a woman."

DeLorio was wearing tennis shorts, a white T-shirt, and sneakers. His sportsman image was ruined by a sullen mouth, a gold chain around his neck, and a very expensive Rolex on his wrist. Coco had always wondered what Dominick's first wife had looked like. She'd seen a couple of grainy photos, but no portraits, nothing in Dominick's possessions to indicate he'd ever had a wife, nothing except DeLorio, who had dark Italian eyes, even darker hair, thinning a bit on the crown. He didn't have his father's long aristocratic body either. He was shorter, more compact, not fat, but the physical package was one of a longshoreman, not a rich man's son. His thighs in the white tennis shorts were thick and very hairy.

"Merkel wants to know if he can go over with Coco," DeLorio said to his father. "He wants to sniff around a bit, talk to Hank, see if they discovered anything."

"He told you about the thing with Marcus?"

"Yeah. You know he's got spies everywhere."

"Tell him to go if he wants to."

"Who's the woman?"

"Her name's Rafaella Holland," Coco said. "I met her yesterday and she wants to have lunch with me." Coco shrugged. "A groupie maybe."

"Why don't I come along?" Paula said, inching past her husband.

Coco gently shook her head. "I don't think it would be appropriate, Paula. The woman asked me. Let me see what she wants."

"You've become a cynic," Dominick said.

"It's boring here," Paula said.

"Let's play tennis," DeLorio said, and took his wife's hand. "Hear anything else about those Dutchmen, sir?"

"No, nothing."

"I don't want to play tennis."

"You need to, you're getting fat on your thighs."

"Fat! That's crazy, and you're just jealous."

"Oh, yeah? Who is it this time?"

"Marcus—you're jealous of Marcus!"

"Devlin is just a nobody who makes a good employee. Come on, Paula."

Dominick said nothing, merely waited until his son and daughter-in-law were out of his hearing.

"I thought she would be good for him," Dominick said to no one in particular. "I really did. I thought DeLorio would get better. He needs to gain his bearings, to understand his position in the world as my son. He's all I have. A wife should have helped him.

"Paula's family is rich, she attended all the right schools—her father even sent her to a finishing school in Switzerland—and look at her, always whining, never content. Didn't you tell me you saw Link come out of her room really late one night while DeLorio was still in Miami?"

"Yeah, but Link's too old for her. Maybe he was just telling her stories about his bad old days. Another thing. The relationship between the two of them—it works, most the time. DeLorio likes to be the one in charge, and unless I miss my guess, Paula very much likes being compliant, submissive. They sort of fit together."

"Only in the bedroom."

"Perhaps, but it's a start."

Coco also knew that the marriage kept DeLorio away from the female help, but she didn't say that out loud. He was dangerous, this uncontrolled boy in a man's body, and he was a sadist and a bully. For the most part, Dominick seemed to wear blinders where his son was concerned. Only when confronted face-on with his son's viciousness, his savagery, would he control him with equal viciousness. He'd told Coco before that he expected DeLorio to mature, to gain his bearings, to become reasonable, but Coco knew this would never come about. She dug her fingertips into a particularly knotted muscle in Dominick's lower back and he groaned with pleasure.

It was eleven o'clock in the morning and Marcus had already learned a bit about Rafaella Holland by making a simple phone call to Marty Jacobs of the Miami *Herald.* Marty knew everything about everybody and loved to gossip, free of charge. Marty told him about the Pulitzer Prize she'd won—yeah, for the bust of that group of neo-Nazis in Delaware some two and a half years before. So she'd been the reporter to crack that story. Marcus remembered it. After the Pulitzer she'd moved to the Boston *Tribune* and gotten a quick promotion to one of two investigative-reporter spots. He'd heard that she was a looker. Did Marcus want to get her in the sack?—Well, then, he didn't need to tell Marcus anything. . . . Marty had then given him another name and number for more personal stuff. Marcus had found out she was twenty-five or twenty-six, smart, stubborn, sometimes she acted before she thought, the impulsive sort, and she'd just cracked another big story about a guy in Boston who had supposedly axed his family. But he hadn't, as it turned out, the little brother had done it, and she'd found out the truth. She was also illegitimate, a little-known fact. Her mother was very rich and had been very young at the time of Rafaella's birth. The identity of her real father was unknown and likely to remain so.

Her stepfather was Charles Winston Rutledge III, a very wealthy, influential newspaperman, and her mother was currently lying in a private hospital on Long Island, in a coma after being hit by a drunk driver who'd left the scene. The cops were looking for a dark blue sedan, no license number, not even an I.D. on the sex of the driver. Long shot to say the least. When Marcus hung up, he leaned back in his chair and steepled his fingers, tapping them together.

She was here to do a book, was she?

And her mother was in a coma in a hospital?

He wanted to know everything about her. There was a lot happening, too much, and he knew that information might be the only thing to keep him alive. He thought back to *Bathsheba,* the attempt on his life the previous evening—if it had really been a true attempt to kill him—pulled out his cell phone, and dialed Savage in Chicago.

He smiled as he listened to the soft ringing through to Savage's number. Marcus's office had been dutifully bugged for his first six months. Then he'd simply brought the bugs to Dominick and told him it was shit and he didn't like it and he'd quit if Dominick didn't trust him enough, at least as the manager of the resort.

Then, two months later he used his cell phone for the first time in his office. Thanks to the ingenuity of the U.S. Customs Service, his was a very special cell phone, one that couldn't be nabbed by triangulation. They'd also provided him with a past life that would prove out, no matter how in-depth the inquiries. What more could a man want?

Now, every two weeks, he had the office electronically checked for bugs. Trust was fine, up to a point.

"Savage here. What's up, Marcus?"

"Several things, John. I want you to have Hurley or one of his guys find out about a Rafaella Holland, a reporter on the Boston *Tribune*. I've already found out a great deal but I have this feeling there's more, and just maybe that *more* could get me killed. Anyway, see what Hurley can discover. Any word on this *Bathsheba* thing? On the woman, Tulp?"

"Yeah, I was going to call you at our usual time about it. The woman is most likely Frieda Hoffman, from Mannheim, Germany, and an assassin. It gets complicated. She has a reputation for being tough and getting the job done. She asked for and got big bucks. What do you think about that? She matches your description to me, and she's also missing. Hurley's trying to find out who hired her to kill Dominick. I'll let you know when there's any word. Now, *Bathsheba*— nothing like that in Holland, no terrorist group with that name, no big organizations, nothing. Hurley's still checking, though. It shouldn't be too much longer now. Ah, Marcus, Hurley told me he was real glad you didn't let Dominick bite the big one."

"He would be. A bullet's too easy for him. He wants Dominick in prison until the second coming. Oh, yeah, John, I've also been wondering why these folk would want the damned name *Bathsheba* painted on the side of the helicopter. It seems needlessly risky, particularly if the logo could lead back to an organization or to a person responsible."

"Because, my friend, no one was to come out of there alive, at least no one who could possibly have seen the logo. Has Giovanni discovered anything?"

"I don't know. He hasn't told me a thing. He's always polite, but inflexible as a stone. He just puts me off. Anything on Koerbogh and Van Wessel?"

"Little crooks for hire. Even if you had questioned them, according to Hurley, they wouldn't have known a thing."

Then why did they poison themselves?

Marcus rang off, gave Callie some dictation, and looked up to see that it was nearly one o'clock. Rafaella Holland was having lunch now with Coco.

"I'm going to lunch," he said to Callie, and left before she could question him, or sidetrack him, or collar him with more messages.

When he saw the two women together, he knew they were discussing something he wouldn't like. Coco caught his eye and waved to him, then said something to Rafaella.

Her head jerked up and she sent him a look that would make the most intrepid man shake in his shoes.

He grinned, feeling suddenly that the world was a very interesting place to be, and strode over to their table.

Eight

Marcus's timing was rotten, Rafaella thought, frowning toward him. She was sorting through various options when, to her immense relief, a woman approached and handed him a piece of paper. Both Coco and Rafaella watched him read it, fold it carefully, give them a small salute, and leave in the opposite direction.

"Probably another disaster brewing," Coco said. "Marcus can solve nearly any problem, and just about all of them swim directly to him." And then she frowned and Rafaella wondered if she was thinking about the previous evening, if she even knew about it. Rafaella wasn't about to bring it up.

"I'm glad he's out of the way for a few minutes. I really wanted to talk to you, Coco."

Rafaella turned her worship approach on Coco Vivrieux, and saw that even though the woman knew what she was doing, she was more or less succumbing with good grace and some laughter. It was a relief. She felt the urge to be candid and ingenuous, and that worked too. She presented Coco with an autographed copy of her book on Louis Rameau, titled *Dark Horse,* and said simply, "I want to do a biography of Mr. Giovanni, with emphasis on the past two years—in other words, on you, Ms. Vivrieux."

Rafaella bit into a fresh shrimp that she'd dipped into a sauce that held just a nip of horseradish, and chewed slowly as Coco sat there saying nothing, looking mildly worried and more than a little wary. Things didn't look promising.

Rafaella rifled through the pile of photos and clippings from her mother's journals. She picked up one and showed it to Coco. "I love this photo of you taken with Mr. Giovanni coming out of that boutique in the village of St. Nicholas on Crete."

Coco blinked, trying to remember. "Good heavens, how do you know of this? Ah, what a week that was. Do you know there's an island right there called Spinalonga that was a leper colony for centuries? Your collection here is terrifying. Oh, look at this one of Dominick in Paris. Is this how you know about me and Mr. Giovanni?"

Rafaella smiled. "I have just about everything ever written and have just about every photo published of you and of both of you together." *Thanks to my mother's obsession with the man.*

She watched Coco pick up another photo, then another. Some brought smiles, others frowns. Rafaella had carefully culled out those before Coco's current three-year stint with Mr. Giovanni. Also, the articles she'd brought were more social than otherwise, except for two. Finally Coco turned to Rafaella and said with a charming Gallic shrug, "Well, you got me fair and square. I can see you aren't going to let this go. You might as well come to the compound this evening and speak to Mr. Giovanni yourself. Just one thing, though, Rafaella, he will be the one to make any and all decisions."

There was one article she'd brought that spoke of some Senate hearings in the late eighties that had seemed innocuous enough to Rafaella. Coco read it, then paused a moment as she stirred her iced tea, gently moving the sprig of mint. "You know, then, that Mr. Giovanni has enjoyed a rather enigmatic past." She shrugged. "Controversial, if you will. Things like Senate hearings, several indictments—no convictions, of course—one, I believe, on tax evasion and another having to do with political bribes back in the eighties . . . there was even a felony charge a very, very long time ago. Of course, all of that is public record. He's still harassed by American agencies for supposed drug trafficking, which he doesn't do. He's very much against drugs, as a matter of fact. Why I don't know, but he would die before he'd touch drugs. He even sponsors some drug-rehab programs in the U.S. But the Americans don't buy it; they believe it's all lies and hype and they want to bury him. I just want you to know—up front—there are always two sides to everything."

"I understand that," Rafaella said, and added, lying without a qualm, "I had heard that he backed some drug programs." She picked up the other article, handing it to Coco. "My preliminary research has also turned up that Mr. Giovanni is an arms dealer."

Coco glanced over the text. "Oh, yes, but that's all aboveboard and quite legal. He does business with the CIA, but of course, if anyone asked him, a reporter, whoever, he'd refute that he did, point-blank."

"Then he doesn't lean into the gray or the black arms market?"

"Certainly not. He knows the men who do it, but he would never be involved. Roddy Olivier, for example. Now, you want to meet an evil man, a man who makes your skin crawl, go to London and talk to him."

"I understand there are vast amounts of money, depending on the risk you take."

"That's true of nearly everything in life, isn't it? These are questions you must ask Dominick, if he allows them. I really don't wish to say any more about it."

"Is he guilty of those things you mentioned earlier?"

Coco chewed on the sprig of mint even as she smiled. "Of course not. Perhaps he did some foolish things when he was younger, but then again, who doesn't? He's older now, wiser—at least that's what he likes to tell me. He doesn't believe in drugs, as I already told you, wouldn't touch them despite all the money involved, which makes me wonder why the DEA has him on their list. He's a very rich man, Rafaella, and he owns this entire island, not just Porto Bianco. There are also his houses in Paris, Rome, a villa on Crete—near St. Nicholas—and a huge cattle ranch in Wyoming. He's a legitimate businessman, but nonetheless, I truly don't believe he'll want anyone to do his biography. Why would he?"

Coco shrugged again. "But you know men, they're so—well, unpredictable, I guess you could say. So, come to dinner at the compound this evening and ask him yourself."

"I'd like that. Thank you again. Could I ask you, Coco—you speak English with no French accent, yet I've read several interviews about you—this one, for example—and, well, in it you seem very French."

Coco smiled easily. "I do the French routine very well. I've perfected it. You see, I was speaking rather loudly to Marcus yesterday when I met you, and, admit it, if I'd suddenly turned on the French, you would have wondered, wouldn't you?"

"Yes, I would. Thank you for telling me the truth. And your name, Vivrieux? Where are you really from?"

Coco gave her a long, very intent look. "I was born and raised in Grenoble, France. Vivrieux is a very old, respected family name."

"I would love to ski there. I hear it's wonderful. It's nice to have an old family name."

"It is," Coco agreed, the pact made. "Oh, here's Marcus, back again." She waved and Rafaella looked up to see him strolling through the tables on the lanai, pausing to speak to guests, to the waitresses—there were only women serving on the Hibiscus Lanai—then stopping at their table. "Hello, Coco, Ms. Holland.

Are you enjoying our perfect weather? Our chef's perfect concoctions?"

"Certainly, Marcus. Join us. If I know Callie, she hasn't allowed you to eat yet, has she?"

"Nope, that one's a soulless taskmaster." He signaled a waitress, and without asking, she brought him a glass of Perrier, two lime slices on the edge of the glass. He squeezed both slices into the glass before drinking.

"Miss Holland wants to do a biography of Dominick."

Marcus choked on his Perrier.

It was rather disconcerting, the way Coco just said right up front what they'd been talking about. Did this man know everything that went on? "Yes," Rafaella said quickly, "with emphasis on the past few years, since Miss Vivrieux has been with him and since he bought the resort and the island."

"I think not," Marcus said, after he'd gotten his breath. He then turned in his chair to answer a question asked by a man seated behind him.

"Who asked you?" Rafaella said, all but snarling.

Marcus made no sign he'd heard her. He spoke for a few more minutes, then turned back to the women.

"So, who cares what you think?" Rafaella asked.

"Coco will agree with me," Marcus said easily. "There are a few unpleasant things lurking on the horizon. I just don't think it's smart to do something of this nature right now."

"I heard about your scrape last night," Coco said to Rafaella. "Marcus told Dominick that you saved his life."

"It was purely by accident, nothing heroic, I assure you." So, everyone on this island knew everything the moment it happened. Not surprising, not really. "I don't suppose he told you he'd managed to find out who did it?"

Marcus just shook his head and ordered a club sandwich. He turned back to her, and he looked so tough

and hard that she nearly missed the baiting gleam in
his eyes. "Let me be blunt, Ms. Holland. No more
talk about horizons. There's simply too much crap
going down right now. I think you should take your
little fanny—wait, not all that little, if I recall correctly—and go back to the *Tribune* and scrutinize everyone else's business, and, of course, go back to your
very nice apartment in Brammerton and your slew of
boyfriends. They'll surely be more predictable and
more to your expectations."

Rafaella picked up her glass of iced tea and threw
it in his face.

"I was wrong," he said, wiping himself down with a
napkin. "Your fanny is very nice. I shouldn't have intimated that there was more to it than was strictly necessary. I keep forgetting that women are so sensitive. They
just can't take even the smallest objective observation."

"Miss Vivrieux, I would like to come to the compound for dinner this evening. Could you tell me how
to get there?"

Coco told her she'd send someone for her, and Rafaella, not looking again at Marcus, left the table.

"What's going on between you two, Marcus?"

Marcus glanced toward the retreating Rafaella.
"She does have a very nice fanny."

Coco laughed. "Why would she save your life, then
toss tea in your face?"

"Who understands women?"

"Jerks don't, that's for sure."

"Can I come to dinner too?"

"Only if you can promise no more violence. Lord
knows, we've too much of the real sort right now. And
no more baiting Ms. Holland, Marcus."

"Scout's word, ma'am," he said, and solemnly laid
his open palm over his heart.

Merkel was willing enough to play tour guide to Ms.
Holland. The island—called Calypso Island before Mr.

Giovanni had bought it—was just a little over three square miles, roughly two thousand acres, and roughly the shape of a watermelon. They were a leeward island, just west of Antigua, about fifty miles southeast of St. Kitts.

The resort took up the length of the east side, Mr. Giovanni's compound the west side. It was mountainous—as mountainous as any island in the Caribbean could be—and the chain nearly met the sea, end to end. It was covered with lush jungle, very nearly impenetrable because of the heavy rainfall. Here on the eastern side, it rained usually every morning for about thirty minutes, but that was about it. When the island had been at its most productive, a good ninety percent of the population had lived on the western side. The natives had evidently claimed there were evil spirits lurking on the eastern side and avoided it. There was more rainfall on the western side. But you could die of mold rot in the jungle that covered the mountains in the center. The interior was unpopulated and had been for a very long time.

Everything Merkel was telling her in his easy, soft voice, coming out of a football lineman's throat, she already knew. She saw her mother's writing, stark and clear in the beginning of the last volume, dated September three years ago. Her mother had chartered a plane in Pointe-à-Pitre and had the pilot fly her to Giovanni's Island.

I know you'll think I'm unwise at the very least; perhaps you'll believe I'm lost now to all reason and logic. Why am I doing this? I'm happily married—truly I am—to Charles, who's wonderful and kind. Oh, I don't know. But, Rafaella, I had to see his island. I had to see where he lived. The island itself is beautiful, a jewel, lush and tropical, with fine white-sand beaches, north to south, and a range of thick jungle mountains down the center.

Even from the air you can see the luxury of Porto Bianco and the harbor with all its myriad sailboats and yachts. Dominick's compound is on the western side. Perfect for its setting, all the whitewashed cottages, the big house with its red-tiled roof, the swimming pool, the two tennis courts, and the gardens. Ah, the gardens— unbelievably beautiful. When we flew over, I saw men, at least a half dozen, and some of them carried weapons.

I asked the pilot to land on the resort side. I just wanted to have lunch at the resort—I knew Dominick wouldn't be there—but he told me that the island was private, members only, and their guests. A very exclusive place indeed. Of course I could find a way to go there, but not with Charles. I dare not go with Charles. He's not a stupid or imperceptive man. And what would I say if he asked me why I wanted to go there? Unfortunately, I'm a miserable liar, at least to him. Sometimes I think he believes there's another man, perhaps not one with whom I'm having an affair, oh no, but a man somewhere in my past, a man I still think about, a man I still love. And when I see his doubts, the pain they give him, what can I say?

Oh, but I would give anything to see him. Just once. Just for a few minutes. Not long. Just once.

Merkel was still talking as they neared the helicopter pad on the northern perimeter of the resort grounds. "There are three paths that traverse the central jungle, and Mr. Giovanni keeps them clear of undergrowth. In normal circumstances, we use the helicopter, it's only about ten minutes . . . Hey, miss, are you all right?"

Rafaella realized her eyes were suspiciously damp. She sniffed. "Allergies," she said. "Just allergies. A pain in the neck. Oh, yes, I would imagine that the middle ridge keeps curious resort visitors away from the western side." Her mother's pale face rose in her mind's eye. Lifeless, so very still. Her condition was still the same. Charles had told her again that morning on the phone: there was nothing she could do. She shouldn't come back. He promised to call her if it became necessary. He'd said nothing about her being in the Caribbean. She'd lied to him; it was a special story, she'd told him.

"That's right," said Merkel, at his most laconic. "Actually, Mr. Giovanni calls the mountainous area *stoámaco di diávolo*—Satan's gut. He said if you got caught in there, you'd be chewed up in no time, never seen again.

"Look over there—we have a huge harbor for yachts and sailboats. Mr. Giovanni doesn't allow cruise ships, of course. Porto Bianco is a private club, as you know."

Rafaella nodded, then climbed into the front of the helicopter. "You're the pilot?"

Merkel nodded, made certain Rafaella was duly strapped in, gave her earphones, then flipped at least a dozen switches.

"It'll take us only nine or ten minutes. It's a small island—at least for planes and helicopters."

Merkel lifted off, and Rafaella forgot her mission for the moment, too interested in the scenery below. Odd how one really didn't see things until one was a couple hundred feet above. The island *was* shaped something like a watermelon, and Antigua was due west. Dominick Giovanni, she'd read, was a personal friend of the prime minister of Antigua.

When they reached the central point, the resort area was sprawled in beautiful detail from the north to the southern tip. All she had to do was turn her head and see Dominick Giovanni's compound. It wasn't as luxurious or as blatantly opulent as the resort, but it was extensive, the main house vivid white with the ubiquitous red-tiled roof, surrounded by small cottages, all in the same style. There was a huge swimming pool, and all the grounds were covered with fat hibiscus bushes, trellised bougainvillea, thick-branched frangipani, and clusters of purple, pink, and white orchids. The jungle looked to be hunkering at the very edge of the grounds, waiting to leap forward and consume the manicured gardens, a thick green maze that looked shapeless as a nightmare and so thick as to be impenetrable.

Not more than one hundred yards from the compound, through the jungle, was the western side of the island, its beaches covered with white sand, smooth and inviting as sin itself, and aqua and pale green water, incredible and almost impossible to describe. Her mother had described it, but it couldn't truly be imagined from just words, no matter how poetic the attempt.

Merkel didn't say anything. He was used to this reaction from people on their first trip over to the compound. It was why he gave his tour-guide talk before getting to the helicopter. If he waited, no one heard a word he said. He expertly set the helicopter down on its pad, then motioned for Rafaella to look to her left.

"Mr. Giovanni," Merkel said, nodding toward a man coming toward the helicopter. He watched her and found himself wondering just who the hell she was. She was staring fixedly at Mr. Giovanni. Something wasn't quite right about her, but he didn't understand what it was. She was a pretty young woman. And she wanted to write a biography of Mr. Giovanni. Merkel couldn't imagine Mr. Giovanni allowing such a thing. Men of Mr. Giovanni's questionable international stature just didn't give free information to writers. But Mr. Giovanni wasn't like any other man he'd ever known. Mr. Giovanni made his own rules, and he obliged others to live by them. He knew how to control; he knew how to ensure obedience. Mr. Giovanni, in sum, did whatever he wished to do.

Rafaella stared at her father. The trip over had temporarily tamped down on her fear, her excitement, her gut-churning anger at this man for his betrayal of her and her mother.

She knew what to expect. She'd seen more pictures of him than anyone would want to. She was afraid for him to come closer; she was afraid of what she'd feel, of how she'd react.

Where, Rafaella wondered, would her father be a year from now? Maybe in a prison with Gabe Tetweiler? In Attica? She suddenly thought of Charles in that moment, sitting beside her mother's bed, her limp hand held so gently in his warm one. Please don't let her die, she prayed, a litany now. And what would become of Charles Rutledge if her mother died? He loved her so very much. It was frightening.

Her hands grew suddenly damp. She didn't want to wipe them on her new white linen Lagerfeld slacks. Her side-tie red silk blouse got the sweat, even though the outfit was equal to a week's salary. She felt an instant of consternation because she felt her control slipping, her focus blurring. She watched him.

Mr. Giovanni himself walked to the helicopter and opened the pale blue cabin door.

"Miss Holland. Welcome to my home." He offered her his narrow hand and she found herself staring for an instant at it before accepting his assistance. Then she looked directly into her father's pale blue eyes, the exact color of hers. They were tilted upward at the corners, just like hers. But there was no recognition in his eyes. No leap of awareness, of feeling, toward her. She took his hand and stepped out of the helicopter cabin. To her surprise she discovered that in her three-inch white sandals, she was nearly as tall as he was. Somehow she'd thought he'd be taller. But his white linen suit made him look tall and distinguished, with its red handkerchief sticking up in a smart triangle from the breast pocket, the only spot of color on his clothes. There was a thin gold watch on his left wrist and an emerald ring on his right hand.

"Thank you, Mr. Giovanni." She waited again, silently, waited for some spark of recognition, but there wasn't any. Nothing. She was a complete stranger to him, just as her mother had been in Madrid. He didn't see a thing of himself in her, but Rafaella, with eyes tuned to her mother's perceptions, saw herself in his eyes—her eyes—the pale, pale blue, tinged with a very cold gray when emotional, and the tilt of the chin, a sharp chin, one that shot up in anger.

She shook his hand, suddenly feeling more relief than disappointment at his obliviousness of his paternal tie to his daughter. This meant she could satisfy her curiosity without jeopardizing herself. She saw Coco behind him and waved.

"Ah, yes, my Coco is responsible for your being here. But I must confess, Miss Holland, it is sometimes lonely here, and new faces are appreciated." He turned to Merkel. "You're returning for Marcus?"

Rafaella tried not to show that this upset her. Certainly she had enough control not to make a scene if he said something baiting. That she'd lost control twice with him bothered her. It wasn't like her, not the Rafaella Holland who was an investigative reporter for the Boston *Tribune*. She didn't want to slip and lose control, she didn't want to do and say things she hadn't mentally cleared before speaking. She didn't want to lose her bearings. She recognized that there had to be changes in her feelings, in her outlook, in her way of examining things, once she'd stepped foot on the island, her *father's* island. Had she really expected to be immune to her new situation? She moved toward the house, watching the helicopter as it lifted off again, heading back to the eastern side of the island.

"You have a beautiful house, sir. I'm glad I could see it from the air."

"Thank you. Why don't you call me Dominick? And I'll call you Rafaella."

"That would be lovely." Rafaella wasn't all that common a name; if he'd bothered twenty-five years ago to ask once about his daughter, he'd have been told her name. But he hadn't even cared enough to view her in the nursery. He hadn't even cared enough to look at her birth certificate. If he had, he'd have seen that her mother's name was Holland, not Pennington. He'd have seen that he hadn't been named as the father. But he hadn't cared enough to look. He'd dumped a check for five thousand dollars on her mother's bed and walked away. And his daughter had grown up a complete stranger to him. And he to her. Until now. She felt a shock of pain so sharp that she stopped cold, not moving. She felt suddenly open and raw, and fought it with all her strength. She turned and smiled at her father.

The house was cool, airy, and spacious, all glass that gave onto breathtaking views of the Olympic swimming pool, impossibly colorful gardens, lush green arbors, and the spectacular mountain range that backed right up to the property. There were fresh cut flowers on every surface, bringing the sweet, heady scents indoors.

The furnishings were homey, a mélange of brightly painted southwestern chests, armoires, low tables, and white wicker love seats and chairs, nothing of great value except the collection of Egyptian jewelry in glass cases throughout the large living room.

Rafaella knew all about Dominick's collection from her mother's journal. There'd even been a photo taken in London, just outside Sotheby's in 1991. *He's collected—probably stolen—many beautiful pieces, all Eighteenth Dynasty. I've read that this period was overly ornate, in downright bad taste even, but some of the pictures I've seen of items show that they're incredibly beautiful. I should love to hold that translucent green glass goblet, the legitimate one he bought at So-theby's for a phenomenal sum. Perhaps I'll see it, Rafa-ella. Perhaps . . .*

Rafaella was offered a seat and a glass of white wine.

She couldn't seem to take her eyes off her father. Her *father*.

He realized she was staring at him and gave her a crooked smile. "Does something bother you, Rafa-ella? Perhaps you'd like a sweeter wine?"

"Oh, no, the wine is perfect. It's just that I've wanted to meet you for such a long time."

"It's like I told you, Dom," Coco said. "Rafaella knows everything about you and me. She has so many press clippings and photos, even one taken by the papa-razzi in St. Nicholas. Do you remember? I was telling her about visiting that Venetian fortress, Spinalonga, that became a leper colony—"

He interrupted her easily, without noticeable insult, his voice as smooth as the wine she sipped. "My Coco is a history buff. Just how long have I been of such interest to you?"

She met his eyes. "Not long, really. But once a sub-ject catches my interest, I tend to go all-out. Just as I did with Louis Rameau."

Why couldn't he see the resemblance? Why couldn't he see it, damn him? Was this what her mother felt? Disbelief? Deep, deep pain that she was a complete stranger, of no account at all to him? For a moment Rafaella couldn't understand, couldn't comprehend, that he, her father, didn't recognize himself in her. If he knew her mother was lying near death in a coma, what would he say, what would he feel? Nothing, probably. He didn't care, probably didn't even remem-ber, after twenty-five years.

"Ah, come here, DeLorio, I have a surprise for you."

Rafaella looked about and saw a young man about

her own age come into the living room. He was dressed in pale green linen slacks and a white polo shirt with a thick gold chain around his neck. He looked like a mongrel, albeit a well-dressed mongrel. He looked like a work-muscled peasant to his father's aristocrat. He didn't look like his father's son, didn't look like her half-brother.

He was compact, athletic-looking—not a long-legged runner, but a wrestler, all muscle and thick neck and thicker thighs. Rafaella couldn't believe she was looking at her half-brother.

"My son, Rafaella. DeLorio Giovanni. DeLorio, this is Rafaella Holland."

"This is an unexpected surprise." DeLorio smiled at her, and even his smile was unlike his father's. It was predatory and sexual, as if every woman he met was weighed, a value placed on her body, and then assessed as to her compatibility in bed. It was the look of a predator sniffing at its next kill. He stared at her breasts, then at her crotch, finally looked into her face, but only briefly. Her chin went up automatically.

Rafaella didn't rise, waiting for him to come to her, which he did. He shook her offered hand, holding it longer than necessary. She wished she could tell him to go shove it, that she was his half-sister, for heaven's sake.

"It's a pleasure to meet you. Your name is interesting, DeLorio."

"Yes, it is, isn't it?" Dominick answered for his son. "It was my mother's maiden name—her family was from Milano."

"Where's Paula?" Coco asked.

DeLorio shrugged. "Soon."

Rafaella watched him walk to the bar and pour himself a Glenlivet, straight up.

"Hello, all," said Paula, sweeping into the living room. It was a marvelous entrance and Rafaella smiled, wishing she could applaud. She knew a bit about Paula Marsden Giovanni. She was twenty-four years old and hailed from old money. Marsden Iron and Steel of Pittsburgh, Pennsylvania. She was spoiled, selfish, quite pretty, and man-mad, according to the most recent clippings in Rafaella's mother's journal. Paula had pale blond hair and hazel eyes, a very nice combination, distorted a bit by the sullen mouth. She had a nice body, a tan that made Rafaella want to tell her to be careful of the Caribbean sun, it would make her a wrinkled mess by the time she was forty.

"My dear. Come and meet Miss Rafaella Holland. Our guest for dinner—"

"And possibly Dom's biographer, Paula," Coco added, raising an eyebrow at Dominick.

Paula looked at Rafaella Holland and forced a smile. Then she looked at DeLorio and saw that he was staring fixedly at the woman. So she had nice hair and an okay face, so what? The so what, Paula knew, was that DeLorio would pursue anything female for the sheer pleasure of catching and subduing his prey. Violently, if need be and if it pleased him.

"Well, how very nice," Paula said. "I trust Dukey is cooking something edible, for once, since we're so very privileged to have Miss Holland here."

"Dukey is my chef," Dominick said mildly, sipping from his wineglass. "And an excellent cook."

Another man appeared in the doorway. He was tall, wiry, with a thick mess of white hair—premature white hair, Rafaella quickly saw, given the youthfulness of his face. He wasn't above forty and he was black. One of the few natives left on the island?

"Marcus is here, Mr. Giovanni."

"Excellent. Please tell Dukey that we'll eat in fifteen minutes. Thank you, Jiggs."

Rafaella wondered how many men Dominick had in his employ. She'd have to find out. Her mother mentioned in her journal seeing half a dozen. But Rafaella could hardly count on that being accurate. Surprisingly, she hadn't spotted any armed men when the helicopter had come down.

"I beat DeLorio at tennis," Paula said. "Two out of three sets."

DeLorio grunted and poured himself another Glenlivet.

"You must be a fine player," Rafaella said.

Paula laughed. "Not really. DeLorio's attention was wandering again. But it—his attention—always comes back to me."

DeLorio smiled at his wife's remark, and his eyes, so cold moments before, were now filled with warmth. Dark eyes, unlike hers, unlike her father's. Dominick said to Rafaella, "Would you like to see my collection after dinner?"

"Yes, certainly I would, particularly the carved alabaster head of Nefertiti I've heard you have."

He suddenly looked sympathetic and approachable, his entire face softening. He looked human, very human, as he sat forward, smiling. "Nefertiti, huh? That's what you've heard? It could be any of the princesses, my dear. For example, Sumenkhkare. Have you heard of her?"

Rafaella shook her head. "But it is of Nefertiti, isn't it?"

Dominick just smiled, saying no more, but the warmth was still there, his excitement over his collection. He didn't look like a criminal.

Marcus came in, a breath of fresh air, Rafaella was forced to admit. He wasn't wearing a suit, just white slacks and a short-sleeved pullover of pale blue, like DeLorio. He looked fit and strong and full of good humor. He looked uncomplicated and clean-cut. She frowned at herself. He *did* have secrets—she felt it in her very reliable gut—but somehow she didn't think Marcus's secrets were evil or terrifying. He searched her out and winked broadly.

"When does the party begin, Dominick? Has Ms. Holland told you how she slammed me in the shoulder with a karate kick, then landed squarely on top of my poor abused body when the first bullet went over?"

"No, she's very modest. I know only what you told me. He was that easily vanquished, Rafaella?" Dominick turned the full force of his charm on her and Rafaella felt herself leaning into him, wanting his vitality, his interest, wanting the excitement he'd shown her when speaking of his Egyptian collection.

"I caught him by surprise," she said, astonishing herself by her reflex to protect his fragile male ego, not, she thought, that he'd care.

"Other things on his mind, no doubt," DeLorio said, staring at Rafaella, and everyone in the room knew precisely what he meant.

"That's not the half of it," Marcus said, grinned toward Rafaella, and gave her another wink. Then he immediately turned serious. "We've found out nothing about the sniper who took potshots at Ms. Holland and me last night. Not a blasted thing."

"I didn't really think you would," Dominick said with a frown.

"Where's Merkel?" Rafaella asked, changing the subject, suddenly afraid that Marcus would go on to tell them all in the blandest of voices how he'd stripped her naked—before she'd even gotten inside the front door of his villa—and caressed her and kissed her. He wouldn't, would he? She hoped he'd just keep worrying about those shots. She was tired of worrying about him. She felt herself slipping again, and fought to clear her mind.

"Merkel sometimes doesn't eat with the family."

This from Paula, who was looking at Marcus. Rafaella thought of the old song "Hungry Eyes."

"He was very informative on our ride over."

"He's a stupid servant," Paula said. "We don't eat

with the help—at least we shouldn't. I never did at home. My mother didn't allow it."

"Paula, that's enough. There's no place for snobbery at my table. Ah, here's Jiggs. Rafaella, may I escort you into the dining room?"

The table was long enough for twelve people, a chandelier hanging over it, with high-backed brocade covered chairs. On the table there was a huge glass bowl filled with fresh fruit, several platters of broiled yellowtail snapper seasoned with lemon and butter, individual fresh green salads, and fresh baked rolls.

Maria, the serving maid, poured a light chardonnay into everyone's glass, then at a nod from Coco left the dining room, Jiggs beside her.

"Now, everyone," Dominick said, looking at each of them in turn, "what do you think about Miss Rafaella Holland writing my biography?"

Nine

Marcus leaned forward and said, "I wouldn't let her near me with a pen or a computer." He added to Rafaella, "No offense intended."

"I don't want to get near you, Mr. Devlin, not with a pen, not with a computer. Perhaps with a muzzle or a leash."

"Would I be in the book, Miss Holland?" Paula asked.

"Look, Dominick," Marcus said, "it's not a good idea, certainly not at the present time." Surely Dominick couldn't be that great an egomaniac; he couldn't believe himself that invulnerable.

"How do we know you'd treat my father fairly?"

"I've written one biography and it was about a man not all that different from your father. A very charismatic man with power and many enemies. He was ruthless, brave—yet he was also a man prone to human failings, who made mistakes that—"

"He made an unforgivable error because of his vanity," Dominick interrupted smoothly. "I'm speaking, DeLorio, Marcus, of Louis Rameau, a man who was de Gaulle's right hand and one of the leaders in the French resistance during World War II. It was in 1943, I believe, that Rameau decided he had to kill a courier who was bringing special orders from Hitler himself to the SS headquarters in Paris. It wasn't any big deal, Rameau had the courier tracked to Paris, knew exactly where he would be when, so he let a young resistance recruit come with him. To watch him, to observe the great Rameau do incredibly brave things. All in a night's work for the great man. I suspect that he wanted her to admire him so much she'd go to bed with him. Sex was also one of his major appetites. In any case, it went wrong and she was killed. It was an error attributable to his overweening vanity.

"And the moral to the story is that Rafaella is fair in her presentation. She shows us Rameau in all the richness of his character, but she doesn't sacrifice the good things to the bad, or vice versa."

"You've read my book," Rafaella said, charmed by him at that moment and hating herself for it. Vanity, that *had* been Rameau's Achilles' heel, his mortal weakness, and Dominick Giovanni had understood her book better than many esteemed reviewers and critics.

Dominick smiled. "This afternoon, my dear. The copy you gave Coco. It's a pity that his vanity cost the girl her life, a grave pity."

"Rameau forgot the incident, you know," Rafaella said, and her voice was cold as she looked at her father. "He forgot about her because it simply hadn't been important to him. I met a very old man in Paris when I was there doing my research. He remembered the incident and the girl. Her name was Violette and she was only eighteen years old when she was killed. Rameau grieved for her for twenty-four hours, according to the old man, but he didn't feel any guilt for what had happened. Within a month he took another young recruit, and luckily, she didn't die in his need to prove himself a great god living among mortals." *Just as you forgot my mother, forgot me. How soon after did you have another affair with another now forgotten woman?*

"In fact," Rafaella continued, "he fathered a child with her. Her name was Marie Denière. She died right after the war, her daughter with her." She shrugged. "Some men's bastards live on, some don't."

"A pity, of course. But as I said, Rafaella, I thought you were fair. That is what struck me. Your fairness."

"All this is fascinating," Marcus said. "But fair? You, Ms. Holland? Fair to a man?"

"Read the damned book!"

"Marcus, really, my boy, she did save your life."

"For what reason I've yet to discover. I think maybe she saved me just to do away with me herself, in her own fashion." But he smiled as he spoke, and Rafaella found herself shaking her head; then, against her better judgment, as if she really had no choice in the matter, she smiled back. She looked up to see Paula staring at her as if she were a snake trapped against a wall, and she, Paula, was a mongoose, ready to do her in on the spot.

She took another bite of the yellowtail snapper. It didn't taste quite as good as the previous bites.

"It sounds to me like no one wanted to kill you," DeLorio said. "Just scare you. How many bullets were there? Three, four? Surely the guy wasn't that bad a shot. Maybe someone just wanted to bring you down to size."

Like you, shithead? Marcus's smile didn't slip.

"But why?" Rafaella said. "And why do it when I was there? That's what I don't understand."

Coco said, "Maybe you were the one to be scared off the island, Rafaella, not Marcus."

"I don't suppose our jackal realized that you were such a fighter," Marcus said. "My own personal bodyguard. If I'd pointed you in the direction of the guy firing, would you have roared off and ripped the guy's head off?"

"Like a good dog—a good bitch?" Paula said, and forked a slice of mango viciously, all the while smiling sweetly.

Marcus didn't say a word, he was just relieved that

Paula was safely seated on the other side of the table from him, next to her husband. She couldn't reach him from there. Instead she was amusing herself by going after Rafaella. She obviously saw her as a threat. Interesting.

He sat back, wondering if Rafaella Holland would be able to control herself and her fury until the end of the evening. And he'd just begun to launch his strategy of sabotage against her and her confounded plans for Dominick. How could Dominick possibly consider for even one brief moment letting this woman—an investigative reporter—onto the compound to write a biography? He was a criminal, after all. Was his vanity so great, his opinion of himself so hallowed, that he didn't see the threat? Surely even he couldn't be that blind, that egocentric.

Marcus couldn't have cared less if it was Rafaella's intention to nail Dominick. He just didn't want her delving into anything that might interfere with his plans. His own cover could fall like a house of cards if given the right push. "Look, Dominick, we've had too much trouble lately. It simply isn't safe for Ms. Holland to hang around talking about your life and taking your mind off business. Don't do it. I vote no."

"I vote no too," Coco said, "because what Marcus says is true."

"What kind of trouble?" Rafaella asked. "Something other than the shooting last night?"

"Yeah," said DeLorio. "Someone tried to take out my father—and very nearly succeeded."

"I was at the resort," Paula said. "I missed it."

"They locked me in a cabana," Coco said. Both women sounded disappointed.

"We are not taking a vote," Dominick said, "and, DeLorio, this is hardly the time or place to air sensitive family business."

"But you said you wanted to know what we thought," DeLorio said, sullen.

"Yes, and now all of you have been good enough to tell me."

DeLorio looked down at his plate, saying nothing more.

Damn, Marcus thought, staring at Dominick. He was going to let her do it. She'd appealed to his vanity, and the damned fool actually fell for it. He had to stop it. She was the last person he wanted involved in this mess, the last person he wanted interfering and learning things she'd be far better off not knowing. He knew Ms. Holland would probably never forgive him for it, but he also knew his only chance was to launch an attack.

"Did our Ms. Holland here tell you about her Pulitzer Prize, Dominick? She won it for specialized investigative reporting three years ago. She ferreted out a nasty little neo-Nazi group involved not only in the usual racist rhetoric but also in the local political scene. They were bribing local officials, intimidating the town council to pass resolutions they wanted, buying local cops. Those who refused to go along with them enjoyed pain. It was in a little town in Delaware. It took you nearly six months. Right, Ms. Holland?"

"Yes."

"You got threats from these creeps, but you persevered, didn't you? You hung in there, never budging, not once. You talked people into spilling their guts to you, despite the fact that one of them got his ribs broken, his foot smashed, and his face rearranged. I think, Dominick, that our little Ms. Holland, given her record, could be counted on to find out who tried to whack you and me. I can certainly see her digging deep, then deeper still, what with her little-bulldog instincts. Digging where she shouldn't. Digging until folks got hurt or until she did."

"That simply proves that she's good," Dominick said, sitting forward. "Doesn't it, Coco?" Coco shrugged.

"Come now, my dear, wouldn't you like to know

who that woman was?" He was toying with her, but she didn't respond. "I haven't been able to find out who hired her. None of us knows a thing yet about this *Bathsheba.*"

Good God, Marcus thought, did Rafaella simply have to be present for people to spill everything they knew to her? Just listen to Dominick. Marcus said quickly, before Dominick could go on, "Then there's the fact that dear old stepdad just happens to be one Charles Winston Rutledge III, a man who owns several large newspapers and a number of radio stations, a man with considerable clout, and more power than any one man needs. Did he buy your Pulitzer for you? Did he talk to his good old buddy Robby Danforth, the owner of the *Tribune,* to give you the investigative reporter's job?"

Rafaella threw her sliced fresh fruit in his face. She stared at him and thought: *I've lost control again.* She couldn't understand it.

"Not again," Marcus said.

DeLorio shouted with laughter. Coco whispered to Dominick, "Marcus and Rafaella have been going at it all day. She threw her tea in his face at lunch."

Dominick nodded. "All right, enough, Marcus. That's right, wipe the pineapple juice off your forehead and keep your mouth shut." He sat back and tapped his knife handle against the edge of his bread plate. "I'm not stupid, my boy. I checked out Miss Holland. Discreetly, of course, my dear—no need for you to worry or be offended."

"Marcus is right," Paula said. "She shouldn't be here. She's a reporter. She'll ruin you, sir. And I agree with Marcus: her stepfather did everything for her."

"I wouldn't mind her staying here at the compound one little bit," DeLorio said, and gave Rafaella a smile that made her skin crawl. "Since I'm your only son, she'll also need to find out all about me."

Rafaella returned DeLorio's look with one so limpid she thought she'd gag. But she didn't want to alienate him yet. She could handle him.

"I think she should do it, Dominick," Coco said. "But not now. There's too much going down. I'm sorry, Rafaella, but it's just not a good idea."

Rafaella was disappointed. She had been counting on Coco's support.

Then suddenly Dominick raised his hand and cut De-Lorio off mid-sentence. "That's quite enough, I think. Are you through with your dinner, Rafaella?—Good, I'll show you my Egyptian collection now. Some other time I'll show you my art collection. It's rather impressive. When we've finished, Marcus, dear boy, you can escort Rafaella back to the resort, if you please. Take the helicopter."

And that was that.

It was nearly midnight when Rafaella and Marcus were escorted to the helicopter by Dominick, Merkel close behind him.

"It's awfully dark," Rafaella said. "There's only a quarter-moon." She didn't want to climb into a helicopter and place her life in Marcus's hands. She didn't want to place anything of hers in his hands. Not again.

"I'll speak to you tomorrow about my decision, Rafaella." Dominick took her hands in his, leaned down, and kissed her cheek. Slowly, very slowly, she pulled away. "Thank you, sir. Thank you too for showing me your collection. I still think the head is Nefertiti. I look forward to seeing your art collection as well."

He chuckled and stepped back.

Coco, DeLorio, Paula, and Merkel watched from the veranda as the helicopter lifted off, turning slowly, and headed to the mountains.

"Come," DeLorio said to Paula, his eyes on the ascending helicopter. "Now, to bed."

"But I don't—"

"Shut up." He took her hand and pulled her back into the house and up the stairs.

Dominick remained outside. The night was balmy, the air redolent with the scent of hibiscus and bougainvillea and roses. The smell of the sea blended with the scent of the flowers. Coco put her hand through his arm and smiled up at him. "Your son is horny tonight. He just dragged Paula away."

"I don't know, Coco," he said, disregarding her words.

"About letting Rafaella write the book?"

He looked at her closely for a long moment, then shrugged. "That and many other things. Would you like to ease me tonight, Coco?"

She smiled at him and kissed his mouth.

The helicopter lifted into the darkness.

"I don't like this," Rafaella said.

"Trust me. There's plenty of light. Besides, if I screw up, it's not just your hide, but also mine that's on the line here."

"That's supposed to reassure me?"

The helicopter lifted higher, barely skimming the tops of the trees at the back edge of the compound, then climbing another two or three hundred feet.

"I really don't like this," she said again. He merely smiled and dipped to the left, scaring her to her toes. Then he headed nearly straight up, higher still.

"Stop whining."

"If I could pilot this thing, I'd kick your butt out right now. Would you just put a lid on it for ten minutes, until we get back home?"

"Yes, ma'am," Marcus said, grinning at her set profile.

He began whistling. He whistled for only about three minutes. They were nearly over the highest part of the range, nearly one thousand feet, the jungle its thickest at this point, dense and tangled, a maze of green branches and roots and brambles. Suddenly there was a loud popping noise and the helicopter began a wild spin.

"Damn!" Marcus slammed down on the tail-rotor pedals. Nothing. He worked them. Still nothing. No more directional control. He auto rotated, finally bringing the wild spinning under control. He quickly looked below for one of the trails. He saw it, winding and narrow through the jungle. He cut the engine, causing it to sputter, then quickly brought it up just a bit. He headed down.

"What was that? What's wrong?"

He shot a quick look at Rafaella, saw that her face was as white as a sheet, and started whistling again. Everything had happened in less than five seconds.

"No problem," he said.

"Don't lie to me, you fool. What was that banging noise? Why did we spin around like a damned dervish?"

"All right, I've lost control of the tail rotor. That means that we're going down because—Oh, shit!"

The cabin was spinning again, lurching clockwise, and Marcus stabbed at a switch on the controls in front of him as he fought with the stick. He lost sight of the trail.

Rafaella watched, silently, praying with all her might.

Marcus saw the trail again, some two hundred yards to the left. "Ah, there's a trail, thank the good Lord. We're going down, my dear girl. Start praying and make sure your seat belt is tight."

The helicopter was French and thus had fiberglass rotor blades that spun counterclockwise. Without the tail rotor, the helicopter was dragging violently clockwise.

Marcus fought it with all his experience, which hadn't been much in recent years. "We're in deep shit," he said finally. "The deepest. Hold on, we're going down."

He cut the engine power even more. Turn just a bit

more to the left, just a bit, down slowly, hold that
stick steady—Jesus, the cabin was spinning wildly
again. About twenty feet above the trail, he cut the
engine. The main rotor kept turning, but he couldn't
help that, any more than he could help—

There was a sharp rending sound and Rafaella saw
the main rotor slice into the undergrowth beside the
trail and break cleanly, ripping loose from the fuselage. The nose of the helicopter was pointed down,
and when they hit the trail, the skids collapsed, ram-
ming up into the cabin, gashing through the floor beside her feet. The cabin shuddered wildly.

Rafaella thought her feet would be shoved up into
her shoulders; her teeth clinked loudly together, sending pain through her head.

Incredibly, Marcus was still whistling. He calmly unfastened his seat belt. The helicopter became suddenly silent.

"Thank God there was enough moonlight to see the
trail. Thank God Dominick keeps them cleared.
Thank God you had me. Now, Rafaella—"

The cabin gave one final shudder and suddenly
kicked up on one side when the right-side skid pushed
through the floor on the pilot's side of the cabin.

"Well, how about that?" he said, more to himself
than to Rafaella, who hadn't moved, hadn't said a
word. He saw that she'd opened her eyes.

"Hi, we're safe."

"I don't believe you."

He pulled loose his seat belt, leaned over, and
hugged her, squeezing her until she grunted. "I promise we're safe. See, you squeaked, you're alive." He
kissed her cheek and flipped open the clasp on her
seat belt.

"I squeak, therefore I am. You're blessedly literate,
you know that?"

"Let's clear out of this thing. I don't think it's going
to blow, mind you, but I'd just feel better if—"

She was out of the helicopter in a flash. He followed her, coming around the back of the helicopter, laughing, but just for a moment. The main rotor had ripped cleanly from the fuselage and it lay against the tailbone like a broken ice-cream stick.

He paused only a moment to look at the tail rotor.

He took Rafaella's hand and ran toward the side of the trail.

"I didn't think that trail would be wide enough," she said, staring back at the helicopter.

"It wasn't. We were lucky as hell. That, and, you see, it's a French helicopter, and the main rotor is fiberglass. It breaks clean usually and doesn't do much fussing around." He pulled her against him and hugged her tight. "It's all right. It's over now."

Rafaella pulled back. "Are you talking to yourself? I'm not the one in danger of nervous collapse here."

"Even though your eyes were closed tighter than a corpse's?"

"That's what I thought I was going to be." She shuddered and made no further move to get away from him. Comfort, whatever the source, wasn't to be scorned at this particular moment.

"Was that an accident?"

"I can't be sure until I go over it," Marcus said, his voice sounding oddly cheerful to Rafaella. "Sometimes even careful examination can't tell you what went wrong. Maybe it was an accident, maybe not. If someone did tamper with the helicopter, they were very good and very precise, calculating that it would go out of control exactly when it did, right over the highest point of the island."

"What do you mean you might not be able to tell? It's just a damned machine."

"Yeah, and it's got literally thousands of bolts and nuts. I think that a bolt came loose in the tail rotor, because I lost all control with the pedals after that loud banging sound. Did someone loosen it? Probably.

Merkel is a sterling mechanic, fanatic about preflight checks with the helicopter."

"This sucks."

"No argument out of me on that one. Now, Ms. Holland, we have a couple of choices. We can either stay—"

"Let's go home."

"All right."

At that instant there came a loud roaring sound. Rafaella jerked back, hitting Marcus in the stomach. "What was that?"

"A wild boar, perhaps. Maybe a lion or a cougar."

The sound came again.

"Actually, I haven't the foggiest idea."

"I think I'd like to spend the night in the helicopter."

"All right. But you know, I can't be sure what brought it down. It could, I suppose, still blow, but—"

Rafaella turned, her hands on her hips. "Just look at my outfit—it's Lagerfeld, dammit. It cost me nine hundred and fifty dollars and it's bloody well ruined, all because you can't drive a damned helicopter. And now you tell me we can't do anything, that we're—"

"Nine hundred and fifty dollars? You spent nearly a thousand dollars on those pants?"

Her once-pristine white slacks were stained with dirt, sweat, and oil. Where the oil had come from, she hadn't the remotest idea. She looked up at Marcus. In a move reminiscent of the previous night, she braced herself, grabbed his arm just above his elbow, and flipped him onto the middle of the dirt trail on his back.

He just lay there sprawled out, arms and legs flung away from his body, and looked up at her. "I think I would have preferred another bowl of fruit in my face."

"Oh, to hell with you," Rafaella said, and offered him her hand. She tried to jerk it back, remembering how he'd pulled her down the previous evening, but she was too late. Down she went, sprawling over him.

"Hi. How's tricks? You kept your head. I like that. I'll tell you something. I do think someone tried to do me in again. With you in attendance, which means that your popularity is at an all-time low, along with mine. Who do you think it was?"

She pushed upward so she could see his face. "During the evening when I was oohing and aahing over Dominick's Egyptian collection, someone sneaked out and sabotaged the helicopter?"

"Nicely put. Yes, that's what would have happened if someone did sabotage us. Whoever it was probably removed a bolt on the tail-rotor control. Who? You're the hotshot reporter."

"Paula. She's vicious and she hates me."

"Yes, but she adores me. And since I was the pilot, she wouldn't have chosen that way to rid herself of you. Arsenic in your wine, perhaps. But she wouldn't off me, not when she wants me in her bed. Besides, what Paula probably knows about tampering with a helicopter wouldn't fill a thimble. No, all her knowledge involves men and their vices and urges, and her own, of course."

"You sound like you know all about it."

"I do, sort of. She caught me once when I was in bed, helpless. I'd been laid out with a bullet—" Marcus broke it off. Here he was spilling his guts to this damned woman, just like everyone else. He was as weak in the head as they were.

"What bullet? When?"

He didn't answer, merely jerked upward, rolling her off him. "You should see your nearly thousand-dollar slacks now."

"The whole outfit was nine hundred and fifty dollars. The slacks can't be more than six hundred. When we find out who did it, that jerk can buy me a new

pair. How about DeLorio? Now, he doesn't adore you.
He hates your guts."

"That's my guess. The kid's—"

"Oh, come on, Marcus. You're not exactly an old
man. What are you, thirty-two?"

"Nearly thirty-three, and DeLorio is twenty-five. He
is a kid to me. He's spoiled, sadistic, probably verging
on being psychopathic, and he hates and fears authority. He likes to dominate women completely—probably something to do with his mother—"

"Who was his mother? What did she do to him?"

He opened his mouth to tell her, then clamped it
shut. Spilling his guts again, dammit. "Here." He gave
her his hand, careful to brace himself, and pulled her
to her feet.

Rafaella was looking at the helicopter. "We could
have died."

"Maybe, but I don't think we were meant to croak.
If I wanted to kill someone, I wouldn't take the chance
with a helicopter—you just can't be certain enough of
the outcome. Anyway, I like the notion of DeLorio
doing something, but then again, I don't think he
knows anything about sabotaging a helicopter."

"Do you think he was the one who tried to scare
you off—his own words from this evening—or very
nearly?"

"It was like a confession of intent, wasn't it? Who
the hell knows? In his case I suppose you have to
believe in bad genes. His grandfather, his mother—"

"More likely from his father's side."

"What's this? Some unexpected bile? I thought you
were overflowing with feminine reverence and awe for
Dominick. Admiration shone from your beady little
eyes this evening." He turned away and kicked at the
helicopter. "Of course," he added, not turning, "you
are very possibly not at all what you claim to be."

"I thought you checked me out thoroughly, as did
Mr. Giovanni. What could I be hiding?"

He turned and grinned at her. "No, I won't say it. I'll be the soul of discretion."

Rafaella didn't attack. "Go to hell," she said, and stomped off down the trail.

"Careful of the mountain lions!"

Ten

Rafaella took two steps. She turned around very slowly, to see Marcus standing in the middle of the trail, his arms crossed, grinning.

"There aren't any mountain lions in the Caribbean," she yelled. Unable to help herself, she actually shook her fist at him. "They would have had to swim here, that or be brought over like the mongoose."

Marcus knocked a clod of dirt off his arm. "Dominick is a very wealthy man. He also likes his privacy. He brought over lions and wild pigs, boars, and a couple of snakes—boa constrictors—and other assorted intimidating creatures to discourage foot communication between the eastern side of the island and the western. There's a sign posted on the resort side."

Despite herself, Rafaella began walking back toward him. "You're lying. That's absurd. He could just post No Trespassing signs. He wouldn't bring in wild animals."

"That's exactly what the signs do say. The wild animal warning is in the fine print at the bottom of the signs. Dominick likes uncertainty in life."

"That's absurd," she said again, but sounded less certain this time. "What if the animals decided to wander all over the island? What if an animal attacked a guest? Just think of the liability. And besides, even if the animals stayed put, who in his right mind would even want to walk from the resort to his compound?"

"You're on your feet, aren't you?"

"Buffoon," she said under her breath, then turned on her heel and started away from him again.

"Do be careful to stay on the trail," he called after her. "Those boas are fat and are perfectly willing to get even fatter. You'd be a succulent morsel, particularly in that snazzy outfit. A dirty but classy meal."

There was another horrendous snorting sound, just off to Rafaella's left. A wild pig? A wild boar?

Rafaella froze in her tracks, then sighed. "Better the tame bore," she said, and chuckled. It was better than gnashing her teeth. She turned around and walked back to Marcus.

"Do you have a gun?"

"Yep. In the helicopter."

He didn't move.

"I'm obviously in your power. What do you want to do? It's still early— . . . well, maybe not all *that* early. Do you want to stay here or go back to the resort?"

All right, he thought, it was time to stop screwing around; it was time to get serious. There were wild animals, but not a single one of them was loose. Dominick kept a private zoo just about a half-mile to the south. The animals had lots of territory to roam, but they were watched and fed and fenced in. And Rafaella had believed him. She hadn't wanted to, but she had. He was hard pressed not to laugh. He wasn't about to tell her the truth about the animals, not yet.

He said, his face as serious as his voice, "Let's stay here. I want to examine the helicopter in the morning. If someone did tamper with it, I don't want to give him or her the opportunity to come and try to cover it up."

She shrugged. "Okay."

He opened the door to the passenger side of the cabin. "Would you like to go in and slip into something more comfortable?"

"I'd rather cozy up to any other reptile than you."

"Reptile?" He looked startled, then laughed and helped her inside. When he joined her in the pilot's seat, he pulled her against his shoulder. "Go to sleep if you can."

"Will someone realize you didn't come back and get worried?"

"No. Will some guy miss you?"

"Don't be an ass. Well, maybe five or six guys."

"Tough not being an ass, but I'll try. Go to sleep."

She tried for about five minutes. "Marcus?"

"Yeah?"

"No one's ever tried to kill me before. I don't like the way it feels."

"I don't like the way it feels either. At least you don't have to worry right now, we're safe and snug. All we need is a fire and some marshmallows and it would be just like camp."

He never lost his humor for long, she thought, and wanted to poke him in the ribs, but didn't. "I liked summer camp when I was a kid. I could row a canoe really well and start fires and hit a target pretty consistently from twenty-five feet with my bow and arrow."

"I liked camp too. My mom sent me to a Boy Scout camp when I was thirteen. I got poison ivy but it was still fun. I had sex for the first time. Her name was Darleen and she had huge breasts and she was seventeen and a counselor for the Girl Scouts just across the lake."

"I had my first crush at camp when I was twelve. His name was Marty Reynolds and he was the only cute guy who didn't wear braces. I only let him kiss me, but it wasn't fun. How did you get the poison ivy?"

"In the woods, collecting wildflowers with Janie Winters. She didn't wear braces either, but I did. It isn't much fun kissing when you've got a mouth full of steel. Darleen didn't wear braces, obviously."

"My mom didn't like camping, so to be perverse, I

went to camp until I was sixteen. Did you camp out
with your dad?"

He stiffened and all the fun went out of his voice.

"No. My dad died when I was eleven. Even before,
he wasn't the kind of man to take off his glasses and
get dirty."

"I'm sorry." A raw nerve, she thought, and kept the
rest of her questions to herself. "I never had a dad."

"I know. At least you didn't until your mom married Charles Rutledge III when you were sixteen."

She jerked away from him, pulling on his arm to
make him face her. "What do you mean, you *know*?"

"You're illegitimate, so what? We both spent our
teenage years without a father and we both survived.
You're awfully pushy, you've got a smart mouth, and
perhaps a father would have curtailed that in you, but
who knows?"

"Did you tell Mr. Giovanni?"

He frowned at her even as he shook his head. "I
didn't think it was relevant." He shrugged. "If he does
a check on you, he'll find out anyway."

"Yes, I suppose you're right."

"Would you like to tell me something incriminating,
Ms. Holland? Any little thing I could use to get you
off this island and back to your safe little harbor in
Boston?"

"No. And Boston's anything but a safe little harbor.
Forget it, Marcus. I don't have a single skeleton in
my closet."

"Sure, and we'll see pigs flying overhead any minute. Go to sleep, Ms. Holland."

"I'll bet you still dream about Darleen."

"To a boy of thirteen, she was the best, the most
wonderful, the sweetest—"

"Go to sleep, Marcus."

Marcus tried to get comfortable, and he did, but
still sleep wouldn't come. He was worried, but more
than that, he found himself thinking that he quite liked

her smart mouth. She was sleeping deeply, her breathing even and deep. He should have asked her if she still liked to camp out. Perhaps, someday, he could ask her that, once his life was his own again.

Marcus stood up and wiped his hands on his dirty pants. "I can't tell," he said. "I really can't. We need an expert, and that, unfortunately, isn't possible."

"How about Merkel?"

"He could take a look, but he's just good, like me, not an expert. We might as well get going. You up for a long walk?"

It wasn't, in fact, such a long walk. They reached the resort at seven-thirty in the morning, sweaty, dirty, their clothing ripped, but otherwise, in Marcus's opinion, they just looked like a couple of lovers who'd gotten carried away. Not a couple who'd walked away from a crashed helicopter on the middle ridge, one half of the couple worried that a lion was going to pounce at any moment, and the other half of the couple thinking he should tell her the truth about the animals, but not doing so.

Marcus stopped her before she turned off the path to her villa. "You're a good sport," he said. "Do I smell as rank as you do?"

"As rank as a mountain goat. Lord, it's hot. I feel like the humidity's eaten through my skin."

Rafaella was walking across the pale gold-and-white marble floor in the bathroom to pour Chanel bubble bath into the Jacuzzi within three minutes of closing the front door. She turned on the gold faucets full blast. In another two minutes she was sprawled in the hot water, her mother's journal in her hand, open to a September 1997 entry.

I've always loved Christmas. So many of my happy memories are of you and me on Christmas morning, me with my coffee and croissant, you with your huge bowl of Cap'n Crunch and hot cocoa. Remember that year I got you that huge stuffed giraffe? I think it was 1981. You named him Alvin, as I recall.

Since I've been married to Charles, Christmas is more complex, I guess you could say. Not richer—ours were that; no, just more complicated, more unpredictable. My stepson, Benny, married Susan Claver in 1994, the year you graduated from high school. There was a baby at Christmas the next year. You haven't seen little Jennifer in a very long time. She's not quite so cute now as she was then.

Why am I prosing on about Christmas? Who cares, really? Charles gave me an incredible ruby-and-diamond ring, five carats of diamonds, on that Christmas of 1994. I didn't like to wear it. I'm always afraid that I'll lose it. It bothers Charles because he wouldn't care if I lost it. He truly wouldn't. He just wants to make me happy.

I tell him he does. I tell him all the time how much I love him. I exhaust him showing him how much I love him. It's funny sometimes about our sex together. He treats me like a Victorian maiden whose sensibilities couldn't take oral sex. Once I went down on him and I thought he would expire on the spot. He looked at me like I should faint rather than love him like that. Strange, isn't it? Dominick always—Oh, no, no more about him!

Sometimes I sense that Charles is looking at me and I sense he doesn't believe me. I realize that he can't know about Dominick. I would never, never tell him. I keep my journals well hidden. He'll never know.

I sometimes think that I would give almost anything to have had one Christmas with Dominick. But there wasn't one. There was the Fourth of July when I was twenty and he told me he loved me, and that was about it. Of course when I was pregnant with you and he made his trips back to see me, he didn't make Christmas. He was with his wife, naturally. The only gift he

*ever gave me was you, my darling. You and that check
for five thousand dollars. The bastard.*

Rafaella fell asleep in the tub with the jets still going
full blast. She came awake abruptly at a noise, her
eyes flying open.

Marcus was standing over the tub.

Rafaella's roommate at Columbia had told her that
it was unnerving the way she came instantly and completely awake. She did so now. Her eyes narrowed on
his face, but she made no sudden jittery moves. She
wouldn't let him get her goat again, not this time.

"What do you want?"

"To see if you're all right. I knocked, but no answer.
I got a bit worried." He'd been looking at the book
on the ledge beside the tub. It was the same one he'd
seen her with that first night when he'd found her
crying.

"I'm just fine. Now, get out of here."

"Did I tell you that I like the way you're put together? No tan, but I'm not complaining."

The bubbles from the bubble bath were long gone.
"Would you just get the hell out of here?"

"You sound angry. I can't imagine why. I'm just
being politely interested and nonjudgmental. As I was
saying, you don't have much of a tan—but I like that
white stomach of yours."

She looked at him dispassionately, an eyebrow
cocked. "What is this? I didn't think you took the
final plunge. You just like to dominate, to humiliate,
to prove what sexual power you have."

"This time I'd like to make an exception," he said,
not taking his eyes off her. "After all, we've been out
on several dates now. I just didn't want you to think
I was too easy. A man needs his respect, you know."

He hooked his thumbs under his waistband and his
shorts. He grinned at her and started pulling them
down.

"All right, stop it, you ass!"

He stopped, then pulled his shorts and pants back up. "I so dislike the teasing-woman bit. I was just being cooperative."

"If you don't want me to throw every drop of water in this tub on you, get out, Marcus. Now."

"I've already seen it all, and—" He got a sopping wet washcloth in the face.

"Rafaella! Are you here?"

Rafaella groaned. It was Coco. Marcus was calmly wiping his face with one of her towels and fastening his pants with the other. She quickly got out of the tub, ignoring him, and wrapped herself in one of the soft-as-sin Egyptian-cotton bath sheets.

"Just a minute, Coco!"

"Hi, Coco. We'll be out in just a minute."

Rafaella knew startled silence when she heard it. Then: "Marcus? Is that you? In there? With Rafaella?"

"I'm just wiping the water out of my eyes, Coco. Don't come in. You'll embarrass Ms. Holland. She's already blushing from her eyebrows to her toes."

"I'm going to kill you," Rafaella said. "With a rock, I've decided. I'm going to pound you all over with a rock. Then I'm going to gut you like a yellowtail snapper. I'm going to debone you and then—"

"Coco is a very curious lady. I suggest you get your robe on. Use the one the resort provides. It covers up just about everything but it manages still to be real sexy. The resort provides different colors, you know. With your coloring, I'm guessing the robe is either a very dark green or a soft pale yellow."

"Then I'm going to skin you, or is 'flay' a better word?"

"With your tongue or with a knife?"

"Marcus? Rafaella? What are you—? Are you in the bathroom?"

"Yes, Coco," Rafaella called. "Please sit down. I'll be right out."

"Me too," Marcus said, and tossed the hand towel to her.

He left the bathroom and Rafaella heard him say, "Good morning, Coco. Why didn't you come to my villa? Why Rafaella's?"

"Dom told me about the helicopter. I wanted to see if you were all right. I did go to your villa first. Then I even went to the gym and talked to Punk. Did you see that stripe in her hair? It's mint green."

"Yeah, the banker from Chicago didn't like the yellow, so she had Sissy change it. So, then, Coco, you figured I'd be here, with dear Rafaella?"

"What are you doing here?"

"He's a lousy Peeping Tom," Rafaella said, stomping into the sitting room. She pulled the sash tighter on her pale yellow satin robe.

"I think I'd prefer the dark green robe on you," Marcus said, rubbing his chin with thoughtful fingertips. "Not that this one isn't nice, mind you."

"Marcus, a Peeping Tom?" Coco stared at Rafaella with a blank expression that said it all. Not only didn't Coco believe her, Rafaella knew she was hard pressed not to laugh.

"Rafaella's good," Marcus said to Coco, nodding with grave understanding. "Quite good. More of the dominatrix than I usually like, but still she's enjoyable. Hey, what's a little pain?"

Rafaella turned her back on him. "This thing with the helicopter, what—?"

"I don't know anything. Marcus called Dominick a little while ago. Merkel flew over in the other helicopter to get some equipment that was here at the resort. I came with him. He's taking one of the motor scooters back to the wreck to check things out."

"It wasn't an accident," Rafaella said. "Marcus thinks someone probably loosened a bolt on the tail rotor."

"That's what I told Dominick," Marcus said. "An-

other scare tactic," he added to Coco. "And it worked,
I don't mind admitting. But it's damned odd."

"What is?"

"Your reporter's genes getting fired up, Ms. Holland? No, don't curse me out. What's odd is that
someone would begin now to scare me off. It doesn't
make any sense. I've been here over two years. Why
now?"

"It's obvious that you did something recently that
scared someone," Coco said. "What could it be?"

"I don't know, but that's a good point."

Rafaella looked from one to the other, shaking her
head. "I don't believe this. You're talking about it as
though it were something about as important as the
weather. We could have been killed. Someone *tried* to
kill us! This is very serious, at least to me. Doesn't
anything shake you guys up?"

"Of course it's serious," Coco said. She paused,
frowning. "Or," she continued slowly, "as I said last
night, someone could be trying to scare off Rafaella.
She's been involved both times."

"We think it was DeLorio," Rafaella said to Coco.

Coco looked thoughtful. "Plain speaking, then. De-
Lorio doesn't like Marcus, that's for sure. He's jealous
of him." She paused a moment, then laid her hand on
Marcus's arm. "It's not because Paula's so obvious
about wanting to get in your pants. It's Dominick and
the very real affection he has for you. I've heard again
and again that all Dominick wanted to do was to build
his dynasty. And all he got was DeLorio, whose
mother was—Well, he doesn't really like his son, and
he's tried to. He realizes it's his responsibility to like
him. His duty. You know that, Marcus. I wouldn't be
at all surprised if DeLorio was behind both the helicopter and the gunshots on the beach the other night.
He wants you out of the picture. You're a threat to
him. Maybe he sees Rafaella as a threat too."

Marcus was staring at Coco. She'd just spilled her

guts to Rafaella, like all the rest of them. It was un-
canny. He started to say something, but Coco interrupted him.

"Rafaella? What's the matter? Did that crash really
shake you up?"

"Oh, no. Would you like some breakfast, Coco? I
can order something and the two of us can sit out on
my veranda and enjoy the early morning and—"

"I'd like some dry toast, please," Marcus said. "And
lots of coffee."

Rafaella walked to the door, opened it, and said,
"My knee is itching, Marcus, it truly is. I suggest you
take yourself off while you're still intact."

"She doesn't like talking afterward," Marcus remarked matter-of-factly to Coco. "No gentleness, no
sweet little nothings whispered about whether it was
as good for her as it was for me, no smoking a cigarette—"

"Out. Now, Marcus."

He nodded to Coco, walked to the door, then at
the last minute grabbed Rafaella and kissed her hard,
then was gone.

Rafaella slammed the door shut. She could hear him
whistling through the open window.

"I've never seen Marcus like this," Coco said. "He's
got it bad."

"He's got what? Oh, no, Coco, all that is just show,
it means nothing. He likes to bait me, and I'll admit
he knows exactly which buttons to push."

"Come on, Rafaella, you've already been to bed
with him. I can tell; it's how you look at each other.
Your eyes give you away—that intimate look." She
shrugged, a very Gallic gesture. "And Marcus, he's
hard on women, but he's got something and you want
it. It's—oh, what the hell!" She gave Rafaella a wicked
grin, shook her shoulders in another very French shrug,
rolled her eyes, and grinned. "*Un homme avec, ah, un*

certain je-ne-sais-quoi." She shrugged again. It was incredible.

"That sounded completely legitimate."

"Of course. My name is Coco Vivrieux and I was born and raised in Grenoble."

"Yes, a wonderful place to ski. But seriously, Coco, you're wrong. We haven't had sex together. I swear it." It sounded like the truth because it was, and Coco bought it, temporarily.

"All right, I believe you. But—" She shook her head. "This whole thing is very strange. Now, my dear girl, the reason I'm here is to invite you over to the compound. Dominick has decided to let you do his authorized biography."

Easy. Just that easy. Rafaella couldn't believe it. So easy. Now what was she going to do? *You're going to get him to tell you everything and you'll get him to let you see his papers, to show you things no one else has seen, and you'll get him to trust you and then you'll publish a book that will blow the damnable bastard out of the water.*

No, she was the bastard. He was the bastard's father. And she was going to have her revenge, she was going to take her mother's revenge, and it would be in print and it would be there forever to haunt him. It would be sweet revenge.

She'd bet he'd even sent weapons and parts to Iraq. She'd expose him, oh indeed she would. Probably he'd sent Russian Kalashnikov automatic rifles and RPG-7 grenade launchers to North Korea. She wouldn't even be surprised if he'd sent RPK light machine guns and those 38/46 heavy machine guns to Libya's Muammar Qaddafi, one maniac that most arms dealers claimed they'd never deal with, according to the research she'd done. She was rather pleased that she still remembered the names of some of those weapons. Suddenly she had an image of herself introducing Dominick to Charles Rutledge.

"*I'd like you to meet my real father, Charles. He's an arms merchant. He claims he's white-market but it's a lie. He's very smart and very shifty, so folks don't know much about him, but he's as black-market as they come. This is only his latest venture into crookdom. I'll tell you so much more in my book. To know him is to love him. Just ask my mother; just ask your wife.*"

Yes, Rafaella was certain that Dominick got State Department clearance once for every six crooked deals. She'd nail him but good. He could still live on his damned island, but he'd never again dare to leave it. She must check to see if there was an extradition treaty between Antigua and the United States.

"Rafaella?" Coco snapped her fingers in front of Rafaella's face. "Where are you?"

Rafaella forced a grin. "Oh, no place very exciting."

"Is it Marcus that's responsible for your swoon?"

"Swoon? Good God, no."

"You know, Rafaella, Marcus was right about one thing. Perhaps it isn't the best time for you to be here writing this book. Maybe it would be better for you to go back home until all the mystery is cleared away."

"Coco, I love mysteries, and this one's a corker. You ready for some breakfast?"

Marcus held the phone tightly. "I don't like it, Dominick." Actually he was worried to death, but he couldn't come across that strong.

"Sorry, my boy, but I've made up my mind. How's your shoulder? You didn't hurt it in the crash, did you?"

"No, everything's fine. Did Merkel find anything?"

"No, not a bloody thing. It could have been tampered with or it could have been an accident. If it makes you feel any better, Merkel agrees with you. Sabotage more than likely. And I don't like it any more than you do. Also, Miss Holland was with you both times."

"Don't do it, Dominick. I don't trust her, but more than that, why risk her life? Send her away for the time being. She really isn't—"

"Look, Marcus, you've told me everything you know. I told you what I'd found out. She's a smart girl, she's published a biography, so there's no cause to doubt her credibility. She's got ambition—she didn't use any of Rutledge's clout, and undoubtedly he offered."

"Still, something just doesn't feel right to me about her, and—"

"Look, Marcus, bottom line, she's still just a woman. If I don't like what she writes, well then, maybe I can use her in another capacity. I don't particularly like her aggressiveness, but her body is quite satisfactory. Perhaps I'll try her out in bed. A woman, Marcus, that's all she is. Do keep your perspective, my boy."

"She isn't like Coco or Paula," Marcus said, his voice amazingly neutral even as anger surged through him. Had Dominick lost it completely? An assassination attempt and two other attacks? What if they'd been on him? Would he bleat about scare tactics? Damnation, what a mess.

"No, not on the surface. Who knows? That pushy mouth of hers just might add a bit of spice to things, to a lot of things. Stop carping."

"Her mother's in a coma in a hospital on Long Island. It was a hit-and-run, a witness said, and the guy driving the other car was weaving all over the highway. I just found that out this morning."

There was a long unbroken silence on the line.

"Don't you think it's strange, Dominick, that she'd be here when her mother just might be dying?"

The silence continued.

Marcus sighed. "You think about it. If you still want her to stay at the compound, I'll bring her over this evening."

"Use one of the motor scooters. I don't want you in a helicopter again anytime soon. Besides, now I've got only one that's operational. I can't spare it." Dominick chuckled and Marcus frowned into the phone.

"Okay. Think about it."

"Good-bye, my boy. Oh, by the way, Marcus, you might consider not mentioning what you learned to her. There are a few more things I want to work out. Leave it all to me."

Marcus hung up the phone and leaned his head back in his chair. He wasn't so sure it was all that smart to have told Dominick about Rafaella's mother. He just wanted her off the island. He didn't want her hurt or dead. But there was no reason for Dominick to hurt her unless—The thought of her in bed with Dominick wasn't a pleasant one. One thing he knew for sure: Rafaella Holland would never willingly go to bed with Dominick Giovanni.

He finally managed to shake the thought out of his mind. Almost immediately the Dutchmen came into focus. He couldn't forget them, couldn't forget that they'd poisoned themselves. But why? To the best of Marcus's knowledge, Dominick had never resorted to torture. DeLorio—now, that sadistic little son of a bitch was another story entirely. But, dammit, he'd been in Miami, supposedly meeting with Mario Calpas. About drug trafficking? Against Dominick's express orders? He remembered the one and only incident when DeLorio had acted on his own and pulled off a drug deal with some Colombians. DeLorio had gotten off scot-free but the DEA had found out enough about the deal to blame Dominick and they'd sworn to get him. DeLorio had made a cool quarter of a million dollars on the deal. Marcus had watched Dominick burn each one-hundred-dollar bill in front of his raging son. He wondered then if DeLorio would snap, but he hadn't. It was later that one of the servant girls, a teenager from Antigua, had been found raped

and beaten. The girl swore she didn't know who had
done it to her. She'd been paid off and shipped back
to Antigua. Marcus had no doubt it had been DeLorio. Dominick had never said a word, merely com-
mented it was high time for his son to marry and
he knew just the young lady who would suit his and
DeLorio's requirements.

Marcus's thoughts veered back to the first assassination attempt. All the checking around about those
Dutchmen had led to nothing concrete. Dominick had
many competitors, fierce competitors, in arms dealing.

Marcus knew that as the white market had dwindled
markedly during the 1990's, the gray and black markets had become bloated with business opportunities.
Antonio Cincelli, a powerful dealer in Italy, for example. He'd come awfully close to being busted by the
Italian police just last year when it was discovered that
a small southern Italian weapons manufacturer he
used was shipping mines and other weapons to Iran.
Cincelli had gotten off, but he'd blamed Dominick,
among others, for the fiasco, and sworn, quite graphi-
cally, to shoot his balls off. Marcus himself had wondered if Dominick had tipped off the Italian police,
used his influence in the corrupt government; but he'd
never found out for sure.

Then there was Oscar C. Blake, an American citizen
born in Munich, Germany, who worked for and
around the CIA, buying mostly Soviet-style weapons
because they were less easily traced to the U.S. and
they were cheap. He was a hard nose, a real professional who claimed everything he did was just business. Never anything personal. Who the hell knew?
Marcus didn't. Nor could he dismiss Roddy Olivier.
Talk about a ruthless psychopath. And powerful, so
powerful it boggled the mind. He and Dominick had
discussed these men and a good half-dozen others. All
powerful men; all ruthless and determined. They

called themselves businessmen, but the kind of hard-ball they played was deadly.

What did *Bathsheba* mean? Why the devil couldn't anyone trace that helicopter? Or that ridiculous name?

Odd, but Marcus would give more to understand that than he would to know the name of the man behind the attack on Dominick. Of course the two were tied together. They had to be.

Marcus didn't want Rafaella at the compound. De-Lorio wouldn't leave her alone. Paula would go after her. Why did she want to do a biography of Dominick Giovanni? Another Louis Rameau he wasn't. He wasn't a hero. He was a criminal. He wasn't a romantic criminal, far from it, even though he could appear that way on the surface with his educated charm. Not all that many people even knew about him, except for all the feds and cops in San Francisco, Chicago, and New York.

He was a criminal, and Marcus had known about him, at least indirectly, since he was ten years old, way back in Chicago. He'd sure as hell known about Dominick's father-in-law, Carlo Carlucci. To think of him made Marcus's guts cramp with remembered pain.

Why had Rafaella chosen Dominick? He planned to ask her this very evening.

At six o'clock that evening Rafaella opened her villa door to his knock. He gave her a cocky grin. "You look quite nice, but I guess you already know that. Another designer thing?"

"It's a silk sundress with flowers on it and you wouldn't know the designer's name so I won't waste it on you."

It was off-the-shoulders and he remarked, "No bra. I like it even more."

"Well, I don't like this," Rafaella said as she eyed the motor scooter and the helmet she was to strap under her chin. "How do I know you can drive this sucker any better than you did the helicopter?"

"Put your arms around my waist and be quiet."

She laughed. "Can't take the heat? A very common male failing, I've noticed."

He revved the motor scooter and spun out. Rafaella grabbed his waist and threw herself forward against his back. "I'll get you for that."

"Not until I stop this thing, you won't."

He didn't stop it until they reached the helicopter remains on the middle ridge. "Off," he said, and swung his leg over.

"Why are you stopping here?"

"I want to ask you something and you're going to tell me the truth or I just might shake it out of you."

Rafaella grew instantly still and braced herself.

"Just as I had expected, I found out a bit more about you. Like the fact that your mother's in the hospital in a coma and you're down here in the Caribbean jet-setting around trying to weasel your way in with Dominick. Why? And don't lie, Ms. Holland. I know you—from the inside out, I guess you could say."

What to say? How had he found out? Well, she hadn't bothered to cover many tracks, because Dominick Giovanni wouldn't recognize from her present connections that she was his daughter. He probably wouldn't have recognized her if she'd walked up to him and said, "Hi, Daddy. You remember Margaret in New Milford back in 1975?"

"Why do you care?"

"Talk. Now."

Rafaella just shook her head. She had to think, and think fast. Then she looked at him, really looked, and knew he was dead serious. His eyes were nearly black with concentration. She knew he'd catch her in a lie, and she wondered suddenly how he could have come to know her so well after such a short time.

She sighed, becoming as serious as he. "All right. I can't tell you."

"Just why the hell not?"

"I just can't. Are you going to tell Mr. Giovanni?"

"I already did. Actually it didn't seem to make all that great an impact. But with him you never know. He's not all that straightforward, holds things close to his chest. I suggest you be very careful. If you're here for reasons other than a book, you should leave while you've still got your sweet hide intact."

"I'm here to do a book on him. That's all, I swear it."

"You'd better be telling the truth, because I think he finds you a bit toothsome. You could end up on your back in his bed if he doesn't like your writing."

Sleep with my father? She very nearly laughed at that. "Oh, no," she said. "Oh, no."

"You prefer younger men, do you? Why did you leave your mother?"

"My mother's accident, her current condition—it's not relevant to this. I'd already planned to do this book, and my stepfather told me there was nothing I could do back home. I was there for nearly a week after the accident. Now I call him every day to check on her condition. Nothing's changed. But then, I assume you know I call every day to Long Island."

"Yes."

"Not a very trusting sort, are you?"

"Since you're about as trustworthy and as up-front as most women, I'd say I'm pretty smart not to trust."

"Sexist."

"Not really. It's Dominick who's the sexist, which, if you stay, you'll discover for yourself. Take Coco, who's one smart lady. She's his mistress; he treats her well, buys her whatever she wants, but she's not his equal—not in his eyes. She's there to service him, to jolly him out of bad moods, to listen to him whenever he wants to talk, to feed his masculine ego.

"He wanted DeLorio to marry Paula because he thought, mistakenly, that she'd straighten him out and produce offspring quickly and frequently. We're talking barefoot and pregnant here. God, was he off target there. She's hot for anything in Jockey shorts, and the last thing she wants is a kid ruining her figure. If she had a child now, no one would know who the father was. Oh, and there's another thing. DeLorio will be after you in a flash. He's like his old man in matters of the flesh. Unlike his old man, I've heard he isn't all that considerate a lover. He likes a woman to be utterly compliant, submissive."

"Why are you warning me, and with such explicit language? You don't even like me. You surely don't trust me."

He gave her a slow smile then, his eyes lighting. "Ms. Holland, any woman I take on my front lawn, I don't like to have despoiled by some other man, particularly one with such tastes as DeLorio has. No, no more throwing me on my back. I'm serious, and if you try your karate on me now, I'll tie you up and take you back to the resort."

"Oh, yeah?"

"You sound just like a little kid in the sixth grade, ready to fight it out. Come on, let's get going. Do you still want to go through with it?"

"Certainly. Thanks for the warning. And, Marcus?"

"Yeah?"

"I'm just here to do that biography. Nothing more, I swear it to you."

"It's Dominick you'll have to convince, Ms. Holland."

Eleven

"I want to drive the rest of the way," Rafaella said, and swung her leg over the motor-scooter seat. The skirt of the dress wasn't full, but it had enough material to keep it from crawling up her legs.

"A pity," Marcus said, eyeing the skirt, then shrugged and climbed on behind her. He immediately hugged himself against her back, his arms around her waist.

"Not so tight," she said, and tried to shake free of him. "It's bloody warm." When he only tightened his arms, she twisted about to face him. "All right, lover boy, let me tell you something. You say you don't trust me. Well, I don't particularly trust you. And it's not a question of my virtue. It's just that you're—well, you don't seem the type of man to me who would be content to run a resort for another man, no matter how swank, no matter how high the salary."

"Hmmm. What else do you see in your tea leaves?"

"You're probably something of a renegade. You like to be in charge—Lord, do I ever know that personally. You value your independence and you don't like to accept orders from other people."

Interesting, Marcus thought. He moved his hands up until they were touching the undersides of her breasts. That should distract her. It sure was getting to him. But she didn't move, just looked at him.

"No, you're not what you seem, but you're not going to tell me, are you? Are you a crook, Mr. Devlin? A plain garden-variety-type criminal? Is Devlin even your real name? You never answered me on that one, incidentally."

"Are you going to tell me what's in that strange looking book I saw you with that first night? The one that made you cry?"

He felt the shock go through her body, but she didn't flinch. She was very good.

He pushed a bit more. "I saw it again on the side of your tub this morning. What is it?"

"None of your business," she said, and gunned the motor scooter.

He could hear her muttering curses under her breath, and he smiled at the back of her helmet.

But he was worried. He'd been very worried since he'd spoken to Dominick.

She was one smart cookie, and perceptive. She was also too impulsive, and that could get her hurt.

It was a clear, sweet-scented evening, and for an unwanted moment Rafaella found herself alone with Paula. Where was Coco? Marcus? Anyone?

Paula wasted no time with preliminary skirmishes.

"So tell me, Miss Holland, which one are you after? Marcus? Dominick? Or my husband?"

Rafaella merely smiled at Paula, who looked innocent and young and vulnerable in a pale peach silk sundress, her long light blond hair hanging straight to her shoulders. She didn't look like she wanted to get in every guy's Jockey shorts.

"I want you to leave. It isn't healthy here, not for someone like you."

The two women were standing on the veranda that faced the swimming pool. The scent of hibiscus and bougainvillea filled the evening air. It was warm but not uncomfortably so. The sun had just gone down and it was that particularly spectacular time of evening in the Caribbean that lasted mere minutes.

"On the contrary, it's beautiful here. Just smell the air. So sweet. Don't you agree?"

"DeLorio's my husband."

"Congratulations," Rafaella said. "Look, Paula, I swear to steer very clear of your husband. Satisfied?"

"And Marcus?"

"Why ever should you care about Marcus? You're not a bigamist, are you?"

"You're not funny, Miss Holland."

"Very likely not, but you know, Paula, it's rather odd to be having this conversation in 2001."

"What do you mean?" Paula's voice was heavy with suspicion.

"Women competing over men, arguing over them. Women not seeing each other as allies, but as natural enemies."

"You mean all that sisterhood crap our mothers preached back in the Dark Ages?"

"That's what I mean. Listen up, Paula. I'm not after any man. You got that?"

"Yeah? For someone who is not out to snare a guy you sure do seem to put a whole lot of care into presenting a pretty package—I mean, that designer outfit isn't exactly sack cloth."

"No, it isn't." Paula had a point there. It wasn't that Rafaella hadn't ever exploited her looks, because she had. She'd played that angle plenty of times for the sake of getting a story. She remembered coming onto that jerk neo-Nazi—Lazarus, he'd styled himself—to get him to talk.

"Would you just believe, Paula, that there's more to life than men?" So much for keeping her mouth shut. So much for coming across like a hypocrite, which she probably was. Really she just didn't want to admit to herself that Marcus, in a revoltingly short time, had managed somehow to throw her so totally off-balance again and again.

"You just try going after Marcus and I'll—"

"You'll what, Paula?"

"Make you sorry."

Such a little girl. At least that was how she was coming across. A spoiled little rich girl who needed the attention of any and all males constantly fastened exclusively on her. Rafaella eyed her closely. Al Holbein had told her time and time again not to be satisfied with surface appearances. "There's always something deeper, Rafe, even if the person comes across like a glowing idiot."

Marcus had dismissed Paula as exactly what she appeared to be. But he was a man, and evidently Paula had come onto him. When he'd been helpless—What had she done?

"What are you grinning about?"

"I was just remembering what Marcus told me about you, when he was helpless and you—" She paused, not knowing how to proceed. She didn't have to. Paula went pale, then turned as red as the mahogany sideboard inside the dining room. Then she looked furious.

"He told you about that?"

Rafaella just shrugged, her smile never slipping. What had she done anyway?

To her further surprise, Paula looked humiliated.

"That bastard. He loved it, he just pretended he didn't at first. He was hard and he enjoyed pushing into my mouth, and he was groaning and pushing, the damned bastard."

And Paula was gone in a whirl of peach silk skirt and long bare legs.

"What was that all about?"

Rafaella jumped guiltily at the sound of his voice. "Oh, hello, Marcus. I don't suppose you were eavesdropping? No, even you couldn't have carried it off in magnificent silence, given the subject matter."

"Which was? Here's a rum punch for you."

She sipped it. It was too sweet and far too potent. She gave him a sweeter smile.

"Paula, er, taking advantage of you when you were down, and how you loved it."

"Well, well," he mused aloud, but Rafaella wasn't fooled for a moment. His fingers had tightened around his glass and there was an interesting tic in his jaw. He was embarrassed. He was mad. He had wanted none of it. Rafaella was watching him and thinking how odd it was that she seemed to know him so well after only a few days. And she knew him, or was coming to know him more quickly than she ever had another human being.

"You were really that helpless? When was this?"

"I was shot here a while back. I was laid up in bed and too weak to fend her off. Coco tried to protect me, but she couldn't be there all the time."

"And DeLorio?"

"He was in Miami. I wasn't safe until he got back." Then Marcus stared at her. He'd just spilled his damned guts and she hadn't really questioned him in a pushy way, hadn't pressured him, just looked at him so warmly, as if telling her would solve all his problems. Only it wouldn't. Telling her anything could get both of them killed. "Look, Ms. Holland. I don't want you here. I don't want you on this island. I doubt that I even want you in the Caribbean. You're dangerous to yourself and you're damned dangerous to me." He was looking at her as though he wanted to smack her. Then he shook his head and plowed his fingers through his hair. "Oh, what the hell!" And like Paula, he turned on his heel and stomped off. Only he walked in the opposite direction, along the side of the swimming pool, toward the far deep end. It was shrouded in evening shadows.

Rafaella watched him, not moving. He was a complex man and she wished desperately that she could have met him in another time, in another place, anywhere but here, with Dominick Giovanni. She recognized this in herself and accepted it, but not willingly. He was making her crazy. Even now she was looking after him, not wanting him out of her sight. She watched him stop suddenly and jerk around. He stared down into the water. Then he dropped to his hands and knees, peering over the edge of the pool, his body tense, his eyes searching. She watched him pull something out of his pocket and toss it behind him. Then in a fluid movement he straightened and dived into the water.

Her heart jumped. Oh, Lord, what was wrong? What had he seen? A body? Something, something—? Adrenaline surged.

She ran to the other end of the pool, stared down into the shadowed water, saw Marcus's outline, and without further hesitation kicked off her shoes and jumped in. She sucked in air and kicked downward, her beautiful silk floral dress billowing up around her chest.

His hands went around her waist and he pulled her to the surface, still holding her.

She sputtered out water and tried to wipe her hair out of her eyes. "What are you doing? What's wrong? What's down there?"

Marcus gave her an evil grin and pushed her against the side of the pool, letting her find her footing on the narrow ledge. It was nearly dark, they were in deep shadows, and the air was soft. Hummingbirds dived about the bougainvillea, pausing to feed, then dipping and fluttering to another blossom. Evening insects hummed. They were alone.

Rafaella tried to pull away from him, but he held on. "You scared the hell out of me. What did you see?"

"There was nothing in the pool."

"Then why—?"

"I just wanted you to come running, and you did."

Marcus wrapped her wet hair around his hand, pulling her forward, and kissed her. She felt him hard and pushing against her belly. The air went out of her and every wonderful feeling imaginable swirled about inside her, and when he pulled back only to push her floating dress up to her breasts, she just looked at his mouth, wanting him to kiss her again. His hand slid up her thigh and beneath her panties. He jerked them down to her knees. Then he cupped her, his fingers closing over her, resting there, and he sighed and kissed her again.

"Very nice, Ms. Holland," he said in her mouth, and she wondered if she'd lost her mind. She kissed him again, resolving to worry about it later. He had the sexiest mouth, and his tongue—

His fingers moved, and she moved with his fingers. His middle finger eased inside her and she jerked against him, sucking in her breath in a loud whoosh.

"Easy now," he said, and nibbled her earlobe.

He pushed his finger deeper, then stopped, resting again, seemingly content, and she looked at him. His eyes were dark with pleasure and lust.

She said the obvious again because she couldn't think of anything else: "You did all that just to get me in the water?"

"It worked." He moved his finger and stroked his thumb over her, teasing and pressing inward until he'd found her. And he just stopped his fingers again. "You're such a little heroine, rushing headlong into the unknown, into dangers unimagined, straight into the pool, not caring what lurking terrors await you. Do you like this, Ms. Holland?" And his resting fingers stopped resting.

She moaned.

"You do. Very nice. Yes, I knew you'd come dashing to my rescue—that or to satisfy your curiosity about what was in the pool. A fleet of marines couldn't have held you back. I like that about you.

You don't think, do you? You could have been Saint Georgia. You don't worry about consequences."

"Evidently not. Just look at what I'm letting you do to me."

"There's a difference this time, and you know it. This time I firmly intend to take the final plunge. How about right now? I thought about your words this morning—your final-plunge joke—and decided to carry through with it, replete with swimming pool and all the water you could want. I admit I would have felt the consummate fool, however, had you merely stood at the side of the pool and stared down at me. I would have had to drag you into the water. This way, you leapt to your fate with great willingness. Now, let's see if everything is working." He pulled back his hand and felt her lower body quiver when his fingers left her. He kissed her even as he unzipped his pants and freed his erect sex.

"Now," he said with deep satisfaction. "Now."

He lifted her off the ledge, keeping her pressed against the pool wall, his fingers parting her, and without warning he came fast and hard into her.

Rafaella cried out at the shock of him, deep and thick, filling her, but then he was kissing her again, holding her tightly against him, pressing her against the side of the pool, making the water swirl around them. And then his fingers found her, and quickly, so very quickly, she was struggling with an orgasm that would overwhelm her, make her lose control, and she didn't want that but she couldn't stop it. She didn't understand this unacceptable effect he had on her, and at the moment she simply didn't care whether she did or not.

She cried out and he quickly kissed her again and moaned into her mouth and pounded into her, and after she'd jerked and heaved and exploded wildly, he let himself go.

He held her close, his cheek against her wet hair, still deep inside her.

He said against her left ear, "You don't have to be concerned about the demise of my credit standing, Ms. Holland. I took time to remove my wallet before I dived into the water. The only things ruined are my Italian loafers, and I must tell you that I consider this well worth it. Do you know where your panties went to? No? Still can't talk, huh?"

"I can't believe I let you do that," she said finally, her mouth against his neck, and she was kissing him. She made no effort to get away from him.

"Why not? You wanted it. I'm an amiable man, a kind man. I hate to see a grown woman suffer."

"A grown woman is going to kill you. With a rock."

"Talk like that makes me shrivel. Ah, well. Would you like to stop kissing my neck? Come back to sanity? To good ole Paula? Who knows? Maybe she's watching." He pulled out of her, not wanting to, held to the edge of the pool with one hand, and zipped up his slacks with the other.

He saw her face in the dim light and smiled. She looked dazed and sated. He liked that. Her eyes were lazy and unfocused and a very light blue, not a dollop of gray. He frowned. Light blue, very light—It was familiar to him. He'd seen—

"You want your drawers? Or do we let Juan, the pool boy, find them in the morning? Yeah, let's. It'll give him a thrill. You don't monogram them, do you? No, of course not. How could I forget so easily? I have a pair of your panties, the ones I pulled off you that memorable evening in my front yard."

"I wondered what happened to them. Do you keep women's panties as trophies?"

"Hmmm. I never thought about that. It would save the bedposts from all those notches, wouldn't it? The ones from the other night are nice—all light blue with a sexy bit of cream-colored lace around the crotch.

Maybe I can just drape them over the bedpost, maybe put your name under them on a little plaque so no one will get confused. What do you think?"

Rafaella shivered. Not from cold, because both the air and the water were warm enough to bathe in. She pushed her hair away from her face. Her beautiful Scassi floral silk sundress, ruined—all eight hundred bucks' worth. And she hadn't cared. She'd done it without a thought, without a whimper. She'd enjoyed herself immensely, flamboyantly.

"I think I should go find myself a rock, a nice big solid rock."

He leaned over her and kissed her again, then pulled himself out of the pool. He squished his feet. "My poor loafers. Well lost, I suppose, to the over-powering needs of love."

"Lust, you fool. Lust."

"You want a hand?" He held out his hand to her and she didn't know whether to trust him or not.

She decided she couldn't get any wetter, and gave him her hand. Evidently he'd decided the same thing, because he jerked her right out of the water and into his arms.

He released her after a quick hug. "I suggest you change. I imagine that Dominick will wonder what happened if you're late for dinner."

"I didn't bring any other clothes. You know that."

"Speak to Coco," he said, smiled down at her as he flicked a fingertip over her cheek, and strolled away, whistling as if he hadn't a care in the world.

"I've got to be the biggest fool alive," she said, and went off in search of Coco.

To everyone she saw in the house, she said, "I fell in the pool," and that was it.

Coco, thankfully, didn't say a word, just looked at her and gave her that I-know-what-you've-done smile. The borrowed skirt and blouse didn't fit all that badly, bought for her, Coco told Rafaella, some eighteen months before when she'd been a size smaller.

"You're so tall and willowy, it's not fair."

"You're quite tall enough, Rafaella, just not as tall as a model. You aren't intimate with Marcus, huh? Now you need to use my blow dryer. You want a curling iron? By that smile on your face I imagine he's as good as his reputation. You've only got ten minutes until we're to be downstairs. Of course by now I assume everyone knows you, er, fell in the swimming pool."

"That's right," Rafaella said, her voice as steady as the rock she intended to find and pound over Marcus's head.

There were quite a few people waiting in the living room. No one said a thing about the pool incident.

Dominick introduced a man to her as his lieutenant, Frank Lacy. It made him sound like part of a police force. He was a gaunt man with a receding hairline and a smile that looked pained. He probably hadn't smiled for real for at least twenty years. He had sad eyes. He didn't say anything to Rafaella, merely nodded when Dominick introduced her. He looked like someone's overworked father.

"And Merkel you know, of course, my dear."

"Yes. Hello, Merkel."

"And Link. He keeps the compound running smoothly. He's my majordomo, of sorts."

"Hello, Link." Rafaella wondered if that was his first or last name. He had a clever face, thin and intelligent. She'd ask later.

"I've invited these three gentlemen to dine with us because they're part of my life and you may wish to speak to them later. Link, you'll discover, is an expert on historical murders and murderers. His current investigations involve—Well, you tell her, Link."

The man was shy. It was a pained voice that said, "Helene Jegado, ma'am. She was a cook who loved to poison her employers. She enjoyed watching them suffer. She ended up as a cook in a convent, but so many of the sisters died that the authorities were called in. They discovered that she'd killed over sixty people."

"And all these people hired her without references," Merkel remarked.

"Good grief," Rafaella said. "That's wonderful. I want to hear more stories, please, Link."

He agreed, and Dominick said, "He told you one of the least sensational and least gory. Now that you've asked, beware. Now, Merkel, the dear fellow, doesn't cotton to murder. He's into fashion. Any advice you need, he'll consult his *GQ*."

Well, Al, she thought, you're quite right. No one is really what he seems to be on the surface, except for Marcus—whom I recognized as many-leveled from the outset. He, the jerk, obviously had another wardrobe here at the compound. He looked utterly unmussed, very well-dressed in white slacks and an open-collar white shirt. With his tanned face and black hair and blue eyes, he looked like a bandit, a bandit who made love like no man she'd ever known in her life. She wanted her fill of kissing him, and she had no idea how long that could take.

She'd never imagined letting a man orchestrate such play with her. What Marcus had done was beyond her experience. It should have been distasteful. He'd played with her, enjoying both himself and her, and she, she had to admit, had had the time of her life. Why couldn't he at least have a roll of fat around his middle or a receding chin?

Marcus strolled over about five minutes later and handed her another rum punch. "It's not so sweet this time."

She sipped it and the rum content nearly knocked off her borrowed panty hose.

"When's your period due?"

"Ah, so you're suddenly concerned about being a daddy?"

"I got so carried away with my daring scheme in the swimming pool that I didn't use a condom. You're on the pill, aren't you? Didn't I see some on the counter in your bathroom just this morning?"

Let the jerk suffer. Rafaella closed her eyes for a moment and said, "That's all I need. To be pregnant by a man who's going to be murdered by me with a rock. The jury won't believe I hate you because of my fat stomach."

"I'm sorry. I shouldn't have rushed the thing."

He sounded sincere, and she looked at him. There was no amusement in his eyes this time. She said, "My period's due in a couple of days. And yes, I'm on the pill. No problem."

"You're regular? You'll tell me if you're not okay, won't you?"

"How in heaven's name couldn't I be okay? And what would you do? Leave the island? Fly to Mongolia and become a monk?"

· "I don't know. I'll think about it." His amused look returned in full measure and he turned away to talk to Coco.

Dominick came on cat's paws beside her and she prayed he hadn't overheard anything. "Something bothers you, Rafaella? Marcus, perhaps?"

"Oh, no. I was just thinking about my fall into your beautiful swimming pool. I'm usually not so clumsy."

"Indeed."

He knew something. Surely Marcus wouldn't brag about it, would he? He wouldn't have had to. Everybody probably had seen that he was as wet as she was.

"You must tell me what your favorite foods are, Rafaella, and I'll pass it along to Jiggs. Dukey's really quite a fine cook. Marcus will bring your clothes over tomorrow. Coco's clothes look fine on you, but I'd imagine that you'd be more comfortable in your own."

That's my father speaking to me, she thought, and he hasn't a clue. She realized he'd just given an order she had no intention of obeying. An order that would mean that Marcus would go through her things. And Marcus wouldn't stop there. He'd search her villa. Her mother's journals were hidden under the edge of the carpet that curved beneath her dressing table. It would take someone good to find them, but Marcus was good, no doubt about that. She hadn't really worried about the journals until now. She probably should have, but she hadn't. She was worried about them now. If Marcus found them, he'd give them to Dominick and it would be all over. Rafaella realized she'd been stupid to bring three of the journals, but she hadn't wanted to leave them behind. She'd wanted to study them. She'd wanted to feel the rage flow through her when she read again and again what he'd done to her mother.

And Marcus already wondered about her mother's journals. What would Dominick do if the journals got into his hands? Kill her? Kiss her and say, "Hello, daughter?"

"Actually, I hadn't realized you expected me to stay here tonight, Dominick. I would prefer packing my own things and returning for the duration tomorrow."

"As you wish," he said, and his slight frown turned to a beguiling smile. "I suppose you've gathered that I want you to write my biography."

Coco had told her, but to hear him say it was quite another thing. "Thank you," she said. "Thank you very much. I'll try to do justice to my subject."

"We'll speak of approaches and ground rules tomorrow. Since I am to be your subject, I do insist upon having full approval over what you write. I'll also be your editor. There will be certain areas that will warrant more emphasis than others, and of course I will be the one to select those areas. For example, you know from Coco that I fund several drug-rehab programs in the States. Not, of course, that I would want to dwell overly on those activities, but a mention would be appropriate. Other areas of my life simply aren't relevant, and those won't be mentioned. I don't foresee any problems, Rafaella. You and I will work well together.''

As long as I do exactly what I'm told, she thought, but nodded all the same. She understood very well what he wanted to do. He wanted to rearrange facts, make himself look like the benevolent philanthropist: he wanted to recreate himself and his life. He wanted to write everything but the actual words. She was to be his secretary, to record the great man's life. Just let him think that. It was fine with her. Also unspoken but very well understood was the threat that she'd better do exactly as he dictated.

After a wonderfully cool dinner of fresh shrimp, lightly buttered rolls, Caesar salad, and cheese and fruit, they adjourned again to the living room. Nothing of any particular import had been said during dinner. Rafaella realized that Paula was interested in both the man Link and in Marcus, but neither man appeared to return her interest. Coco hung on Dominick's every word, yet managed at the same time to direct general conversation to each guest in turn. She was the perfect hostess, the perfect mistress, cool and gracious and beautiful. Paula was sulking by the time the Caesar salad arrived, no longer giving Marcus heated looks whenever she thought DeLorio wasn't looking, and as for DeLorio, Rafaella's half-brother stared at her breasts for two-minute stretches. Merkel and Lacy ate remarkable amounts of food and said little. Link looked faintly worried.

Rafaella was ready to bolt when she saw Dominick in private conversation with Marcus. Dominick used his hands when he spoke. He should have looked insignificant next to Marcus—after all, he was much slighter of build and shorter and older—but he didn't.

He looked powerful and strong and decisive. He was her father and she hated him more at that moment than she ever had before. He was very real, very solid, and she felt a shiver of fear.

What were they talking about?

She was determined to get back to the resort. She'd been a fool to leave the journals in her villa, no matter how well they were hidden. No way would she allow Marcus into her villa without her. What could she do with the journals? Not the resort safe—Marcus would be in there in a flash. And the journals told everything. And he'd already told her he didn't trust her.

She was a fool, a thousand times a fool. Becoming more of one every day, in fact every time she was with Marcus. She'd had a wonderful time making love with him—in the deep end of the swimming pool— just after giving Paula a woman-to-woman talk about self-esteem and self-reliance and sisterhood. Rafaella decided she'd been full of it. She was hourly learning things about herself that weren't at all comforting.

She was relieved when Dominick didn't raise a fuss about her leaving that evening. Merkel accompanied them as pilot.

"It ain't as if Mr. Giovanni doesn't trust you, Marcus," Merkel said, then smiled and shrugged.

"Well, I don't. I'm glad you're here, Merkel," Rafaella said, and indeed she was. His presence saved her from Marcus and his mockery and his teasing and his wonderful mouth and equally wonderful hands and fingers. She wondered if he would have made love to her in the helicopter, a thousand feet up.

Unfortunately, it was Marcus who walked her back to her villa once they'd set down on the helicopter pad.

"I'll wait with you," he said shortly. "Dominick's decided he wants you to come back to the compound tonight."

"No," Rafaella said with a perfectly pleasant and

final voice. She was scared, very scared, but she couldn't let Marcus see it.

"No what?"

"No, I'll go back to the compound tomorrow, just as I told Dominick I would. I have no intention of going back tonight. I'm too tired. I don't want to rush my packing, and no, I don't want your help. Good night, Marcus."

She closed the door in his face and quickly locked it.

She didn't hear a sound for many moments.

"I have a key, Rafaella."

"Try using it and you're a dead man."

Nothing but silence.

Then she heard him walking away. Whistling.

Twelve

Giovanni's Island
March 2001

Marcus waved good-bye to Punk, who sported a pale blue stripe through her hair today, and walked down the immaculately trimmed walkway to the executive wing of the resort. The Chicago banker, Punk had told him in some disgust, was a dud, but she'd found a guy from San Diego who was a hunk, and what did Marcus think of him? The guy in question was about twenty years old, a beautiful blond California surfer who did his workouts directly in front of the mirrors.

"The three of you should have a great time," he'd told her, and Punk had laughed and laughed. She'd just join him, she told Marcus, and they'd have an orgy.

His workout had gone well. He had nearly full rotation back in his shoulder, and if his strength wasn't yet at one hundred percent, it was close. He could take on Ms. Holland. He went directly into the private entrance to his office, not wanting to see Callie just yet. He quietly locked the door, then pulled the small electronic device from his pants pocket, flipped the blue switch, and walked slowly about the room. Nothing. No bugs. He was more relieved to find nothing than to find a listening device. It meant he was trusted. Then he pulled out his cell phone and punched in

Savage's number in Chicago. Savage answered on the second ring.

"Yeah, Marcus? What's going on?"

"Giovanni's made another deal. He told me about it last night. This one will go through a munitions factory in Lyons, France, with an end-user certificate showing the stuff is going to Nigeria. It'll be rerouted to Bombay, of all places, then to the Middle East, to Syria. It's all aboveboard, approved by the French government, Giovanni's name isn't being used at all, and the man who's rerouting the arms to Syria is so crooked I can't believe he can still walk straight— Jack Bertrand."

Savage whistled. "That fellow's worked with the CIA in the past, hasn't he? Getting arms to places they don't want to be involved with directly?"

"Yes, and he's used this French munitions factory a couple of times in the past, but not for the CIA. You know the scam well enough."

"When was the deal approved?"

"Yesterday."

"Giovanni's proved his trust now." He heard the optimism in Savage's voice.

"Not so fast, John. It would appear so, but I wouldn't swear to it still. He wants me to fly to Marseilles and oversee the packing and crating and delivery of the goodies—mines, for the most part, on this shipment—onto the ship that is, in actuality, bound for Bombay, not Nigeria. It's Bertrand he doesn't particularly trust on this one, so he wants me to finalize the deal and handle the money transfer before the mines leave France. It's Bertrand's job to see that the stuff gets to Syria. My bet is the stuff ends up in Syria. Giovanni didn't consider that a need-to-know for me, so he didn't tell me."

Savage whistled. "Really, old buddy, it sounds like you've finally got him."

"No, not yet, unfortunately. Now, don't get hot

under your collar, Savage. Giovanni's clean on this one; no one could prove he's involved, except at the highest levels, and even my testimony wouldn't be enough. I've been through this same kind of deal too many times to think it'll soon be over. Maybe we won't even get this Bertrand character. It will take more time."

"Do you think the French authorities will put the munitions factory out of business when they find out about this deal?"

"No, but hopefully they'll investigate and find the greedy little sons of bitches doing the stealing from the factory. As for Bertrand, he has powerful friends. And those powerful friends have other powerful friends. Tell Hurley to let the mines go through, at least until they get to Bombay. He can stop them there. Of course everyone will throw up their hands and claim they know nothing about anything and just look at the end-user certificate. Also, I won't be suspected. If anything, it'll be one of the little guys at the munitions factory, playing off both ends. We'll just have to bide our time."

"It's past time for you to get out, Marcus. I know we've had this conversation before, but dammit, listen to me. You've done your duty. Just blow off this assassination thing, let whoever it is have another go at him. Let him get killed. Who cares?"

Marcus sighed. "You do, John, and so do I, not to mention Uncle Morty."

"Damn Uncle Morty. Oh, hell, I don't mean that. All right, have it your way. Incidentally, your mom is with him a great deal of the time. You just be careful, particularly in Marseilles. You're dealing with real scum. Bertrand's connected to Olivier, isn't he?"

"I doubt it, but Dominick didn't tell me. You know what he and Olivier think of each other. Working together on this? Hard to believe."

"How's your reporter doing?"

"She'll be going back to the compound this morning. She's stubborn, wants to fracture my head with a rock, she knows karate as well as I do, and—"

There was a deep chuckle. "Sounds like you're having a fine old time. I saw a photograph of her. On the back of her hardcover."

"So?"

"She looks fascinating, those bright eyes of hers . . . what are they, green?"

"No, pale blue. When she's mad, they're flecked with gray."

"She'll be all right with you off the island?"

"Yes, at least she'd better be." Marcus rang off after a few more minutes, and he wasn't thinking of Rafaella as a killer anymore. He was thinking of her as a woman who was vulnerable and naive and arrogant. Yeah, she had a smart mouth. He was worried about her. He'd be gone for three days, maybe longer. The good Lord only knew what kind of trouble she could get herself into during that time.

He rose and slipped out through the private entrance of his office. He wondered if he could talk Ms. Holland into some good old-fashioned necking before he took her over to the compound. He'd even be content with more talk about camping when they'd been kids. There were so many off-limit subjects. It only added to his frustration. He wanted to know her, really *know* her. He wanted to talk to her, really talk. He wanted to get beyond the superficial jokes and baiting.

Probably she wouldn't even speak to him. She'd been pretty pissed with him last night. And he thought he knew why. There was the swimming-pool thing, of course, but she'd enjoyed herself immensely. No, she'd refused to stay at the compound because she'd been afraid he'd search her villa.

And he would have. He wondered if he could get her out of there even now so he could search. He should have thought of it sooner. A phone call from the States? No, he couldn't do that. She'd think it was about her mother. He didn't want to frighten her like that just to search her villa.

He wanted to read that strange-looking book of hers. It occurred to him now why it was strange. It was because it wasn't a published book. No, it was something like a diary or a journal. He wanted very much to know its contents.

But Rafaella wasn't stupid. When he asked her if she'd like to have breakfast with him, she agreed immediately, and he knew that she'd already hidden the book and he'd never have a chance of finding it.

He took her to breakfast. No choice. She looked fresh and young, guileless as a nun, in white slacks and a pale blue blouse. She'd French-braided her hair and was wearing next to no makeup. She looked just fine to him. More than just fine.

"You look chipper this morning. You sleep well? Or were you too busy burying things?"

Her fingers tightened around the coffee cup. "I ran last night and took all my valuables, all my collectibles, all my secret documents with me, and buried them deep. You'll never find them, so you can just forget it."

"That's what I thought you'd done." He sighed, sat back in his wicker chair, and crossed his arms over his chest. "I hope you took high tide into consideration and didn't bury the goodies too close to the shoreline."

She slapped her hand to her forehead. "Oh, goodness me. So silly of little old me, and so stupid. It must be my hormones acting up."

"You did say last night that your period was due soon." That earned him a hiss that he chose to ignore. "All right, so you're good. I should have coshed you over the head last night and searched your place. You're making my life difficult, Ms. Holland. But then you start kissing me and I find I'm ready to forgive you just about anything."

She opened her mouth but he raised his hand to stop her. "No, don't say it. You've got a rock in your villa now, with my initials on it."

Rafaella smiled at him. "You're good-looking, Marcus. Even while I carved your initials in that rock, I thought you were good-looking. Even when I think you're the biggest jerk alive, I still think you're good-looking."

"And a superb lover? Given the constraints of eight feet of water, of course."

She just looked at him. Finally she said, "Yes, I've never done anything so crazy before. I just didn't care, didn't think. That's odd, isn't it?"

He wished she wouldn't talk like that. It scared him to death and worried the hell out of him. He decided superficial talk was better. At the very least, it was safer. He said abruptly, "Yeah, it's bloody odd."

"I've never trusted good-looking men before. Not that I trust you, of course. There was that Spanish boy who was a senior when I was a lowly freshman, and he was divine-looking, at least that's what all the girls thought. But I didn't trust him. And I trusted him even less when he turned his Latin black eyes in my direction." She stopped and her look was one of profound worry. "I wish I understood this thing about you."

"I'm a plain and simple man. There's nothing to understand."

"Sure, and my managing editor is an evangelist bound for heavenly climes."

"Well, we're even. I've never particularly trusted good-looking women."

She laughed, no hesitation, no guile, she just laughed at him. "That's absurd."

"You're trying to make me believe that you don't

know you're good-looking? Able to shiver my timbers if you really try?"

She looked at him then, her laughter dried up. "I'm not in your league, Mr. Devlin, or whatever your name is. I should be the one running a check on you, but I'll bet whatever you are, whoever you are, no one would find out. You're that good, aren't you?"

"I wonder, Ms. Holland. If anyone had asked me, I would have assured them that you could play well in any league at all. I'd also tell them that you made the cutest little noises in your throat when you were nearing your climax. And your legs are strong from all that running. I like how they—"

"I wonder where the waitress is," Rafaella said, and looked around.

"Did you go to your senior prom? Did you wear a guy's senior ring? Do you like football?"

She cocked her head at him, the waitress forgotten. "Yes, no, and yes, I love football."

"Who's your favorite NFL team?"

"The Forty-niners. I'm in love with Bryant Young and J.J. Stokes and—"

He held up a hand, laughing. "More lust. Do you watch the games on Sundays?"

"Yes I do. I have the Sunday *Tribune,* coffee, and croissants from my neighborhood bakery. Also I'm in on the betting pool at the *Tribune.* I've won over three hundred dollars the past couple of seasons. How about you?"

"I'm a Bears fan, what else?" He fell silent, picturing suddenly being in bed with her on a fall Sunday morning watching a game until the half, then making love, watching more of a game, arguing about plays— He hurt suddenly and said abruptly, "I'm leaving the island today."

Rafaella, startled, quickly looked back at him. She realized she didn't want him to go. It was disconcerting and vastly annoying. "Why? Or is this another one of your secrets?"

"I've got some business in France, nothing much. I'll be back by Friday. One thing, Ms. Holland. Be careful at the compound. I'm very serious. Don't trust anyone. Don't act first without thinking. You understand me?"

"What I don't understand is why you're warning me."

He shrugged and waved a hand toward Melissa, one of the waitresses. "You're terrific in the deep end. Just be careful. Hi, Mellie. A jolly beautiful morning, isn't it? Toast and half a grapefruit, please. Ms. Holland?"

"Do you have three initials or just the two? Coffee, please, Melissa, and a croissant."

Marcus watched Melissa's long legs as she made her way toward the kitchen. "I wonder if Juan found your panties in the pool yet. He's eighteen and horny. He'll go mad, probably frame them on the wall next to his bed."

"What's your business in France?"

"Or maybe old DeLorio found them. He likes to swim early in the mornings. You be careful of him." Marcus sat forward and grabbed her hand, squeezing it. "I mean it. Don't trust a soul. Now, what was in that journal you hid?"

No information from him, Rafaella thought. The closemouthed slippery clam.

"Ah, here's our breakfast." He released her hand. "Keep up your strength, Ms. Holland. When I get back, I'll have thought up new and even more exciting ways of easing you out of your virtue."

The Bridges, Southampton, Long Island
March 2001

Charles Winston Rutledge III carefully laid the phone receiver back in its cradle. Still the same. The doctors had detected some improvement in the EEG, but they remained guarded in the prognosis. There's always a chance, Mr. Rutledge, they'd say. It was their litany. He'd flown in Dr. Jacob Phillos, one of the foremost neurologists in the world. There was a chance, Dr. Phillos had told him following a bout of profound thought on his part. He'd then patted Charles's arm as if he were a worried parent or a five-year-old patient and told him not to worry. Damned old fool.

And the other doctors would gather around and chant their litany. There's always a chance, Mr. Rutledge, don't give up. Always a chance.

It had become his litany as well. Margaret had to live. She would live. He literally couldn't go on without her. He knew it, had known it for a very long time.

He punched in a call to B.J. Lewis, a private investigator in Manhattan. He identified himself and was put through instantly to the great man himself, a self-image that Charles found amusing at the best of times and ludicrous at the worst of times, like right now. But Lewis was good, more than good.

"Rutledge here. Anything?"

Charles prepared himself for disappointment, ready to grunt neutrally to cover his irritation, his annoyance with everyone around him who professed an expertise and didn't come through. Not, of course, that there'd been much for B.J. Lewis to go on. A dark sedan, four-door; the driver probably drunk, a car that should be damaged on the passenger's side, since it had hit Margaret's car on her side.

But he wasn't to be disappointed, not this time. He sat forward in his chair, clutching the phone. "My God, are you certain, B.J.?"

He listened again, his hand shaking with excitement. "Of course I don't know." Then, "Keep on it," he said finally. "You know as well as I do that we can't rush this. Keep gathering evidence. I've got to do some thinking." He listened for a few more moments, then rang off.

B.J. had very probably found the individual who'd struck down Margaret, then speeded off. At least he'd firmly identified the car and the owner, who'd probably been driving. Charles didn't know what he'd expected, but it wasn't this. A woman owned that car. A damned drunk woman had hit Margaret.

Her name was Sylvia Carlucci.

And B.J. had wondered rhetorically if Charles knew of this woman. She was infamous for the sheer number of dollars she flung about, the number of martinis she could belt down, and the number of young studs she took to bed.

Charles rose slowly to his feet. When he'd hired B.J., it was out of a need to do something, anything, to make him feel he had some modicum of control. But he hadn't expected this. No, anything but this. A drunk kid, perhaps, scared and panicked. But not Sylvia Carlucci. Even if she'd been a nun, people would have known about her; she'd never been a low-profile lady, because her father was Carlo Carlucci of Chicago. Sylvia Carlucci—about fifty years old now, and still going strong, strong with the booze, strong with the young studs she hauled around, and there was her husband, of course, who'd kicked her out of his life many years before, not that they'd been close for a decade before that. But no divorce, of course no divorce, not the daughter of Carlo Carlucci, who still lived in a penthouse on Michigan Avenue, all of seventy-five years old now, still surrounded by his cronies, scores of parasites.

The irony of it nearly bowled him over.

The phone rang. It was his private line. He knew that no one in his household would answer this line. He walked back to his desk and picked up the phone. Only six people knew of this number. "Yes? Rutledge here."

"I've missed you, Charles."

This was all he needed. He pitched his voice low and filled it with false patience. "Listen to me, Claudia, I don't know why you called, but I don't need this. My wife is still in the hospital, still in a coma, and I'm rather busy, what with my business and worrying about her."

"But it's been so long, and I do miss you."

Charles looked across the expanse of his library, through the bow windows that gave onto the east lawn. It was a lovely prospect even with the winter naked trees and the brown grass and the pruned rosebushes. Everything was dormant. Even Margaret.

But Claudia wasn't dormant; beautiful talented Claudia. He couldn't remember why the hell he'd even let her into his life. But then, of course, he did. It was her mouth. Quite simply, it was the lady's mouth.

"Look, Claudia, I just can't—we broke it off over six months ago. I meant it then, I still mean it. I'm sorry."

She ignored his words and started talking to him, describing what she would do to him, in great and imaginative detail. She knew he was aroused in a flash when she did it, and he was now, only this time his brain was more in control than his cock. He waited until she finished her expert performance—another litany, this one designed to arouse him beyond thought.

Finally she paused and he said, "Claudia, I would very much like for you to accept a small token of my appreciation." He forgot that he'd already given her quite a fancy token, many months before, when he'd finally broken with her. "Let's say a diamond bracelet? From Cartier? I'll have it delivered to you this afternoon. No, no, I can't bring it myself." As he said the words, he knew he was weakening, knew in his soul that he wanted the thoughtless release she would bring him. Just a moment out of time, just an hour out of twenty-four, with nothing in his consciousness, nothing in his brain, just the sexual release of the appalling tension in his body. And afterward, she'd be so sweet, she'd listen to him, sympathize, be anything he wanted her to be. . . .

He was weak and he hated himself, but he was a man, and his father had always said that men were strong in those things that counted. Men also needed sex, and they deserved pleasure for all their hard work. Men could stray. He'd used those arguments his entire married life with his first wife, Edith. But there'd been another reason with Margaret, a reason that made him furious and sick and frightened. But that wasn't important now. Claudia was gone from his life, long gone, his decision made months before.

He remembered how several times he'd caught Margaret staring at him, worry and love in her eyes, and he'd wondered what she was thinking and wondered if she might have heard of Claudia, and then he'd taken her to bed and told her with his body how much he loved her, only her. Of course there was so much more now, always more to understand, more to be explained, to know and deal with.

Charles then called Clement, his chauffeur, and told him to drive to Manhattan, to Cartier, and pick up a package for him. Then he called Mr. Clifford, the manager of Cartier, and ordered up the small token of his appreciation.

When he hung up the phone, he found that he was thinking of his son's wife, Susan. Susan with the soft white hands, the boomy deep voice, and the beautiful big breasts. Benjamin was such a bloody fool, such a nice boy, but with no guts, with no push or drive. If only Charles had sired Rafaella instead of Benjamin. Now, there was a child to be proud of. But no, he wasn't her father and it wasn't fair.

He should probably call her soon, find out how she was holding up. He shook his head at himself.

God, the irony of it, the blissful irony. Charles had

never been one to appreciate irony for the simple reason that he'd always had control in his life, until now.
Irony hadn't ever slipped in unnoticed, until now. Now
he felt he was in an ocean of irony, floundering about
like a helpless fool. But he wouldn't be the one to
drown. No indeed he wouldn't.

All during his drive to New York City, he thought
of the irony of Sylvia Carlucci hitting his wife.

Sylvia Carlucci *Giovanni* hitting his wife. But even
as he thought about it, examined it, he found he just
couldn't bring himself to accept such a coincidence.
Coincidence was just fine in fiction, but in his experience, coincidence just didn't happen in real life. Did
it?

Giovanni's Island
March 2001

DeLorio held up the wet panties. "Isn't this interesting?"

"They belong to that little slut," Paula said, and
tried to grab the panties from her husband.

"They could belong to Coco," he said, raising them
out of her reach.

"No, they're hers. Where did you get them?"

"They were on the bottom of the swimming pool.
The deep end. No, I think I'll return them personally
to the lady. I must say that Marcus has excellent
taste." He grinned at his wife, then touched the crotch
of the panties to his mouth. "Wonderful."

"What is? The chlorine?"

"You have no imagination, Paula. It didn't take
Marcus long, did it? I did wonder when they both
showed up wet before dinner. Is she the one who's
the exhibitionist? Do you think she went after him
on purpose?"

"Yes, to show me."

DeLorio paused. Very slowly he laid the panties on the dresser top, smoothing them into shape. "Show you what, Paula?"

"That she could take, no, to prove to me that she was better than—"

"I know," he said, and turned away from her. "It's hard to explain, isn't it? But all your little confusions and conceits—they only make me love you more. I'm going to Miami this afternoon. I have business meetings and arrangements to make. Do you want to come with me?"

"Yes, oh, yes, Del. Let me pack. How long?"

He turned and smiled at her. "Don't you find it interesting that my father evidently didn't mind Marcus screwing Rafaella Holland in the swimming pool? My civilized, well-bred father? No, he didn't say a word. I'd like to see what he'll do— First, Paula, I want you to change into a dress. That pretty blue sundress I bought you just last month. You know the one, it has a very full skirt and narrow straps over the shoulders?"

She nodded happily and turned to do as he'd bidden her, but he stopped her, his fingers curling around her forearm. He smiled down at her. She would love this. His fingers caressed her arm and his breath was warm against her temple.

"When you have the dress on, I want you to bend over the balcony with your arms balanced on the railing. I'll just lift your skirt a bit and stand behind you. And while I push inside you I want you to wave to the gardeners and speak to whoever wanders by. If it's Link, I want you to ask him all sorts of questions about his gruesome murderers of the past, keep him looking at you, until I come inside you."

"But they'll know—you'll be behind me, pushing, and they'll know—Link will know, and I—"

"But you'll have your dress on. No one will see a thing," but he was thinking, *Yes, I'll just bet he'll know.* And the bastard would know what DeLorio was doing and that Paula belonged to him and that he'd better keep his sniffing distance of Paula or he, DeLorio, would castrate him.

Link didn't come by, but Merkel did, dressed immaculately as always in his three-piece white linen suit and pale blue oxford shirt, and when he saw DeLorio standing behind his wife, his hands on her waist, he knew what he was doing, and it made him want to puke. But it was also powerfully erotic for all its crudity, and from the brief look he'd gotten at Paula's face, it seemed to him that she was enjoying it as much as she was hating it. He shook his head. He would never understand the two of them.

And when Paula called out to him, her voice high and embarrassed and shaking with excitement, he refused to look up at her again, just nodded and kept walking.

He was vastly relieved when the two of them flew to Miami that afternoon. He himself had gone earlier to fetch Ms. Holland from the resort. She was in her room, changing, Coco with her.

And he remembered Marcus's request just before he'd left him that morning at the airport in St. John's. "Watch her, Merkel. She's too unthinking, too impulsive, and that can be dangerous. And she has that talent to attract confidences, and that can be even more dangerous."

Merkel wondered what he'd let himself in for. At least one worry was down—DeLorio. He'd said he'd be gone for a week. God willing, it would be longer. He wondered if Mr. Giovanni had sent DeLorio away. If he had, then did he want Rafaella Holland all to himself? Just to work? Or did he want all competition out of his way? Was that why he'd sent Marcus to France? No, no, he was being crazy. Marcus had to go to Marseilles to deal with Bertrand. And, after all,

Coco was still here, still the head mistress, and Rafaella was her friend. No, he had to be wrong.

When Mr. Giovanni requested his presence after lunch, Merkel was impatient to know what was in his boss's mind. Hopefully, more than writing his biography with Rafaella Holland. Maybe he'd gotten information about the assassination attempt, about *Bathsheba.*

"Both DeLorio and Marcus are gone," Dominick said. He was sitting in a high-backed wicker chair, sipping a glass of lemonade laced with gin. "Now we will get Rafaella Holland settled in and everything back into, ah, balance."

Merkel was smart enough to keep still. He simply stood there waiting for his boss to get on with it, and silently cursed.

"She likes Marcus. She knows it but she just isn't ready to admit it."

Merkel looked at the beautiful Picasso over Mr. Giovanni's desk. It was from the artist's Pink Period, Mr. Giovanni had told him once. He didn't particularly like it. Most of Mr. Giovanni's other paintings were in a private vault, located just off the master suite. He'd gotten the Picasso some twenty years before, he said, at an auction.

"As for my son, well, I wanted him out of the way so he wouldn't be tempted by her. Also I wanted him to concentrate on other things. He will take my place in the future; he must learn about the responsibility, the strategy, all the tactics. He must learn the personalities of all the men he'll be dealing with. He must learn humility." He paused, and Merkel tried not to choke. Humility?

"Sometimes the boy shows so little breeding, so little class. He's just like his mother, that stupid drunken woman, and his grandfather, the rotting old bastard."

Merkel wasn't about to tell Mr. Giovanni what De-Lorio had done to Paula that morning, and how she, all red-faced with embarrassment, had probably had the best orgasm of her short life. He shifted his attention to the Vermeer that was artfully hung exactly seventeen inches from the Picasso, with its own lighting, stolen from Sir Walter Wrentham's collection three years before. He himself preferred the Egyptian stuff in the living room. You could touch the jewelry, pick it up and feel how warm it was, press it against your cheek, and know that real people had worn it, and still it was so old that you couldn't even begin to understand how those people had felt, what those people had been.

"Not that I don't think DeLorio will straighten out. He will. He's my son. He'll have to. As for his wife, well, she is just a girl, young and silly and unthinking. Ah, forgive me, Merkel, carrying on like this and embarrassing you. You're taken with the Vermeer, hmmm? I like it. Soon though I'll exchange it with the Turner that's in the vault. Just look at those colors—so soft, almost blurry, yet so real and stark. It sounds impossible, yet it's true, that wondrous effect Vermeer achieves. If only life could hold such beauty dear and unchanging, but it doesn't, does it? No, it's always changing, mostly for the worse. It isn't really fair, but there you have it.

"Now, Merkel, I wanted to see you because I will start working with Rafaella this very afternoon. Marcus is seeing to business, the dear boy, and I have nothing else to worry me.

"Yes, Rafaella will do a fine job. I explained things to her last night, slowly and carefully. She understands her role. She won't try to cross me, I'm certain she won't. She won't play the ruthless reporter out to find dirt. She'll write exactly what I want her to write. She will present me as I should be presented to the world: a man of ingenuity and imagination, a man of great vision, an intuitive man, a philanthropist. She will be my amanuensis, if you will.

"You, Merkel, you will ensure that peace reigns

here. You and Link and Lacy. Poor Link, he's such a
shy fellow, so diffident. He doesn't seem to be able to
grasp innuendo. Well, he's still a fine marksman and
he does please me with his tales of long-dead murderers." Dominick paused and sipped more of the gin
lemonade.

Finally Merkel said, "Mr. Giovanni, you sent Marcus to France because you wanted to be alone with
Miss Holland?"

How odd of Merkel to speak his mind so frankly.
How unexpected of staid old Merkel. "Oh, no, I
needed him there, to handle Bertrand. Don't you
think I can trust Marcus?"

"Yes, of course. He saved your life. Didn't give it
a second thought, you know, and—"

"Ah, that's exactly what worries me. A man who
just rushes into something, a man who doesn't weigh
his options, a man who doesn't stop and think. I don't
think that such a man is all that trustworthy."

Merkel just stared at him. "He saved your life,"
he repeated. "He took a bullet in the back to save
your life."

Dominick picked up a gold pen, fiddled with it a
minute, then tossed it into the air, deftly catching it.
"Perhaps you're right. Marcus has been with me over
two years now. He's bright, seemingly loyal, has made
a good deal of money for me and for himself." His
voice suddenly turned hard, his eyes cold. "Keep everyone away from me and Rafaella. I want her to
myself. She is to write the story of my life. There are
to be no distractions."

Merkel was afraid he did understand. He nodded
and left the library. But what about his promise to
Marcus?

Dominick didn't move for many more minutes. Certainly he trusted Marcus. Hadn't Marcus told him just
this morning before he'd left for France that he'd finally
gotten the opportunity to search Rafaella's villa? There

hadn't been a bloody thing there. That's what Marcus had told him. Marcus hadn't told him that Rafaella was illegitimate. Dominick wondered why. It wasn't important; that was what Marcus had decided. Still—

And Marcus had told him about Rafaella's mother, lying in that hospital in a coma. And Marcus had counseled him not to let her come to the compound. He'd said it was too dangerous. Marcus was timid and a coward. He didn't realize that Dominick controlled everything and everyone. Controlling one more woman was child's play.

Dominick tossed down the rest of his drink. His book would be a masterpiece. He would be seen by the world as he should be seen. It was about time.

Thirteen

Rafaella opened the journal. The date April 5, 1994, was neatly entered at the top-left-hand side of the page. She looked at her mother's rather crabbed, very straight handwriting and felt tears sting the backs of her eyes. She closed her eyes a moment, dealing with the pain. It would be endless pain, because even if her mother fully recovered, the other pain would still be there for all of those who loved her. Rafaella's throat felt wet, and she swallowed.

She had to succeed. She closed the journal just for a moment and thought about calling from her father's compound every morning to the Pine Hill Hospital on Long Island. Surely Dominick monitored all calls that went out from here.

But he already had to know that Rafaella called Long Island every morning. Marcus would have told him, just as he'd told him about her mother being in the hospital, in a coma.

She would simply, very matter-of-factly, ask Dominick if she could call the hospital every morning. If he asked her what she was doing here in the Caribbean with her mother so very ill in New York, well, she'd just tell him what she'd told Marcus, more or less.

She'd be more convincing with Dominick for the

simple reason that she had to be. There was too much to gain, too much to be lost.

And he had no more idea who Margaret Rutledge was than who his daughter was. Even if he remembered a Margaret, it was Margaret Pennington, not Margaret Holland.

Rafaella smoothed open the journal again, picturing her mother in her mind, sitting at her small Louis XVI writing table, pen in hand, her eyes staring off, remembering the pain of the past, wondering about the future, obsessed in the present.

It's Tuesday today, my dear Rafaella, and you're here on spring break from Columbia. It still makes me grin to think how very appalled Charles was when you told him you didn't want to go to Yale—his alma mater—but rather to Columbia, locked in Spanish Harlem, dangerous to the unwary, but the best school of journalism in the United States, in your estimation. How Charles started at that. "Columbia," he nearly yelled at me. "For God's sake, Columbia!"

I cajoled him, flattered him, loved him until he was silly, but I refrained from telling him that it was, in fact, none of his business where you went to school. He's very fond of you, Rafaella. It troubles me because I think he's more proud of you than he is of his own son, Benjamin. Sweet, unpretentious Benjie—proof that genes do come through, only not necessarily in the configuration one could wish. Benjie's an arty type, as you know, as was his mother, Dora. He really does fine watercolors. But Charles disdains all modern sorts of endeavors. He does, however, approve of those masters who had the good fortune to paint at least three centuries ago, e.g., Hals, Rembrandt, Vermeer, Brueghel. Practically all those masters are Dutch; his library is filled with them, some, er, acquired through less than pristine means, I doubt not.

But I digress. I will tell you, Rafaella, even if the

great Michelangelo himself had been Charles's son, Charles would have given him hell.

Am I mocking my husband? I suppose so, but it's healthy, not malicious. He's human, and that's just fine with me. Oh, yes, he's all too human—not at all like Dominick, who cared nothing for anyone except himself and his dynasty and—I never understood his obsession with founding a dynasty unless it was his own overweening need to see himself immortal—was there anything else?

He's had only the one son. His name's DeLorio and he's only eight months younger than you are, Rafaella. I don't know much about him except that he lives with his father, and has for years. So much for his blessed dynasty. As for his wife, Sylvia Carlucci Giovanni, she doesn't live with him, hasn't for more than a decade. She gave him a son, started drinking like a fish because he probably didn't give a damn about her and showed it, and is now living near us, of all the ironic things. She lives in a small hamlet called Hicksville, a very exclusive place, private, and the word is that she has a succession of handsome young men coming and going. Ah, here's your mother, gossiping like an old fool. Which I am. No doubt about that. What else can a young fool become anyway?

There was another rumor about Sylvia. After DeLorio's birth, she had her tubes tied—to spite Dominick, the word was. Her father, old Carlucci, was peeved with her, but he ended up siding with her when Dominick would have divorced her in a flash. The old man, it was said, threatened to kill Dominick if he ever tried to divorce his daughter. So Dominick has only one son and won't ever have any more legitimate ones unless Sylvia dies and he marries again. Irony, Rafaella. Life seems to abound in it. It's quite frightening sometimes.

There was a knock on the door and Rafaella quickly closed the journal.

"Just a moment."

She placed her mother's journal haphazardly in among a pile of books—novels, travel guides, biographies, a couple of reference books on the Caribbean, two more of the journals—on top of the fireplace mantel, all in full view of anyone who happened to look, then opened her bedroom door.

"Oh, hello, Merkel. How are you? It's so quiet. Is Mr. Giovanni ready to begin our work?"

Merkel didn't like this, not at all. She was young, far too young for Mr. Giovanni, honest and open, and she'd made her preferences clear. It was Marcus all the way.

"I like that tie you're wearing. The stripe is very classy."

"It's the latest style, according to *Gentleman's Quarterly.* It's made in Britain and can only be ordered from there. Thank you for noticing. Mr. Giovanni would like to begin now."

Rafaella gave him a sunny smile. "I'm ready to go. Let me get my tape recorder. Oh, yes, Merkel, as you might know, my mother is in a hospital on Long Island. I like to call her every morning. Do you think it will be a problem?"

Merkel just stared at her. Marcus had been wrong. She was exactly what she seemed to be. She wasn't trying to hide anything. She was a reporter who wanted to write Dominick's biography and she didn't have any secrets. She could be trusted, at least to a point. "Certainly, Ms. Holland. I will speak to Mr. Giovanni."

Dominick was in the living room, looking at his Egyptian jewelry. He motioned her over to where he stood.

Rafaella joined him and peered down into the palely tinted glass case.

"Do you recall my telling you these pieces were from the Eighteenth Dynasty? Of course you do.

You're young, not old and forgetful. Well, many people consider the jewelry from this time to be overly ornate, decadent, but I don't think so. It's lovely, isn't it? Especially this." He lifted a wooden box carved in the shape of a small dog and opened it. Inside was a sweet-smelling scent Rafaella couldn't identify, and a child's bracelet of pounded gold sat atop a swell of blue velvet. It looked so delicate she was afraid to breathe on it.

"Very lovely," she said, and to her relief, Dominick closed the lid and gently placed the box back under the glass case. He flicked a switch on, wiped his hands on a pristine white handkerchief, and smiled at her.

"Anytime you wish to look at any of these things, simply ask me, Rafaella. Just touching the pieces, just knowing that they're here, that they're mine for a brief period of time, brings me peace, serenity. They connect me to the past, make me realize that all of time is fluid and unending, that all of us will continue to exist, in some fashion, into the future, into infinity. Ah, but I pretend to be the philosopher when I am but a simple man."

"You're anything but simple, sir."

" 'Dominick,' please," he said, and looked pained. She wondered what effect "Father" would have.

"Very well, Dominick."

"We're going to become quite close, Rafaella. As long as you understand what it is I expect of you—" He paused a moment and she nodded. Oh, yes, she understood his ground rules, his plans for her, her place as the recorder of his greatness. She would agree to whatever he said in order to remain here on the compound. She was still very curious about him. He was her father and she now accepted that. She also accepted the fact that she was going to do her best to ruin him. She would write his biography and hold it up to the world.

"Good. You won't deviate from what it is I wish.

You will produce a masterpiece, you'll see. Oh, yes, I also have a fondness for art, as you know. When you would like to see the pieces in the vault, you have just to ask." And he touched his long cool fingers to her cheek and caressed her.

Rafaella didn't move. She was too surprised. She hadn't considered, hadn't even thought, that he would possibly be interested in her as a woman. Even if he didn't recognize her as his daughter, she was young enough to be one. She smiled and managed to step away from him, hopefully not showing her shock and distaste.

"Come into my library, it's cooler."

"I would really prefer being on the veranda that faces the swimming pool. The smell of the bougainvillea and the frangipani is so wonderful." It was also more open there. "Is there a plug for the tape recorder?"

He nodded, his smile never slipping.

"—so my papa was a man dedicated to getting all his family out of Italy and over to beautiful San Francisco. By the time he died in 1965, he'd succeeded. His brothers, sisters, cousins, the whole bloody lot of them, most moochers, but it didn't bother him, he had this strange sort of drive, to be the dependable one, to be the one everyone could count on, everyone except his only son, that is."

Rafaella dutifully wrote in her own specialized shorthand, adding her own personal notes to his reminiscences on the tape recorder, filling page after page. So he'd felt neglected by his father, had he? Too bad he hadn't choked on it. She could tell that he'd thought about this, thought about the order in which he would present his life to her, and what in his life he would tell her. There was no deep bitterness, no hurt in his voice when he spoke of his father. Just a sullen kind of whine she'd heard once from DeLorio. It shocked her to hear it from him.

Finally he paused and raised a hand. Jiggs appeared, dressed in his usual waiter-white, and received his orders.

"I asked for a lemonade for both of us, Rafaella."

"That's fine."

He stopped talking then, pressed the off button on the tape recorder, sat back in his chair, and steepled his fingers, tapping the fingertips together.

"Merkel told me you wanted to call your mother from here."

"That's right. She was in an accident—perhaps Merkel told you—and she's in the hospital, in a coma. There has been improvement, more EEG activity. I pray every day that she will just wake up one morning and smile and want to get on with her life."

"It must be difficult for you to be so very far away from her."

Rafaella looked down at her hands. She was holding her pencil very tightly.

"I assume you're close to your mother? Although I don't know why I should assume anything of the sort. My son isn't at all close to his mother—in fact he hasn't seen her for a goodly number of years now."

"Goodness, why ever not?"

Dominick shrugged, nodded to Jiggs, and watched as he set the glasses and pitcher on the glass table between them. Dominick handed her a glass. "To our future together," he said.

"Our future," Rafaella said, and clicked her glass to his. She saw that he would begin again, and quietly pressed the play button.

"You asked me why DeLorio hasn't seen his mother. It's very simple, really. My wife is an alcoholic, has been for more years than I care to count. She didn't want him, not really, except as a means to hurt me. So I simply removed him from her care. He asked me to, you know, begged me in fact. She lives on Long Island, has all the servants one could wish for, all the money any ten women could spend in a single lifetime, and she sleeps with very young men."

Rafaella felt her heart pounding, but her voice was steady, thoughtful. She shook her head. "I've never been able to understand that. The older women with the very young men and, of course, the older men with the young women. Just imagine how you'd feel if someone asked you how your son or daughter was doing. Nothing particular in common, no shared experiences or memories, no—"

"You're forgetting sex, my dear, the most powerful and common of all things that bind. That and of course the illusion that even an older man, such as myself, is still attractive, still alluring, can still entice and please a much younger woman. Such as you, for example."

"But it's an illusion. It's not real."

"Isn't it? Maybe not to the older man who's living it, but it's certainly real enough to all those who look upon it. Don't be naive, Rafaella. Throughout the centuries wealthy men have used young women to prove their virility, their influence, their power, to their adversaries. And that, my dear, is real, as real as it gets."

"Perhaps, but it's also despicable. It's people using each other for the most base of reasons."

"You're very young, Rafaella, and the young are more dogmatic than religious fanatics, more passionate in their beliefs, be they absurd or not."

"Perhaps," she said, then glanced down at her notepad. "Your wife, Dominick, you never divorced her?"

His face seemed to go stiff all over. "No, I'm not that kind of man. I made vows to her before God. I keep my word. No matter what she's done—Well, it doesn't matter. She's my wife until she dies, and that's the end of it. A pity she gave me only one son. Yes, a pity. And she was unfaithful to me. From the very beginning, she was unfaithful."

He sounded sincere, hurt, yet stoic. She'd never before met a person who lied with such earnestness. He was good. *Just as her mother had said.* She looked down at her pad, fiddled with her pencil a moment, then said straightly, "And you weren't ever unfaithful to her?"

"Not until she had broken her vows. I wanted sons, Rafaella, I wanted to found a dynasty, to show my father that he wasn't the only one—I digress. But Sylvia wanted revenge on me, she wanted me to suffer—"

She listened to him enthusiastically ride what she was certain was one of his favorite hobbyhorses, his voice sounding more and more bitter, and she knew that her mother had been right. He was a man possessed. And he was a liar. He stopped suddenly and smiled.

"Are you ready for a break yet?" Rafaella asked quickly.

"Ah, Coco, come here, my dear. Of course we're ready. Poor Rafaella has been listening to me carry on for longer than one should have to endure."

"It's all been fascinating," Rafaella said, and it was true.

"We got twisted about in the chronology. Is this a problem for you, Rafaella?"

"Not at all. In fact, if you don't mind, Dominick, I would prefer speaking about things in any order you wish, or in any lack of order. It makes for more spontaneity. If you would excuse me now, I think I'll go listen to what we've got on the tape recorder and transcribe all the marvelous notes I've taken."

"Oh, Rafaella, you never did tell me why you're here while your mother is lying in a coma three thousand miles away."

His voice was like silk and honey, but she wasn't stupid. She must go carefully. She turned slowly and gave a very sad smile. It wasn't difficult. Her eyes blurred. "I was with her for nearly a week. There was nothing I could do. My stepfather encouraged me to come down here. You see, I'd already made the arrangements. He told me he'd send a jet for me if there was any change. I think it's better. At least you, sir, are helping to keep my mind off it."

"Your stepfather is Charles Rutledge."

"Yes, a very nice man and very good to my mother." And he's not like you. He's loyal and honest and real.

"It's curious, you know," Dominick said in a faraway voice. "A man of your stepfather's stature, his wealth, his obvious power, and yet he chose a woman not that much younger than he. Very curious."

"Perhaps he is a man who prefers what is real, what is solid, what is honest, over the chimera, the illusion. Excuse me, Dominick, Coco."

All the way to her room, Rafaella wanted to kick herself for baiting him. He was far from undiscerning. God help her if she had gone too far.

Marseilles, France
March 2001

Marcus had always liked the fog, at least in London, but not here in the south of France, in Marseilles. It had been raining steadily since he'd arrived six hours before. Now the rain had slowed to a light drizzle with a thick blanket of fog over the harbor. Periodically the horns rang out loud and ghostly. Men huddled together on the ship decks, along the pier, in doorways, talking low, their Gauloise cigarettes glowing red-tipped like spots of fire in the darkness. The long rotted docks were slimy with old rain and smelled of wet, dirty wool and moldy mackintoshes.

Marcus took another drink of his beer, Italian beer

that was god-awful, and was thankful that he was inside and not out there in the bone-chilling damp.

The bar, Le Poulet Rouge, was noisy, dank, filled with the raucous laughter that resulted from cheap booze. There were a half-dozen prostitutes lounging about, accepting drinks from the sailors, and avoiding the foul-breathed dockhands in dirty coveralls.

Marcus leaned back against the cracked, dirty vinyl booth. Cigarette smoke had turned the air blue and there were swirls of blue snaking up around the naked light bulbs hanging from the black ceiling. He felt anxious and wished for a moment that he smoked.

Where was Bertrand?

A very young girl, not more than sixteen, he guessed, made her way through the throng of men to his booth. He saw her wince when several men patted her bottom or fondled her bare leg. She was slightly built, pretty in a childish way, with long black hair hanging down her back, and a very white face that Marcus realized finally was the result of a thick layer of white powder.

"Monsieur? Vous voulez quelque chose d'autre, peut-être?"

He grinned up at her. "You know the beer's undrinkable, do you?" Then he shook his head and switched to French. *"Non, mademoiselle, non, merci."*

He watched her thread her way among the small crowded tables, accepting stoically as her punishment all those lewd comments, all those free feels. Poor little girl. He wondered if her father owned the bar. Probably so. Cheap labor. Maybe she smeared her face with all that white powder so no one would recognize her, so she wouldn't recognize herself. Marcus shook his head. He thought of Rafaella and wondered what she'd think of this bar and its denizens. She'd be wide-eyed and shocked to her toes, but she'd try to act like it was as normal as attending Carnegie Hall. He grinned and wished she was here with him.

Where was Bertrand?

A prostitute eyed him, blew him a kiss, and arched an artistically drawn black eyebrow. He shook his head, smiling. She started to rise and he shook his head again, not smiling this time.

She shrugged, took her seat again, and leaned forward, her arms pressed inward, so that her breasts, full and sagging, nearly spilled out of her chemise top. A man laughed and plunged his hand down her top and fondled her breasts. She shrieked and slapped his hand, then shoved him off his chair, sending him sprawling to the floor. The room erupted with laughter.

A jukebox started up, a youth howling out some acid rock that smothered the bar noise. Marcus coughed, the smoke was so thick. He'd just about decided to leave the bar when Bertrand came through the door.

Marcus stared a moment, thinking: This is just like a 1940's movie with Humphrey Bogart. Bertrand was wearing a slouch hat low over his left eye and a light brown raincoat belted at the waist. A Gauloise was dangling from between his thin lips.

He looked Marcus's way, nodded very slightly, and slowly, as if the cameras were following his every move, made his way between the tables to the booth.

"You're late," Marcus said.

Bertrand sat down and raised a hand to the young waitress. "It was unavoidable," he said, then added, looking at the girl, "She's nice. Her name's Blanchette, she's only fifteen, and she wasn't a virgin when she first had sex with me. I wondered who'd done the deflowering. Maybe it was one of these intellectual customers." He was smiling at her all the while he spoke of her to Marcus.

"*Ma chère, une bière, s'il te plaît.*" She nodded, smiling nervously at him. Bertrand waved her away.

"You're late," Marcus said again. "Why was it so

unavoidable?" He hated Bertrand and all he stood for. Some thought him a comely man, in his early forties, fit, and with a dark brooding look that drew the women, and evidently the young girls as well. But Marcus thought his face showed his black soul. Bertrand was vicious, ruthless, amoral, and so unpredictable that both men and women had constantly to be on their guard.

"Business," Bertrand said, and leaned back. He unbelted his raincoat, showing a black turtleneck sweater and black jeans beneath. "I had some more checking to do. My contact at the factory had screwed things up and I didn't get all the mines I'd ordered." He quickly raised his hand, seeing Marcus's color heighten with anger. "I got it straightened out, don't worry. Tomorrow morning, at six o'clock, on Pier Twenty-seven, you and I will oversee, along with one of the stupid bureaucratic Frenchmen, the loading of the mines aboard the *Ionia.* Bound for Nigeria, you know. Everything's right and tight."

"You'll then travel aboard the ship?"

"That's the plan, yes. Ah, my beer. *Merci, ma chère.*" Marcus watched the girl walk away slowly, looking back at Bertrand several times, and this time she was smiling shyly. Bertrand smiled back at her as he said to Marcus, "You want her, Devlin? She's so very young, but I've taught her quite a bit in the last two weeks. She'd been savaged before, not taught how to please or be pleased."

"No," said Marcus, trying not to show his disgust, his revulsion. "She's a child. She could be your daughter."

"Yes, she could, but the point is, she isn't, thank the good Lord. And I like them unspoiled. They're spoiled by the time they're twenty."

"I want the money. I've got to start the transfers as soon as the banks open tomorrow."

"You'll get it, just after the loading of the mines on the ship."

"Why then?"

"Because I'm not stupid. Everyone's heard about the assassination attempt on Giovanni, and I can't imagine that he's filled with the milk of human trust right now. No, you'll get the money tomorrow when I'm certain that everything is just as it should be. I don't mind telling you that I was concerned about the screw-up at the factory. Giovanni should have had it all in order, you know. Yet someone slipped. On purpose? Because they thought Giovanni was weak?"

"It was your responsibility this time."

Bertrand shrugged. "Is that what Giovanni told you?" He drank down his beer in one long gulp, the muscles in his throat working deeply. "Well, it *wasn't* my responsibility. Giovanni's on top of the dog heap right now, Devlin. Everyone's watching, wondering what will happen, waiting. You really don't want to join me with the little girl? I've always had a fancy to have another man around, watching, playing the way he'd like to play while I did the same. Ah, well, you're a puritan, huh, Devlin?"

"No, I'm just not a degenerate."

Bertrand's left hand shot to his right sleeve. Marcus saw the glitter of a silver-handled knife.

"Don't do it, Bertrand. I've got the sweetest little derringer here, palmed, aimed right at your crotch. I'll blow your cock off, boyo, if you don't just calm down. Now."

Bertrand eyed Marcus's right arm. The forearm and hand were under the table. "I don't believe you, Devlin."

"Try me."

Bertrand became very still. His expression didn't change. Then he shrugged. "I'll leave now. Pay for my drink, like a good stooge." And he rose, wended his way between the tables, and was gone, blurred in a haze of blue smoke.

Marcus raised his arm from beneath the table. Gently he shoved the derringer back into place, lightly fastened to the strap around his wrist. He'd never blown a man's cock off before. He wondered if he would have felt any remorse at removing Bertrand's manhood. Probably not. He tossed francs on the table, grabbed his raincoat, and left Le Poulet Rouge.

He looked carefully both to his right and to his left. Bertrand had either really gone about his business or was hiding in an alley waiting to slit Marcus's throat. No, Marcus thought, business was more important than insults.

He walked quickly back to his *pension,* a run-down excuse for a bed-and-breakfast three blocks from the harbor. A loudmouthed old harridan ran it. She was still up when he returned, and he was aware that she was searching for a woman, waiting in the shadows, to follow him up to his room.

"*Pas de femmes,*" he told her, and marched up the two flights to his room.

He heard her cackling below. "*Je puis vous aider, monsieur! Une jolie femme, eh? Très jeune, eh?*" At his bellowed "*Non!*" she just cackled again and retreated.

He couldn't wait to leave here. This part of Marseilles was a pit, and had been for as long as he could remember. Was it more so now? The men and women who roamed through here seemed just as bereft of hope, just as hard and cruel as before. The endless rain and damp didn't help. It made the dirt look filthier and everything else moldy and dingy. He didn't undress, just lay down on the narrow bed.

What was Rafaella doing? Was she safe? Had she managed to keep her smart mouth shut? What would she have thought of Bertrand? Of Marcus's derringer?

He missed her. It came as something of a shock. He hadn't missed anyone in so very long. Sure, his mother, and John, even Uncle Morty, but it wasn't this same kind of bone-deep emptiness. It was unwelcome; it made him sad and even more frustrated at his situation. Savage was probably right. He should get out of this before he got himself killed.

The dream came that night, beginning with the seductive soft colors, romantic stage settings like in old movies, then speeding up, losing softness, gaining edges, sharp and hard, and there he was with his father, Ryan "Chomper" O'Sullivan, and his old man was helping him with math, and his mother, Molly, was there, laughing, teasing her husband, who was always too serious, and she nipped his earlobe with her sharp white teeth. Then there were loud noises, louder still, and the scenes tumbled out of sequence and there was the blood, red and redder still, and it flowed over everything, and his father was there, and the blood was flowing over him and it was everywhere, so much of it, and—

Marcus jerked awake on a moan. He was wet with his own sweat. His heart was pounding. He felt the terror very slowly begin to recede as his mind settled into the present again. Would it never end? He didn't want to go back to sleep, but he did. This time it was dreamless.

In the dark of the night he awoke, fully alert, and knew something was very wrong. Someone was opening the door to his room. He'd locked that door. Slowly he turned onto his side, facing the door. He watched the knob turn slowly.

Hicksville, Long Island
March 2001

Charles sat quietly behind the wheel of the rented Ford Taurus and watched the two-story Tudor house through the black iron gates. He was stiff, and so tired his eyes felt gritty. He reached for the carry-out coffee and pulled the plastic top off the Styrofoam cup. The coffee was cold, and awful, and he drank it down, all of it.

He continued to wait silently. He had to see the woman, the drunken woman, who'd run down Margaret. The coincidence of it, the outrageousness of it, still unnerved him, but B.J. Lewis, his private detective, had been certain. Perhaps it wasn't so impossible. Margaret's car had been in this vicinity when she'd been struck. Not more than two miles from here. But why? He hadn't wondered before, but now he did. What was she doing around here? To his knowledge, she didn't have any friends in Hicksville.

Sylvia Carlucci Giovanni. *His* wife. *His* familiar.

Charles just had to see her.

But how could he possibly know if she'd truly hit Margaret just by looking at her? And if she had, had it really been an accident? Charles shook his head; he was losing his mind.

Suddenly there was activity. He stiffened, hunching forward against the steering wheel to better see the entrance of the house. A man emerged from the front door. He was young, handsome in a male-model sort of way, and built like a sleek young bull. One of her lovers? Evidently so. He turned in the doorway and leaned back, as if he were embracing someone; then he straightened, smiling, and walked away. He was wearing a white T-shirt and tight faded jeans that clearly outlined the bulge of his cock. He was whistling.

Charles watched him flip a set of car keys into the air, then catch them with a jaunty move. He got into a white Porsche, revved the engine like a teenage boy with his father's car, and gunned it, making gravel spew upward. He must have pressed a button inside the car, because the iron gates opened slowly. Charles could practically feel the young man's impatience with those gates, feel his bubbling energy, his pleasure at what he was and who he was and what he had. Charles wondered how long that would last. Then the Porsche roared down the road, headed west.

Charles continued to wait. What else could he do? It was silent again, no sign of her, no sign of anyone. He thought of Margaret, lying there so still in her hospital bed. This morning he'd stayed while her private nurse had massaged her, keeping her muscles as firm and supple as possible. Muscle atrophy and bedsores were the worst enemies. Margaret was massaged three times a day. Her body was white, innocent of scars, her breasts still firm and high, and he'd wanted her very much, just as he'd wanted her since he'd met her on the beach at Montauk Point.

She'd looked so young lying there, her hair neatly brushed, her gown not hospital regulation but a pale blue satin Dior confection he'd bought her some months before for her birthday.

He held her hand, caressed her long fingers, noting that her nails needed trimming. Still holding her hand, he leaned back in his chair and closed his eyes.

And now he was sitting here in front of Sylvia Carlucci Giovanni's two-story Tudor home, waiting. It would be dark in an hour. Then he would have to leave.

He cursed softly. He wanted to see her, had to see her. For a brief moment he pictured himself shooting her; then he laughed at himself.

First he had to just see her.

Shadows were lengthening over the road. He dozed, then awoke with a start. There she was, coming out the front door. He couldn't make out her features clearly. Then she walked beneath a bright outdoor house light that had just come on, and he felt a stab of recognition.

Sylvia Carlucci Giovanni had his wife's blond hair, her graceful walk, her slim figure and slightness of build. There was no resemblance he could see in their facial features, but the general initial impression was that they looked to be related. Sisters perhaps.

That petite lovely woman was the drunk who'd struck Margaret? That was Sylvia Carlucci Giovanni?

Fourteen

The knob kept turning, slowly.

Marcus eased up, silently cursing the squealing of the old bedsprings as his weight shifted.

There was little light in his room, merely a sliver of new moon coming in the narrow window, but it was enough. His eyes never left that door. The door was all the way to the left.

He watched the door ease open.

He was off the bed then, in a low crouch, his derringer in his right hand. He saw a hand on the doorknob, saw that hand continue to push the door open. Suddenly he grabbed the wrist and yanked forward.

He realized at once that it was a woman's wrist he held and that she'd cried out in pain.

"*Monsieur, non! C'est moi, Blanchette!*"

He looked down at the pale-faced girl. Her mouth was working. She was terrified. "What are you doing here, creeping into my room in the middle of the—?" He paused and pulled his French together. "*Quest-ce que vous faites ici? Vous venez comme une voleuse.*"

He shook her, not hard, but she'd frightened him, and now he was angry.

"Answer me. *Répondez-moi.*"

She did, her voice a thin wail, a whisper, and he realized she was now as frightened as he'd been. He'd

sent her, her lover had, he'd told her to come here
and pleasure Devlin, yes, yes, the man in the bar,
Monsieur Bertrand, her lover, the man Devlin had
spoken with.

"*C'est tout, monsieur, je vous assure.*"

He looked down at her pale face, dead white from
all the face powder, her eyes still blank and wide from
shock. What was he to do now?

Even as he weighed his options, sorted through possibilities, he felt something cold that was near, coming
ever nearer, and it was like the dream—cold and hard
and relentless. He whirled about, saw the glimmer of
silver, the shadow of an arm raised, poised, and he
hurled the girl to the floor, dropping on top of her,
covering her as best he could, and as he plunged
down, he felt the hiss of the knife as it went past his
ear, felt the air split, and he saw it hit the headboard,
embedding itself in the cheap pine.

He heard a curse, and saw the shadow of the arm
rise again, and the glint of silver in the pale moonlight
from the window, and slowly, calmly, Marcus raised
the derringer, rolled off the terrified girl, and came to
his feet, facing Jack Bertrand.

"You bastard! You should be in bed, screwing the
little tart's eyes out!"

Bertrand brought the knife up in a fluid motion and
angled it for Marcus's throat. It came slowly and deliberately, as in the dream, and Marcus saw himself, fast
and urgent now, the dream speeding up in crazy
spurts, pull up the derringer, distinct and deadly, and
fire it once, and it struck the knife blade with a loud
ping and ricocheted backward, tearing through Jack
Bertrand's throat. Venous blood poured out, so much
blood, not spurting, just pouring out like water
through a dam. Bertrand stared at Marcus, then at the
girl, who was staring up at him from her crouch on
the floor.

He grabbed at his throat, and the blood poured

through his fingers like rivulets as he fell heavily to the floor. Marcus came down to his knees beside him. He lifted him. "Why? Why, damn you?"

"You're a fool, Devlin," Bertrand whispered, his voice as liquid as blood. "If you weren't so isolated on that island, you'd know that the king is dead, or very nearly. Olivier will take over. I should have been with him, all the way, and I should have killed you. When they found your body, everyone would believe *Bathsheba* had done it."

Marcus just stared down at him.

"I thought I had you. I failed—failed—" There was a soft hissing sound and Jack Bertrand's head fell to the side. His blood-covered fingers slid away from his throat.

There was so much blood. Marcus heard Blanchette sobbing from behind him, turned and saw that her hands were covering her face, her long black hair curtaining her profile.

"Shush," Marcus said automatically, his brain racing. The bullet hadn't been all that loud, but one never knew. The last thing he wanted to do was to become embroiled with the French police. They'd probably throw him in jail and let him rot there. The neighborhood was on his side—derelicts, petty criminals, but mostly empty warehouses.

Marcus quickly pulled Jack's body into his room and closed the door as quietly as possible. He locked the door but knew it wouldn't keep anyone out who wanted to come in. He could just picture that old harridan climbing up here, demanding to know what was going on in her respectable *pension*.

He came down on his haunches next to Blanchette. He shook her shoulders, gathered his French together, and spoke softly, firmly. He told her to leave quickly by the window and go home *vite, vite!* He told her to keep her mouth closed or she would find herself in grave trouble with the police. He would take care of things. She had to trust him. She had to leave now. "*Ne parlez pas aux gendarmes*," he told her over and over. "*Vous comprenez?*"

She stared at him, mouth open, eyes vacant. Had she lost her wits?

"*Vous comprenez, Blanchette? Répondez-moi!*"

Finally she nodded, words still beyond her. He helped her to her feet and out the window. She didn't look once at Jack's body, sprawled by the bed, his eyes staring toward her from his bloodless face.

Marcus didn't move until she'd disappeared from his view. He walked quickly to the window, watched her climb down the fire escape and disappear into the misting dank fog and the filth of the alley.

He turned back to Jack Bertrand. "I wish you hadn't tried that," he said, and got to work.

Giovanni's Island
March 2001

Rafaella didn't trust him. She wasn't afraid, but she knew that if he tried to seduce her, the jig would be up, as her mother used to say. She'd been relieved when the phone call came through. Dominick dismissed her for the afternoon. She heard Lacy say that the call was from Marcus.

Was Marcus in trouble? She didn't want to think about him, but she couldn't help it. She didn't want to worry about him, but she couldn't help that either. He was insidious, that man, and in weak moments she admitted he was there, in her mind, always there, a permanent resident. Could he be in trouble? She didn't want anyone else hurting him, just her, and only when he deserved it, which was, admittedly, quite often.

Rafaella dismissed the idea of swimming in the pool. There were too many guards about and she didn't feel like being stared at. Nor did she like the notion of Dominick seeing her in a bikini. She changed quickly, pulling shorts and a baggy top over her suit. She grabbed several books from the mantel, including one of her mother's journals, and headed for the beach.

The day was clear, warm, and saved from misery by the breeze from the Caribbean. Beautiful, beautiful Eden, but she was already growing tired of its perfection. A little Boston rain wouldn't have been horrible. A lot of Boston rain was another matter.

She nodded to Merkel, told him where she was going, and kept on her way. She saw Frank Lacy, looking as gaunt as he had the other night, waved to him, and tried to ignore the half-dozen men, all of them armed, who strolled around the grounds. Their movements looked unrehearsed, their direction unplanned, which she knew wasn't true at all. They all appeared to be excellent at their jobs, and Rafaella, for one, even knowing a martial art, never wanted to face any of them.

She strolled through the lush jungle that separated the compound from the beach. About fifty yards of thick vegetation, now damp from a thirty-minute rainfall, made it almost difficult to breathe. She began to feel closed in, despite the cleanliness of the path. She imagined that the encroaching growth had to be cut back every day of the year.

Marcus had to be all right. Why had he phoned? Perhaps the call hadn't even been from Marcus, and if it had, he was just reporting to Dominick that all was going well. She prayed with all her might that that was the case.

She gained the beautiful white beach and chose a shaded spot under a palm tree. The air was so clear and clean, it made the suffocating thick jungle seem like a bad dream.

She stripped down to her suit and crashed through

the gentle waves, swimming strongly out beyond the breakers.

Link regarded the woman from the protection of the jungle. He'd been told by Mr. Giovanni to keep her in sight at all times if she left the grounds. So she wanted to swim? Who the hell cared?

He watched for ten minutes or so until he was bored enough to sit down and light a cigarette. Finally she came out of the surf, and he watched her walk to her spread-out towel and sit down. Almost immediately she pulled on a loose-fitting top, leaned back against the palm tree, and pulled an apple out of her bag.

At least she wasn't bad to look at, he thought, wishing now that he also had an apple, too.

Soon she pulled a book out of the bag, settled back, and opened it. At that point, Link decided to nap. What could she possibly do with a damned book?

Rafaella turned to a journal entry dated July 1997:

He's taken a new mistress. She's an incredibly beautiful French model by the name of Coco Vivrieux. From what I could find out, he met her in France and immediately they became an item, as the Hollywood rags say. I close my eyes and see them together, naked, in bed, his hands all over her beautiful body, his mouth clinging to hers, and I hear the noises she makes when he comes inside her. God, I can't bear it.

I had to put my journal away for a few days. I couldn't bear to write, but I know I must accept her in Dominick's life. I have no choice, and after all, he doesn't remember who I am. I might never have existed for him. I've tried to make excuses for him for that day in Madrid in 1989 when he looked right through me. After all, I've told myself countless times over the years, I was very slender when I was twenty years old. I'm fuller now, a woman, and my hair is darker than it was then. Yes, I had pale blond hair when I was twenty, I've told myself. And dark glasses—I'm almost certain

*I was wearing dark glasses in Madrid, the kind that
hide your eyes completely. After all, isn't the sun so
very strong and bright in Spain? Doesn't one always
wear dark glasses? My own daughter wouldn't have
recognized me. That's what I've told myself, Rafaella,
over and over, until I hate myself, my weakness.*

*The word was that his new French mistress is in her
early thirties and getting a bit long in the tooth to stay
on top much longer in the modeling world. Thus she
accepted Dominick's offer without too much hesitation.
He's taken her to that bloody island he recently bought
in the Caribbean.*

*I must go there. I must see it. It's stupid and obsessive
and I am aware of it, but there it is.*

*My hatred for him grew by another good-size bound
when he took Coco. He's had so many women over
the years, but I know, I'm certain that she will last. The
funny thing is that she doesn't seem to be an evil
woman, a greedy kept woman. I'm trying to find out
everything I can about her. No, the hell of it is, she
appears quite nice.*

*I must stop thinking about him. I did for a while,
when you graduated from Columbia and Charles and
I attended and Charles threw that wonderful party for
you at the Plaza. You were so gracious, Rafaella, even
when Charles wanted to call the newspaper in Wallingford, Delaware. Charles, of course, is furious. He
counted on handing you the moon, at the very least. I
threatened him with loss of all sex with his wife if he
said anything to you, and the dear man managed to
swallow his bile.*

*You told me at your party that you were worried
about Benjie. Well, I am too. Benjie is a nice man but
he'd take anything his father offered him, in a flash.
No, really it's more Susan who wants things, so many
things, and she is really very talented. Charles doesn't
at all mind being manipulated by her. Or so it seems
to me. She's also teaching little Jennifer to be manipula-*

tive, conniving. Poor Benjie, he'll never be the success
Susan expects him to be. Or the success Charles expects
him to be, for that matter. His watercolors continue to
improve in their beauty and quality. He loves sailboats
and the ocean, and they are mostly his subjects. I al-
ways buy several of them for Christmas presents for
my friends. What else can I do?
  I must see the island. I must see where he lives, with
her, with that damned French model.

  Rafaella closed the journal. Her mother had actually
seen the island, studied it, willingly engulfed herself in
pain. And to think she had never imagined that her
mother had been suffering such torment, had spent
her life gnawing over painful memories, creating new
ones with every stroke of her pen in the journal, with
every newspaper and magazine clipping she cut out
and so relentlessly and neatly placed inside the journals. Rafaella wished very much that her mother
hadn't come to the island. Until then she'd kept herself physically away from him.
  When would it stop? Perhaps with the publication
of the biography Rafaella would write about Dominick, the very unromantic illegal-arms merchant, the
purveyor of death?
  Rafaella wished she were with her mother at this
moment. She felt awash with guilt, even though intellectually she knew that a vigil at her mother's bedside
would have no bearing on anything. It would change
nothing. She leaned her head forward and rested it on
her knees. She prayed. She hadn't prayed, not really,
since she'd been sixteen, and then it had been a selfish
prayer, one that had been answered, one she hadn't
deserved: Oh, please, God, let me have a convertible
for my birthday, please, God—
  And there it had been, more than she'd prayed for,
a Mercedes 450 SLC, red with white leather interior,
jaunty and ready for her, sitting on the gravel drive

in front of the house, Charles and her mother holding out the keys to her, smiling, smiling—

Stupid selfish child. But that was years ago and she had changed and grown up. But her mother hadn't; she'd remained locked into her hatred of Giovanni, her obsession with the man.

Link watched Rafaella, wondering what she was thinking. She was obviously upset. He hoped she wouldn't cry. His grandmother, who'd raised him, hadn't cried except when he'd hurt her, and then it was great gulping sobs, and as an adult he simply couldn't bear a woman's tears. He was vastly relieved when the young woman seemed to shake off her funk, gather her things together, and rise. She was pretty, no doubt about that, and her eyes were particularly fine, that pale blue that darkened with emotion, like now. Those eyes of hers—Link shook his head. He needed to get off this bloody island; he was going stir-crazy. He quickly shrank back behind a palm tree when Rafaella walked toward him. As he watched her progress through the jungle until she was lost from his sight, he wondered if he were protecting her by shadowing her or protecting Mr. Giovanni from another assassination attempt.

Link began his trek back to the compound, keeping a goodly distance between himself and Rafaella. There hadn't been another assassination attempt. Of course, that first failure had been quite a fiasco, and the island was a fortress in itself, quite a deterrent. And the men, keyed up after the first attempt, shamed to their toes for their failure to guard Mr. Giovanni, were now losing it, boredom getting to them again, making them careless, not obviously—no, never that, they were professionals, after all—no, it was their judgment, their reflexes if there were a sudden attack. Link decided to speak to Lacy, who probably already recognized the problem. If there were a second attempt—*when* there was a second attempt—Lacy and the men would be ready.

Funny, Link's thinking continued, funny that those Dutchmen had poisoned themselves before Mr. Giovanni could question them. Funny that they should have poisoned themselves at all. Did *Bathsheba* have such a fanatic hold on its men?

Link sighed. None of it made much sense to him. And he'd searched the Dutchmen before locking them in the shed; searched them personally. They must have had the poison glued between their toes.

Link was continuing his ruminations when he heard her scream, high, thin, filled with terror and surprise. He sprinted forward, veering right at another cry, this one choking, pain-filled. He came to a horrified halt to see Rafaella Holland just off the path, the one and only boa constrictor on the bloody island, all ten feet of it, wrapping itself lazily around her body, its dark brown crossbars glistening as they slithered to her waist, tightening, ever tightening.

She saw him, and he saw the sudden hope in her eyes. "Shit," he said, and drew his knife as he sprinted forward.

Rafaella forced herself to hold very still even though she wanted to continue her struggles. She wanted to vomit, she wanted to yell, but she didn't move a muscle. The boa's coils were heavy, so very heavy, and she was being bowed to her knees, but there was Link, and she instinctively closed her eyes when he cleanly slashed his knife through the snake, just below its head. There was no sound, only the loud thud as the head hit the ground. Did she expect a scream of pain from the snake? She was shuddering now from shock as the snake's heavy coils began to loosen their hold on her. Her ribs, released from the gripping pain, heaved as she frantically sucked in air. She felt Link pulling the snake off her, knew he was unwinding it, and it was all she could do not to vomit.

She opened her eyes and saw the blood, blood everywhere, on her bare arms, all over her baggy top, on Link, and covering the knife blade. And the boa constrictor lay headless at her feet, giving spasms still that made the coils hump upward, and she jerked away quickly, and raced away, only to fall on her knees and vomit. There was little in her stomach, but she couldn't seem to stop the spasms. She dry-heaved until she was weak and shaking and ready to fall over. But she didn't; the snake was too near.

She felt Link's hand on her shoulder. "It's dead, Miss Holland. Come along now, let's get back to the compound and get you cleaned up."

Rafaella looked up at him and slowly shook her head. "I can't, Link, I just can't." She pulled herself to her feet, avoided the snake, and raced back toward the beach.

Link let her go. Quickly he wrapped the snake's now-limp coils about his arm and dragged the rest of it into the jungle, out of sight. The other animals would devour the carcass. And Miss Holland wouldn't have to see the thing again.

He waited another moment, then walked toward the beach. He stopped at the edge of the jungle and looked out toward the sea. She was standing knee-deep in the surf, wildly and frantically splashing water on herself. Her hair was matted down and he could practically feel her skin crawling with revulsion as she scrubbed the snake's blood out of her clothes.

"Get hold of yourself," Rafaella said over and over, even as her fingers fretted madly with the pale pink stains on her shorts. Then her fingers stopped and her arms dropped to her sides. The rush of adrenaline was over. She stood there utterly still, weary to the depths of her, the warm water slapping at her thighs, and she knew now that she was safe, quite alive, and the horror was slowly receding. She looked up then, took a deep breath, and saw Link standing patiently at the edge of the white beach, watching her. She waved and she fancied he smiled as he raised his arm and motioned her back to him.

"Thank you, Link," she said when she reached him. "You saved my life, and to me, sir, that is quite a wonderful gift."

"It's all right," he said, and he was smiling at her, a sweet smile, a gentle smile, and she was nearly undone. She wanted to cry, but she saw the appalled expression on his face and swallowed convulsively. She even managed to grin. Link understood and awkwardly patted her back.

"There aren't any more of those monsters," he said presently. "That one's dead as a bloody doornail—whatever that means. My grandma always used to say that when I was a boy—'You keep doin' that, Everett, and I'll make you deader than a doornail'—and so it is, Miss Holland."

Rafaella looked up at him, sniffed, and wiped her nose on her sleeve. "Everett? Your name's Everett?"

Well, he'd done it to himself. "Yes, ma'am. I'd appreciate it if you'd keep it to yourself. Merkel would batter me into the ground if he knew. And old Lacy, well, he just might roll off the island, he'd laugh so hard."

"You can count on me, Link. But I think it's a lovely name."

"So did my ma," he said. "So did my ma."

And there was the snake story to tell again and again, until Rafaella began to think it was but a tall tale, nothing more than a snake story that she and Link had embroidered to terrify the listeners. And Coco, mouth agape, cried out several times, "Oh, my poor Rafaella," and folded her against her breasts, patting her back.

Dominick said nothing in her hearing. He studied the bedraggled young woman, wondering where the devil that blasted snake had come from. Boas rarely left their own territory even when free to do so, and that snake had been cozy and happy high in Dominick's private zoo on the middle ridge, and yet it had somehow gotten free of its pen, providently come down and waited just off the path, and given Rafaella the scare of her life. It didn't make sense; he happened to look at Link at that moment and knew that the other man was just as confused.

It was near to evening when one of the men found a large wooden cage in the jungle. And then things became clear. Someone had brought the boa here, loosing it on the trail to the beach. But the timing? Who had been the intended victim? It was accident, purely, that Rafaella had been on the path. Unless, he thought, unless that someone waited until Rafaella started back from the beach, waited and then opened the cage and loosed the boa.

He said as much to Coco as they dressed for dinner, but before she could reply, Merkel was at the door, out of breath because he'd run upstairs, and told Dominick that Marcus was on the phone again and that Jack Bertrand had tried to kill him but Marcus had got him instead.

Dominick merely nodded to Coco and followed Merkel from the room. He allowed Merkel to remain as he sat down at his desk and picked up the phone. "Dominick here, Marcus. Tell me what happened."

He listened, saying nothing, for a good five minutes. Finally, "I'm glad you survived it. There's nothing to be done about the rest of it at the moment. Come home. We'll decide what's to be done when you get here."

Dominick fell silent again, listening intently. "You're right, of course. We'll go into it when you've returned. Oh, by the way, my boy, our Rafaella just had a very close call."

Even Merkel could hear Marcus shout, "That brain-defective woman! What did she get herself into this time?"

Dominick chuckled, but Merkel, tuned to his boss's every expression, his most subtle body language, saw that the chuckle didn't mean what it was supposed to.

"She had a run-in with a boa constrictor, Marcus. Link was with her, of course, not with her knowledge, and he killed the snake. She is rather upset, as you can imagine." He paused, listening. "Yes, I'll keep Link with her. Don't worry. Come home."

Dominick gently laid the phone back into its cradle. He said, not looking up, "Bertrand never intended to pay up, and there were no arms. It was all an elaborate setup, a ruse, to kill Marcus and make me look like an ineffectual fool, a buffoon, a weakling. 'The king is dead, or very nearly dead'—those were Bertrand's dying words. But at least we have a lead on *Bathsheba,* this group or organization or man or whatever the hell it is."

Fifteen

Over dinner, Dominick calmly told everyone in general terms what had happened in Marseilles. When he began speaking, he glanced at Rafaella, and she knew that he was assessing the wisdom of speaking so frankly in front of her. To her relief and chagrin, it appeared he decided she could either be trusted or it didn't matter. It was the latter, she had no doubt, and she imagined he saw her only as a woman who was bright enough to be the recorder of his glorious life, and a woman, any woman, could be controlled. She accepted it; it didn't matter. Only knowing what had happened to Marcus mattered. She forgot the boa constrictor that had nearly caved in her ribs and clutched her fork so tightly her knuckles showed white. "How did this Jack Bertrand try to kill him, Dominick? Marcus isn't stupid."

"He tried to kill him stupidly. He sent over a girl whose responsibility it was to get Marcus into bed. And when Marcus was otherwise occupied, Jack would creep in and cut his throat for him."

"I take it, then, that Marcus refused to do as expected?"

"Marcus isn't indiscriminate in whom he takes to bed, nor is he a pedophile. He told me the girl was fifteen years old."

Dominick looked as if he would say more, then abruptly stopped. He took a chilled shrimp and forked it into his mouth. He chewed slowly. "I would just

add, Rafaella, that this arms deal was all aboveboard.
There was an end-user certificate. It's just that these
arms weren't going to Nigeria as the French believed.
They were going to a group of rebels in East Africa,
to fight the communist-backed dictator there. Since
this group is off-limits, we had to bend the rules a bit
to get the arms to the rebels."

And goats sing opera, Rafaella wanted to say, but
kept both her mouth and her expression closed. Dominick continued, saying, "We haven't yet spoken of my
profession. I admit I'm an arms dealer, but I deal
openly, Rafaella, despite what you might have read or
what you might have heard. I'm not an outlaw; I'm
not a criminal; I'm not a man who supplies terrorists
with weapons to kill innocent people; I'm not in the
black market. Sometimes I am forced to stray into the
gray market, but not often. This time was the first in
quite a while that I was prepared to bend the rules. I
never send arms to our country's enemies—not to
Qaddafi, nor to Saddam, not to North Korea. I have
dealt often with the CIA in the past, but unfortunately
that can't be included in our book. An arms dealer
would never admit working with your government or
he'd be thought a fool or a braggart. He'd be laughed
out of the country by his peers."

"We are out of the country," Coco said.

"You jest," Dominick said, but he didn't smile.
"Nor, I might add, would our government be pleased
with such an admission."

"What were you sending to the rebels in East Africa?" Rafaella asked.

Dominick fanned his hands in front of him. "Lord
knows they need everything. I'd made a deal for a
large shipment of mines, primarily. The mines are very
useful to the rebels, given the desert terrain in their
country."

Rafaella didn't ask which country in East Africa.
He'd have to step up his lying, and for some reason

she didn't want to admit, she didn't want him to, not so blatantly. She was too worried about Marcus, blast his careless eyes.

"I'll teach you about the white arms market, Rafaella," Dominick said. "So few people know anything about it, except the feds, of course."

"I'd like that," she said. She'd read a good bit about arms dealing before she'd left the United States. There wasn't much to be found, as Dominick had just said. As to the black market, even less was known. Many of the major players were recognized, of course, but not much else. And of all the major players, least was known about Dominick Giovanni. She wished she could have spoken to someone in the know at the CIA. That or the U.S. Customs Service.

She sought out Merkel after dinner, drawing him outside on the veranda. "Please tell me more about this *Bathsheba* thing. What does it mean?"

Merkel didn't know what to say, so he tried backing off. "Look, Rafaella, I can't talk to you about Mr. Giovanni's business. He wouldn't like me talking, and he wouldn't like you asking. You've got to ask him or Marcus."

She'd ask Marcus. Oddly enough, very suddenly, she was afraid to ask Dominick. "So tell me about this now-deceased Jack Bertrand."

"You *are* a reporter, aren't you? Again, ask Mr. Giovanni or Marcus. I'll just say that he wasn't a nice man. He was also something of a free-lancer until this thing." Merkel shrugged. "Ask Marcus," he said again, gave her a small salute, and went back into the house.

Rafaella was on her way to bed when Coco stopped her in the second-floor hallway. "Are you truly all right, Rafaella?"

"Shaky still, but that's understandable. I'm okay, Coco."

Coco paused a moment, then seemed to make up

her mind about something. "Come with me out onto the balcony. It's private there."

Rafaella dutifully followed her to the balcony through a wide set of glass French doors at the south end of the hall. The iron railing could scarcely be seen through the tangled mass of bright red and purple bougainvillea. The night was calm, the air perfumed with the scents from the hibiscus, roses, and frangipani. Rafaella took a deep breath, turned, and smiled inquiringly at Coco.

"Just plow forward, Coco. Get it off your chest, whatever it is. My phenomenal bout with the killer boa? Marcus almost getting his throat cut in Marseilles? The book? What?"

"All right. It's gone too far, Rafaella. Much too far. Someone took the boa from its preserve, brought it down from the middle ridge in a cage, and probably waited to release the snake when you were seen coming."

Rafaella, still not immune from the experience, felt a tremor of fear race through her. "Yes," she said, "the cage. It does give me pause, I assure you. But it isn't a very reliable method of killing somebody, Coco. Who would be sure the stupid snake would decide to come after me? It could have simply napped while a dozen people strolled along that path. Why me? It's all a very iffy proposition."

Coco shrugged, but she looked worried, very worried. "Listen, for whatever reason, the boa went after you. If Link hadn't been close by, you would have been killed, the life literally squeezed out of you. Tell me this. What if the snake hadn't gotten you, what if that huge monster had just been lying on the path in front of you or dangling from a branch? How would you have felt?"

"Petrified. Scared out of my skin. I probably would have screamed my head off and run all the way to Antigua, all the way to the airport."

"That's what I think you should do. Leave, Rafaella. Tomorrow." Coco paused a moment, drawing her beautifully arched brows together. "We've all assumed that the shot on the beach was intended for Marcus. We've assumed the helicopter crash was intended for Marcus as well, as a warning. Maybe both things were intended for you, Rafaella. Maybe someone doesn't want you here."

Coco had a point, and Rafaella wasn't indifferent to it. She listened, then said simply, "Why, Coco? I'm just here to write a book, nothing more, nothing less, nothing remotely threatening to anyone. I repeat, who? Why?"

Coco said very slowly, not looking at Rafaella, but staring inland, toward the high middle ridge where the boa had lived, "I'm not an alarmist, not at all. I've thought about this a lot, quite a bit, in fact, even before the snake incident today. And I think it's DeLorio. I think he's jealous of you and he's afraid, afraid that his father will come to value you more than he does his only son. He didn't want to leave before you arrived here, but his father ordered him to Miami. It's the same thing with Marcus, you know. The other times, both of you were together. This time you happened to be alone. I would have suspected Paula—for obvious reasons. She loathes you and wants nothing more than to see you hurt or off the island for good. But Paula doesn't seem to me to have the smarts for such planning. I could be wrong, who knows? The bottom line, however, is the same. I think you should just put off writing the biography for a little while. There are other things going on, things that could also harm you."

"Like *Bathsheba?*"

It had grown quite dark, and Rafaella wished she could see Coco's expression more clearly. Coco wasn't surprised, because Dominick had mentioned *Bathsheba* at dinner, but she stiffened nonetheless.

"What do you know about *Bathsheba*?"

"Just the name, that's all Dominick said at dinner."

"Well, just forget it. It's not important to you—forget *Bathsheba* and think about all this. I'll see you in the morning, Rafaella." She stopped, turned, and said, a smile on her face, "You're stubborn, but I am very fond of you and I don't want to see you hurt."

When Marcus saw Rafaella the following evening at nine o'clock, alone on the east lawn, he was so relieved to actually see that she was still in one piece that he bellowed, "Why the hell can't you be more careful? What were you doing, hiking up in the middle ridge by yourself, trying to be the macha of the month? However could you attract a boa? Did you open its cage? You drive me crazy, you know that?"

He knew very well, of course, where the boa had been. Rafaella just smiled at him, a very sweet smile that should have put him instantly on red alert. She walked toward him, stopping a half-foot away. "Welcome home, Marcus."

Without warning, she grabbed his arm, gained the leverage she needed, and sent him flying onto the grass on his back. He just stared at her, arms and legs sprawled. "You know, you're going to do that to me one too many times and I'll get you, but good."

"You and who else?" She gave him a crazed smile.

"Just me."

"Yeah? How?"

"You want specificity, huh? I think I'll tie you down and make love to you until you're silly. That should keep me relatively safe."

She didn't say anything to that, just stared down at him, her legs spread, her hands on her hips. She was wearing a wraparound denim skirt and a pale pink blouse.

It was her turn now. He was lying there, safe and fit and quite well, and he'd come close to death, and she realized how frightened she'd been, and yelled at him, "Just what did you get yourself into in Marseilles? How could that Jack Bertrand possibly have thought that you'd go to bed with a fifteen-year-old girl? You must have given some indication that it would be just fine with you, you jerk. So then he tried to kill you. Weren't you being at all careful? I told you—several times, in fact—to watch yourself and look wh—"

In the next instant Rafaella was on her back, Marcus straddling her, his knees on either side of her chest. She was winded, but quite unhurt. He quickly grabbed her wrists when he saw the counterattack plan in her eyes, and pinned them over her head.

"Are we even now?"

"How'd you do that? It was faster than you usually are. Have you been practicing? Come on, let me up now—and no, we're not even."

"I guess I'll have to. I see three of Dominick's men all staring at us, their guns slack, grinning like fools. I would just as soon kiss your face off and make love to you until both our feet get numb, but . . ."

"Feet get numb? What kind of a pervert are you, anyway?"

He leaned down and kissed her lightly on the tip of her nose. "The kind of pervert who doesn't leave undershorts in the deep end of the swimming pool for just anyone to find."

She closed her eyes at that remark. She'd forgotten all about her panties. "Oh, dear, no one's said anything. Do you think they're still in the pool?"

He ducked his head again and nipped her nose. "You wanna go check it out tonight, late, after everyone's gone to bed?"

It was Rafaella's turn, and she executed her move quickly and efficiently, pulling him to his side, rolling the opposite way and onto her feet, smiling down at him.

"How about midnight, Ms. Holland? I really have quite a bit more to say to you."

She looked down at him, just sprawled there. She hadn't realized how much she'd missed him—his mouth in particular, that easy wit of his that flowed from it. She shouldn't lie to herself. She'd missed all of him like crazy. "Aren't you afraid that I'll think you're too easy? That I won't respect you in the light of dawn?"

"I won't be easy. You'll have to pull off your finest tricks to get me going properly. What do you say, Ms. Holland?"

"I do have quite a bit more to say to you too." She regarded him thoughtfully. "You'll probably come to a bad end. But I'll tell you what, Mr. Devlin—or whatever your name is—I really do want to speak to you in private. About *Bathsheba*."

That removed the sexual gleam from his eye in a flash. He said carefully, "What do you know about that?"

"Dominick told us at dinner what had happened, and he mentioned it. I want to know, Marcus. I want to know everything and I won't be put off."

He said nothing as he came up to his feet and brushed off his slacks.

"Well?"

"Your belligerence doesn't move me, Ms. Holland. I've got to see Dominick now. I'll meet you at midnight by the pool. Oh yes, I do want to know why you're a Forty-niner fan and not an avid Patriots fan. You do live in Boston, not San Francisco."

"I won't tell you," Rafaella said to herself as she watched him stride away from her.

She returned to the house and was told by Link that Marcus was indeed closeted with Mr. Giovanni. She nodded and made her way upstairs to her room. She pulled her mother's second journal out of the pile of books on the mantel and lay down on her bed.

She'd been rereading the journals, out of order, given her mood at any particular time. She opened the journal to March 2000, nearly one year ago today. But she read only a bit about the visit her mother had made with Charles to England and the god-awful fight Charles had had with Susan when they returned. *Money,* Margaret had written, *damned lousy stuff. If people don't have it, they'll do anything to get it. If they've got it, they'll do about anything to keep it or get even more.* Rafaella closed the journal and thought instead about her two-hour interview with her father that afternoon.

He'd been, understandably, on edge. Withdrawn, somewhat absent. She'd offered to leave him, but he'd insisted that they keep on with it. And so she'd asked him about his years in Chicago. He'd raised a thin eyebrow. "What do you know about Chicago?"

"You forget, Dominick, I think I have every newspaper and magazine clipping ever done on you. I remember this one article that referred to you as a crime boss second only to Carlo Carlucci in Chicago. He's not exactly a household name, but still, as a reporter, I'd heard of him. But that was after you'd married his daughter, I believe." She kept her voice even, emotionless. She couldn't let him sense that she was more than an ardent worshiper at his shrine, couldn't let him feel her contempt for him.

"That was a very long time ago," Dominick said finally, his voice remote. "A very long time ago. Did you know that old man Carlucci is still alive and still living in Chicago? He has this penthouse on the thirty-second floor of a building just off Michigan Avenue. He doesn't have much active control anymore, but oddly enough, no one's tried to bump him off. He's evidently beloved for his fairness to his fellowman." This was said with such bewildered derision that Rafaella didn't know how to respond, so she simply waited for him to continue.

"I met him when I was twenty-eight years old and fresh from San Francisco—"

He made it sound as if he'd been fresh from college, when actually he was just fresh from San Francisco, the SFPD hot on his trail, she thought, but again, she merely waited.

"I was very young—"

"You were twenty-eight."

His head whipped up and he stared at her, growing anger darkening his eyes to the same shade of gray hers reached when she was caught in emotion. She stared back at her father and said deliberately, "I'm almost twenty-six and am old enough to accept the consequences of my behavior."

His entire body eased in the next moment. "You're right, of course. I was a grown man. I knew what I was doing, and if what I did was unwise, well, there it is. I went into legitimate business. My businesses have always been legitimate. I bought a restaurant and immediately ran into trouble. I needed a liquor license and for some unknown reason the city wouldn't give me one. Well, things like this are the same all over, so I simply made inquiries as to whose palm had to be greased. It was Carlucci's, only his palm was immense, and the palm could turn into a fist on a whim.

"I met Sylvia, his daughter, quite by accident. She came into my restaurant one evening with another man, a creep who looked like a bodyguard."

"What was the name of your restaurant?" When he just looked at her, Rafaella added, "A book that has specifics is more interesting. It makes it more real, you see, less generic."

"I changed the name from The Golden Ball to The Golden Bull."

Rafaella just arched an eyebrow at him.

He grinned. "Yeah, I know. I was real macho in those days, and full of myself. Hell, I was young, with my life ahead of me, and I thought I could do anything." He paused a moment and his eyes faded with memories. Rafaella just waited until he'd shaken them off.

"I met Sylvia. It was in 1962, in November. The weather in Chicago was already too miserable for humans." He unconsciously rubbed his arms. "I hate the cold, always have. She was really quite lovely then. Not at all innocent, of course, but who cared? We married in February, her old man decided he liked my zeal, my ambition, and things began to go well. The Golden Bull became well-known, and my other ventures prospered as well."

"Such as?"

Dominick waved his hand vaguely. "Just branching out into other areas—like oil and food markets and shoe stores—things like that, legitimate things."

Did he honestly believe that she'd take any of this seriously? "Tell me about your marriage."

"Before we married, Sylvia told me she wanted a dozen kids. After we married, she didn't get pregnant. For a very long time. I was patient with her, Lord knows. I liked her father . . ."

Ha! You were scared to death of her father.

"Then she finally got pregnant in 1975 with DeLorio. I was thrilled. I wanted many children, many sons."

"Just sons?"

"Oh, no, of course not. I would have loved daughters, lots of them."

She stared at him, unable to tell him that he was a liar. But oh how she wanted to.

"Boys first, that's all I asked, boys to follow in my footsteps, and I would have trained them and they would have been successes, my successes." He paused a moment, staring beyond Rafaella's shoulder. Then he shrugged. "After DeLorio was born, she began being openly unfaithful to me. It was then that, to get revenge, I suppose, I began to sleep with other women. We spoke of this before, Rafaella. In any event, I have never divorced her, as you know. Also, I never see her. Nor does DeLorio. He knows the sort of woman she is."

Rafaella was jerked away from those memories by the shouts from her open French doors that gave onto her balcony. Men shouting. An intruder?

She jumped from her chair and raced out onto the balcony. It was very dark tonight, but she saw the jerking beams from flashlights.

Then she heard DeLorio's voice, cold and furious. "Stop it, you idiots! It's me—put down those guns!"

She heard Dominick, his voice sharp, worried. "What are you doing back here? Did something go wrong?"

"No, nothing's wrong. I left Paula there to do some shopping and flew back to St. John's. I took a helicopter to the resort and a motor scooter over the ridge home."

"Why didn't you call me? I would have sent someone for you."

DeLorio didn't answer.

And Rafaella knew the answer at that moment. DeLorio hadn't called because he feared his father wouldn't have wanted him to come home. She felt fury at Dominick and a wave of pity for his only son. But then, there'd been the worry in Dominick's voice.

DeLorio mumbled something, then yawned loudly. "I'm tired, sir. I think I'll go upstairs."

Then there was silence. Rafaella turned away from the balcony and closed the French doors. She went to bed fully dressed because she planned to go to the swimming pool at midnight. To see Marcus. She told herself she just wanted to talk to him, to find out what all the secrecy was about. She needed to know.

She didn't sleep. She just stared at the digital clock on the bedside table. When it was five minutes to midnight, she left her room and as quietly as possible made her way downstairs and outside. She was stopped by one of the men and identified herself. Everyone would know that she was meeting Marcus.

It couldn't be helped.

He was waiting for her down by the deep end, near the diving board. "Good evening, Ms. Holland," he said, giving her a grin. "Yes, I know, you needn't say anything. Every man in the compound knows that we're meeting out here. And no, I don't see your panties. And no, I don't plan to let you seduce me, even though I know that's what you came out here for. Let's just sit over there on the recliners and talk. All right?"

"You've said about everything," she said, and with a sigh sat down.

"We can hold hands."

She slipped her hand into his. He kept both their hands between them.

"Now, tell me about the snake."

"You've already heard everything. It's already reached tall-snake-tale proportions."

"The sucker attacked you?"

"Yes. It was horrible."

"What I find interesting about the whole thing is that whoever put that snake there also knew that Link was keeping an eye on you. So, no matter that the snake would try to squeeze the life out of you, Link would save you."

"I hadn't thought of that," she said slowly. "You're probably right. Then it was just another warning—Coco was probably on target."

"About what?"

"The other accidents. Maybe I was the target all along, not you."

"I've thought of it, and it's possible, so I want you to leave the island tomorrow."

"No way."

He sighed. "I know you must have been terrified."

"I was, but I'm not a coward. Well, so I am, but it doesn't matter. I want to know who's behind this, Marcus, and I'm not about to be forced away. The thing is to go ahead and be scared witless, but regardless, you just don't give up, turn tail, and run. I won't do it. Now, tell me about Marseilles and this fifteen-year-old girl of yours."

He did, omitting nothing.

She was silent for a moment, warming up, he thought, looking at her mobile face. "*Bathsheba* now, if you please."

"I would have told you a couple of days ago to forget it, but now it seems that everyone who counts in this business—all over the world—already knows all about it, so who cares if one more nosy reporter knows?" He began talking, telling her about his trip to Boston. "It was so bloody cold there—"

"I was there and didn't even meet you."

"I've thought the same thing. I could have taken you to a hockey game. In any case, Dominick called me and told me everything had been finalized and to come home." He paused a moment, watching one of the guards light a cigarette. All he could see was the fire-red tip. And he thought of Jack Bertrand and his Gauloise cigarettes.

"—and there were green letters on the cabin of the helicopter. *Bathsheba.* That was all. The two Dutchmen killed themselves before they could be questioned. I was laid up in bed for nearly a week. And that's it. We don't know who or what this *Bathsheba* is. But all Dominick's competitors know that he was nearly taken out, and it will destroy him."

"That woman—Tulp—she really shot you?"

"Yep, right in the back. I didn't want to kill her. Merkel did, with a kick in the nose that—Well, she died then. It was weird about the Dutchmen, though."

"Poisoning themselves?"

"There was no reason for them to do it. No reason

at all. It made no sense then, and it makes even less now."

Rafaella had a sudden very sharp memory. "What day was that? The day of the assassination attempt?"

"March 11."

She was silent for a moment, counting back. Suddenly she whirled to face him, grabbed his arm, and shook it. "You won't believe this—hell, I'm not sure I do! Marcus, that night the night of the eleventh—I awoke from a violent dream. I heard several gunshots, crystal clear they were, and I felt tremendous pain—in my left side—my shoulder, my arm, all my left side, as if I'd been shot. I got up, nearly certain that the shots had to have come from outside my apartment. There wasn't a sign of anything, of course, but the pain didn't go away for a while."

He felt the gooseflesh rise on his arms, then laughed. "You're talking fate here, Ms. Holland? You felt the pain when I was shot, as if we were somehow joined, even then?"

Even then.

"Not that I don't like the idea," he continued, amusement in his eyes as he looked at her. "Joined spiritually or psychically, then physically. I guess the deep end of the swimming pool was also inevitable, also fate?"

"Go ahead and poke fun, but it happened, Marcus, it surely did."

It occurred to her then that her father had also been shot in the left arm. That made her shiver violently. She much preferred the connection to Marcus. She saw that Marcus was focusing in and quickly said, "But there was just the one assassination attempt."

"Yes, just the one. Then the three attempts on my life or on yours—"

"Or just warnings."

"Yes, or warnings. If you turn your face this way, I'll kiss you."

She turned to face him. He just touched his mouth to hers. He was warm and she wanted more. She leaned toward him, but he pulled away. "No, sweetheart. Not now, more's the pity. Have I told you everything your reporter's little heart yearns to know?"

"Yes. I must think about this, or at least try." She sighed. "You've shorted out my circuits. But you know, it doesn't make a whole lot of sense. Who would want to kill Dominick? Who would want to warn you away, or me, for that matter? Who would advertise *Bathsheba,* and what does it mean?"

Marcus shrugged. "We now have a lead. Olivier."

"As in Roddy Olivier?" At his nod she said, "I read about him. From all accounts, he's not a very nice guy."

"No, he's not. Olivier is primarily a gray- and black-market arms dealer. He and Dominick have hated each other since three years ago when Dominick cut Olivier's legs out from under him in a deal to Iran."

It was then, quite suddenly, that it struck Rafaella with renewed force: Marcus was just as much a criminal as Dominick Giovanni. She swallowed. He was a criminal, and she hated it. What about fate? Surely fate wouldn't fashion a criminal for her.

"In any case, we now have a lead, as I said."

"Dominick will send someone after this Olivier?"

Marcus nodded.

"Why did you make love to me in the pool that evening and not tonight? Aren't the same guards hanging about?"

He grinned down at her. "No, ma'am. They were having supper. I'd checked. There was no one anywhere close."

She poked him in the ribs, and for the sake of the guards, Marcus kept his grunt to himself.

"If you've had enough, why don't we go to our respective beds? Just know that I'll be thinking about you, Ms. Holland, and my thoughts will be carnal as hell."

"I like the sound of that. I guess my thoughts will be carnal too."

"It makes a man happy to hear that from his woman."

His woman. It should have sounded macho to her, but it didn't. She rose and straightened her skirt. "Will you be here in the morning?"

"No. I've got to go back to the resort. I *am* the manager, you know. I'll be back for dinner. I imagine that Dominick will want a war council." He rose then, ducked his head, and kissed her throat. "Good night."

"Marcus? Do you like to fish?"

"No, but I don't mind if you do it and then scale the critters, all the dirty work. Salmon I like."

"Good." Rafaella walked slowly back into the house. It was dark and very quiet.

She fell asleep quickly and awoke just as quickly. It was a dull gray morning light, and she opened her eyes to see DeLorio standing beside her bed. He was naked except for a pair of Jockey shorts, and he was staring down at her, holding her panties.

Sixteen

He was built like a Dallas Cowboy linebacker, all compact muscle, no flab, even around his stomach, and a thick neck. He was covered with black hair, thick on his legs and his chest, and there he was holding her panties in his big man's hands, looking down at her.

"You're awake now. Good."

She wasn't about to let him realize he'd frightened her. And after the first shock, she wasn't afraid. The house, after all, was full of people and the guards were everywhere. She managed to hold perfectly still until she had herself firmly together. He was there to rape her, no doubt about that. Or did he believe she wanted him? Or maybe he was thinking seduction. Only one way to find out. She asked easily, "What do you want, DeLorio?"

"To make love to you, of course. I found your panties. They're dry now. Would you like me to put them on you? Then I could pull them off again, just like Marcus did. Only I'm better than he is, Rafaella, much better. I'm not a stupid Irishman. You won't believe the things I'll do to you, the things I'll make you feel."

She stared at her half-brother, wishing she could just blurt out: *Well, you know, DeLorio, I've never been much into married men or incest, for that matter. Whatcha say you just get out of here and quit trying to screw your own half-sister?* Instead, she said quite pleasantly, "I want you to leave now, DeLorio. This is my room. I have no sexual interest in you. Further, you're married. Go, now."

She was wearing only a sleepshirt from Columbia University that said JOURNALISTS LOVE BIG ERASERS across the chest. She watched him rub her panties against his cheek.

"Go away," she said again. Slowly she inched up in her bed, bringing the sheet with her.

He moved in a flash, coming down beside her, his strong arms pinning hers to her sides. He tried to kiss her, but she jerked her head and his mouth landed on her ear.

"Hold still!" He tried to grab her jaw to hold her head still, but he couldn't get a firm grip. He jerked her arms over her head and grasped both her wrists in one hand. She let him think he could hold her like this. She didn't want a scene. She didn't want Dominick to find out what his son was trying to do. She didn't know how he'd react. In her short acquaintance with her father, he'd shown himself to be very unpredictable. No, she had to protect DeLorio, if she could, or else Dominick just might make her leave the compound. She couldn't leave, not yet, not until—

She drew a deep breath and waited. DeLorio was trying to kiss her again, his free hand clamping around her jaw to hold her still.

She said very calmly, her mouth an inch from his nose, "Let me go or I'll scream. I'll bring every guard in here down on your head, and your father as well. They'll all see you in your Jockey shorts, looking quite ridiculous, trying to rape me. I can't begin to think what your father will say to that."

"You want my father, don't you?" His free hand closed over her breast and she jerked with the shock. "Yeah, that's why you're here, to get my father away from Coco. She won't let you, nor will I. You won't get my father into your bed." He paused, then added in a voice of bewilderment, "He's an old man."

"I don't want to be your father's mistress. Believe it, DeLorio. I'm not lying: I'm here to write his biography, nothing more, nothing less. Now, get your hands off me or I swear you won't like the consequences."

He shook his head, and his fingers were furiously kneading her breast, stopping just this side of pain. "Marcus was just a means to an end, wasn't he, Rafaella? You slept with him so you could get here, get to my father, that stubborn fool. He's old, worn out, wrinkled. Are you just like all the rest of them, Rafaella, are you—?"

"Where's your wife? Where's Paula?"

That drew him up, but just for a moment. "She's probably screwing a bellhop, for all I know. Who cares?"

"She's just unhappy, DeLorio. She's also your wife. You owe her better than this. Now, get out of here or you're going to be one very sorry boy. I've really had it with you."

He suddenly grabbed her left hand and brought it down to clutch his swollen penis. She flinched and he gave her a smile that froze her.

"I'm big," he said, forcing her fingers up and down the length of his penis. He was big, very big. "I'm bigger than any man you've ever had. And you'll love it when I shove into you. All the way up into you."

He was taking a big risk, she knew, having her anywhere near his cock. Adolescent fool. She'd had enough. If he was so far gone to any kind of reason—

He shoved her hand inside his shorts. "There, Rafaella. Feel that."

"That's enough, DeLorio." He'd left himself vulnerable, and even more than that, he was on the verge of orgasm. His body was shuddering, his breathing harsh and deep. She quickly twisted her hand free and sent it into his belly, hard. Her other hand went against his throat even as she brought her legs up and kicked his chest. He gagged and fell backward onto the floor with a crash. He lay there, his legs drawn up in the fetal position, his breathing harsh and uncontrolled.

Rafaella rolled out of bed and hurried to her bedroom door. She eased open the door and peered into the dawn-lit corridor. There was Coco peering around hers and Dominick's bedroom door.

Coco said in a stage whisper, "What's wrong, Rafaella? I thought I heard something."

"Nothing, nothing. I just had a nightmare. I was just checking to make sure I didn't bother anyone, but I did anyway. I'm sorry, Coco. Go back to bed."

Rafaella quickly jerked back into her bedroom and firmly closed the door. DeLorio was still lying on his side, holding his stomach. He wasn't moaning now, at least, just lying there, his eyes closed, his face gray. She stood over her half-brother, wondering what she should do now.

What Rafaella hadn't expected was someone coming to her bedroom by way of the balcony.

"What have we here?"

She looked up to see Marcus standing in the open French doorway, wearing only a pair of jeans and raised eyebrows. His hair was mussed, there was stubble on his jaw, he was barefoot, and he looked so good to Rafaella she could easily have tackled him and pinned him down on her bed and kissed his face off.

She was instantly irritated to be caught in such a ridiculous situation, wearing a nightshirt that said JOURNALISTS LOVE BIG ERASERS. "Shush, for heaven's sake. Come here—you might as well help me."

"What did you do to our roving Don Juan?"

"DeLorio and I just had a slight misunderstanding. He mistook my room for his, nothing more."

DeLorio rolled onto his back and stared up at Marcus. His mouth was still tight with pain.

"Is that right?" Marcus said, and his voice was full

of amusement, which Rafaella saw enraged DeLorio. "You just happened to be having a dawn stroll and you just happened to walk into Rafaella's bedroom?" That swarmy smile of his would have enraged her, Rafaella thought, had she been the one lying on the floor in her underwear, clutching her belly.

Rafaella offered DeLorio her hand. "Come along, now. Go back to your room." To her consternation, Rafaella saw that DeLorio still held her panties crumpled in his right hand. Then his fingers released them. Please, she prayed, don't let Marcus see that.

"What's he doing here?"

"He thought I was in trouble—that, or having a bad nightmare. He came to see if I was all right. Go along now, DeLorio."

DeLorio tried for a bit of bravado, but it was difficult with that employee of his father's, Marcus, standing there, and knowing, *knowing* that he'd been thrown to the floor by a woman half his size, that she'd hurt him. He looked at Rafaella Holland. Rage surged through him, uncontrollable and dark. He wanted to hurt her, but he also wanted to pleasure her. He wanted to treat her just like he treated Paula. Paula liked it, craved it. So would Rafaella, once he could—His mouth worked, but he didn't say anything, and he quickly left her room, closing the door very quickly and very quietly behind him. Next time he'd know to be careful; next time he'd take care of her before he let her wake up. He could picture her with her arms pulled over her head, her wrists tied to the bedpost—Yeah, Paula really liked that game.

Rafaella stood there in the middle of her bedroom in her sleepshirt and sighed.

"I guess I should thank you for coming, but I wish you hadn't. And you really didn't do anything except push DeLorio more than necessary. He's got a hair trigger on his temper. Since you came, that means other people might have heard the noise and other people just might have seen DeLorio going out of my room. Oh, damn."

"No one saw anything unless he or she was standing outside in the hall."

"I saw Coco there just a few minutes ago."

"My room is just around on the western side. Your balcony doors were open, as were mine. That's the only reason I heard anything. Stop worrying." He suddenly grinned, shaking his head. "Poor DeLorio, he hadn't a clue what he was getting himself into. Hey, what's this?" He bent down and picked up the panties. His grin nearly split his face. "Well, they were found. Dear DeLorio, I presume? They're home—or very nearly—nice and dried out."

She snatched them from his hand. "Go away, Marcus."

His humor vanished in the next moment. "You all right, kiddo?"

"Yes. If I couldn't have handled him, you'd better believe I would have yelled my head off for help."

"Why did you protect him?"

"I couldn't begin to guess what Dominick would do. He might kick DeLorio off the compound or he might kick me off. He does love his son, no matter how he treats him sometimes."

"He's afraid of his son. Dominick feels he has to control him completely or DeLorio just might turn on him."

"I hope you're wrong. Perhaps that's part of it, but he still loves him."

Marcus just shrugged. "This book is so very important to you?"

It was dawn, with only ghostly gray highlighting the darkness. "It's more important than anything."

"More important than staying alive?"

"No, of course not, but I can't leave, not yet. I have to finish what I've started."

"Why is the book so important?"

He saw too much; even in the early morning, when there was no real light, he saw far too much.

"None of your business."

"Ah, that's like pleading the Fifth, you know. It's a tacit admission that there's far more to things than you let on. Are you here under false colors, Ms. Holland?"

"No more so than you are, Mr. Devlin—or whatever your name is."

"Shush, keep your voice down. I don't relish being caught in your bedroom either. I manage the resort, Ms. Holland—and very well, as you know. Plus I work in other areas for Mr. Giovanni."

"Do you, now? Illegal things? I wonder about you, Marcus Whatever-your-name-is. I've already told you that you just aren't the kind of man to work for another, even if the money is spectacular. You're a loner, a man who's his own boss. No, you don't make a great deal of sense. And no, I don't believe you."

"Rafaella—" he began, then caught himself and yawned. She was really quite good. She'd neatly turned his attack and put him soundly on the defensive. And he'd wanted to tell her the truth, tell her he wasn't a criminal, tell her—But he couldn't. He had to wait, to be patient. It was an impossible situation for both of them. And she wasn't leveling with him either. "Since your room seems to be clear of young Don Juans, I'll take myself back to my lonely mattress. Or would you like me to check under your bed?"

"If you do, you'll have to bend over. I wouldn't even consider that if I were you."

He cocked a black eyebrow at her. "Are you saying you'd kick my rear?"

"Be quiet and get out of here. The way you came in, if you please."

He gave her a little salute and walked toward the balcony. Suddenly he strode back to her, grabbed her, and kissed her, running his knuckles along her jaw.

"I'll go deep-sea fishing with you, all right? Then we'll fry the fish over a wonderful fire that I'll build—I was a Boy Scout—on our own private beach, and then we'll sit by the fire—Do you play the guitar? No? Well, we'll sing love songs to each other, *a cappella*."

She nodded. "Yes, I'd like that. I play the flute a bit." He kissed her again and said, "The flute? Well, I'm pretty hot on the harmonica. Good night, you damned pain. Oh, and, Rafaella, I'm not that much of a loner." And he was gone.

She stood there, staring toward the balcony, wishing more than anything that things could be different. But they weren't.

She slept soundly until eight o'clock. It was Coco who woke her, bearing a tray with a cup of coffee and a croissant.

"What is this? Breakfast in bed, Coco? Have I got the plague and just don't know it yet?"

"I figured you'd need it. Sit up and let me get the tray settled."

As Rafaella ate her croissant, Coco sat in the chair facing her, saying nothing. She was beautifully dressed, as usual, in white cotton walking shorts, dark blue tube top, and a red-and-white-checked blouse artfully tied at the waist. Her legs were long and smooth and tanned. Her hair was long and smooth and very blond. Rafaella gave her a dirty look. "How can you look so beautiful this early in the morning?"

"I have to," Coco said matter-of-factly. "When I was your age, I never minded if someone flitted into my room to wake me up, because I knew that I looked gorgeous even with on-end hair and no makeup. But now, well, it's a very different thing now."

"I don't believe it," Rafaella said, and drank down half the cup of coffee. "Anyway, not for you. You'll be gorgeous when you're eighty. It's the bones. They're perfect."

Coco wasn't immune, and she smiled, straightening

her shoulders just a bit. She waited until Rafaella had another mouthful of croissant, then said suddenly, "What happened early this morning? I saw DeLorio coming out of your room in his undershorts."

"I wish you hadn't seen him. Please, Coco, don't tell Dominick. I don't know what he'd do. I just set DeLorio straight, that's all. He won't try anything again."

"If you say so. Will you be meeting with Dominick today?" At Rafaella's nod, she rose and said, "Well, then, I'll see you at lunch."

Marcus spoke quietly to Savage, telling him about Marseilles and Jack Bertrand. When he finished, John Savage said, "Okay, buddy, that's it. Hurley would agree. You're out of there, Marcus. There's no reason to get yourself killed when Giovanni's the target. You were lucky once, hell, twice. No more. We'll cut a deal about Uncle Morty. Come home."

It was tempting, very tempting, but Marcus shook his head even as he said, "No, not yet, Savage. We'll never get a thing on him until this *Bathsheba* thing is destroyed, resolved, whatever. Giovanni's effectively out of business until it is." He paused, sighing. "Another thing, there's more to it now than just Giovanni."

"The reporter."

"Yes. And don't try to sell me on the notion that you're a fatalist or, worse, a psychic." And he told Savage about the boa constrictor.

There was a whistle on the other end of the line. "This is becoming more complicated than our country's foreign policy with Central America. What are you going to do?"

"I've been thinking about it," Marcus said. "I think Ms. Holland and I are going on a *Bathsheba* hunt. Once it's resolved, Giovanni will doubtless pull a big deal to prove he's back on top where he should be, a very big and daring deal to impress all the competition, and we'll get him."

He smiled as the very suave John Savage sputtered on the other end of the line.

Five minutes later Marcus was in the gym, headed for the men's locker room.

"Hiya, boss. How's tricks?"

Marcus smiled at Punk, who sported a lime-green streak in her bleached blond hair today. He'd missed her, and he liked the blond hair and its lime-green stripe. He realized as well that he'd miss Callie and most of the other people who worked for him when he eventually left here.

"Tricks is just fine. How you doing with the stud from San Diego?"

"Oh, him." Punk shrugged and whipped her gym towel with a loud thwack against a Nautilus machine. "Yesterday's news. You were right, he was more interested in watching himself come than being with me. I'm off men now, I swear it."

Marcus looked around the gym, stopping when he spotted a new man doing bench presses. "Who's that, Punk? That man with the dark brown hair, the flat gut, and the all-over tan?"

She turned to the direction he was pointing and stared. "How about that," she said, smiled up at Marcus, then turned to saunter over to the newcomer, hips swaying, long legs sleek in pink tights, the lime-green stripe radiant as a beacon.

"Good luck," he mouthed after her. He worked out for forty-five minutes. Then he returned to his office, only to be collared immediately by Callie, who had a sheaf of papers for his signature. "Now, boss," she said, and followed him into his office. "Think of yourself as my captive. Please." She didn't let him out of her sight for two hours.

Then there was the gardener who'd gotten drunk

and made a pass at a female guest, who was now yelling for the guy's head.

There was a professional gambler who'd gotten into the resort under false pretenses. Abramowitz, Marcus's chief security man in the casino, had spotted him within an hour. He'd been hustled out before he could make a dent in the bank. Marcus himself put the man on a helicopter bound for the airport at St. John's.

Marcus was making his rounds in the casino that evening, wishing he was at the compound, worrying despite himself about that damned female irritant, when he was charmingly accosted by three women from New York. He was stuck. It was all he could do not to hurt any feelings when he went to his own villa alone at two o'clock in the morning. The worst part of it was, he was hornier than he could ever remember. But the strange thing was, he was only a tad interested in any of the three women. Not enough to take any one of them to bed. He'd prefer Rafaella on his front lawn, truth be told, or in any mode possible.

He was still stewing things over the next morning when the kicker arrived. It was a special-delivery envelope waiting for him, marked PERSONAL in heavy black marker. Callie handed it to him silently, her expression faintly puzzled.

He smiled at her and took the envelope into his office, closing the door. There was a single folded sheet of paper inside the envelope, and its message, in hand-blocked black letters, was short:

> THERE'S NO ESCAPE FOR YOU, GIOVANNI.
> BATHSHEBA IS VERY NEAR NOW.
> YOU'RE A DEAD MAN.

It was bloody melodramatic, stupidly and childishly melodramatic. And effective. A messenger from *Bathsheba* was on the island. And no one had any idea which of the guests it was. If it was a guest. It could be someone on the compound. It could even be Rafaella.

Marcus cursed in frustration.

He left the resort and took one of the motor scooters over the middle ridge to the compound. He arrived around lunchtime and was shown into Dominick's library, where he and Rafaella were seated, her notebook open on her lap, her pen poised. There was a tape recorder on Dominick's desk. Was it Rafaella's idea, or was it Giovanni's vanity?

When Marcus came in, Rafaella looked up, briefly met his eyes, and was aware of a rush of pleasure. A rush of pleasure for a man who was very likely a criminal, though she prayed he wasn't, but it didn't matter, because she was falling for him. For the first time in her adult life she was in love with a man.

How to save him from himself? How to get him out of here, away from Dominick Giovanni, without getting either of them maimed or killed? That brought up another thing: What did Marcus want?

"Hello, Marcus," Dominick said easily. He hesitated only fractionally, then continued just as easily to Rafaella, "Why don't you take a break, my dear girl. I've been talking your ear off. I'll see you a bit later." He leaned forward and pushed the off button on the tape recorder.

She'd been dismissed. Rafaella only nodded to Marcus on her way out. She wanted to remain by the door and listen, but Merkel, ever-present Merkel, was there, and he smiled at her, shook his head, and pointed her toward the living room, where Coco sat with Paula, who'd just arrived a few hours earlier.

Paula was the last person Rafaella wanted to see. All her attention, the source of all her WASP angst, was still back in the library. What had happened now? She felt a frisson of concern and began planning how she'd worm it out of Marcus later.

"Well?" This from Paula, who was drinking a martini.

"Hello," Rafaella said absently. "No booze for me, Jiggs. Just iced tea. Thank you."

Jiggs smiled at her. "Just plain, Miss Rafaella?" At her nod, he took himself out of the living room.

"Well? Is my dear father-in-law quite through with you yet?"

Rafaella didn't take the bait on that innuendo. "How was Miami?"

"Hot but exciting, not boring like it is here. There are shops and shows and people I don't know, people to talk to, interesting people."

"Island fever," Coco said. "You should have stayed away a bit longer, Paula."

"I wanted to. Dominick called me this morning and ordered me back. Like I was a teenager or something."

And Rafaella thought: Oh, dear, he's guessed. That, or Coco told him about DeLorio. She sent a look toward Coco, but the other woman was studying her fingernails and didn't look up.

"And DeLorio wasn't very happy to see me," Paula added. "Did he give you back your panties?"

Rafaella smiled. "Why, yes, he did. They were a favorite pair."

Paula jumped up from her chair, her face suddenly pale with anger.

"Oh, for heaven's sake, do can it, Paula. Sit down. I don't want your husband. Stop being dramatic. It's too hot."

"I hope you die," Paula said, and left the room.

"How old did you tell me she was, Coco?"

"Twenty-four going on eight."

"Sounds about right."

"What did Marcus want? Link said he'd just gotten here. He wasn't expected until this evening."

"Yes, he's here, and I don't know what's going on.

Dominick dismissed me before I could find out anything."

"I suspect you'll get it out of one or the other of them," Coco said mildly. "Do you like this shade of peach polish? It's called Caribbean Sunset."

In the library, Marcus said after a long stretch of silence, "Well, Dominick, what do you think?"

"Our absent villains are no longer absent. You know about Bathsheba in the Bible. She was Solomon's mother, the wife of King David. You remember how David married her after he'd sent her husband to his death in a battle?"

Marcus nodded. "Vaguely. My mother was always one for reading from the Old Testament on Monday evenings." He was standing by the open windows, and the prospect was incredibly lovely. The mixture of colors—all the bright oranges and purples and reds—so beautiful, like a hothouse full of lush, nearly overripe blooms and scents and colors. An Eden, but now there seemed to be danger everywhere. Here, very close. Who had written the threat? Marcus wondered suddenly if he'd acted on an insane impulse to volunteer his life to get Giovanni. And had it become some sort of macho power trip now? He just didn't know. He hoped not. He turned back to Dominick. "What's your point?"

Dominick shrugged. "Nothing, I suppose. That's the story from the Bible."

"Are you telling me that it's possible someone thinks you sent a man to his death?"

"So I could have his woman once he was dead? I don't know, Marcus. The whole thing's fantastic. Take Coco. She had this hefty, rather stupid boyfriend when I met her. I got rid of him easily enough because he was as poor as he was handsome. It cost me ten thousand bucks, but the guy was tame and uninterested in

Coco really. Chances are the name *Bathsheba* doesn't have any relevance to anything at all."

"I've thought about it, Dominick, and it's time we took direct action. I have a plan."

Dominick listened. When Marcus was through he said nothing for a very long time. Then, slowly, he nodded.

It was late, nearly ten o'clock, and Marcus was seated across from Rafaella on the swimming-pool patio. He purposely kept the distance between them. He needed it. He wanted to deep-six another pair of her panties in the pool. The more he thought about it, the more his fingers itched and his groin ached.

"Let's go to the beach."

She looked at him, faintly puzzled, but just for an instant. She ran her tongue over her lower lip. "Do the guards go down there?"

"No."

"All right. Shall I get my swimsuit?"

He just shook his head.

"Oh? Would you like to tell me why?"

"Because I'm leaving. I'm going after *Bathsheba,* which means tracking down Olivier, who's our main lead. I don't want to leave you here alone. If DeLorio doesn't get you, then whoever is trying to scare you will finally succeed at something more. I don't want you on my conscience."

"I can't leave. I won't. I'm not afraid, nor am I a fool."

"You're not a lot of things, Ms. Holland."

Seventeen

Charles held her hand to his lips. Her skin felt dry and he was irritated. The private nurses he'd hired weren't taking proper care of her. Annoyed beyond reason, Charles rummaged about in the drawer beside her bed until he found some hand cream. He gently massaged her forearms, her wrists, the backs of her hands, until the flesh was once again soft and supple. He spoke to her, his voice pitched low, as he massaged.

"Please wake up. I need you, Margaret. I need you more than you can imagine. I saw that woman, the one who ran into you. I told you about her, honey, you remember? She's married to him and I know he sent her to kill you. How could it have been an accident? A coincidence? I can't buy that. But then, you were driving near her house. Why? Did you want to see her? And she looks a little like you, maybe close enough to be your older sister or a cousin. Maybe she tried to kill you because she found out that you had had an affair with her husband, and a child; and she was jealous. What am I to do? Have her arrested? Have her face plastered next to yours in all the newspapers? No, no, that's impossible.

"What should I do, Margaret? I could keep the lid on what goes in my newspapers, but all the others? It would be more than just embarrassing. The reporters would camp out here at the hospital like bloody ghouls, waiting and asking everyone questions and more questions: Did they think you'd die? Did you ever mumble about your lovers? What did they think of me as your husband? You don't know, honey, you can't imagine. I'm so afraid they'd find out about you and that criminal, and then they'd go tooth and tong after us.

"I found out one of the reporters for Rafaella's paper had stepped on a woman's foot so she couldn't get away from him, all because he wanted to know how she felt when she found out her son had died in a military plane crash.

"How I hate that bastard for what he did to you. What he's still doing to you. And you don't even know that I know. No one does. You're so certain that you've kept it from me. Remember when you flew to Palm Springs last August and I couldn't go with you? I found the journals then—by accident, I swear it to you. I read them, every last word in them. *God, I hate him.*"

Margaret moaned. Her lashes fluttered, her fingers closed over his, a light pressure, nothing more. She opened her mouth and said very clearly, "No . . . Dominick, no. Rafaella, please, you must understand."

"Margaret? Oh, God, Margaret!" He was shaking her now, babbling, lightly patting her cheeks, jerking at her hands.

She'd said *his* name. Charles felt a surge of pain, pain so deep, so sharp, he nearly cried out with it. Dominick. Dominick Giovanni. That criminal was Rafaella's father. Thank God she didn't know. And Margaret had said his name in the same breath with Rafaella's. Charles stared down at his wife's pale face. But Margaret's eyes were closing—No, no!

Margaret was quiet, her hands limp, her head turned slightly away from him on the pillow. Charles jabbed the call button again and again. Then he sprinted to the door and yelled, "Come here! Hurry! She woke up!"

Giovanni's Island
April 2001

Marcus lifted her, his fingers digging into her buttocks, and he smiled painfully at the feel of her panties, thin but still a barrier, and he ripped them off her, jerking them down her legs.

He was naked, and now she was too. He told her to wrap her legs around his hips and he lifted her to help her and she never stopped kissing him, his mouth, his nose, his ear. "Marcus," she said over and over. "Marcus, Marcus," and he loved the sound of his name when she said it.

And when her legs were tight around him, he spread her with his fingers and brought her down over him and slid upward into her, moaning with the pleasure of it, and felt her body tighten around him, jerking and easing, then closing tighter and tighter, and it drove him crazy.

"I've missed you too damned much," he said against her ear, then turned his face and took her tongue into his mouth.

"It's—just—sex."

He managed to laugh even as he worked her with his hands, lifting her, then bringing her down fully over him. He went deeper still, and when he felt his orgasm nearly upon him, he grabbed her hips in his hands, pressing her tightly against him, holding her still.

"Don't—move. Don't. I don't want to leave you."

"No," she said into his mouth. "No, I won't move." But she did, unconsciously clenching her muscles, squeezing him, and he cried out, his hips thrusting upward, and he knew he was a goner—and he hadn't brought her to a climax. He tried to stop, but it was too late.

When he'd quieted the deep hollowing breaths that made his chest heave, when his hands just cupped her buttocks, no longer working her, Rafaella laid her head against his shoulder, her face pressed against his neck, and felt her legs relax, felt the building tension ease just a bit.

Slowly Marcus let her slide down his body, but he hated coming out of her, and for a moment he held her there, his cock just inside her, until, with a sigh, he let her leave him. They were standing only ankle-deep in the warm Caribbean. It was as far as they'd gotten before he'd grabbed her and lifted her and brought her legs around his hips—

"Rafaella?"

"Hmmm?" Her arms tightened about his waist. His chest hair was tickling her nose, so she kissed his chest, wetting his hair with her tongue.

Even the feel of her tongue on his chest turned him on. He held her away just a bit. "Look, I'm sorry about being a male pig. But I'm over it now. And I've got plans for you that include having you on your back with your legs wide apart and me between them and you arching your back and pressing up against my mouth. Do you remember that first night when I had to put my hand over your mouth, you were crying out so loud?"

She ran her hand down his stomach and her fingers closed around him. He was still aroused and he was wet with her and with himself, and her fingers moved and she felt him swell and grow hotter against her palm. "Perhaps I've more plans for you too, Marcus."

Marcus knew about sand and where the gritty stuff ended up, so he forced himself to take the time to spread out his shirt for her to lie on. But he begrudged every second his mouth wasn't on her.

"Lie down," he said, then tripped her up himself, catching her as she fell, and laid her out as he wished to see her. Rafaella was languid and cooperative and excited. "Bend your knees," he told her, then came down between her legs and bent her knees himself, then spread her thighs wide, then wider still. And she lifted her hips, unknowingly wanting, and he brought his mouth immediately down on her, his tongue searching through the soft folds of flesh to find her, and she imagined that she could hold back for a while, but it was impossible, and her body tensed, her legs muscles tightened and flexed, and she cried out and this time he let her, and listened to her while he probed her body with his tongue, scraped her flesh lightly with his teeth. When she came, he lifted her hips with his hands, and her fingers were winding in his hair, pressing his face closer against her.

When she'd quieted just a bit, Marcus slid into her, deeply, as he covered her.

"Rafaella?"

"It's nice," she said with great inadequacy.

He pushed deeper, and she smiled and lifted her hips.

"Why don't you come with me this time? You up to it?"

She started to shake her head, to say that she was exhausted and there was nothing left in her, but it wasn't true. She was more than able to come with him. She'd always considered herself quite healthy in her responses, but two orgasms she'd never before considered as all that healthy or normal, yet it was happening again, and when his fingers worked her, his belly pressing against his hand and her, she felt the ache deepen and widen through her lower body and grow stronger, and she cried very softly against his shoulder, her body tensing incredibly with pleasure, and he kissed her, his tongue in her mouth when he reached his own climax.

"That's it. I'm a goner." He lay on top of her, his full weight, and she didn't mind it at all. "I've also got sand in my parts."

She laughed at that and felt him easing out of her.

He came up on his elbows and looked down at her, studying her face. It was a dear face now, and it made him intensely uncomfortable because he didn't want this, not now. Because if he let himself care, he'd have to worry; but that was stupid, because he already did worry about her, had worried, in fact, for so very long now. So, he decided, knowing he was a fool, it was just too late for him now, and to hell with it.

What to do?

He knew, even as the words hovered on his tongue, that she wouldn't leave Dominick's compound. She saw herself as here to stay, and nothing he could say would budge her. Stubborn and bullheaded and committed—but committed to what? It drove him mad. It wasn't just the damned biography, it was something more. He also knew that he didn't particularly want her with him to hunt out *Bathsheba,* but given that those were the only two choices, he had to take the latter.

He kept his mouth closed. He knew now what he had to do, and even though it wasn't remotely honorable, it was the only sure way.

"It's just sex," she said, her first words, and he wanted to throttle her.

"Really, Ms. Holland?"

"Yes, that's all it is, and because you're pretty good, you make me care about things that are detrimental to my own well-being."

Her words so paralleled his own thoughts that he was momentarily surprised into silence, even though he knew she didn't feel about him the way he felt about her, however that was.

"What things?"

"You. I now find I worry about you. I nearly went

crazy when I found out that awful man had tried to kill you in Marseilles."

"You did go crazy. You kung-fu'ed me flat on my back."

"You did the same thing to me." In the next breath she added, "And it was just sex. You're a wonderful diversion, but nothing more. You can't be."

"I agree completely. You're keeping things from me—"

"You're doing the same thing! No, don't go. Come back. I like you where you were."

"Sorry, but my arms are tired." He lay on his side beside her, his palm on her stomach. "You ain't exactly an affliction yourself, at least at the moment."

And at that moment she wanted to tell him so badly: *Look, Marcus, you're a criminal. More than that, you work for Dominick, and I want nothing more than to destroy him. I can't let you anywhere near me.* Instead she asked, "You're not a murderer, are you?"

"No. If I had killed that woman—Tulp—it would have been self-defense. Just as it was with Jack Bertrand."

She sighed and leaned up, kissed his chest. He liked her to kiss him, but he didn't want to tell her that, so he just leaned down and kissed her nose.

"You won't tell me anything? I can whine until cows swim the Atlantic, and you still won't tell me?"

"Please spare me," he said. "And no, I can't, won't, tell you anything. Not yet. Be patient."

"It's just sex."

"Yeah, sure. And Saddam always invites the Kurds for Thanksgiving dinner."

"Really, Marcus, let's leave it at sex. It can't be anything more, surely you understand that."

"Yeah," he said again. "I understand."

And he did, too well. "Let's get back." He helped her up.

*   *   *

Link turned back to the beach to check that they were all right. They were standing, dressing, speaking in low voices. He sighed and turned away to hide himself in the dense foliage of the jungle until they passed him. Things were getting more complicated by the minute. He didn't like it, and he couldn't begin to predict what would happen now.

Rafaella jerked up in bed at the knock on her bedroom door.

"Yes?"

It was Marcus who opened her door, and he said abruptly, "Pick up your phone. It's the Pine Hill Hospital on Long Island. They routed the call from the resort over here."

She went cold. She picked up the phone, vaguely realizing that it too felt cold, and said, "Yes? This is Rafaella Holland."

"This is Dr. Bentley. I'm sorry to have to call you, but Mr. Rutledge asked me to. He didn't want to leave your mother for even a moment. She's worse, Miss Holland. We think you should come here as quickly as possible."

"But what happened? What's changed? I just spoke to my stepfather yesterday."

And Dr. Bentley reeled off words and phrases that made little sense except the "she's deeper in coma—sinking—"

"I'll be there right away," Rafaella said, and hung up. She stared blindly toward Marcus, who still stood in the doorway. "It's my mother—"

He hated the numbed pain in her voice, and said, "I'm leaving in just a little while for Miami. You want to come with me?"

"Oh, yes," she said, and was dressed, packed, and downstairs in ten minutes.

To the gathered family in the living room she said simply, "My mother's condition has gotten worse. I'm leaving right away with Marcus." And to Dominick, "I'll be back when I can, sir. You can count on me."

He stood up and walked over to her. He looked down at her for a long time, gently touched his fingertips to her cheek, and said, "I understand. You'll be back when you can. If you need anything, anything at all, you will call me. All right? Good. Now, off with you. Marcus will see to everything. Good luck, my dear."

Coco hugged her, and even Paula wished her luck. DeLorio was nowhere to be seen.

Rafaella and Marcus reached Miami at eleven o'clock in the morning. Marcus said, "I've booked you on a flight to New York that leaves in an hour. Come have a cup of coffee with me."

She nodded, still numb with fear. He ordered her coffee in the small airport snack shop and set it in front of her.

"Drink up."

She did, then set her cup down and smiled painfully at him. Odd, but he was still standing there beside her, just standing, saying nothing. "Thank you, Marcus. You've been more than kind. I really appreciate your being here for me. Funny that it should end this way, isn't it?"

"This isn't an end, Ms. Holland. Now, come with me. I'll take you to your gate."

He led her through security, and when she weaved slightly, it felt natural for his arm to go around her waist. And when she fell asleep in the waiting-room chair just outside Gate 93, it was natural that her head fall on his shoulder.

And when she finally woke up, it was natural that Marcus's face was the first one she saw. Only it wasn't natural. He shouldn't be there. Something was wrong, very wrong. She couldn't seem to think straight.

She smiled at him. It felt natural to do so. "Are you going to New York with me? Are we in the air?"

"No and yes. How do you feel?"

She yawned, stretched, and rubbed her eyes. There was lots of room. They were in the first-class cabin.

"Boy, I didn't realize I was so tired. How long did I sleep?"

"About an hour and a half. You were upset. I'm sorry for that, Rafaella."

"You're very kind. I really was out for that long? Goodness, you checked me in and dragged me onto the plane?"

"Yes." He lifted his left hand and pushed her hair out of her face. He smiled. "Do you know that it's dangerous to do any kind of martial arts on an airplane that's thirty-three thousand feet in the air?"

"I guess so."

"So you wouldn't?"

"No. Unless there was a hijacker or something. That's a crazy question. Why do you ask me that?"

"The bottom line is, Ms. Holland, I outfoxed you."

"What?"

"That phone call was a fake. I'm sorry about scaring you like that, but I couldn't think of anything else to make you move off that damned island."

"My mother isn't dying?"

"No. I talked Dr. Haymes, our resort physician, into scamming you. He wanted me to apologize to you for doing it. Your mother is fine. In fact, she woke up for a few seconds yesterday."

Her mother wasn't dying. She'd been so afraid, felt so guilty because she'd been off tilting at windmills when her mother was lying in that wretched bed in that wretched hospital and she hadn't been there beside her, and now, to find out it had all been a lie. A rotten lie because Marcus had wanted her off the island. She no longer felt numb from sleep. She no longer felt numb from guilt. "What did you put in my coffee?"

"The proverbial mickey. You're very responsive to

the stuff. Of course, since I've known you, you've always been responsive. Oh, by the way, we're going to London, not New York."

It was always better to keep one's mouth shut until one understood the situation fully. That's what Al Holbein had always preached to his reporters. Rafaella tried, she truly did, but it was harder than she imagined.

"Tell me why," she managed, her mouth dry with relief that her mother was okay, drier with fury at what he'd done. "Tell me now or I'll send you through that six-by-twelve-inch window."

"I love it when you talk tough and mean."

"Marcus—"

"All right. Are you feeling sharp enough, or do you want some untampered-with coffee?"

Before she could tell him what she really wanted, a flight attendant, a chirpy grandmotherly woman, sharp in her British Airways uniform, said, "You're awake. Your husband said you'd had a hard night. One of your children was ill?"

"Yes," Marcus said. "Little Jennifer. An earache."

"Oh, earaches are the dickens, aren't they? My two boys were plagued with them until they were nearly in the first grade. Your little girl's all right now?"

Marcus said easily and quickly, "She's just fine, and with her grandmother, as well as Rory and David, her brothers."

"It sounds like you have a wonderful family. Would you like something to drink? Champagne? Juice?"

Rafaella ordered a huge glass of water for her dry mouth. She just waited, saying nothing to the man beside her until she had her water. It was tempting to throw it in his face, but she drank it instead.

"Your eyes look positively vicious."

"Little Jennifer? Rory? David? For heaven's sake, I'm only twenty-six. And just barely that!"

"You're precocious. As was I, of course."

"That six-by-twelve-inch window is looking like the best idea I've had in a very long time."

"Good. You're much better now. Are you ready to listen? Here's what's going to happen, Ms. Holland."

"My name is Rafaella, and if you call me Ms. Holland in that snide, patronizing voice again, I'll knee you until you're singing soprano at St. Pat's."

"Talk about cutting off your nose to spite your—"

"Don't finish that thought. Sex I can live without, and that's all you are. A sexual diversion. I told you once, I don't trust good-looking men. My gut was accurate as usual. All right, tell me what you've gotten me into."

"But you keep interrupting."

"Sometimes it's difficult to get in a word edgewise with the noisy children. And of course Jennifer and David and Rory are little devils. One forgets when they're not around. I won't say another word."

"I had to leave the island, but I didn't want you to be there without me. It's too dangerous—no, keep quiet, you promised. I decided I had to go *Bathsheba* hunting, no choice now. I wanted you gone, but I knew you wouldn't leave because you're obstinate, inflexible as hell, and you have this thing about writing Dominick's biography that I don't understand. I knew I couldn't trust you not to get into more trouble if I left you on the island, so here you are."

"Here I am," she repeated slowly. "You took this all upon yourself—you decided to make all the decisions—"

"Okay. Serious, now." And he was, all amusement gone from his face. "Yes, I've made these decisions. You're coming with me. I figure this is dangerous, but not as dangerous as leaving you by yourself on the compound, at the mercy of an unidentified maniac."

"We're going to find the man or the organization behind the assassination attempt on Dominick?"

"Right. I've got to. Dominick can't resume his business activities until it's all over and done with. He's got to resume it, you know, and I can't afford to wait any longer."

"One way or the other."

"Exactly."

"That sounds suspiciously mysterious. What do you mean, 'exactly'?"

"Nothing. Just—"

"I know. Be patient. Trust you. Trust the man who faked a call from my mother, scaring the wits out of me, trust the man who spiked my coffee and put me on a plane to London, of all places. Why London?"

"Good, the reporter's back. London because that's where Roddy Olivier is at present. Isn't this a kick— his middle name is Masada. Anyway, he's our only lead. Jack Bertrand was working for him at the time of his untimely demise in Marseilles. Olivier's very civilized, he knows everything that's going on in the international community, and he's not just amoral like Dominick. He's very dangerous, and he's evil—flat-out evil. We have to be very careful."

"I've been careful before, in tough situations."

"I know. That's the only reason I thought I could pull this off. But one thing, Rafaella. There can be only one boss here, and it's me. Anything happens, anything comes up, and you do what I tell you to— immediately—none of your infernal questioning. You got that?"

"What makes you think I won't take the first flight back to Miami from Heathrow?"

He'd considered that, she could tell by his expression—part worry, part weary resignation. "Don't. You weren't really worried about DeLorio and his clumsy attempts to get in your panties. Well, Rafaella, worry about Dominick. He saw you as nothing more than a bright girl who seemed like she could be put to good use. His vanity is enormous, and what more could he ask for than a lovely female wanting to write his biography? Actually, writing what he tells her to write. But face and accept this as well: he wants you in his bed, no matter your other uses to him."

The thought of her father attempting seduction— She'd considered it before—DeLorio had said it—but not all that seriously, and it was strange in the extreme to hear it from Marcus.

"You still don't believe me. All right, I remember asking him, wasn't he worried that you could be hurt—this was after that assassination attempt. He told me you were only a woman, after all, so who cared when it came right down to it? Women are expendable to him. I wish you'd believe me."

"I believe you."

"Just like that?" He looked as if he couldn't take it in that she'd capitulated so quickly.

"Hardly 'just like that.' I believe you," she said again. "All right. I'll stay with you for a while."

Marcus wondered what "for a while" meant.

"You said Dominick's vanity is enormous; it's also obvious that you don't like him. In fact, I'd say you're close to feeling like he's scum and dirt. Why, then, are you risking everything to find the group who tried to kill him? *Still* trying to kill him, for that matter."

"Good question."

"You got an answer?"

Marcus's agile brain failed him. He just looked at her. Her lipstick was long gone, her mascara had smeared beneath her eyes, her hair was hanging over her right eye, and he was so afraid she might not be safe with him that it made him mute.

"I know," she said, poking him in the ribs. "Trust you. Have patience. Make love to you in the swimming pool, ankle-deep in the Caribbean, on your front lawn—"

"I wasn't all involved that time, if you'll recall."

Rafaella looked out the small window. "Do you think we've reached our cruising altitude yet? Usually it's over forty thousand feet to Europe. It's a long way down."

"You know, you might consider quality rather than quantity. For example, just the other night you—"

She held up her hand. "You win. I'm retreating. And since I have no choice but to trust you, I'll pretend that I do. The truth, you know, Marcus, might not be too bad."

"Sometimes the truth is the very devil."

When he was right, he was right, Rafaella thought. She fell asleep three minutes later, and the grandmotherly flight attendant just clucked as she viewed the beautiful rare sirloin steak that had to go back to the galley.

Eighteen

Dominick let out a yell, and Merkel, terrified, dashed into the library, coming to a stunned halt. Dominick was seated behind his desk, and in his hand he was still holding the phone. It was buzzing loudly. He let out another whoop for Merkel's benefit, then waved him to a chair. "I can't bloody well believe it," Dominick said, and Merkel wondered for a moment if the strain had been too much and Mr. Giovanni had gone berserk.

"No, it's the best news I've had in more years than I can count." He beamed at Merkel.

Merkel was dying to ask what had made Mr. Giovanni so happy, but he knew better. Mr. Giovanni never liked to be questioned. Merkel waited.

Dominick clapped his hands, threw back his head, and laughed deeply, showing a molar that needed to be capped. "Pour each of us some champagne, Merkel. Don't stint. Get the best stuff we've got. We've got some celebrating to do. My dear father-in-law, that interfering old bastard, Carlo Carlucci, is dead. He's finally dead. *Dead!* In his bed, of heart failure. I hope he rots in hell. You can't imagine, Merkel, you can't believe—I was beginning to think he'd live forever."

Then Dominick laughed yet again, a deep, rich laugh that made Merkel smile even though his skin crawled at the same time.

"Dead! The old fool's dead. Dead. Get the champagne."

When Merkel returned to the library carrying a silver tray with champagne and fine crystal flutes, Dominick was standing by the wide French windows, looking out.

"Here, sir."

Dominick turned slowly, and the look in his pale blue eyes was frightening as hell itself. "I'm free now, Merkel, or I soon will be," he said very softly. "Free. After all these years, I'll be free of my drunken, unfaithful wife."

Merkel carefully poured the champagne and handed the flute to Dominick.

"Pour yourself a glass, Merkel. Quickly, man."

After they'd drunk two glasses, Dominick said, "Send Lacy to me. Tell him I've got a wonderful job for him."

That evening at dinner, Dominick announced that he and Lacy were flying to Chicago on Thursday to attend his father-in-law's funeral. "I wouldn't miss it for anything," Dominick said. "Besides, I think my wonderful wife just might be there as well. It's been years. Years since I've had the pleasure of seeing her."

"Mother would be at the funeral," DeLorio said thoughtfully. "I think I'll come as well, Father. I haven't seen her for a long, long time."

Dominick looked startled, then smiled, shaking his head. "No, my boy, you're needed here on the compound. Both heads can't leave the body, DeLorio. No, you stay here and I'll attend to this unpleasant business." He paused a moment and smiled toward Paula. "You keep Coco company, my dear girl. You understand?"

The threat hung implicit in the silence. Merkel knew the threat was very real, and he hoped that Paula realized it too. She did. She was alarmingly pale. DeLorio was frowning at his father, and Merkel didn't like the look on his face, his very young face that didn't look young at all at times.

"How long will you be gone?" DeLorio asked.

"Just three or four days."

"You must be careful," Coco said, leaning forward, her hand on his forearm. "It's dangerous for you away from the island."

"I know. Lacy will be with me, won't you, Frank? He'll keep any bad guys at a goodly distance." Dominick laughed again, and continued laughing even as he dipped some lobster in hot butter and chewed on it.

Late that night, just as the downstairs grandfather clock struck twelve times, Dominick was saying very slowly to his son, "No drugs, DeLorio. I've told you this more times than I care to count. *No drugs*. I won't get involved with the Colombians or the Cubans or the trash from Miami. Never. I'd have to do more than burn your money if you tried it again. You got that, kid?"

"I don't see the difference. Death by illegal weapons or death by drugs. The suckers are dead either way."

"No drugs. Since when do I have to explain things to you? You'll obey me and forget about this. Trust me, DeLorio."

"The money—there's so much money, and the damned DEA, they don't have enough people to check even a tiny fraction of incoming boats and planes. It's so easy, and I've already been contacted, in fact I've already—"

"No drugs. You try anything, you try going against me, kid, and I'll cut your balls off."

DeLorio stared at him, mute.

Dominick ruffled his son's hair. "You're a good boy, DeLorio. You're not like your mother. Don't blow it."

Hicksville, New York
April 2001

Sylvia Carlucci Giovanni wasn't drunk. She hadn't had a drink since that awful night when her beautiful young Tommy Ibsen had been high on cocaine and had struck that woman—that poor woman who was still in a coma in the hospital. She could still see Tommy's white face as he told her what he'd done, how he'd been singing as he drove, and he'd been feeling so wild, so powerful, and then suddenly there was this BMW driving just down the road, and he'd hit it, straight into the driver's side. He could still see the woman's face—her surprise, her utter astonishment, her terror. And he'd thought somehow that she'd known him, but he didn't recognize her at all. The woman had known she was going to be hit, hard. It was as if, as she'd stared at him, she'd somehow accepted the fact that she would die.

Sylvia shook it off. It was over, the woman would live, she had to. Sylvia had found out that it was a Margaret Rutledge, the wife of a very wealthy newspaper magnate, Charles Rutledge. She had the best medical care—she'd live. Sylvia was safe; Tommy was safe. The cops didn't know a thing.

Sylvia looked down at her two-year-old hybrid roses. She'd tended them faithfully, sung opera to them, mostly an aria from *Madama Butterfly,* and yet they weren't as deeply red, their petals as velvety soft as she'd wanted. Of course, it was still very early in the year, but the promise she'd held for them, the awards she'd dreamed of winning at the Long Island Flower Festival—all seemed for naught now.

She looked up to see her Taiwanese houseboy, Oyster Lee, approach, a frown puckering his ageless forehead.

It was a phone call. Very urgent, Oyster told her. And when she, her own forehead puckered with a frown, took the call as she was stripping off her gardening gloves, she turned white as a sheet.

"Oh, God," she said, and fainted.

The Bennington Hotel, London, England
April 2001

The call went through immediately.

"Hello, Merkel? It's Marcus. I need to speak to Dominick. It's important—*What?* You're kidding. Don't let him off the island! No, I know you can't do a bloody thing. All right, get him. I'll try to talk some sense into him."

Rafaella was making hand signs at him, and he covered the mouthpiece of the phone and said, "Carlucci died and Dominick's going to the funeral in Chicago. There's also his wife, Sylvia, who—Hello, Dominick?"

"Marcus. You're in London?"

"Yes, and there are two things I need to talk to you about. The first is that I've got Ms. Holland with me."

Rafaella strained, but of course she couldn't hear what Dominick was saying. Marcus's face remained expressionless, curse him.

"If you'd just hold it a minute, I'll tell you," Marcus broke in. "Listen, her mother is fine. It was an overreaction. I talked her into taking a bit of time away from the island and the book, and I'll provide her with some background information. Sorry you don't approve, but there it is. She's staying with me for the time being—Yes, Dominick, with me."

Dominick stared into the phone, wishing he could see Marcus's face, and knowing, even without seeing him, what his expression would be. Determination in that hard jawline, the usual faint amusement in his eyes. Damn him, he'd taken Rafaella! He was sleeping with her, he'd freely admitted it. And Dominick had plans for her. The moment she returned from Long Island, he'd fully intended to take her to bed. If that had gone as well as he had guessed it would, well, then he'd planned to marry her.

Just like that.

Once Sylvia was dead.

Once he was a widower, he could marry again. Coco was too old. He was sorry about that, but she was. Her years of use were nearly over. Soon he'd send her on her way. He remembered the abortion she'd had some three and a half years ago. But it had been a girl. What else could he have made her do? And she hadn't seemed to mind. She hadn't said much about it.

Rafaella was the perfect age. Even if she had a girl child first, she was young enough to bear him a battalion of boys.

Now she was with Marcus. Sleeping with Marcus. And there was possible danger if she stayed with Marcus. He thought of Roddy Olivier and blanched. The man was a treacherous snake. There was nothing to be done about it, and he hated to feel powerless.

He jerked back at the sound of Marcus's smooth voice. "You what? Say that again, Marcus."

"I said, Dominick, that I think you're crazy to leave the island. Wait until I catch the man or men behind the assassination attempt, behind *Bathsheba*. There's no way Lacy can guard you completely, no way at all. And you're talking Chicago here. Who cares about Carlucci? You hated his guts for the threat he made, but now you can just—" Marcus broke off as he realized Dominick's motive. The man was insane, certifiable, if he thought he could get away with it.

Dominick would do it. He'd lived on the island too long; he was king there, the feudal lord, the entire justice system rolled into one. He'd forgotten how very vulnerable one could be off that wretched little island. Marcus said very mildly, "You plan to see Sylvia in Chicago? Will you ask her for a divorce?"

Dominick laughed. "Marcus, you never cease to amaze me. See Sylvia? More than likely—that is, if my little wife isn't afraid to come to Chicago. If she doesn't show, well then, we'll see, won't we?"

Marcus felt helpless. He rang off, knowing Dominick Giovanni would do precisely as he wanted; he also knew that Dominick was enraged with him for taking Rafaella. He turned to face her now.

"Well?"

She still wasn't very happy with him, and after adding a goodly dose of jet lag, she looked ready to tear him to shreds. Her hair was limp, her clothes a wrinkled mess, but he smiled. He couldn't help himself.

It was nice to outsmart someone like her every once in a while.

"Well, Dominick didn't tell me to send you his love. He is, to put it bluntly, pissed. With me, not you. Like the true macho man I am, I shouldered all the blame, not even hinting that you were the one who continually seduced me. Dominick realized there was nothing he could do about it." Marcus stopped, running his hand through his hair, making it stand on end.

Rafaella chuckled.

It was so unexpected that Marcus just stared at her.

"You're a mess, and now you're even more of one."

"Go take a look in the mirror yourself."

"I already did. You should get me a large paper bag. Now, this other thing. What is it about Dominick leaving the island?"

Marcus told her. "—he's always hated the old man. He's responsible for Dominick still being married to Sylvia."

"I know all of that. He told me."

"Maybe you don't know this. I could be wrong, but I don't think so. Now that Carlucci's dead, Sylvia's not far behind."

Rafaella just looked at him. "You think he'd kill her? That's absurd. He could just divorce her. You're losing it, Marcus. It's jet lag." But of course she knew he was perfectly right. She looked around the smallish room. "You really know how to pick hotels. The lobby is infinitesimal, the staircase is really quite beautiful, to be fair about it, but this room, Marcus, it—"

Marcus said easily, "Forget the Savoy, Ms. Holland.

I want us out of sight, the essence of discretion. Just consider yourself in the enemy camp. You don't want to be out front doing the dance of the seven veils."

"I couldn't even manage one veil right now." She sighed. "Sorry I jumped on you."

"You're tired. We both are. You wanna sack out for a while?"

"With you, I suppose."

"I'm too tired at the moment to do more than twitch. Which wouldn't get me very far at all."

"All right. I'm going to take a quick shower."

He thought of her naked in the shower and did more than twitch. He stretched out on the bed, waiting for her to come out of the bathroom. When she did, ten minutes later, he was snoring. Rafaella looked down at him and shook her head. Dead to the world. *Dead as Sylvia would be?*

Rafaella shook her head. No, Dominick couldn't be that—that corrupt. Besides, it wasn't logical to kill his wife. But what did that matter?

Dominick would do whatever took his fancy, and there were years of resentment and hate for Sylvia.

Yes, he would kill her, without blinking.

She pulled the covers over Marcus, then slipped in beside him. She was asleep within minutes.

Chicago, Illinois
April 2001

April in Chicago could have been beautiful, the air fresh with spring, flowers bursting with scent and color. But it wasn't. It was gray and cold and drizzling. The service was held at FairLawn at graveside. There were some seventy-five people there, mainly old men, and at least three Chicago cops, come, Dominick thought, to wish the old man a speedy trip to hell. Dominick kept his head down while the priest intoned an epitaph that sounded far more suited to a man like Father Sabastiani than a villain like Carlo Carlucci. Carlucci's buddies had probably paid the priest to extol the obscene old fool. The rain suddenly thickened, thudding loudly and obscenely on the coffin lid. Scores of black umbrellas snapped open. Faces disappeared. A convention of crows, Dominick thought, all come to pay respects to Carlucci's rotted carcass.

Where was Sylvia? His wife had probably been too afraid of him to come.

He saw a flash of blond hair and tensed up. The woman turned her head suddenly and looked straight at him, and he saw that she was young, not more than thirty, and ugly as sin. But her hair was pretty, like Sylvia's used to be, like the other women's used to be—soft blond. Like Coco's used to be until she'd started fooling with it. It was too light, too white, not a soft-enough blond. She'd told him she was beginning to look faded—

Where *was* Sylvia?

Frank Lacy sneezed beside him. Dominick smiled at his henchman. A man with Lacy's credentials shouldn't have something as paltry as a cold. But he did. Leaving the warm island in the Caribbean and coming to cold, dank Chicago had done it to Lacy. But it didn't matter. For what Lacy had to do, he could be sneezing his head off and it wouldn't affect anything.

The priest was finally drawing to a close. A woman, heavily veiled in black, stepped forward and tossed a singularly beautiful red rose with petals as soft-looking as velvet on the coffin. Then a man scooped a shovelful of dirt onto the coffin lid. Then the priest blessed the assembled company, rain dripping off his fingers as he made the sign of the cross. It was over.

The woman turned on her high heels, then made the mistake of looking furtively back toward Dominick. He smiled at her. It was Sylvia. He had her now.

He waved at her and she scurried away toward a big black limousine. Quickly and quietly, Dominick made his way through the tangle of black umbrellas until he reached her side at the limousine.

"Hello, Sylvia."

She'd known he'd be there, of course. To gloat over her father's grave. She'd been a fool to come, but how could she have avoided it? "Hello, Dominick. It is good of you to come."

"Why? I came just to see the old bugger finally laid underground. He's dead, and if it weren't raining, I swear I'd do a dance right now. So, dear Sylvia, I hear from Oyster that you've knocked off the sauce."

She stared at him. "That's right. I don't drink anymore."

"Why?"

She shrugged. Never would she tell him that her lover had struck a woman and she felt responsible because she'd provided him the coke. She couldn't begin to imagine what he'd do with that information. "I've changed, Dominick. I didn't want to be like I was. I have changed, truly."

He just looked at her, that look that had always made her frantic with lust and fear, both at the same time. Odd, but it didn't affect her at all this time. She looked back, waiting, tense, afraid.

"Folks don't change, Sylvia. You of all people should know that. You're beginning to look your age."

"As do you," she said, refusing to back down, to cower, even though her palms were wet with the sweat of fear.

"But with men, my dear, with men, it's different. They become only more exciting as they get older. Of course, money is an integral part of the equation. But enough about our respective looks. Do you plan on staying long?"

"No. Goldstein will read father's will; then I'm returning to Long Island." She waited now, waited for him to ask her for a divorce. That woman he was living with, that French model, he'd probably want to marry her. And try to have children. Or was the woman too old now?

She said finally, unable to wait longer, "I'll give you a divorce, Dominick."

"That's certainly thoughtful of you. But a little late, I think. I wanted the divorce twenty years ago. What makes you think I'd want it now?"

She felt a shaft of fear. "I don't know. Don't you?"

He didn't bother to answer her.

"How is DeLorio? And Paula?"

"He's much the same, as is Paula. She's disappointed me."

"You'll recall that you selected her. Good stock, I remember you saying." The moment the words were out of her mouth, Sylvia cursed herself for a fool, which she was, but he looked unfazed by her words.

"Why don't I see you to your hotel? Or are you staying at your father's penthouse?"

She didn't want to go anywhere with him. She turned him down as politely as she could, but she knew she could have responded like Saint Ursula and it wouldn't have mattered. He let her go, no fuss. She nearly ran from him. Dominick smiled. She knew; she'd guessed. Sylvia was many things, rocket scientist not being one of them, but she had an odd streak of shrewdness. Oh, yes, she knew. He considered different options on the drive back to the Clarion Hotel.

Sylvia wanted to leave Chicago. She had no intention of returning to Long Island, not for a very long time, if ever.

So Oyster had betrayed her. She wasn't surprised, not really. He was loyal, but his concept of loyalty could easily accommodate several masters. Undoubtedly Dominick had paid him well over the years. She wondered what he'd reported to her husband. She shuddered. She was terrified of him. She'd wondered if she would still be terrified of him when she finally saw him again. Her fear was far greater than she'd expected it to be.

Samuel Goldstein came over to the penthouse several hours later and read her father's will. Sylvia sat in that prized antique Regency chair, disbelieving. She had him read it again, more slowly this time. Goldstein obliged her. Indeed, she thought, he was enjoying himself thoroughly. He'd always hated her, taken every opportunity to speak ill of her. And of course, she'd given him tons of fodder over the years.

Carlo Carlucci had left his only child nothing. He'd willed everything to his only grandson, DeLorio Giovanni. She couldn't believe it. She left Goldstein sitting there, left the penthouse, and walked quickly to Michigan Avenue. She had no coat, no umbrella. She was stunned and thus quite numb. Her father had left her destitute. He hadn't even continued her allowance, leaving it to DeLorio to decide if he wished to give his mother anything. She thought of how much the mansion on Long Island would bring. Enough to keep her in her current lifestyle for a year. Things were just so very expensive now. And there was Tommy Ibsen—and oh how he loved nice things. Her father had never complained of the million a year he'd given her—even more than that the past three years.

Now she had nothing except what her son might choose to give her. DeLorio wasn't normal, but she knew things that Dominick didn't know, knew things her father had never known. She knew, for instance, about the teenage girl: her name has been Marie, and she'd been fourteen years old when DeLorio abused and raped her and left her nude in a field some three miles from her parents' house. She'd survived—and hadn't named her assailant. Sylvia had managed to see to that. DeLorio had been thirteen at the time. She'd paid the girl's family over eighty thousand dollars to date. She wouldn't pay them another cent. Let DeLorio do it. Let Dominick know the whole dirty story. He could pay. She was through. She could even call them up. *Hello, Mr. Delgado. This is Sylvia Giovanni and I just wanted you to know that you'll not see another dime from me. My son's father owns an island and he's very rich and here's his address.*

She hated her father at that moment. She'd told him about DeLorio. Not all of it, no, but she'd had to tell him something so he'd provide enough money for the girl's family. And he'd still left the money to his grandson. There had been other incidents, lesser infractions, but each with DeLorio's individual earmark. She'd been frankly relieved when Dominick demanded custody of his only son. She'd rather thought at the time that DeLorio had called his father himself and made up stories about how his mother had abused him and about how unhappy he was with her. She'd wanted to sing hallelujahs when he'd finally walked out of her life. And then she'd remember at odd times how sweet he'd been as a little boy. Innocent and sweet, pure, and all hers. When he'd changed at puberty, the pediatrician had merely smiled and told her not to worry. He was just a normal boy and he'd get over the raging hormones. A fat lot that doctor had known.

Evidently her father had blamed her for DeLorio's leaving. He'd punished her, but good.

Sylvia waved down a taxi and returned to her father's penthouse. Even that was now owned by DeLorio. She packed her things and was at O'Hare within an hour. Within three hours she was on her way to Los Angeles. She'd wanted Japan, but she didn't have her passport and she wasn't about to return to Long Island for it.

Let him go there to find her. She'd sell the mansion, kiss Oyster Lee off, and let him go rot. She'd learn how to economize. But how she'd miss her roses.

She flew first class, momentarily forgetting that her financial status had changed drastically. She immediately ordered a whiskey, neat. Then another and another.

After four of them she fell asleep, much to the flight attendant's relief. "All I need in first class," he remarked to his friend. "A rich lush."

Dominick wasn't notified until late that afternoon by Samuel Goldstein about Carlucci's will. He also told Dominick that Sylvia had left, and she hadn't told him where she was going. Probably gone home, Goldstein thought, pondering. Probably not a wise thing to do. Not that he felt concern about her. He'd even given her a head start.

Dominick just smiled into the phone. He was pleased on both counts. He decided to remain in Chicago another day. He wasn't as yet certain how pleased he was about Carlucci's will. DeLorio needed his firm hand or he'd do something stupid with drugs. It was something to think about—DeLorio and all that money that was his and only his.

As for Frank Lacy, after checking around, he was on a flight to Los Angeles. His cold would improve in the warmth of southern California.

The Bennington Hotel, London, England
April 2001

Rafaella spoke quietly into the phone. Marcus was still sound asleep, sprawled fully clothed on his back. She didn't want him to hear what she was saying.

She said to her stepfather, unable to keep the excitement from her voice, "She really woke up? She really said something? What did she say?"

Charles stared at the phone. Well, there wasn't any reason not to tell her the truth now. When he'd gone to get the final journal the previous night, it wasn't in Margaret's desk, nor were any of the others. Rafaella must have taken them. There was no one else. So now she knew. Knew about her real father, knew all her mother's pain and obsession. He said harshly, "She called out *his* name and then yours and said 'No, no.' That was about it."

It was Rafaella's turn to stare at the phone. So Charles had read the journals too; her mother certainly hadn't confided in him. He'd found the journals and read them, and now he realized that Rafaella had read them too, because some were missing.

"How long have you known about Dominick Giovanni? And about me and my antecedents?"

"A long time," Charles said. "A year, but it seems like forever. I might as well tell you something else, my dear. The person—the drunk—who hit your mother was none other than Sylvia Carlucci Giovanni. I hired a detective and he discovered it was her car. Your mother was driving near where the woman lives. I can't figure out why."

Rafaella absorbed the shock of it and shook her head even as she said, "I can't either. Mother didn't think Sylvia had had any contact with Dominick in years. I don't know why she would have been driving near there. I don't like it, Charles. You're right: coincidences like that don't add up."

"You should come home, Rafaella. Either here or back to Boston." He paused, then said deliberately, "I don't know exactly where you are right now. Al Holbein told me you'd gone to the Caribbean for a rest. I pray you aren't anywhere near that man's island, but if you are, you'll have to get out of there now. I want you to come home."

"It seems you know everything. I can't come home, Charles. Not just yet. Dominick went to Chicago for the funeral. Now I'm in London, not on the island."

There was a startled silence. "Why?"

"I can't go into it, Charles. I'll be very careful, you can count on that. Giovanni can't hurt me here."

"That man could hurt the devil."

"I'll be very careful," she said again. "Please tell Mother I love her. I'll call again tomorrow." She paused a moment. "Charles? I'm sorry, very sorry. For all of us, but particularly for Mother." Rafaella rang off before Charles could say anything.

"I knew you had a talented mouth—"

She said as she turned to face him, "Don't finish that, Marcus."

She looked worried, so he didn't tease her anymore. "Did you get some sleep?"

"Enough, I suppose. You're awake," she added, seeing that he hadn't moved, that he was still sprawled on his back. But he was alert; he was always alert.

"How's your mother?"

"As you'd told me, she woke up, then slid back into the coma. What you didn't know was that she spoke a few words before going back under." Rafaella stood up and pulled her robe belt tighter around her. "I'll call room service. What would you like?"

He started to try out his morning wit but decided against it. She looked on edge. A lot had happened in a very short time, things that had been beyond her control. So he kept his wit firmly under wraps and contemplated breakfast. "Oat bran, please. I care about my cholesterol level."

She was momentarily distracted. "I can't insult your choice, since you look like you could run a marathon. I think I'll change and put on my face. Do you really play the harmonica, like a western cowboy sitting cross-legged in front of a campfire?"

"Yes, ma'am, I do. I've always dreamed of a flute accompaniment."

"I've always thought a harmonica would be nice to play along with."

"Soon, Ms. Holland." They were just staring at each

other, and Marcus felt the urgency between them but knew that there was just too much uncertainty in both their lives to allow for mutual trust.

She said quickly, "Why don't you go shower?"

Since there was little choice in the matter, Marcus agreed.

After Rafaella called room service with their order, she changed as she listened to Marcus sing opera in the shower at the top of his lungs. He wasn't bad. He even knew the words in Italian. That was impressive. The opera was *Don Giovanni.*

When a knock sounded on the door, Rafaella had just finished brushing her hair. She looked toward the still-closed bathroom door, shrugged, and opened the door. A fresh-faced waiter rolled in a trolley with beat-up covered silver trays on it. She signed the bill and tipped him three dollars. Marcus had changed some money at Heathrow but she didn't want to go through his trousers. After the waiter had left, she sniffed at the domed platters for a whiff of the eggs Benedict she'd ordered. Nothing. She lifted the lid on one of the trays.

She yelled, then instinctively covered her mouth with her hand as she gagged. The silver tray banged against the table and thudded to the floor.

Marcus burst through the bathroom door, wearing nothing but surprise on his face.

"What the hell—?"

Then he saw, and winced. There was a large rat on the plate, mangy and gray and still warm. It was quite dead. A folded piece of paper was sticking out from beneath it.

Nineteen

Rafaella wanted to look away, but she couldn't. She just stared at that mangy gray thing. She couldn't think of a thing to say; she just stood there gagging.

"Well," Marcus said, looking a bit green around the gills, "that's enough to make a grown man puke." He gingerly pulled the folded piece of paper out from under the rat, then picked up the cover and gently replaced it over the platter. He unfolded the paper and read the bold black lettering.

"What does it say?"

He handed it to her and Rafaella read:

My dear Mr. Devlin:

   Not unlike Jack Bertrand, my friend. The symbolism can't escape you. I will see you at my club. Tonight at eight. Do bring your lovely companion.

"Olivier, I presume?"

"Yes, I guess so. Some sense of humor, huh? Although he's right about the symbolism." He sounded preoccupied and Rafaella said, chuckling, "You're naked, Marcus. Not that I'm complaining, mind you. You came charging out of the bathroom every bit like Saint George, *sans* armor."

He looked down at himself. "Not much of a dynamic stallion at the moment."

"What's the opposite? Oh, yes, a gelding."

"Just keep looking, and yours truly will soon rise to the occasion. If I get a robe, will you have breakfast with me?"

Rafaella looked at the covered platter and shivered. "Move that thing out of here first—No, let's go out."

They ate lunch near the British Museum, at the Running Fox Inn. He told her not to order beer, but she did, just to be contrary, then wished she'd listened to him. It was warm and heavy and flat.

"You've got to ask for your Coke in a glass filled with ice," he said, and raised his hand to the waitress.

Once they'd gotten their corned-beef sandwiches, Rafaella said, "This Olivier person, how did he find out so quickly that we were here?"

"You got me, kiddo. As I said, he's got spies everywhere. This club of his—it's called The Occidental Club. It's in Piccadilly, if I remember my notes correctly. We'll dress up, go see him, and you'll be my decoration, nothing more. You got that?"

"Decoration? Kindly elaborate on that, please."

"My lady, my companion, my mistress."

"Like Coco."

Marcus looked startled, then said slowly, "Yeah, like Coco. You're to look expensive, beautiful, and must keep your mouth shut when the men talk business."

"I feel like a gun moll from the thirties. Shall I wear a pistol in my garter?"

"If he knew you were a reporter, I doubt he'd invite us to his inner sanctum, and this is important. Think you can pull it off?"

"Yeah, I can pull it off. I did well playing different roles as a reporter." She added thoughtfully as she took another bite of her sandwich, "I don't know why he doesn't know about me. He seems to know everything else."

"Good question, but I guess he disregards women as a threat to him. Just hope he doesn't ever think you're more than my moll."

That evening they stood in front of The Occidental Club, a tall narrow building just off St. James's Street, a building discreet in the extreme to any passerby. For one of the hottest gambling clubs in London, it wasn't close to what Rafaella had expected. Had she really been naive enough to think it would be loud and garish with overdressed people dripping with jewels hanging out the windows?

They were ushered in solemnly by a man garbed in black evening clothes. He had a very bald head and a Vandyke beard. "Mr. Devlin," he said, nodded, turned, and walked through an arched doorway. The main salon was at least thirty feet by seventy—the entire length and width of the building. Soft lighting from opulent crystal chandeliers radiated a pleasing glow on the men and women standing beneath them. No garish loud folk here, Rafaella saw. Just very wealthy and discreet people winning and losing oodles of money.

"I hear tell," Marcus said just above her left ear, "that on a good night Olivier hauls in almost three hundred thousand pounds. Incidentally, you look gorgeous."

"And expensive? And sexy? And kept?"

"Yes, all of those wonderful things."

She gave him a look that spelled out some kind of retribution, but he just kept smiling. He'd sent her that afternoon to forage on Fleet Street, where all the newspapers were housed, to find out about Olivier. She hadn't found much because the man avoided publicity and Scotland Yard like the plague, but she had met a reporter for the London *Times* who'd wanted to help and also wanted a date with her. Marcus had disappeared, turning up late that afternoon back at their hotel room carrying several boutique boxes. At her raised brows he'd said, "I needed a tux and so did you."

Her "tux" was a Halston white jersey gown that was incredibly simple and so suggestive that she'd just stared at it for several minutes. "It's indecently elegant," she said finally.

She tried it on at Marcus's urging, and when she came out wearing the gown and the matching white pumps, she looked indeed like a very rich man's very expensive lady. "The heels should be higher," Marcus said, rubbing his jaw judiciously, "but you never know when you'll have to sprint out of a tight spot."

Then he'd just stared at her, walking around her, viewing her from every angle, telling her to straighten her shoulders, and she could read the look in his eyes with ease. She looked him straight in the eye.

"You, Marcus Whatever-your-name-is, kidnap me, drug me, lie about my mother, and scare me half to death, and then you expect me to fall into bed with you."

He sighed. "Yeah, it's true. But not really *expect*. 'Hope' is more accurate. Behold a hopeful man who's never approached you properly in bed. And the fact is, Rafaella, now that I think about it, you're the one who's always been seducing me. Do you need help with that zipper?"

She'd laughed, she couldn't help it, but she wanted him and she knew that he knew that she did, but in the end, sex in the very late afternoon with Marcus wasn't to be, nor the possibility of talk between them—not banter, but real talk, about each other.

The phone rang. Marcus looked at it with both surprise and annoyance, but after a minute of silent debate he answered it. He said nothing, absolutely nothing, merely listened, his eyes narrowing a bit, no other sign on his face that the call was good news or bad or neutral. It frustrated Rafaella to no end that he had such a poker face. Then he hung up and sighed deeply.

"I've got to go out for a while. No big deal. Be ready to leave for Olivier's club when I get back."

He gave her no time to say anything, just kissed her quick and hard, cupping her jersey-covered breasts and fondling them for just a moment, and he was gone.

Rafaella walked to the phone and asked for the hotel operator. "Excuse me, this is Room Nine-two-seven, and our caller forgot to leave his number. You do have a record, don't you?"

Rafaella, who'd had no real hope, nearly whooped when the operator said, "Why, yes. Your caller is Mr. Anton Rosch in Room Ten-twenty. Shall I ring him for you?"

Rafaella quickly demurred. "I don't believe it," she said, then said it again, shaking her head in amazement. She quickly changed into jeans and a pale blue sweater and jogging shoes. Mr. Anton Rosch, huh? What was he to Marcus? What *was* Marcus, anyway? Some kind of foreign agent? What nationality was the name Rosch? It sounded Czech.

Rafaella took the stairs to the tenth floor. She'd wondered with every step how she was going to get the truth out of Marcus. Truth serum? Then she thought of her own motives, but not for long. Her motives were personal; they had nothing to do with anyone but Dominick Giovanni, her father. Whereas Marcus—Who was Marcus Devlin?

Room 1020 was just another brown door near the end of the brown-carpeted hallway, which was, thankfully, empty. She pressed her ear to the door. Nothing. She went down to her knees but could see only empty room through the keyhole. Marcus had evidently gone somewhere outside the hotel to meet this Rosch fellow.

She'd wandered into the small coffee shop just off the lobby, but Marcus wasn't there. Then she'd returned to their room and brooded. To deal with Marcus, one needed finesse. She must have enough of that, somewhere.

His voice suddenly sounded through her thoughts. "Well, you've been staring off into space for quite long enough. What do you think of this place? Decadent enough for your rich trust-fund tastes?"

Rafaella jumped at the sound of his voice, then quickly brought herself back to The Occidental Club. She smiled up at Marcus, trying for a mysterious sort of smile that looked, in truth, more like Betty Boop playing vamp, but Marcus appreciated her efforts. She wished she could just spit it out and demand to know who the hell this Rosch was. But she knew better. Marcus was fast on his feet, nimble-tongued, and too slippery to be caught like that.

No, she needed finesse, and here in Olivier's den wasn't the place to try it.

"Yes, it's plenty decadent enough," she said finally. She looked around. "Shall I go lose my mistress allowance at the baccarat table?"

Marcus started to flip out a suitably lighthearted answer, when he saw their bald Vandyked escort wending his way through the guests toward them. "Well, here goes," he said. "King Olivier will see us, evidently. Remember, Rafe, keep your mouth shut— be a good mistress, nothing more. Act sweet, stupid, and suitably deferential to the men, and—"

"I've got the picture, Marcus. How's this?"

He grinned at the vacuous expression. "Quite fine, but a bit more sultriness in the eyes, I think."

"Don't push it, Devlin."

They followed their escort out of the main salon, through a dark door marked PRIVATE, down a wide hallway. Rafaella was reeling from his calling her Rafe. Only Al Holbein, her Boston editor, had ever called her that. It had come off Marcus's tongue so easily. She felt his hand cupping her elbow. Ah, she liked the sound of "Rafe" when he said it.

"Do you think you could manage to swing your rear end just a bit?"

Rafaella calmly eased her arm out of his hold and reached down. She lightly stroked her fingertips over him. He sucked in his breath and she grinned evilly. She felt him springing to life and was well aware that several people, probably employees, coming toward them down the corridor saw what she was doing. She gave him the sexiest look she could dredge up, then walked a bit in front of him, swinging her rear end outrageously.

She heard him say behind her, "I'll get you for that, Ms. Holland. You can count on it."

She waited for him when their escort stopped in front of a double set of thick oak doors. The man knocked, then, after nodding to them, opened the doors and eased in, shutting the doors behind him.

"You calm again, Devlin?"

"You really like to live dangerously, don't you, Fifi?"

"Fifi?"

"Yeah. I think that's a good name for my mistress."

Roddy Olivier's office was an opulent oak-paneled affair that reeked of turn-of-the century wealth and privilege. The man himself sat behind a dark and heavy Spanish desk. For a man of sixty or thereabouts, he was in remarkable shape. He looked much better than the couple of grainy newspaper photos Rafaella had seen of him. He had a full head of stark white hair, a very pale long face, a very clever face, and the coldest gray eyes Rafaella could imagine. He wasn't smiling, he wasn't doing anything, just reposing and taking in everything about them. Then, after nodding to Marcus, he turned those nearly colorless eyes on Rafaella. He looked her over slowly and thoroughly and with complete indifference. So much for her sexy Halston.

Roddy Olivier lifted a very thin beringed hand. "Devlin," he said in a low, soft voice. "Do sit down. The lady will sit over there. Bufford, do bring us drinks. Whiskey for Mr. Devlin and myself and ginger ale for the lady."

"That will be fine," Marcus said, even though Olivier hadn't asked for their preferences.

Olivier said nothing more until they were both seated, Marcus in a soft leather chair opposite his desk, and Rafaella on a chaise against the far wall. Here sits the high-class tart, she thought, forced to hold herself very straight because there was no back to the chaise. She crossed her legs and tried to look like a high-priced tart.

Olivier wasn't looking at her as he said to Marcus, waving a hand in her direction, "Very nice."

"Yes."

"Is she worth what you pay for her?"

"So far. I haven't had her long."

"If you tire of her, I would consider taking her over."

"I'll think about it."

"You took out Bertrand," Olivier said then, softly, easily. He steepled his thin fingers together, tapping the tips.

"I had no choice in the matter. Did he come after me on your orders?"

"No. Unlike Bertrand, I wouldn't have underestimated you, Mr. Devlin. And if I'd wanted you out, you'd not be here now. No, Jack had ambitions of his own, I fear. You saved Dominick's life in that first attempt."

"You have amazing sources."

"Of course. Not many men could have managed that; not many men would have even wanted to try to save Giovanni's hide. I do wonder why you did it. You were shot; were you not?"

Marcus merely nodded.

"Why did you come to London? To find out if I'm the man behind *Bathsheba*?"

"That's about it. You see, Bertrand spoke of *Bathsheba*."

At that moment Bufford came back into the office, carrying a silver tray. He silently offered whiskey to Olivier, then Marcus, and last he walked to where Rafaella sat and handed her a glass of ginger ale. Olivier nodded to the man and he left again. "One should always pick one's tools wisely," he said. "One wonders if Giovanni has forgotten this simple truism.

"Bufford, for example, is faithful as a hound." He raised his whiskey glass. "Mistresses should also be faithful, don't you agree? Certainly you do. It's odd, isn't it, about mistresses? Well, to your quest for *Bathsheba*, Mr. Devlin."

"Yes," Marcus said, and sipped his whiskey. It was Glenfiddich and slid smoothly to his belly. What, he was wondering, had Olivier meant by those cryptic words?

Rafaella, who wouldn't touch ginger ale unless she were thirsting to death, sipped at the rim of the glass but didn't take the stuff into her mouth. She felt the power of Olivier, the absolute belief in himself and in his ability to accomplish whatever he pleased. She'd met other men who had the same aura about them, but they hadn't also given this unmistakable impression of almost eager ruthlessness. He was a very scary man. All her movements were slow and discreet. She didn't want his attention to shift to her again. What was Marcus thinking? She had never before in her life felt so distinctly out of her league. It was frightening.

"Bertrand knew about *Bathsheba*. At least he spoke as if he did. I assumed you would be able to tell me something about it or them or him, or whatever it is. If you wished to, of course."

"I would be a fool to tell you anything. Whoever it is, wants Giovanni dead. I wouldn't mind seeing him nailed. He's arrogant, a thorn in my flesh. He thinks he's all-powerful, a proper little god. He's also effectively out of business for as long as this *Bathsheba* threat exists.

"But just to add some sport, I will tell you this much, Mr. Devlin. You know about the Dutchmen and the woman, Tulp, of course. Tulp shot you. She was tops in her profession until she took this job. She went to New York. So whoever or whatever it is you're looking for is likely there, in New York. I'll bet you also wondered, Mr. Devlin, why the Dutchmen killed themselves. Where did they get the poison? And did they take it themselves? But that's another question for you to answer, and it's not to this point. The name *Bathsheba* is odd, isn't it? What do you think its genesis is?"

"*Bathsheba* from the Bible? David's consort?"

"Yes, that's a good guess. It could make sense symbolically, with some men. But there's something more immediate, more of our time, at least closer than biblical days. Are you an art lover, Mr. Devlin? No, I can see by your blank look that you're not. Well, sir, become one and I think things might get clearer. Now, you may leave. I expect you to be shortly gone from London. I imagine you will be traveling south. Will you leave your lady here?"

"No, she goes with me."

"A pity." Olivier didn't rise; he merely nodded to Marcus. "If you decide to leave Giovanni, I could use you in my organization. Good night, Mr. Devlin. I won't be seeing you again."

Neither Rafaella nor Marcus said a word until they were in a taxi bound for the Bennington Hotel.

Rafaella had never felt so very cold in her life.

Los Angeles, California
April 2001

Sylvia checked into a small hotel off Wilshire Boulevard. It was cheap and looked reasonably clean. Her head ached like the devil, her mouth felt dry, and her stomach wasn't happy. She had a hangover and she hated herself. She'd seen the looks the first-class-cabin flight attendants had given her—pity, disgust. Never, ever again. Never would she touch booze again.

She had no luggage, but she still had a credit card with an exquisitely high limit on it. She drank three glasses of water, all the while looking at herself in the small bathroom mirror, and decided she needed to treat herself. She needed to feel good about herself; she didn't want to feel like a drunken sot. No, certainly not. She ordered a taxi and had it drop her at the line of boutiques on Rodeo Drive. This was what she needed. A pick-me-up. Some pretty clothes. But no more booze. She thought of Tommy Ibsen, but with no regrets.

It was hot, nearly ninety degrees, and she hurried into the first boutique, a dress shop. Sylvia immediately felt right at home. The salespeople knew it too; they were at her side within moments, offering her champagne, offering to have their models show her whatever dresses she chose to see. Sylvia felt the balm of their goodwill flow over her.

Because her stomach was still rebelling from her indulgences on the airplane, she did drink one champagne. She selected four dresses, three pairs of slacks, tops and silk blouses and blazers, nodding at the deferential saleswomen, pleased when they offered to go next door and select shoes to go with the various outfits. Sachs, Adolfo, Blass, Perris, Chanel, Ricci—all lovely names she knew well. Yes, oh, yes, that Saint Laurent cashmere coat would look wonderful on her, the woman was perfectly right. White was her color, and the very long coat, more cream than the stark white of the slacks and blouse, was electric. That was the exact word she was thinking. And the matching hat, delicious.

Sylvia was very happy at that moment. This was where she belonged. She wouldn't think about her situation just now. Not when all these exquisite clothes belonged to her. Not when she could dress up in that beautiful de la Renta satin-faced red organza and visit the "in" place for lunch—was it still the Polo Lounge? Men would ask her out; women would want her secrets. Oh, yes, life would be grand.

Sylvia handed the woman her beautiful gold credit card. She smiled at the models and watched the assistants lovingly fold her new clothes or hang them on the elegant padded hangers, and they were asking her if she wished them delivered to her home.

But the woman who owned the boutique was frowning, frowning toward Sylvia. Then another look took over her face, a look of embarrassed uncertainty. She was coming toward Sylvia, and in that instant Sylvia knew what was wrong. She knew. She cried out, covering her mouth with her hand.

"No," she said, and rose, staring toward the huge pile of clothing that should be hers but wasn't because her credit card had been canceled. "No," she said again, and grabbed her purse and ran out of the boutique. She heard the woman calling after her, but she didn't turn back. She dashed out onto Rodeo Drive. The sun was hot and there were cars, so many convertibles, and they were honking at her, but she didn't notice.

Then there was a dark blue sedan and it was right there and it hadn't honked, nor had it slowed down. Sylvia saw Frank Lacy, saw him clearly, knew his intent, and she whimpered just before the car struck her and flung her back over the hood onto the sidewalk, nearly at the feet of the woman who held Sylvia's gold credit card in her hand.

The woman screamed and the credit card fell from her hand. It was ten minutes later that she was telling Sergeant Grimes about the woman. "Sylvia Carlucci Giovanni is what is printed on the credit card, as you can see, Sergeant. I went to ask her for I.D. since the credit card shows a New York address. She looked very strange and she cried out and turned quite pale and ran out of the store. I hurried after her and saw the car strike her. I didn't see the driver. I think it was a man, but I can't be sure. I guess it was an accident and the guy just panicked. It was awful."

Sergeant Grimes didn't know what to think. One of the older men on the force had mentioned that an ancient gangster, Carlo Carlucci, had just died in Chicago. Was this dead woman his daughter? If so, had it really been an accident?

"I don't know what to do with all these clothes. Nearly thirty thousand dollars' worth. Of course, she hadn't signed for them yet. Oh, dear, oh, dear." The woman sighed as Sergeant Grimes took himself off to question possible witnesses.

Reporters and TV cameras started arriving, but the coroner had already taken the body away.

Carlton Hotel, Miami, Florida
April 2001

Dominick heard the news in Miami from Frank Lacy. He had some business to conduct with a very old friend, Mario Calpas, and planned to return to the island in the morning. But that evening he would celebrate. Mario provided a lovely young woman for him, and Dominick treated her to a wonderful dinner and a diamond bracelet because he felt so good about Sylvia's death and the future and what it would bring.

Rafaella. He would have her, despite her fling with
Marcus. She was young and malleable and bright, he
supposed, for a woman, which boded well for the intelligence of their children. Poor DeLorio hadn't had
a chance with Sylvia for a mother, much less with that
old mobster Carlucci for a grandfather. But DeLorio
had improved; he had. It was just the problem with
all this money.

He stopped his thinking and his planning. Melinda
was very talented, and at the moment she was on her
knees in front of him. He was seated in a big armchair
in his suite at the Carlton.

She was good. He sighed and closed his eyes. It was
wonderful, and he felt his climax drawing close. But
he didn't want to come in her mouth. He wanted to
come inside her. He gently tugged her hair and she
raised her head, her eyes questioning. Her mouth glistened with her own saliva and him. He nodded toward
the king-size bed. "Stand up," he told her. "I want to
really see you."

Melinda was naked and she had the longest legs
and a very nice rear end. Her breasts were small but
Dominick didn't mind. The bush of hair at her crotch
was a rich deep brown, at odds with the platinum
blond of her head. He quite liked the contrast. He
told her to lie down on her back on the bed. She did
as she was told, with no hesitation.

Dominick looked at her for a very long time, appre-
ciating the newness of her body; then slowly he began
unbuttoning his shirt. He was on the third button
when he heard a key turning in the suite's door. Such
a soft sound, a whisper of sound that a man wouldn't
hear if he were plunging into a woman's body.

Immediately he looked down at the young woman
and saw it in her eyes—fear and knowledge. He
grabbed her, hauling her off the bed and in front of
him as the front door opened and a man jumped into
the room, his gun up. He fired from reflex when he

saw Dominick, and the bullet struck the woman. Dominick felt the impact of it as her body jerked back
against him. He dropped her and had his own pistol
in his hand in an instant. The assassin saw what had
happened, saw Giovanni's pistol, and was out of the
room, all within a second of time.

It was silent, dead silent. Nothing, not a sound. Melinda was on her side, dead, and there was a small
pool of blood collecting on the carpet, dripping from
the hole in her chest.

Dominick was on a privately chartered helicopter in
less than an hour, headed back to Giovanni's Island.

Twenty

She was so still and pale. Charles wanted to shout to her to wake up, to come back to him, but she didn't move. She remained away, remote. On some deep level he could never reach, she was thinking about Giovanni. She'd come to so briefly, speaking of him— *to* him? Charles shook his head violently. He couldn't bear to think about it.

Wake up, Margaret, wake up.

But nothing happened. Charles waited for the nurse to finish her checklist and leave the room, then turned on the TV. It was Dan Rather with the national news. Charles really didn't pay much attention until he heard Rather say, "Sylvia Carlucci Giovanni, fifty-one-year-old daughter of crime boss Carlo Carlucci, who died on Monday in his bed, age seventy-five, was killed today by a hit-and-run driver not twenty-four hours after her father's funeral. She was struck while crossing the famed Rodeo Drive in Los Angeles. The identity of the driver is unknown."

There was a bit more, but Charles wasn't listening. Rather then turned to the Middle East.

Dead, that horrible drunken woman was dead. There was such a thing as divine justice. Sylvia had been killed by a hit-and-run driver, just as she'd hit Margaret and raced away. And her estranged hus-

and, Dominick Giovanni, had ordered her killed. No doubt about that. The cops probably knew, but were keeping it under wraps for the moment. They needed proof. Well, he, Charles, didn't.

He looked over at his wife. *She's dead, Margaret. Wake up, Margaret, she's dead.* Margaret didn't move.

Charles was too keyed up to sit there and talk to Margaret, as was his usual habit. Besides, how could he care about what he'd done when he'd been at Andover and all of sixteen years old? He'd already told her about it before, if he remembered aright. And he wouldn't want to hear *his* voice anyway. No, Giovanni was there, deep in her mind, where Charles couldn't get.

The Bennington Hotel, London, England
April 2001

Marcus locked the hotel-room door and fastened the chain. He turned to face Rafaella. She said without preamble, "I want to take a very long, very hot shower. I'm cold and I feel incredibly dirty."

"Throw out the dress—that should help."

She looked startled at that, then smiled at him. "It just might."

He could only imagine how she felt. He nodded and she disappeared into the bathroom. He called room service and ordered up bottles of whiskey and soda. He stripped down to his shorts and sat in the chair by the window. There was a small park across the street, but he hadn't noted its name. It would be nice, once spring had come to England and turned everything green again.

He thought of Coco, not Coco the woman he'd come to like and respect, but Coco, Dominick's mistress, his property, his possession. It wasn't right. Olivier had spoken as though Rafaella hadn't been present, as if she were a commodity. And as a mistress, that's how he'd seen her. And that's how Dominick viewed Coco as well. Marcus wondered what Coco thought about it, if she'd accepted it, or if, deep down, it was a wound that wouldn't heal.

Marcus rose and began pacing the room. So Olivier wanted to be sporting about Giovanni, did he? Well, good thing he did. It just might give Marcus time to find this *Bathsheba* person or organization and neutralize it. Art, Olivier had said. Art? Marcus knew next to nothing about art. What did art have to do with this mess? And what did Olivier mean by "go south"? Marcus shook his head. He hoped Rafaella would have some ideas about that. He heard the shower turn on and imagined her stepping into the stall, naked and shivering and feeling dirty because of the way Olivier had looked at her and spoken of her.

He didn't blame her a bit. Olivier scared him to death. Marcus wondered why this was so, and decided it was because the man felt deeply about absolutely nothing at all. He was devoid of humanity, and it showed. After room service left, Marcus quickly poured himself a whiskey, neat, and drank it down. He poured another and drank it. He felt the warmth curling in his belly. He began to relax. He heard the shower spray.

He rose and walked into the bathroom.

He kicked off his shorts and opened the shower door, quickly stepping inside. Rafaella was staring at him, her wet hair plastered to her head and face. "Come here," he said, and pulled her against him. He buried his face against her throat.

"I'm so sorry about all this, Rafaella. So sorry, love. I didn't realize it would be that bad."

Rafaella burrowed against him. He was wet and warm and he was now very hard and pressing against her stomach, but his hold on her wasn't the least bit sexual. It was comforting, soothing. He was offering

er consolation. She pressed closer. "It was horrible,
Marcus, so horrible."

"I know," he said, and kissed her forehead. "Let's
et bathed and go to bed, all right?"

He felt her nod against his shoulder. Marcus didn't
athe her—he didn't trust himself to. The last thing
he needed was sex or any kind of reinforcement of
the idea that sex was all she was good for.

Once in bed, Marcus arranged her against his side,
er head on his shoulder. He said, his breath warm
against her temple, "I like you there, Ms. Holland.
Very much. It feels right."

She was silent for a long moment, then just nodded
gain against his shoulder.

"It would help, you know, if you'd spit out how
you'd like to roast Olivier on a barbecue. Righteous
anger's good, better than wallowing in this show of
debasement."

That got to her, as he'd guessed it would.

She reared up in his arms and stared down into his
ace. "What do you mean 'debasement'? I have noth-
g to feel debased about!"

"Are you sure about that?"

"Of course. Olivier's the one who's debased; he's
depraved monster, a—" She leaned down and bit
is shoulder.

"Yes, he is, and was that a love bite?"

She just looked at him, saying nothing, just looked,
d slowly she smiled. It was a sweet smile, one that
eld relief and comprehension and love.

"You really do belong here, you know," he said,
ressing her head back to his shoulder.

"Maybe."

He reached over and turned off the lamp beside the
ed. "Go to sleep." Very soon her breathing evened
d she relaxed against him.

He didn't sleep. He was too wound up. There were
o many unknowns, too many things happening he

didn't understand. Anton Rosch hadn't been much
help either. He was here on Hurley's order to keep
an eye on Marcus, to try to keep him safe just in case
Olivier tried anything nasty. Marcus liked and trusted
Rosch, a man who knew the dens and denizens of
England and Europe as well as Marcus knew Giovanni's Island.

Marcus sighed and tried counting rabbits. That
didn't work either. He wasn't really surprised when
Rafaella said quietly, after about twenty minutes,
"Are you asleep, Marcus Whatever-your-name-is?"

"Naw, I'm a real man. I don't sleep, I don't drink
milk, and I don't wash my own underwear." He'd
hoped for a chuckle, but wasn't too disappointed when
he got nothing. She was still too raw, but at least now
she was talking.

"Tonight was awful. I've never felt so out of my
depth before in my life, so on display. I thought it
would be fun, amusing, to role-play a tart, but it
wasn't. It was disgusting, repellent. It was a killer for
the soul, Marcus. Olivier—he's a very creepy man."

"True. Have you barbecued the bastard in your
mind? You're firmly off the debasement kick? You're
back to being superior and obnoxious?"

"Almost. I still don't even have the slightest wish
to throw you or stomp on you, though. I want to stay
right here where it feels safe."

"You feel safe with me?"

"Yes." She fell silent a moment, then added, her
voice puzzled, "I've never even thought about that
before. Being safe with someone. We're still in a
mess, Marcus."

"Yeah. Now, are you feeling smart right now? Just
nod, that's right. Okay, what could he have meant
about art? About going south? And the main thing,
he knew that Tulp had gone to New York, which
means it's probable that *Bathsheba* is in New York.
Does that make sense?"

Rafaella shivered; she couldn't help it. She was still thinking about Olivier and feeling his eyes on her and hearing his voice, so soft and quiet and cultured. She realized she hadn't been able to focus on anything else, except for the comfort Marcus gave her.

"Earth calling Rafaella Holland. Anyone home?" She scratched her fingernails over his belly. She felt he shudder go through him and drew back her hand. "No more of that. Now, I just remembered that real men don't beg women to listen to them. Either you soak up my brilliant words or I'll just shut up and go to sleep."

She laughed and hugged her arm over his chest. "I like you, Marcus. That is, you're okay when you're not being a jerk. I fry divine fish. I'll even make you hush puppies, southern-style, with lots of honey and butter oozing over the sides."

"I like the thought of that. What do you know about art?"

"I took a couple of classes in school—some medieval courses and Renaissance—" Suddenly Rafaella jerked upright in bed. "Oh, my God," she said, staring off into the darkness. "Dear heavens. No, no—I've got to be wrong, it couldn't be—"

"What are you talking about? What's wrong?" He sat up, hugging her to him, shaking her. Her damp hair slapped his face when she whirled her head about to face him.

"I—Nothing. At least not yet. We need to go to Paris tomorrow, Marcus, all right? We've got to see if something's still—where it should be. And if it isn't, then maybe, just maybe, we'll know."

"Know what?"

"No, not yet. I don't want to say anything yet. It's just too crazy."

"Now, look, Rafaella, you're supposed to be my partner in all this, not go haring off on your own. So just tell me what's going on." But she kept shaking her head. "Trust me, dammit!"

Rafaella wanted to pour it all out. She wanted more than anything to trust him. But the dam held and she shook her head. If it were only her, it would be different, but it was no longer just her. "I can't, not yet. Please, not yet. And what about you, you clam?"

They were back to their familiar impasse. Finally, so frustrated he wanted to yell, he drank another finger of whiskey, gave her a very sour look, rolled over on his side, his back to her, and pretended sleep.

Trust was just too dangerous for both of them. It was damnable, but it was true. They were going south.

Giovanni's Island
April 2001

Coco stared at him. "What did you say? Someone tried to kill you in Miami? Mario Calpas set you up?"

Dominick waved away Merkel and Link. He shook his head, saying nothing. Reaction had set in and he was at once very tired and feeling limp from the terror of that moment. Every movement of Melinda's, every movement the man had made when he'd come into the suite—all of it was printed right before Dominick's eyes. Who had set him up? Was it Mario? But why? Mario couldn't have anything to do with *Bathsheba*, could he? And it was *Bathsheba*. Dominick knew it.

"No," he said to Coco. "Mario didn't set me up. Someone else did. *Bathsheba* did."

Coco got him a drink, telling him curtly, "Drink it—you need it. Then we'll go to bed. But first, tell me what happened."

He drank, then said easily to his mistress, "I was with a very beautiful young woman, about Rafaella's age. I thought Mario had set her up for me. Now I'm not so sure. She was sucking me off and then I wanted er in bed, and when she was naked and lying there, I heard a key turn in the front door of the suite. I looked at her and knew that she knew what was going to happen. Before she could get away, I grabbed her and pulled her in front of me. The assassin panicked and shot her. She's quite dead."

Coco was suddenly very pale. "You were with another woman? She's dead?"

"Right." He paused, staring off into space. "She was good, Coco. She was very good." He paused a moment. "I guess you heard that Sylvia is dead?"

"Yes, there was a mention of it on the news. You didn't have anything to do with it, did you? It was an accident, wasn't it?"

"Of course."

Coco looked at him closely, then said, "What did you do with the girl's body?"

"Melinda? I called Mario and told him to get rid of it. An efficient man, our Mario. He was scared out of his wits. It was his permanent suite, you know, at the Carlton Hotel. I'm sure he took care of everything just right."

Coco waited. "And now?" she said finally, searching his face.

"Now what?" He was irritated because he was tired, and now Coco was asking cryptic questions.

She placed her hand on his forearm. She looked down at the perfectly manicured nails, the soft peach polish. "Now, what about us, Dominick? What are your plans for us? You're free, finally."

"Yes," he said, but he still didn't look at her. He was looking out the front windows, and saw DeLorio in conversation with Merkel. DeLorio was gesticulating wildly with his hands; he'd heard about his mother. Or was he upset about his father's near-demise? Probably not.

But he'd wanted to go to his grandfather's funeral and perhaps see her. Why? Dominick had to think.

He had to figure out how he would explain things to the boy—the fact that DeLorio Giovanni was now a very wealthy twenty-five-year-old kid with a hair-trigger temper and the judgment of a pubescent teenager. Old man Carlucci must have hated her too, Dominick thought. He'd cut her off without a dime. For a moment he regretted killing her. It would have been wonderful to know she was broke and alone. No more sexy young studs for poor Sylvia. He should have let her go about her business, watched her turn into a slovenly sow. She probably would have drunk herself to death within the year. Well, it was done.

Dominick had always made it a practice, a personal philosophy really, not to worry about the past, to keep it back there, out of mind and sight, never to delve, to pick, to regret. What was done was done, and there was nothing that could change it. Why think about it? He turned to Coco, trying to remember what she'd said. Oh, yes, she was pushing him, but she was too old now and he'd have to tell her soon. But not tonight.

"Yes, at last I'm free. Come with me. I'd like you to get me off before I go to sleep."

Coco did get him off, and soon he was snoring lightly, his head against her breasts. She was on the point of getting out of their bed when he moaned, then started thrashing around. She stroked him and caressed him and crooned soft words to him, telling him it was just a nightmare and she would take care of him. And finally he quieted and held on to her tightly.

The Louvre, Paris, France
April 2001

They stood in front of the painting and Rafaella read slowly, "*Bathsheba*, by Rembrandt, 1654."

Marcus just shook his head. "A painting. It is Bathsheba, of course, but I didn't even know Rembrandt had painted her." He looked more closely at the canvas, frowning. "She's fat, our Bathsheba. Do you think she was this hefty before David sent her husband off to battle?"

Rafaella remained silent. She didn't know what to think. Here was the painting, right where it was supposed to be. Perhaps she'd been wrong. What with all that had happened, it was possible she was remembering something else, another painting, one that looked something like this one—but not this one, just another stout woman, naked, in the classical pose. It was certainly common enough. Yes, she'd been wrong. She sighed with relief, relief that she'd kept her mouth shut and hadn't told Marcus. But the room in her stepfather's house was kept locked and monitored to keep the temperature constant, and she hadn't been meant to see it at all, but she had, by accident, returning from a date before she was supposed to and seeing her stepfather there, in that room, looking at the paintings that lined the walls. And she'd realized that here was something that wasn't any of her business, so she'd kept quiet about it and crept quietly to her room. She'd never mentioned that room to either her mother or her stepfather, not in the ten succeeding years.

Now she had to make Marcus forget all her admittedly weird behavior. But the painting was named *Bathsheba*. How to explain that? "Oh, rats," she said, adding as she turned to Marcus. "Fat? Hefty? Aren't you ever serious? For heaven's sake, Marcus, this isn't a joke. Don't you realize what this means?" She was suddenly terrified that she knew exactly what it meant.

"I've never been more serious in my life, and no, I don't know what this means. We have here a painting of Bathsheba, a painting, not just a Bible story. So what? So it's seventeenth-century and not B.C. before the Greeks. So what's the significance? So Tulp used two Dutchmen as her backups and Rembrandt was also Dutch. What is the profound significance of that? I'm angry, Rafaella—you can't begin to imagine just how much. You act mysterious, you drag me over to Paris, to the Louvre, of all places, to stare up at this painting of a fat woman named Bathsheba. And you won't tell me a thing. You won't tell me why you're so upset."

"Tulp is a Dutch name too."

"Very likely, but she lived in Germany."

"How did you know that?"

"Dominick might live on an island, but he does manage to learn some things. Old Tulp operated out of Mannheim."

"Could that be what Olivier meant by going south? Should we go to Mannheim?"

"No. Why won't you tell me what you realized or remembered or whatever? Why can't you trust me?"

She looked away from him.

"Rafaella!" He grabbed her arm and jerked her around to face him. One of the guards took a step forward, then at the frown from Marcus quickly retreated. Several tourists, whispering among themselves, detoured a goodly distance away from the Rembrandt.

"Trust you? Okay, here's trust. Who is Anton Rosch?"

That got him, but good. He stared at her, then exploded. "Ah, so now you eavesdrop on my phone calls."

"No, I was just smart enough to call the operator after you took yourself off, and she told me it was this man Rosch, and what his room number was in the hotel."

"So you just scampered upstairs to spy on me?"

"You're making a scene. Who is Rosch? Some foreign agent? What does he have to do with you? Are you a foreign agent?"

"Forget Rosch. He's not important at the moment, and don't be a fool, of course he's not a foreign agent. Why won't you trust me?" He shook her. "You do know something. And it's something close to home, isn't it? It's something you'd know that I couldn't possibly know." He saw it in her eyes. "Yeah, something real personal. What is it, Rafaella?"

She struggled with herself. She drew a deep breath, her decision made. "Let's find an expert. Let's have this painting authenticated."

He stared at her, then up at that painting. It looked authentic to him. "Who *are* you, Ms. Holland?"

"I'm just what you see—almost. But stop doing that, stop putting me on the defensive. You've got more secrets than a pig in a space suit."

"Don't try to explain that one. You want an expert, okay, let's find one. Do you think the officials here at the Louvre, one of the most respected and famous museums in the entire world, are just going to nod and say, 'Why, certainly, Ms. R. Holland. You think this wonderful picture is a fake? Let's find out.' Get serious, Rafaella."

"I don't know if I can get them to go along with it. All we can do is try."

The name of Charles Winston Rutledge III did help in the end. The art expert, a Monsieur André Flambeau of Gallerie de la Roche, was allowed the following morning to examine the Rembrandt. Monsieur Didier, one of the assistant directors of the Louvre, hovered over him, alternatively frowning, pursing his thin lips and looking vastly worried. He kept reminding all of them, "Of course it's genuine, *certainement. C'est ridicule, vraiment, ridicule!*" He talked of the painting's papers, its provenance, all provable and quite authentic, of course. On and on. Hours passed. Testing continued into the late afternoon. Monsieur Flambeau requested the assistance of another expert, associated with the Sorbonne. He arrived, all agog, and the two men closeted themselves from the Louvre officials. Testing continued well into the night. Finally, near to midnight, Flambeau raised his head and stared off into space.

Monsieur Didier was dancing about with impatience, his nails, Rafaella saw, nearly bitten to the quick. He looked ready to explode. Flambeau said slowly, in very precise English, looking directly at Rafaella and Marcus, "I don't know how you guessed, how you—admitted amateurs—could possibly tell. But you were quite right. It's one of the finest forgeries I've ever encountered in all my career, but a forgery it is."

All hell broke loose the following day in Paris when the announcement was made to the international press.

Giovanni's Island
April 2001

Dominick stared down at the newspaper with the grainy photo of Rembrandt's *Bathsheba*. Well into the article it was said that two Americans—their names were withheld—had brought the possibility of forgery to the officials at the Louvre.

Was it Marcus and Rafaella? Dominick was sure it was; deep down, he knew. Odd how the painting simply hadn't occurred to him; it hadn't occurred to anyone except Rafaella. Stupid, really. He, of course, should have guessed right away. He was an art lover, something of an expert, yet the painting just hadn't come into his conscious mind. Further, he'd had no idea at all that the painting was a fake.

Since it was a fake, it shouldn't be difficult for him to discover who'd bought it. He'd e-mail Ammon Civita, a broker in stolen art from Amsterdam. If Ammon hadn't done the actual procuring, he would know who had.

An hour later, Dominick sat back in his chair. *Bathsheba* was a forgery, replacing the original in the Louvre at least ten years before. Ivan Ducroz had done the job.

Ammon Civita had handled the painting. Now Dominick knew who had bought it, who had to keep it hidden for all time because it couldn't be insured.

Dominick felt the sour taste of betrayal fill his mouth. Oh, yes, he knew, and he would now take the necessary steps.

The man who had bought *Bathsheba* was Charles Winston Rutledge III, Rafaella Holland's wealthy and powerful stepfather.

For the moment Dominick didn't wonder about Rutledge's motives. They didn't matter for the present. He just thought of revenge—sweet, very tough, exquisitely thorough revenge.

He thought for two hours and then he reached for his phone.

Twenty-one

They were questioned until the French officials literally threw up their hands, shook their heads, and let Rafaella and Marcus go; they had no choice: there was no proof of complicity, of motive, of anything.

Rafaella had seen enough interviews with the cops to know their methods, although she had to admit that the suave French *gendarmes* had a bit more flair. One *gendarme* had the plummiest voice imaginable and was all sympathy; another growled; and yet another cursed with majestic originality. Certainly their threats to the Americans were more colorfully gruesome in their detail, and far more bloody. The guillotine—outlawed nearly a hundred years before—was mentioned in frustrated, sour voices. Rafaella held firm. She was polite and consistent and soft-spoken, respectful Boston at its best. There was nothing she could tell them, nothing. She knew art, what else could she say? And there had been something about the painting—No, she couldn't be more specific—it was an elusive feeling she hadn't been able to ignore. She'd been drawn to it, drawn to examine it closely. Certainly they understood that? This perception, this *awareness* that all wasn't right—ah, yes, she could see that Monsieur Labisse understood, such depths he appeared to have, such sensitivity.

Monsieur Labisse thought this perception, this awareness business sounded like *merde*, but he was a smart man and he was politically astute. The young lady's stepfather was the powerful Charles Rutledge III, a close friend of the Minister of Assistance. No, Monsieur Labisse wasn't stupid. Whatever was going on, he would discover it soon enough, and if this young lady was involved, well, what could he do? For the moment, he'd go very carefully, very discreetly.

As for Marcus, he quickly perfected an elegant Gallic shrug and a wonderful look of bewilderment. He was good, Rafaella thought many times during those long hours at the police station. He hadn't a drop of sensitivity about the painting, he said over and over in a forthright guileless voice; he was just along for the ride. Very good indeed. Again she found herself wondering just who he really was.

They weren't released until nearly three o'clock in the afternoon the following day, bedraggled, so tired they could scarcely think; but it was over, until they got outside the station. There were media people clustered there, and like media people from all over the world, which indeed they were, they were ready to do anything to get a sensational story.

"No comment!" Marcus shouted in English.

He looked at Rafaella's pale face and said, "Come on, kiddo, we can get away from them. You've just got to move. Come on. Rafaella?"

Marcus came to a sudden halt, whirled about to see Rafaella stopped dead in her tracks, slightly bent over, clutching her stomach.

"What's the matter? Rafaella?" He was at her side, holding her up, seeing the paparazzi closing in and not knowing for a moment what to do. The hospital? "What's wrong? Your stomach— Do you have cramps? Appendicitis?"

Rafaella didn't move any part of her body for at least ten seconds. She saw the photographers and reporters closing fast, seeing that something was wrong, but she couldn't be bothered. She felt Marcus's arm around her. She felt dizzy, light-headed, then cramps ripping through her belly. The cramps worsened, and because she didn't understand why, it was all the more terrifying. Then suddenly the pain stopped. Just plain stopped. Slowly, very slowly, she straightened. Nothing now.

"I don't know what happened," she said, all businesslike again, and Marcus just stared down at her, not knowing what to say, what to do.

"Let's get back to the hotel, unless you'd like to go to a doctor right now."

"No, no, let's go back to the hotel. I'm okay now. It must have been something I ate."

"I ate the same thing you did—a rubbery pizza with long-dead pepperoni."

"That must have been it. You're so macho and therefore don't get food poisoning. Quick, Marcus, the vultures are closing fast."

Marcus hailed a taxi, and when they were on their way, he said, "Is this all an act just to postpone telling me what's really going on?"

"No, no act. For a while there I really felt bad. But there's nothing now, so forget it." Actually, she'd felt periods of pain occasionally during all those long hours at the Louvre and then at the police station. But not now, thank God. "And as for the other—not yet, Marcus. Please, just not yet. It's fantastic, and even I can't believe it yet. It involves others, not just me, so I've got to—"

He cut her off with a slash of his hand. "So you're not going to tell me anything? I'm like the *gendarmes* and you're going to lie to me, treat me like a blithering fool, like the enemy?"

"It's not like that. Please, Marcus, if it were just me, it would be different, but—"

"Enough. I'm tired of it, too tired to argue with you

anymore about it. So much for your trust, so much for us and any future." He tapped the taxi driver on the shoulder. "*Arrêtez! Laissez-moi descendre!*"

He took one last look at Rafaella and said, "You're right: it's just lust."

Rafaella didn't say a word. How could he be so bloody obtuse? Let him go off and sulk, the stupid jerk. Even though she didn't feel any pain, she wrapped her arms around her stomach. She motioned the driver to go on. He gave her a look, then a Gallic shrug. Typically male, she thought. Of course it was all her fault, she was a shrew, kicking her poor man out of the cab.

Marcus realized he'd been a fool within ten minutes. He was walking down the Rue Carrefour, head bent, hands stuffed in his pockets. He was furious with her, he didn't understand what she was hiding, and he wanted to tell her she'd better begin trusting him soon, since he was going to be her husband.

Her husband.

He came to an instant stop, bumping into a very fat woman who dexterously held a baguette under her bare armpit. He apologized profusely, in fractured German, not remembering where he was, and kept walking. Oh, yes, he wanted to marry her, the damned irritant. He stopped in front of a jewelry store and stared at the array of wedding rings. He was on the point of going in, then remembered their situation and the fact that Rafaella just might be sick. Where was his sense, his brain? He felt strangely suspended, out of time, and he supposed it was the confusion of a strange city, the bewilderment of spending too many hours being grilled by men who had to make their threats through translators—oh, no, he hadn't been about to let them know he spoke French moderately well—the confusion of realizing he was in love with a woman for the first time since poor Kathleen. He'd accused her of keeping things from him, but he was blacker than either the pot or the kettle.

Marcus walked into their hotel room a half-hour later. He called out her name and saw her coming out of the bathroom, bent, like before, clutching her stomach, only this time there was blood running down her legs, staining her wrinkled light blue skirt, puddling on the carpet between her feet. And in that instant he knew what was wrong.

Rafaella looked up at him, her eyes dumb with pain and confusion. "Help me, Marcus. Please help me."

He didn't know much about miscarriages but he knew about hemorrhage and knew he had to get the bleeding stopped. He was at her side in an instant, scooping her up in his arms and laying her flat on her back on the bed. He quickly got towels, all four heavy white cotton ones that were in the bathroom.

"It's gonna be all right, Rafaella, just hold on. Let's get the bleeding stopped." He pulled her back onto her back and pulled a pillow under her hips. He worked her skirt up to her waist, then pulled off her bloody panty hose and panties, saying over and over, "It'll be all right. Let's get you elevated—try to stay this way, love. Just hang in there, just another minute, that's right. Oh, sweetheart, I'm sorry, so very sorry about this. You'll be okay, just hang in there with me. Don't forget about our date on the beach, you with your flute."

She felt the rhythm, the cadence of his voice, not particularly his words, and it calmed her, took away the numbing fear. But the pain was worse now, and she cried out, unable to keep it in, and tried to bring her knees up to her chest, but he was sitting beside her, holding her down, and finally her belly felt like it was twisting over onto itself and she felt a rush and it was warm and liquid and it was her blood and that of the fetus.

Marcus saw it was over. He bathed her again, stuffed

the smaller hand towels against her, and quickly covered her with every blanket in the room. "Just lie quietly now, don't try to move." He added unnecessarily, "You've had a miscarriage. You'll be okay now."

So much blood, he thought, gathering up the sodden red towels. Too much blood.

When he came back to the bed, he saw that she was asleep, and he was relieved. Exhaustion, he supposed, that and worry, had brought about the miscarriage. He felt her pulse and it was steady. Her color was better. Still he knew he should get her to the hospital. He wasn't certain about the blood loss and if she needed a transfusion—that and whatever else should be done following a miscarriage.

He opted for a taxi, not an ambulance. They didn't need any more publicity. He wrapped her in blankets and held her close until the taxi pulled up at the emergency entrance of Saint Catherine's Hospital. He calmly told the reception people he was her husband and she'd suffered a miscarriage on their holiday.

He prayed none of them would recognize the two Americans who'd just turned the art world on its ear.

They weren't recognized. Marcus used his real name. Marcus Ryan O'Sullivan. He thought, as he signed their names, that Rafaella Holland O'Sullivan had a very nice ring to it. Too, it did provide a bit of cover and he prayed as he thought it, prayed for a future for them.

Two hours later he was allowed into her room, a private one that he'd paid cash for. There was no point in taking any chances with another patient recognizing her. She was awake, pale-faced, her eyes shadowed, but she was back with him, thank God.

"Hi, Ms. Holland, or rather Mrs. O'Sullivan." He sat beside her on the bed and took her hand. He kissed each of her fingers.

"Thanks, Marcus. I didn't realize what was happening. I can't believe I was just standing there like an idiot, playing the helpless routine."

"Sometimes you're entitled. I shouldn't ever have gotten in a snit and left you. I knew you hadn't been feeling well, but I still had to go off and sulk."

Rafaella ignored that. "The doctor told me to assure my husband that the miscarriage hadn't caused any damage. He also called me Mrs. O'Sullivan, in a very charming accent, just like you did. Is that your real name, by any chance?"

"Yes. I hope you don't mind, but I wanted to give us a bit of cover. Now, would you please listen to me? I'm sorry about this, Rafaella. But I don't understand. You're on the pill."

"Yes, I am."

"Remember after our bout in the swimming pool I asked you when your period was due? And you told me any day?"

She looked frighteningly pale. "I didn't have a period," she said slowly. "I didn't even think about it. There was so much happening. I didn't even realize that I hadn't had a period. And now this."

She was crying, not making a sound, but tears were seeping from the corners of her eyes, streaking down her cheeks.

Marcus gathered her against him, kissing her hair, stroking his hands down her back, saying over and over, "It's all right, sweetheart, really, it's all right. You'll be all right now, I swear it. Shush, you'll make yourself ill. Damnation, you're supposed to be safe with me."

Rafaella sniffed loudly, accepted a French rendition of a Kleenex from him—it was about as soft as the French idea of toilet paper—and blew her nose. She was falling apart, and it wasn't just because of the miscarriage. No, it was the other. She knew he was frightened and concerned, and so she forced a smile and pulled back, out of his arms, and said, "You're

macho, remember? Macho men can overcome anything, including impregnating supposedly impregnable
ladies. You are, evidently, frighteningly virile and
potent."

"I like the sound of that, but not what happened."
He plowed his fingers through his hair. "Oh, Rafaella,
I'm sorry about this."

"It's not your fault. Stop with the *mea culpas*. All
right? Really, Marcus, it just isn't you. And I *am* safe
with you."

"You mean you got pregnant that first time in the
deep end?"

"It would seem so. Get that look off your face. Men
are the strangest creatures," she added, still smiling at
him. "Marcus O'Sullivan. I like the sound of that.
Very, very Irish. Your hair is standing on end."

"You're tired," he said, abruptly rising. "Please rest,
and I'll be back this evening."

"What are you going to do?"

"I'm going to do some checking around and see if
I can't find out who bought *Bathsheba* on the black
market. There are a couple of people here in Paris
who might know." He saw it in her face—knowledge,
pain, deep uncertainty about what she should do. He
raised his hand, knowing excuses would come out if
she chose to speak at all. "No, you don't have to tell
me a thing, ever, if that's what you decide. But if you
can't give me the answers, I've simply got to go out
and try to find them myself. You do understand that,
don't you, love?"

She nodded, splaying her fingers over her stomach,
so flat-looking beneath the stark white sheet. "I'm
sorry, but I just can't, not yet—I have to speak to—"

He leaned down and kissed her, then was gone. Ra-
faella lay there staring a moment at the closed door.
He was a good man, and his real name was O'Sullivan.
She liked it.

What am I going to do?

There was no answer, no sound at all in her room.
I just had a miscarriage, she thought blankly, and
to her surprise, she felt the tears welling up again.

Giovanni's Island
April 2001

DeLorio couldn't believe it. He was a millionaire.
Nothing had changed except an old man he'd rarely
seen in his life had died, and now he was filthy rich.
He just stood there grinning like a fool; he couldn't
believe it. He was free; at last he was out from under
his old man's thumb. His old man had tried to be cool
about it, to play it down, but DeLorio wasn't stupid.
He knew what was what now. There would be new
rules to the game, and he'd be the one to write them,
no one else.

His old man had done more than play down his
inheritance, he'd tried to make it seem like a dung
pile, but DeLorio had an idea of his grandfather's
worth. It was a lot, more than his old man had, he'd
wager. And there wasn't any more money to be spent
on his mother—not that he would have minded, of
course, if she'd been willing to cut back her expenses.

His old man was stupid. He was too old to know
what was good for the family, what family there was
left. Just the two of them now.

His father had told him, looking him straight in the
eyes, that he was sorry Sylvia had been in that accident. And DeLorio had said, "Did you have her
killed?" Dominick had smiled sadly and replied, "Of
course not. She was your mother, she was once my
wife. It was an accident, a terrible tragedy. Shocking."

No more would his old man tell him he couldn't
go into drugs. He had no more power over DeLorio
Giovanni. DeLorio was the man of the future: Domi-

nick Giovanni was a relic of the past. He might as well hang it up; DeLorio was ready to take over.

It wouldn't be long now. He had the money, he had the brains. And he had the connections in Cartagena. And in Miami. The old man didn't know it, but Mario Calpas respected him—DeLorio. He believed in him, believed that the old man was over the hill. But Mario hadn't ordered the hit on him. No, that was *Bathsheba*. Maybe if his old man asked him real nice, he'd try his hand at wiping out the assassins. That smug-mouthed Irish jerk, Marcus Devlin, was a useless imbecile. He'd done nothing, not a damned thing. The fact that he'd saved the old man's life, well, that was just the luck of the draw. All Marcus was interested in was screwing Rafaella Holland. DeLorio's hands fisted. Then, slowly, he relaxed, splaying his fingers, smiling. He shouldn't let little things get to him anymore. Things were looking up now. He was in control.

In the hallway, Merkel took a call from Callie at the resort. She wondered if he could tell her Marcus's plans. There were decisions that had to be made and besides, everyone was asking for him. A popular guy was Marcus, Merkel thought, and told Callie that he'd have to get back to her. Marcus was off on business for Mr. Giovanni, somewhere in Europe. Callie rang off, telling him that he should come over to the resort and see Punk's new hairdo—it was called big hair and it was still very blond and had a gorgeous purple stripe running from the cowlick down to her neck. Merkel said he'd do that. Punk was a hoot. Then he went to see Mr. Giovanni, who was alone in the library and didn't look pleased to admit Merkel. That made Merkel nervous and uneasy.

"I wanted to ask you about Marcus, Mr. Giovanni. Callie called from the resort, asking about him and his plans. I told her I'd ask you."

"Maybe you should be asking me what my plans are for Marcus."

Mr. Giovanni was using his soft, smooth-as-honey voice that made Merkel's flesh crawl. Merkel didn't understand that, and he wasn't certain, all of a sudden, if he ever wanted to.

"I've just discovered who our *Bathsheba* is, Merkel. Aren't you interested in knowing?"

"Yes, sir, Mr. Giovanni. Certainly, sir."

"It's our dear Rafaella's stepfather, Charles Winston Rutledge III. What do you think of that, Merkel? Speechless, I see. I must admit that I was speechless as well, in a manner of speaking. It does make me wonder about Rafaella and her motives, doesn't it you? Sure it does. And now our Marcus is compromised, shall we say. He's in Miss Holland's company, in her bed, and in all probability he's in her confidence. Oh, yes, Marcus is definitely compromised."

It was more than Merkel could take in. It sounded incredible, yet somehow— He shook his head and said, "Is there anything I can do, Mr. Giovanni?"

Dominick shook his head. "No, just stand ready, Merkel. I can trust you, can't I?"

"Mr. Giovanni! Sir!"

"Yes, certainly. You are my man, my creature, as a character of Shakespeare's would say. Yes, my dear creature, stand ready."

Paris, France
April 2001

Marcus held her hand. He didn't want to let it go even though she was asleep. Her flesh was soft, firm, pale as her face was still. A nurse had brushed her hair back from her face. It was lank and dull, but that didn't matter. She was all right, thank God, and no thanks to him, Marcus, the horny bandit. He still couldn't believe he'd gotten her pregnant when she'd been on the pill. In the future they'd have to be very careful, since it appeared that his sperm was happily at home in her womb and quite ready to stake claim.

The future.

It didn't give him pause now. He'd discovered over the past couple of days that all the insanity that had defined his life for the past two and a half years—all the deceptions, the damnable assignments, Dominick Giovanni himself and his devious, quite ruthless mind, the danger—all of it was out of the limelight of his mind. No, his priorities had definitely shifted, and now he viewed all the other as simply things to be taken care of before he and Rafaella could get on with their lives.

She'd feel the same way. At least she'd better. When she was feeling back to normal, he'd tell her the truth. Maybe if he were open, she would be also. Actually, as soon as she cracked her eyes open, he'd start talking. He'd been a fool not to prove his trust of her sooner.

"You're looking awfully serious. For a change, I should say. How are you, Mr. Marcus O'Sullivan?"

"I'm tired and worried and skinny because I haven't eaten forever, and lonesome as hell. I am not, however, horny. Those days are long over."

Rafaella smiled and squeezed his fingers. "You're not, huh? I wonder how long that will last."

"Probably until we're married." He looked thoughtful. "I'll plan a real kinky wedding night, though, one that will sizzle you so that you make all those cute little noises deep down in your throat."

She had no answer to that, just stared at him as if he had a loose bolt somewhere in his brain. Finally she said, "There's so much happening, so much that has happened in the past, and all of it touches me—us—and it's a mess. I don't know what to do, Marcus."

"It'll stay a mess until you tell me all about it. No, don't start shaking your heard at me. I decided you needed an example set for you. A good example from a good man. Here goes: my real name is Marcus Ryan O'Sullivan and my home is Chicago. I'm a partner in—it's true, I swear it—in a munitions factory that earns its livelihood from government contracts. For example, we provide parts for the F-15 fighter. Also, we develop high-density mines that the government pays us a bundle for. We sell to the NATO countries, but we've never, ever, in our professional lives sold to any countries not specifically approved by the State Department. My partner's name is John Savage and I keep in touch with him and through him with a man named Ross Hurley, my contact with the U.S. Customs Service."

"You're not making this up, are you?"

"No. Why?"

"To get me to spill my guts to you. Oh, no, I take that back." She sighed, then said, "You're not, are you, Marcus? Oh, no, you're as honest as my Great Aunt Mildred, who wouldn't lie to the postman about including a letter inside a package and paying more postage. I always knew you couldn't be a criminal, it just didn't fit, but your association with Giovanni, well—tell me the rest of it and I'll believe everything you say."

"It's not just sex."

She giggled. It was a wonderful sound, and Marcus laughed. His first laugh in more days than he could count. He leaned down and kissed her mouth. "You can keep your maiden name, I don't mind. I'm macho—we've proved that countless times—but sensitive macho. Besides, you make lots of money and I'm not stupid. Yeah, I like it: Rafaella Holland O'Sullivan. It has a ring. All the newspapers in the country are going to want that byline."

"You're crazy. Get back to your tale."

He kissed her again. "A hard woman. You'll like John Savage, my partner. We drew straws and I won—or lost, depending on your viewpoint. Here's what happened nearly three years ago. Our business was just taking off in a big way. We had credibility with all the bigwigs and the Defense Department, with all the other feds too, even Congress; we kept to our bids and we rarely ran over our target dates or upped our initial bids. Now, here's the fly in the ointment. John and I are first cousins, and our Uncle Morty—my mother's older brother—was on our payroll. Come to find out, we were under investigation by the U.S. Customs Service and they accused Uncle Morty of selling goodies to foreign agents, notably guys selling stuff to Iran. Not a particularly wonderful thing to have happen to a relatively new company that could use all the credibility it could get.

"Neither John nor I believed Uncle Morty guilty, but there was evidence, and the bottom line was that good old Uncle Morty had been netted by a very gorgeous woman. He's about the most benign guy you can imagine—short, bald, and tubby—but the truth is, he's just plain naive, incredibly so in this case, and he did whatever this woman told him to do. She, unlike Uncle Morty, was one smart cookie, and she was long gone before everything cracked wide open.

"But we ended up making a deal with Hurley of the Customs Service. One of us would go undercover and nail this very elusive fellow whose name was Dominick Giovanni. When he was safely under wraps—that is, when the feds had gotten him—Uncle Morty would be off the hook. Understand, Uncle Morty was looking at life imprisonment and we couldn't find that woman or any of the middle guys who'd done all the circuitous routing of the F-15 parts to Iraq. He's been in protective custody ever since, free but not really, not completely. He'll be really free the day Dominick isn't.

"And that, my dear Ms. Holland, is the truth. What do you think?"

"I'm overwhelmed. But why would they offer that deal to you, two businessmen?"

"Both John and I had been field agents in Europe. We were well trained and were really very good. We stayed in the CIA for five years, then started up our own arms company. That's why I speak some French and a smattering of German. It seemed a good idea, and we'd met a lot of people in the Defense Department and made good impressions."

"I wonder if you guys were set up," she said thoughtfully. "You know, by this guy Hurley."

"Naw, but I'd like to believe it if I could. No, Uncle Morty had been played for a fool. The funny thing is, you will like him when you finally meet him."

Rafaella suddenly grabbed his hand and shook it. "But the danger, Marcus. If Dominick ever found out, he'd—"

"Right. He'd blow my head off. I'd be history."

"No wonder you couldn't tell me anything. I can't get over the fact that both of us are here pretending to be what we aren't, only I really am a writer and I really did write that biography of Louis Rameau and I did truly intend to write a biography of Dominick Giovanni, it's just that it wouldn't have been written the way he expected it to be."

"I'm beginning to see. You want to nail him too?"

"Yes, nail him but good. I wanted to write a book that would hold him up to the world, to show indisputably what a horrible man he really is: amoral, ruthless, cruel."

"This *Bathsheba* thing came as a complete surprise to you."

"Yes, it truly did." She looked over at him, and he hated the pain he saw in her expression.

"Tell me, Rafe. I'll do my damnedest to help."

"The painting *Bathsheba* was stolen ten years ago by my stepfather, Charles Winston Rutledge III."

Marcus stared at her, unconsciously squeezing her fingers. "Good grief."

"You've got that right. I don't understand this serendipity, this calling himself *Bathsheba*, but I do know why he's tried to kill Giovanni." Rafaella broke off when a new nurse came soft-footed into the room, closing the door behind her. Marcus hadn't seen this one before. She was older, more formidable-looking, her white uniform pristine and starched crisp. She was smiling, however, and carrying a tray with a glass of water and a paper cup holding several capsules. She said in perfect English, "You're looking much better, Mrs. O'Sullivan. Now, I have some pills your doctor ordered for you. You must take all of them now, please."

"But—"

"Go ahead, love. I haven't known anything this long, what will a few more hours matter? We'll finish this off later. Your health is the most important thing."

She looked at him. He was perfectly serious. Rafaella took the four capsules. The nurse was taking her blood pressure, speaking softly to her. She lay back, almost instantly feeling the drowsiness pull at her. The nurse finished with the blood pressure and was straightening to stand beside her bed. Rafaella heard her say to Marcus, "Now, Mr. O'Sullivan, it's your turn. No, sir, don't move. You recognize a silencer, I'm sure."

A gun. "No," Rafaella whispered, and tried to pull herself upright in bed. But she couldn't move; she felt heavy and strangely numb, and the room was turning dark.

"Who are you? Another Tulp?" Marcus's voice, low and calm and furious.

"Let's not waste time, Mr. O'Sullivan. Now, listen very carefully. Your little tart here will shortly be quite unconscious. I've got two men dressed as orderlies outside with a gurney. We're all leaving here shortly. You try anything, anything at all, and I'll kill her. Do believe me. Then I'll kill you and maybe some of the hospital staff. And then I'd get away. I've got the gun and the element of surprise. Now, will you cooperate?"

Marcus took stock, weighed his options, all in under two seconds. "Who sent you?" he asked, his eye on her gun. "Who are you working for?"

"You'll know soon enough. Good, she's out. Don't move, Mr. O'Sullivan. You wouldn't look particularly sexy as a corpse." Marcus watched her walk to the door, open it just a crack, and motion to someone outside. In a moment, two men wheeling a gurney came into the room.

"Don't underestimate me because I'm a woman, Mr. O'Sullivan." She watched impassively as the men lifted Rafaella off the bed and onto the gurney. They smoothed the covers over her, a very professional-looking job with neatly tucked-in corners, then nodded to the woman.

"I believe we're ready to leave this place. Don't forget, Mr. O'Sullivan." She lowered the gun under the cover and he could make out its outline, the muzzle pressing against Rafaella's left breast.

"I won't forget," he said, and meant it. He wanted to go after her, but he knew the chances were slim indeed that he'd disarm her without being hurt himself or Rafaella being shot. He walked beside the gurney into the hospital corridor. His chance would come.

Who had sent the woman? Two choices, only two. *Bathsheba* or Dominick. No, there was Olivier as well. But Rafaella's stepfather? He'd threaten his own stepdaughter? And how could *Bathsheba* be her stepfather? How could he try to kill Dominick, knowing she was there on the island? None of it made any sense.

Marcus couldn't seem to take his eyes off the gun muzzle against Rafaella's breast. He kept cool and kept walking. There would be other opportunities. The two men, dressed in their white jackets, looked slightly bored, like orderlies anywhere. The woman's face was impassive.

She reminded him a bit of Tulp: hard, tough eyes as mean as nails.

Where would they be taken?

"Mr. O'Sullivan! *Un moment, s'il vous plaît!*"

It was a young, fresh-faced nurse who was calling to him, and she was trotting down the corridor toward them, waving a sheet of paper. Marcus saw the gun jerk, felt the alarm of the two men. The young nurse was smiling at him, unsuspecting, waving the piece of paper.

Twenty-two

Long Island, New York
April 2001

Charles Rutledge left Pine Hill Hospital just after ten
o'clock at night. It was cold, only forty-six degrees,
and thick leaden clouds obscured the quarter-moon.
He shivered in his cashmere coat and pulled on his
soft York-leather driving gloves.

The hospital parking lot was well-lit, but there
weren't many cars at this time of night. Charles was
bone-tired and depressed. Life—once a Garden of
Eden created especially for him by a beneficent fate—
now seemed pallid and cold and empty as a desert,
and he hated it. It was like purgatory—the uncertainty
of each hour, not knowing when it would end and
what the ending would be, the paleness of Margaret's
face, the damnable doctors just nodding and trying to
pretend optimism. He'd noticed today how Margaret's
hair seemed duller than just the day before, and it
scared him. Was it a sign that she was failing?

He couldn't bear to go home, to hear his own footsteps on the Italian marble tiles in the vast entrance
hall, to know he would be alone. The house was shadowed with memories, yet empty of any present, and
even the Rutledge housekeeper, Nora May, who'd
been with him for twenty-two years, was silent, re-
proachful, as if he, Charles, were somehow responsible
for what had happened.

And even when he was with Margaret, he was alone, because that one time his wife had regained consciousness, she'd said *his* name.

Charles shook his head. Just for now, for the next hour or so, he'd forget Dominick Giovanni, forget his plots, forget his plans, forget his failures. It was like a canker and it would kill him if he let it. He was fast taking over Margaret's obsession. He was already obsessed, had been for months before the accident.

Charles drove his BMW to Claudia's apartment, stopping first at a 7-Eleven to call her and ask her if he could come. She sounded pleased to hear his voice, and he hoped it was true. He was becoming a cynic. Claudia liked him, she really did—at least she had before he'd broken things off with her. It wasn't sex he wanted from her tonight. No, he never wanted sex from her again. He just needed someone he could trust, someone who knew him, someone he could talk to, someone he knew would listen and commiserate and be patient and kind.

Claudia met him at the front door. She helped him off with his coat and scarf, gently pulled off his gloves. She led him into the living room, which was all soft pastels and creams. He sat on a pale peach silk sofa opposite the fireplace. She told him to relax and raised his legs, placing his feet on a squat hassock. She brought him a brandy, then sat on the floor beside him. She simply looked up at him and waited. No recriminations, no sulking, no guilt.

He sipped at his brandy and began to talk. She didn't interrupt him, just listened intently, watching his face.

"Claudia," he said, pausing a moment, "do you know it feels good being here, just as a friend, knowing that you'll bear with me, knowing that you'll expect nothing more from me?"

"Perhaps I still expect something more," she said, "but not now. Yes, I'm your friend, though it isn't what I'm used to." Some minutes later she was sitting beside him, a glass of burgundy in her hand. And he continued to talk. It was late when he stopped, but Claudia merely smiled at him and said, "Why don't you stay the night? You're so tired, Charles."

Charles shook his head, even though he felt so tired, so very enervated, that he could fall asleep where he sat. "No, I can't, but thank you for caring, Claudia."

"I worry about you," she said, lacing her fingers through his. "I truly do, Charles. Your wife will be all right. I know it."

He nodded, saying nothing, and looked toward the fireplace. There were no flames now, no sparks shooting upward, just warm embers, glowing orange. And he felt old and tired and terrified of what tomorrow might bring. He turned suddenly to Claudia and said, "Did I tell you that he murdered Sylvia Carlucci Giovanni?"

Claudia frowned. "I remember hearing that name on the news. Wasn't she some Chicago gangster's daughter? You knew her, Charles?"

"Yes. Not really knew her personally, but she was the drunk who struck Margaret's car. It's complicated." Charles cursed himself for cutting loose to Claudia, and quickly rose to his feet. "Forgive me for carrying on, Claudia. Forget what I said. Thank you for letting me talk my head off."

"Will I see you again?"

"Perhaps, if you wish, but as a—well, as a person, a friend."

She grinned at him. "I suppose that's possible, but a pity, Charles, a great pity. I've always loved our other relationship, you know."

He placed his fingertips over her lips. "I must go now. Good night." He left her. He felt the frigid air slap him hard, and hunched forward, jerking his coat collar up, quickening his pace to his car. The wind had come up and was blowing cold and hard.

He nearly yelled aloud at the shock of it when he
heard the soft voice say from behind him, "Mr. Rutledge, do as I tell you and everything will be all right.
I've got a gun pointed at your spine. We're going to
leave your car here. You're coming with me.

"No, sir, don't turn around, don't say anything. Just
walk, that's it, to your right."

"But who are you?" Charles whispered, his heart
pounding so hard it hurt to breathe. "Please, what is
this about? Do you want money?"

"No, sir, no money. Be quiet or I'll have to hurt
you. Hurry, now. I don't want us to be seen."

Charles speeded up, and his heart pounded wildly
because he was afraid he was going to die, that this
was finally the end for him. He was frightened beyond
words. Maybe it was a kidnapping. What would happen? Margaret—what would happen to Margaret? He
couldn't leave Margaret, not the way she was, in that
frightening limbo.

He felt light-headed with fear, and the man behind
him, as if sensing it, said in that same calm voice,
"You're doing just fine, Mr. Rutledge. Now, here's my
car. You just get in here and slide across the seat."

Charles did as he was told. There was a gear between the two front seats and he had difficulty, but
the man said nothing, merely waited for him to settle
into the passenger seat. He was terrified to look at
the man's face. He wasn't wearing a mask, Charles
knew that. He was terrified to look because he'd heard
that terrorists, if their hostages saw their faces, killed
them, saying they had no choice because they couldn't
leave witnesses. But Charles had heard they didn't
wear masks on purpose because they wanted to kill,
they wanted to see a victim's terror before they killed
him. No, he wouldn't look. But the man was in the
car now, turning the key in the ignition.

"Where are we going?"

The man turned on the heater, adjusted the rear-

view mirror, then said, turning to face Charles, "To
beautiful place, actually. Right now, to the airpor
Just hold still, Mr. Rutledge."

Before Charles could react, he felt a needle sin
into his upper arm; sharp and cold, having penetrate
easily through his thick cashmere coat, his jacket an
shirt, and buried itself deeply into his flesh, and h
gasped with the knowledge of it and the horror of
and tried to jerk away, but it was too late, the ma
had smashed his thumb against the plunger, and the
the man was saying, "It's just something to make yo
sleep, Mr. Rutledge. That's all, just sleep. Just a mir
ute now."

"No," said Charles, and even though his single wor
wasn't slurred, his mind was already becoming cloude
and he turned and stared at the man full-face. Th
man looked benign, a kindly father who was too thir
his features sharp and gaunt, and Charles said, h
voice now slurred, "What's your name?"

"Frank Lacy."

"All right," Charles said. The man was real. He ha
a name and he'd said it aloud and it made Charle
feel better. He slowly fell over on the seat, his hea
lightly hitting the car window.

Paris, France
April 2001

Marcus turned and smiled pleasantly at the youn
nurse, who was flushed and bright-eyed, her fresh lip
stick very red. He said in French, "Yes, what is it yo
have there?"

And she dashed up to him, not noticing anything a
all odd about the trio beside him, because she wa
clearly infatuated with him and had not a thought fo
anything or anyone else. Marcus saw it as she move
closer to him, and wanted to pray that it would co

nue. Her infatuation just might save her life as well
his and Rafaella's. He gave her the sexiest smile he
uld dredge up.

"What have you got?" he asked again, and she
nded him a single sheet of paper, smiling shyly up
him, her very red lips parting a bit, her eyes never
aving his face even as he looked down and read. It
as an insurance form. He said to her, "I've already
id everything in cash. I don't have insurance here
France."

She looked blank; then her face flooded with color
d he knew at that moment that she knew and that
had been only an excuse to talk to him. She backed
and looked squarely into the woman's face. Marcus
ld his breath. The woman looked cold and hard and
e nurse said, flushing even more, "I'm sorry, truly,
very sorry—"

He smiled as he handed the paper back to her.
Thank you, but it isn't necessary. I'll see you later."
She turned and he heaved a sigh of relief, his eyes
mediately going to the gun beneath the cover
essed against Rafaella's left breast.

"Well done, Mr. O'Sullivan. You seem to collect
tle tarts, don't you?"

"Are you next?"

"Me? Sleep with you? A stupid, egotistical Irish-
an? The only thing on your brain is your cock. Now,
st as soon as that little slut is through staring at your
otch, we'll get out of here."

He nearly lost it; he wanted so badly to smash his
t in her face. His fingers flexed spasmodically. No,
, he had to keep his mouth shut.

Monique took one last furtive look at the American
e thought so handsome. It occurred to her now to
onder why they were moving Mr. O'Sullivan's wife
another hospital. It didn't make any sense. Mrs.
'Sullivan would be able to leave the hospital tomor-

row. Ah, what a lucky woman she was to have M
O'Sullivan for her husband. She frowned. It w:
strange. She saw Mr. O'Sullivan speaking to th
woman, and he seemed tense. They both seeme
angry. A doctor? Monique didn't recognize her. Sl
probably wouldn't ever see him again. She sudden
saw the woman's arm jerk. Her hand was under th
cover, touching Mrs. O'Sullivan. How very odd
looked. And Mr. O'Sullivan had said he'd see h
later. Did he mean he'd call her? Monique wasn't eve
sure he knew her name.

Over the Atlantic
April 2001

The private jet was spacious, with seats and tabl
along the right side of the cabin, several small sof;
along the left side, and enough room for Rafaella t
lie on her back, her legs stretched out comfortabl
There was a bedroom in the rear of the plane, b
Marcus had been told to put Rafaella on the floc
near the bulkhead. He supposed their captors didn
want them out of their sight. Rafaella was still uncor
scious from the drugs the woman had given her.

Marcus held her, his hand unconsciously rubbing t
and down her arm. He wanted her to open her eye
He was frightened, not for himself, oddly enough, n
for what awaited them, but for now, right this minut
because Rafaella continued so still and so deep
unconscious.

Marcus leaned back against the bulkhead and gent
laid her head on his thighs. He kept her well-covere
He watched one of the men serve himself a drink
the bar on the left side of the cabin. The other ma
was sitting on one of the sofas reading one of tho:
soldier-of-fortune magazines. The woman sat close
a chair opposite them, the gun in her hand. It was

38. He remembered Tulp's 9-mm and felt a slight che in his shoulder.

The ride from the hospital to a small private airfield ust to the north of Paris outside Neuilly had been amaz-ngly routine. The two men had simply lifted Rafaella ff the gurney outside the hospital in the parking lot, iven her to Marcus, and left the gurney and their white rderly coats there in an empty parking space. They lidn't care that anyone would notice, would wonder, vould question. They obviously didn't care because hey'd be out of the country very shortly. And then, f course, they'd driven to a private airfield, not more han thirty miles north, driven directly onto the tar-nac, and Marcus had carried Rafaella onto the pri-ate jet.

He realized now who had given the orders, who'd lone the planning, who'd settled on the personnel. It ad all the meticulous earmarks of a Giovanni opera-ion: smooth, flawless in execution, quiet, not a whis-er of fanfare, so very discreet.

Dominick had obviously found out about the paint-ng being stolen, since the media had announced it vorldwide, and he'd probably known who to call to ind out that it had been Charles Rutledge who'd ought it ten years before. And then he'd deduced hat Rafaella must somehow be involved, and thus Marcus, because he was with her and sleeping with er. They were undoubtedly being flown back to the Caribbean. To face whatever brand of music Domi-ick had decided they deserved.

Marcus looked down at Rafaella. He wanted her to vake up. He wanted to tell her he loved her, to tell her hat they would have a future together, that they would ever again have lies between them. He wanted to hold er, feel her warmth and her giving.

Rafaella was aware of a soft rumbling sound, a deep ibration that was continuous and soothing, and she ighed, hearing things more loudly now but not wanting to wake up. Somewhere in her subconscious she knew she wouldn't like it when she opened her eyes. She felt fingers on her arm, gently smoothing over her flesh, and she knew it was Marcus and she knew she had to come around soon or he would be worried about her.

She opened her eyes suddenly and stared up at his chin. He needed to shave. "Hi," she said, and was surprised at the hoarse quality of her voice.

"Hi, yourself," Marcus said, and looked down at her. His relief was palpable.

"I'm okay, Marcus, really. Tell me."

"Are you sure you want to know?"

"Might as well." She paused a moment, then said, "We're in a plane?"

He nodded, then told her what had happened, concisely, quietly. "We've probably got another eight hours or so until we get to Miami. I suppose we'll refuel there, but who knows? Maybe we'll just go directly to St. John's. You sure you feel all right?"

In that moment she knew she had a problem. She wanted to shake her head because she was so embarrassed, so humiliated. She saw the woman who'd faked being a nurse and she was just sitting there, looking toward them, her face impassive, ugly, and cold. "I'm bleeding."

Marcus automatically lifted the covers and looked down. He winced at the sight of the bright red blood smeared on the white sheet, soaked through her hospital nightgown.

"Is it normal bleeding or do you feel it rushing, like a hemorrhage?"

"Normal, I think."

"Okay. Do you want me to help you to the bathroom? How weak do you feel?"

"I'm okay. I'd like to bathe and dress too."

Marcus rose and leaned down to lift her up.

The woman straightened suddenly, raised her .38 and aimed it directly at Rafaella.

"I can't miss from this distance, Mr. O'Sullivan. What are you planning to do with her?"

"She needs to use the bathroom."

The woman looked at Rafaella's face a moment, then said, "Her suitcase is in the bedroom. I'll watch her while you get it and put it in the bathroom. Put her on the floor." Marcus moved quickly. When he returned, he pulled Rafaella to her feet. "You sure you'll be okay?"

The woman said, "She's bleeding on the white carpet. Get her to the bathroom." And when they walked past her, she added, "It would serve her right to bleed to death, stupid girl."

Marcus just stared at her.

The bathroom was a marvel. It was equipped with a shower, a bidet, a toilet, and a pink marble basin, and there was adequate space, with hooks to hang things on. And a rod that warmed the towels. Marcus left her at the door, his brows drawn together, not moving until the woman ordered him back. He still didn't move until he heard the sound of the shower.

He was getting worried. Fifteen minutes had passed. The shower had stopped eight minutes ago, not that he was looking at his watch every second. He sat on the floor, his back to the bulkhead, his knees bent and his arms wrapped around them. What to do? The first thing, he supposed, was to hear what Rafaella had to say.

When she came out of the bathroom, he stared at her, then broke into a wide smile. It was *his* Rafaella, healthy-looking and standing tall, her hair nearly dry and pulled back from her face and held with clips. She was wearing lipstick and dangly earrings, dark blue wool slacks, a blouse with a white sweater over it, and running shoes. "You look great," he said, and patted the spot beside him. "Don't tell me this outfit put you out eight hundred dollars."

"This is some of my old working-woman stuff, actu-

ally part of my bright-young-graduate-student persona.
With a pencil tucked behind my ear, it's perfect.''

The woman said nothing, just pointed the pistol at
them. The men were quiet too. They just watched,
drinks in their hands, not guns. Rafaella fell quiet.

When Marcus asked for lunch, it was provided
quickly by one of the men. "Drink all the orange
juice," he told Rafaella. "I remember reading some-
place it was good for anything that ailed you.''

They ate the ham-and-cheese sandwiches. The low
hum of the jets drowned out the noise from their three
captors. They could have been alone, but they weren't,
of course. Marcus held her hand, his eyes searching
her face for fatigue, for pain, but he saw none. He
said, "Did I tell you that I haven't had a single nightmare since you took over things?''

"What do you mean, took over things?''

"Well, since you took over me, inside and out.''

"I like the sound of that, kind of like I'm the boss.
What nightmare?''

He told her about his father, Chomper O'Sullivan,
a pallid man with fanatic eyes, whose only weapon
was a powerful pen, a father who couldn't toss a football but could quote famous remarks from all different
sorts of professional athletes. And how all he wanted
all his life was justice and fairness and how he'd been
murdered when Marcus had been eleven and his murderer was probably Carlo Carlucci but he'd been too
powerful, too protected, to be brought to justice.

"He was killed in front of me and my mom, shot
three times." And he told her how the dream had
started then, and sharpened, adding exquisite terror
over the years. And it had stayed with him until now.
He smiled at her and said, "Anyway, Rafe, for what
it's worth, that nightmare is dead and buried.''

"You've got a mom?''

He grinned and told her about Molly. "One tough
broad, my mom, and the biggest heart, almost as big

as her biceps, big mouth, all full of advice." He gave her more orange juice and another sandwich and watched her eyes begin to close. What she had to tell him about her stepfather and *Bathsheba* could wait. They had plenty of time. They weren't going anywhere for the moment. He wanted her strong again.

While she slept, Marcus did too. He wanted both of them to be as close to the top of their form as possible. He awoke to night, and the woman said to him, "You were stupid, Mr. O'Sullivan."

So she'd gotten bored with her two stooges and herself and she wanted to talk. How long had she been savoring that line?

"Could be," he said mildly. "Being the brain of the western world ain't all that easy."

"You shouldn't have screwed Mr. Giovanni."

"That's interesting. I don't suppose you'd know why he thinks I screwed him?"

She shook her head, but he could tell that she was angry because she hadn't been told what he'd done. She was a hired gun, nothing more. He wondered if she was free-lance. Whatever, she'd accomplished her assignment.

Dominick had moved with incredible speed. It was impressive, but Marcus didn't like being on the other end of all that impressiveness. He wondered who owned the jet. It wasn't Dominick's. Then he remembered Mario Calpas. He owned a jet, probably this one.

"Obviously it's got something to do with her." The .38 waved in Rafaella's direction. "He was very clear that he didn't want her killed. I guess he wants to do it. Was she his mistress first?"

"Nope, she's his biographer."

The woman snorted, a very unattractive sound. She wasn't a pleasant sort. It was after midnight. Marcus wished she'd just go to sleep.

So she'd had orders not to kill Rafaella. But Marcus

knew that if it had come down to it, the woman would have killed Rafaella without a blink, both of them in fact, and any other person who got in her way.

"She's a very good writer," he said.

"Bull. She wouldn't be lying there bleeding if she'd been writing."

"She's multitalented."

The woman snorted again.

"I don't suppose you had a sister who lived in Mannheim, named Tulp?"

"No."

"Oh, well, you look a bit like her."

She didn't tell him her name, which was just fine with Marcus. No, she held her tongue and turned to stare into the dark night from the window at her elbow.

When Rafaella woke, she had to go to the bathroom.

"You swear you're okay?"

"Yes," she said, and he believed her. He helped her up, aware that the woman was watching every move. Didn't she ever sleep? He waited outside the bathroom door.

He fetched them more food. When Rafaella came out of the washroom, he knew her well enough to realize that she was ready for business, any business. She'd nearly gotten it together again.

Rafaella drank down more orange juice. When she finished, she felt almost ready to take on the woman, who still sat there, holding the pistol at the ready, watching them. It was scary, that soulless stare of hers.

Rafaella looked at Marcus, then leaned toward him, her nose practically touching his, and whispered, "Dominick Giovanni is my father."

As a bombshell, it won highest marks. She'd never before seen him utterly speechless; in fact, she'd begun to believe that her suave, smooth-talking Marcus couldn't be caught off-guard, but she'd gotten him this time.

"My God," he said finally, and a black eyebrow shot up toward his hairline. "You've got to be making that up."

"My mother is married to Charles Winston Rutledge, just in case your brain hadn't leapt to make the connection."

"My God," he said again.

"Dominick doesn't even remember her. Her name is mine—Holland—but when he met her, Dominick knew her only as Margaret Pennington. She was—and still is—very rich, you see. Her aunt and uncle insisted that she use their name, to keep away men who wanted heiresses."

"Your eyes—damnation, your eyes. I thought they were familiar. They're the same color as Dominick's."

"I hope that's all I inherited from my dear father. My mother is lying in a coma because she was hit by Sylvia Carlucci Giovanni—that's what Charles was told. I can't buy it myself—the coincidence goes too far."

Marcus stared at her. "And here I thought my secrets would blow you out of the water. I'm not in your league."

"Just keep listening. It's hard even for me to believe it all. My mother wrote journals. I didn't know about them until after she'd been struck by Sylvia or whoever. Then I found them and read them all. That red book you saw beside me that first night on the beach? Well, that was one of her journals. It's so sad, Marcus, so sad. Anyway, Charles found out about the journals and read them too, nearly a year ago. I guess he decided to murder Dominick, get him out of her life once and for all. The painting *Bathsheba*—I suppose he saw a sort of irony in it, the king, himself, dispatching the man who had an incredible hold on the woman he, Charles the King, loved. That explanation would probably make a shrink cringe, but it's the best I can do.

"I just happened to see the painting a very long time ago, by accident. I didn't recognize it at the time, but it made an impression that finally came back to me. And that was when I made the connection. I couldn't tell you then, Marcus. He's my stepfather and—"

"I understand. Forget it. This is crazy, utterly crazy, but I still love you, and we'll get out of this somehow." Marcus took a deep breath. "Dominick will kill your stepfather."

"We must stop him."

"I hate to remind you, Ms. Holland, but you and I are also prisoners and our future isn't the brightest I would have planned for us. Dominick doubtless thinks you're in on the assassination attempts, but he doesn't know why. Which is why he didn't want you killed."

"We'll think of something, Marcus, we've got to."

"Yeah, just not at the moment. I want you to tell me everything, Rafe, don't leave anything out, not even a semicolon. But first hug me and tell me you can't live without me."

But it wasn't to be. Even as Rafaella put her arms around Marcus's waist, the woman said suddenly, her voice an odd mixture of envy and anger, "That's enough. Mr. O'Sullivan, move away from her. It isn't smart to let you two go on and on, because I can't hear what you're saying. If you want to tell her how cute she is, then do it in my hearing."

Marcus gave her a long look, then moved away. "Go to sleep, sweetheart," he said. "Dream of solutions while you're at it."

"And no nightmares for you, okay?"

Twenty-three

The two men stared at each other. Finally Dominick said, "Welcome to my island, Mr. Rutledge. I have heard a lot about you, of course, particularly from your lovely stepdaughter. Do sit down, sir. Do you mind if I ask your age?"

"Fifty-six," Charles said, staring at the man who'd betrayed Margaret, the man who'd killed his own wife, the man who'd made Charles's life a mockery. Margaret had never been all his own, and he'd known it deep down even before he'd found and read her journals, known there was someone else, a man who haunted her. This man, Dominick Giovanni, had always lurked there in the shadows of her mind, always locking Charles out. Charles wanted to kill Giovanni with his bare hands.

"I am fifty-seven."

Somehow that one year made Charles feel a bit better, which was, of course, ridiculous. "Why did you bring me here, Mr. Giovanni? And in such an unorthodox manner?" He looked over at Frank Lacy as he spoke.

"I believe you know quite well the answer to that, Mr. Rutledge. However, if you wish to begin the game in an obtuse fashion, well, in just a little while I'll accommodate you." He stared for a few more moments at Charles Winston Rutledge III and said aloud, "You must, among other things, tell me why you chose the name *Bathsheba*."

"What are you talking about?"

"Pretending ignorance at this stage is truly unworthy of you, Mr. Rutledge. The game is mine. This final match is mine. I have won. Now, why don't you accompany Merkel here. He will take care of you."

Merkel himself was still feeling tremors of shock. The man behind the assassination attempts—this educated easterner, his voice clipped and aggressive. Why? It made no sense, none at all.

Why did this man want Mr. Giovanni dead? Because he didn't like his name? Because Mr. Giovanni had stolen a painting he'd wanted? Merkel said nothing as he directed Mr. Rutledge to a guest room with an adjoining bath. He gave him fresh clothing, not telling him that the clothing belonged to Mr. Giovanni. The clothes would fit, except for the length of the trousers. Mr. Rutledge was the taller of the two.

Merkel left him and returned to the library to report to Mr. Giovanni. He drew to a halt outside the door at the sound of DeLorio's voice.

"*He's* behind the assassination attempts? He's *Bathsheba*? That old man? But why? What did you do to him?"

"That man is my age, DeLorio. He isn't an old man. His name is Charles Rutledge and he's a very wealthy American entrepreneur and newspaperman, and I don't know yet why he wants me dead. We will discover the truth shortly."

There was silence, and Merkel raised his hand to knock on the door, only to lower it again when DeLorio said in a low, vicious voice, "You can't pretend anymore that Grandfather gave me a pat on the head and two quarters. He left me millions. More than millions. All for me, and there's nothing you can do about it. I called Goldstein in Chicago. Yes, I found his phone number in your private book. He told me everything. And you had my mother killed, didn't you? You lied to me!"

Mr. Giovanni, his voice smooth and deadly: "Listen to me, boy, your mother died in an accident. I had nothing to do with it."

"I don't believe you."

"I'm your father, I rescued you from her. I also know about that girl you hurt in New York."

Merkel could practically see DeLorio turn white. His voice was suddenly shrill and high and scared. He didn't sound like a millionaire anymore. "She didn't die, I didn't really hurt her. She's fine now, not dead like my mother."

"No? Physical abuse and rape are frowned upon, you know, DeLorio."

DeLorio's voice was even thinner now. "Mother told me, she swore to me she'd never tell. She took care of it, she told me she did—and she never lied to me!—she paid off that girl's father, she's still paying him off. Except she can't now, can she, because you killed her."

"No, DeLorio, I told you, but I'll tell you again. Your mother's death was an accident."

Merkel backed away. He didn't want to hear any more. He turned around and saw Link standing only two feet away. From the look on Link's face, Merkel knew he'd heard it all as well.

"I don't want to stay here," Merkel said, and turned on his heel. He wasn't surprised that Mr. Giovanni knew about a girl DeLorio had brutalized in New York. Mr. Giovanni usually found out whatever he wanted to know. He'd found out all about Mr. Rutledge, hadn't he?

Link didn't have a chance to escape because the library door burst open at that moment and DeLorio rushed out, his face gray, his eyes wild and dilated. He pushed Link aside, nearly knocking him down, and ran up the stairs. And Link thought: *Poor Paula. No fun and games this time, just uncontrolled rage.*

"Come in, Link, do come in."

Link wanted to join Merkel, to get far away from the house. But he couldn't; he was a soldier, and this man was his colonel. He nodded and came into the library, shutting the door behind him.

"It would seem," Dominick said slowly, his brow puckered in thought, "that dear Sylvia protected De-Lorio, had protected him for years. Did you know about that incident in New York?"

Link shook his head. He wasn't surprised. He wasn't surprised about anything anymore. He was as sure as could be that Frank Lacy had killed Sylvia on Mr. Giovanni's orders, although Frank hadn't said anything. Then again, Frank never said anything. Frank wouldn't hesitate to tell DeLorio to his face that his mother had died in a tragic accident. Nor would Link, for that matter.

"It would appear that I misjudged Sylvia, at least in this instance."

Link wanted to puke. He said nothing.

"I can't let the boy have all that money, Link. I can't begin to imagine what he'd do with it, the kind of twisted power he'd wield with it. It's my responsibility to control him, to direct his steps. I can see that now, more than before. He's still immature; he needs my guidance. He just doesn't understand how to operate yet, how to deal well with the men in this business. He'd get into drugs, the young fool. He still doesn't think beyond his next lay or his next easy dollar."

Link knew well enough that it was the first thing DeLorio would do. All DeLorio saw in drug trafficking was the promise of quick and easy money, lots of it. Mr. Giovanni was right about that. As for sex, the kid had the sexual appetites of a healthy young bull.

Like Merkel, Link wanted to leave the island, go

far away, but he waited patiently to see what Mr. Giovanni wanted from him.

"Charles Rutledge," Dominick said, seeming to savor the man's name as he rubbed his hands together. "Frank did a good job of fetching him here. The man's scared to death. I can tell. He thinks he's such a patrician, so cold and in control of himself, but he'll talk soon enough, he'll break."

"He has every reason to be scared," Link said.

"He'll tell me everything. I can't wait to have him face his stepdaughter. Ah, Rafaella." His face hardened. "She betrayed me. Am I to be surrounded by traitors? And Marcus. I've given him everything—my trust, money, more freedom to do as he wished than one could imagine. And he disappointed me, failed me."

"You don't know that for certain yet, Mr. Giovanni. Maybe Miss Holland didn't know anything about *Bathsheba*, Marcus either."

"Oh, don't I, Link? He took Rafaella to London with him, didn't he? He's slept with her, seduced her as soon as she arrived at the resort. He was with her when they proved the Rembrandt painting to be a forgery. He was part of it, he had to be."

"That's true, sir, that he was there with her. But I don't understand why he and Miss Holland did it. If they were in on the *Bathsheba* thing, why would they want to announce it to the world? Why would Miss Holland want to tell the world that her stepfather was the man behind *Bathsheba*? Why would Marcus save your life? It doesn't make sense."

Dominick frowned, then shook his head. There was simply too much happening, too many outsize details, for him to keep everything straight. It was a good question, one for which he had no answer. "Perhaps Rafaella brought Marcus in on it after he took her to bed. They'll be arriving soon now. I'll ask them then."

Coco knocked lightly on the library door, then entered. She smiled at Link and turned her attention to Dominick.

"DeLorio left the house with Paula. She looked frightened, and DeLorio looked deranged, out of control. This wasn't one of their games. I'm afraid he'll hurt her badly."

"Who cares? She's failed me too, she's—"

"He's got to be stopped or he'll hurt her, maybe even kill her. What happened? What did you say to him?"

"I said nothing. Link, ask Frank to bring him back in, both him and Paula. Tell Lacy to make sure DeLorio doesn't hurt his wife."

Link nodded and left the library. When he told Lacy what Mr. Giovanni wanted, Lacy merely said that he hoped the girl was still alive when he found them.

"Well, Coco, you've seen our guest? Mr. Charles Winston Rutledge III?"

"No."

"You don't look pleased, Coco. He's *Bathsheba*, you know. Now he's mine. Frank took him so easily. You'd think the man would have taken precautions. Did he believe me stupid? Unable to discover who it was who had bought the Rembrandt? He was visiting his little tart when Frank got him. He believes he's such a well-bred patrician, his damned *noblesse oblige*—hell, like every other man, he has little tarts on the side."

Dominick skirted his desk and poured a brandy from the crystal decanter on the sideboard. "He isn't admitting a thing at the present, but I'm not worried. He'll come clean very soon. There are things I've got to know. Do you think Rafaella was in on the assassination attempts with him? That she was his inside plant, so to speak?"

Coco shrugged. "First of all, you're not completely certain that Mr. Rutledge is behind *Bathsheba*, much less that his stepdaughter is helping him. Nor that

Marcus is helping her. There are a lot of ifs. Too many ifs."

"And coincidences, my dear Coco? All these parts and pieces just coincidences? Happenstance? Shall we wallow in them and ignore that they will make a whole, a perfect and complete whole, once assembled properly?"

"No, we won't ignore anything. But you will wait and ask Rafaella and Marcus?"

"Yes, I'll wait. Where is Jiggs? I'd like some lemonade. While I wait, maybe I'll have him tell me some more stories about how things used to be on the island."

It was eight o'clock in the evening. The night was perfectly clear, the stars bright points of light overhead, the air sweet and fresh with the mingling flower scents and the salty tang of the Caribbean. The helicopter they'd changed over to in St. John's now hovered, then set down on the pad outside the house.

Four guards, heavily armed with Uzis, immediately surrounded the helicopter. Dominick emerged from the house, Coco with him.

Dominick called out, "Well done, Marta! Well done."

Marta, Marcus thought, the woman's name was Marta. Marta the Sadist. Tough as nails, stronger than a stevedore, mean as his mother's scarred tomcat, Clancy. Marcus turned and lifted Rafaella down from the helicopter cabin. She looked tired, but not that weary-sick-tired that had so worried him. He straightened and looked at Dominick.

"Why did you do this?" he asked. "And where in the name of insanity did you find *her*?"

Dominick came to within a foot of him and said, "You're a traitor. I brought you home to die a traitor's death. A firing squad."

Dominick nodded to Marta, and she backed up to

stand with the compound guards. Then he said
"You're a turncoat, Marcus. It pains me to have you
shot, but I have no choice."

"No trial? No hearing of the charges, no marching
out of the evidence against me?"

Dominick just smiled. "We'll see, Marcus." He
turned to Rafaella. "Hello, my dear. You've gravely
disappointed me as well. And Coco. You've disappointed her too."

"Anyone else I've disappointed? How about your
son? I'm to be shot too?"

"Perhaps. Come inside." He turned to the woman
and the two men. "Thank you, Marta. You did an
excellent job. Give my thanks to Olivier. I owe him
and I don't forget my debts."

Marcus stared at Dominick. Olivier! Had the man
called Dominick just because Marcus had refused to
give him Rafaella? Now Olivier was Dominick's con-
fidant and helper? He glanced toward Marta. Olivier?

Marcus supposed that he shouldn't be surprised by
anything now.

Merkel was standing in the front doorway. He nodded to Marcus but said nothing. Marcus raised a brow
but Merkel just looked away, saying, "Please come
into the library, Marcus, Miss Holland."

But Dominick was there before them, opening the
door, smiling at them, then stepping aside for them to
enter. "Do allow the lady to go first, Marcus."

Rafaella strode into the room; then stopped dead
in her tracks. Her stepfather was standing there
dressed in one of Dominick's white linen suits, looking
like a plantation owner whose trouser legs were too
short. He didn't look afraid, but when his eyes met
hers, she read suffering there.

"Oh, no," she said and with a small cry ran into
her stepfather's arms. "Oh, Charles, what happened?
He got you because I uncovered the Rembrandt fake!
I'm sorry, so sorry. It never occurred to me that he'd

know. It's my fault, dear God, I was so stupid. It's all my fault."

Charles just hugged her, but he was frowning over her head. "Who are you?"

"My name is Marcus Devlin, sir, and—"

"Don't you mean Marcus O'Sullivan?" Dominick interrupted smoothly. "It was stupid of you to use your real name in Paris. Marta told me you had. O'Sullivan. Very Irish. It allowed me to do some checking, Marcus. I should be hearing back very soon now. I'll strip your cover away and then we'll see how much of a traitor you really are."

Marcus freely admitted to himself that he'd been a fool, a colossal fool. But he hadn't thought, hadn't realized, that there could be any danger. It had been a hospital registration, nothing more, done just to protect Rafaella from the vultures of the press, and look what had happened—

"You'll be disappointed, Dominick," Marcus said. "There's not a thing to find out about me. I'm just a soldier, your soldier, and a damned good resort manager." He took Rafaella's hand and looked at her stepfather, in Dominick's clothes, complete with a pale blue silk handkerchief in the breast pocket of the white linen jacket. Even though the pants were too short, he still looked self-possessed and intelligent. "You're Mr. Rutledge?"

"Yes."

"Shall we all sit down?" Coco waved a hand toward the plush wicker furniture.

Dominick frowned at his mistress. "Rafaella, you will sit here, beside me."

"Why should she?"

Dominick's eyes narrowed on his mistress's face. "Because I said so. Come here, Rafaella."

Rafaella said nothing, merely sat beside him on the wicker love seat. She felt suddenly weak—she hated her body for betraying her—and afraid. Oh, yes, she was afraid. Dominick would kill all of them. And Charles, poor innocent Charles. She didn't care that he'd tried to kill Dominick. She didn't blame him for that for a moment. She just wished he'd succeeded. At the moment, he looked tightly controlled and oddly gallant.

"Now," said Dominick, "I see that we're all here."

"Where's DeLorio?" Marcus asked.

"I don't want him here. It's not necessary."

"Why not?"

This time Dominick openly frowned at Coco, who was sitting just across from him. "Why are you questioning me? You will be quiet or you will go to your room. You have no right to question me, now or ever."

Coco just looked at him, and said patiently, "Of course I have every right. I've lived with you for over three years. I've slept with you for over three years. I've pandered to your every whim for over three years. I've listened to you expound on the stupidity, the selfishness, the immorality, and the cupidity of women for over three years, their general uselessness except as vessels for men's seed. I've been faithful to you for over three years. And when you insisted, I even aborted a child for you three years ago because it was a girl and you only wanted a boy."

"Shut up, Coco!"

Coco smiled then, a cruel smile, vicious, and frighteningly sad at the same time. It was, Rafaella thought, insight hitting her, as if the dam had burst, and at long last she was seeing this woman without her mask.

"Ah, yes, I forgot that women were also rapacious and self-indulgent. Also, you made certain I wouldn't ever get pregnant again. You pretended you didn't know, but I found out that you did. That butcher of a doctor you hired told me when I saw him eight months ago. He told me that you'd told him to tie my tubes because you didn't want any more accidents and

I was getting too old for such risks. You couldn't take
a chance that I'd produce a Down's-syndrome child.
The doctor told me you'd acted so concerned, so loving, and you were just protecting my health."

"That's a lie! You will not speak of such things
now! You will get out of my sight!" Dominick jumped
to his feet, yelling. He was beyond caring that everyone was listening, and seeing him not as the suave
civilized man, smooth and controlled, but as a man
with anger—pale flesh, eyes dilated with rage. Coco
was looking up at him, insolence and contempt obvious in the way she'd crossed her arms over her breasts.
He said to her, his voice vicious, "I was going to tell
you that I was through with you. Oh, yes, just as soon
as Frank told me Sylvia was out of the way, I was
going to tell you to get out. That was my plan all
along."

"Why?"

That bloody word again! Dominick's eyes glazed
with fury. Blood pounded in his temples. He wanted
to kill her, stuff his fist in her mouth.

"Why?" she repeated. "You haven't already found
a sweet young thing to replace me, have you? Tell
me, Dominick, *why*?"

"Because I plan to marry Rafaella. You're too old
to give me children, to provide boys for my dynasty.
And you can't anyway—oh, yes, I made sure of that.
I didn't want any more whining from you, any more
inconvenience. You were a mistress, nothing more. My
mistress. You didn't have the right genetic makeup to
make the kind of children I wanted."

"Oh, you mean the kind of genes Sylvia had? The
kind of genes that produced DeLorio?"

"Shut up, damn you!"

"I suppose you'll have Frank kill me, just like you
had him kill Sylvia?"

"Get out!"

Coco didn't move. There was a moment of stunned silence.

Then there was laughter, stark, ugly laughter. It was frightening because it was so unexpected. It was Rafaella who was laughing, loud and raw, deep in her throat. Now she was throwing her head back and laughing harsher and deeper.

Dominick felt out of control, and he couldn't allow it to continue. He yelled, "Stop that!"

Rafaella looked at him, stopped, then hiccuped. She giggled. "Oh, dear, it's so funny."

"What's going on here? What's funny?"

Dominick's question was aimed at no one, so he didn't really expect an answer.

Then Rafaella said, "Sir, I wouldn't be your wife if you were the proverbial last man in creation. Marry you? That's a sick, very ugly joke."

Dominick's face darkened with blood. He knocked a chair from his path and stumbled toward her. "Let's just see, Rafaella. Let's just see. You've been screwing Marcus, and now you'll try me out. I'm better than he is, you'll see, he's just clumsy Irish scum. I'll make you love it, just like all my women have loved it—"

Rafaella felt Marcus tense, his body ready. She said easily, "That's what your son said. *He* said Marcus was nothing but a bungling bull compared to him. *He* said he was the world's greatest lover, that he'd teach me what pleasure was all about. That was before I kicked him in the groin, of course. Then he was a pathetic whimpering little boy. Something else he has in common with his father, I'll bet."

Marcus was ready to spring, quite ready to kill Dominick if he had to. Why was she pushing him like this? Why had Coco all of a sudden turned into a different woman, baiting him beyond his limits? Had the worm finally turned? He remembered the ugliness Rafaella had felt after the meeting with Olivier, her rage, her feeling of helplessness. Had Coco finally rebelled against being a possession, a thing? Merkel, Link, and three guards stood by the library door, their faces impassive, all except Merkel's. He looked both appalled and disgusted. What could Marcus do? The guards would mow him down in a second if he attacked Dominick. Their Uzi submachine guns were ready, stocks folded down.

In slow motion, colors soft and blurred and people's faces faded, all of it just like in his nightmare, Marcus saw Dominick reach out, so slowly, so precisely, to grab Rafaella's arm. Marcus said, his voice loud and cutting, "You can't sleep with your own daughter."

Time stopped. Dominick froze, staring down into Rafaella's face, into her pale blue eyes, eyes that shaded toward gray when feelings ran deep and strong.

Action teetered, spun out of control, speeded up, colors became distinct and raw and far too real. "No," Dominick said, but he dropped Rafaella's arm and took a step back. "No, Marcus, you're lying. She can't be my daughter. It's absurd. You're making it up."

Charles Rutledge said quietly, "No, he's not lying. Rafaella is your daughter, more's the pity. Her mother is my wife, a beautiful woman whom you seduced and betrayed a very long time ago."

Dominick suddenly straightened and walked to his desk. He kept his back to everyone. Then he said, not turning, "Just what is your mother's name, Rafaella?"

"You knew her as Margaret Pennington. You met her twenty years ago in 1975 in New Milford, Connecticut. You charmed her, wooed her, seduced her, lied to her, got her pregnant, and deserted her. Do you remember the five-thousand-dollar check you tossed on her hospital bed? After, of course, you discovered she'd given birth to a girl. And then you walked out and you never looked back. You miscalculated there. She was very rich, an heiress. That's why she didn't tell you her real name. Thank God, at least she didn't trust you all the way. I don't believe she's ever realized that even if she'd had a boy, you still wouldn't have left your wife. There were no threats then from Carlucci as yet, but Sylvia was pregnant, wasn't she? With DeLorio. And she was your legal wife, and Carlucci was rich and powerful beyond your wildest imaginings. Poor Mother. You fooled her to the very end, perhaps even into eternity.

"Would you like to know something else ironic? Sylvia, your wife, your now very dead wife, was possibly the drunk who hit my mother. She could be the one responsible for my mother being in a coma in the hospital. You betray my mother and your wife kills her. You're quite thorough, Dominick."

Dominick turned finally to Charles. He was in control again, calm, his voice quiet. "This is why you've tried to have me killed. You created this assassination squad to come here to the island to kill me. You tried again in Miami. You hate me because of what I did to your wife. But I still don't understand why you painted the word *Bathsheba* on the helicopter. What meaning does it have?"

Charles Winston Rutledge III looked from his stepdaughter to the man he wished dead. He looked at Coco, who slowly nodded at him, saying nothing now, but her eyes were clear and deep, accepting. Charles said slowly, his features expressionless, "I remember staring at that painting—it is one of the favorites in my collection—and thinking about Bathsheba, the woman. Who was she, really? What was she really like? She was, of course, the seduced woman, powerless, manipulated and used. But unlike Margaret, she hadn't been discarded; David had kept her, his obsession for her lasting an eternity. But you threw Margaret away and it was she who became obsessed—with you, a mirror image of a man, not whole, not complete. I liked the irony of it, I suppose. The man who'd had you killed was the man to gain Margaret's revenge for her, the man to free her from her obsession with you. I suppose that's why."

Charles turned to smile at Rafaella. "My stepdaughter knew nothing about it. I was gravely concerned when I discovered she'd come here. She did it on her own, without consulting me. She acted on impulse. She's completely innocent."

Charles shook his head, adding, "I didn't even know she'd ever seen the Rembrandt."

"I did see it once, a long time ago, in that special room you had, and then I finally remembered. I was stupid not to consider the consequences when I got the officials at the Louvre to have the painting authenticated. I'm sorry, Charles. Nor did I tell you about the biography. I didn't want you involved, you see."

"Ah," Coco said, smiling ironically toward her lover. "The biography. The infamous biography. I told you, Rafaella, that this wasn't a good time for you to be on the island."

"Biography?" Charles looked perplexed.

Rafaella said quietly, "I didn't want you to know. I didn't want to worry you, to involve you in any way. I was going to write his biography—oh, yes, Dominick, that was very true. It's just that I would have told the complete truth about you. Not all that sugar-coated rubbish you were telling me. None of that garbage about you being such a philanthropist, running all those drug-rehab programs. The world would have seen you as you truly are. A common criminal who sells guns to terrorists, a man who rivals Roddy Olivier in being dead inside."

Dominick looked toward Marcus, and frighteningly, he was smiling. "Well, are there more confessions? More demonstrations of hatred? You wanted a trial, a hearing, my dear Marcus, well, that's what has come to pass. Everyone has spilled his or her guts, even my dear Coco. Would you care to add to it?"

"No," Marcus said.

"I remember now," Dominick said suddenly. "I remember Margaret. She was so very young, so vulnerable—her parents had just been killed, you know—and she was so fresh and innocent, and yes, I wanted her. She looked a bit like Sylvia, isn't that an amusing coincidence?" He shook his head and turned to stare out the French windows. "Yes, so very beautiful she was, and she was ready to learn about life, about sex, and so I taught her. I didn't hurt her. I gave her a wonderful summer."

"You got her pregnant!"

"True, Rafaella, with you. Surely that was a good thing from your point of view. I had to tell her then that I was married. And then Sylvia was pregnant with DeLorio. It was complicated until Margaret birthed you, my dear, a girl. But I was fond of her for a while. And perhaps you're right. Perhaps I wouldn't have married her even if she'd presented me with twin boys. My father-in-law was powerful, was wealthy beyond my wildest dreams at that time. I saw him as above the law, as above God."

Rafaella said, "I wish she could see you, see you as you really are, right now, right here, surrounded by those you've hurt, by those you've used, by your mercenaries hired to keep you alive."

"Rafaella. That's a lovely name, my dear. Even if your mother had used Holland for her last name, I doubt I would have remembered her. One forgets, you know, particularly women." He paused a moment, then continued, his voice softer, more faraway, "I wish I hadn't learned you were my daughter until after I'd made love to you. I fear I view incest in the same way I view drugs. I'm irrevocably against both. You're quite lovely, Rafaella. I'm drawn to you, of course, because you're so like me. And you are, you know. I see that now. I wonder if I had made love to you whether Coco would have tried to kill you."

"No, Dom, I wouldn't have killed Rafaella. I would ave killed you. Slit your throat."

Dominick didn't rise to this bait; indeed, he ignored 'oco, and said, still looking out the French windows, Ah, look, here's Lacy, and he's got DeLorio with im. It looks like Frank had to rough the boy up a it. I'm sorry for that, but DeLorio must learn to gov- rn himself, must learn self-discipline."

"Are you really sorry?" Rafaella said. "DeLorio ants to be free of you, but you can't bear the ought. He's more like you than you think, Domi- ick, an ambitious little mobster, a—"

Dominick moved quickly, more quickly than Marcus uld react. Dominick slapped Rafaella hard, sending er head snapping back on her neck. Then Marcus as on him, his hands around his throat, and he was ghtening his grip, feeling the slack flesh of his neck umple and wrinkle beneath the pressure of his fin- ers, and he could feel the flexing of Dominick's roat muscles, hear the ugly gurgling sounds—

"Let him go, Marcus. Let him go." Merkel was be- ind him, speaking softly, speaking slowly, trying to ake him understand and stop, to get hold of himself. arcus felt Merkel's .357 Magnum in the small of is back.

Marcus understood finally, felt the blind rage re- ede. He didn't want to die for nothing, and that's hat it would be at this moment in time. He wouldn't e saving anybody, certainly not himself, not Rafaella. e eased his hands from Dominick's throat. He ushed him back, sent him stumbling into his desk. e watched him clutch at his throat, gently massage e bruised flesh.

There wasn't a sound in the room. Marcus turned Rafaella. "Are you all right?"

She nodded. Dominick's handprint was bright red n her cheek.

Frank Lacy ushered DeLorio past Merkel and Link

into the library. They stood staring at Dominick, ben
over his desk, his face blotched red, his throat muscle
working convulsively.

"Sir," Merkel said, striding toward him.

Dominick waved him back. "I'm all right." Hi
voice was a raw croak. Marcus smiled.

Then Dominick raised his eyes to Marcus's face. "
really cared about you, Marcus O'Sullivan, was nearl
ready to trust you completely. But you're nothing bu
ragpicking Irish scum. You'll die an exquisite deatl
for this. Yes, you will."

"Where's Paula?" Coco was on her feet now, facin
DeLorio, but she was speaking to Frank Lacy
"Where's Paula?"

"She fought me," DeLorio said, his voice sulky, hi
face sullen, his lips puckered like a child's. "Sh
wouldn't do what I told her to."

"She's hurt bad," Frank said. "I brought her back
She needs a doctor. One of the men took he
upstairs."

"No doctor," Dominick said. "Link, you go shoo
her up with morphine. That'll keep her quiet." Domi
nick then turned to DeLorio. "You were foolish, De
Lorio. You must learn to control your temper. Yo
need my help, and you will need it for a long time
You must trust me."

"Who cares? Paula's just a stupid girl, a greedy lit
tle whiner."

Coco's voice rang out, filled with cold laughter
"Doesn't that sound familiar, Dom? Doesn't tha
sound just like a chip off the old block?"

Marcus, unable to stop himself, said to Rafaella'
father, "You taught him everything he knows. Jus
look at him."

Dominick didn't say a word. He didn't even look a
Marcus. As he lunged forward, he hissed, "You'v
turned him against me, you bastard!" But it wasn'
Marcus he struck. His fist caught Rafaella hard agains

e jaw, and she crumpled. As her world was going
ack, she saw Marcus leap at Dominick, heard the
lling, saw the men dragging him off, saw those black
bmachine guns that could empty thirty-two-round
agazines in no time at all, saw so many of them,
ised, ready—

Twenty-four

Rafaella lay stunned on the floor, her breath hitching, her muscles throbbing from the fall. She heard the key turn in the lock, heard a guard's retreating footsteps.

Slowly she came up to her knees. Her head was still spinning from the blow. Dominick had caught her unawares and his fist had cleanly struck her jaw, sending her reeling backward.

She had been unconscious for only a moment, and the first thing she'd seen when she opened her eyes was Dominick fighting off Marcus. She had watched dumbly as Frank Lacy and three men dragged him off. Dominick had walked to him, pulled back his arm and sent his fist as hard as he could into Marcus's stomach. And Rafaella had cried out, "Hit me, you coward! I'm the one! Hit me, not him!"

Dominick had turned to her and said with a slight smile, "You will get what you deserve, Rafaella."

Rafaella decided against moving for a while. She was alone in her bedroom, locked in, to be kept from everyone else. For how long? She'd heard Dominick order that Marcus be taken to the toolshed. What would they do to him? Beat him? Kill him?

What about the rest of them? Were they to be separated as well? Taken singly out to be shot?

She shook her head again, but still didn't move. She prayed hard and fought off tears. When Dominick discovered Marcus was a government agent, what

uld he do? She heard a soft moan and realized it
s from her.

What to do?

She was scared, so very scared.

She heard a noise outside the French doors that
ve onto the balcony, and froze. Heavy brocade
apes were drawn over the glass doors to keep out
e harsh afternoon sun. She couldn't see a thing. Or
erson. Perhaps that was a shadow she saw, moving
althily, furtively. Then she heard a key turn in the
ck, and slowly, so slowly she thought she'd die of it,
e door eased open and the drapes fluttered toward
r. Any second now, whoever it was would pull back
e drapery. She jerked herself upright, preparing her-
lf physically and mentally.

She moved off to one side, out of the direct path
the doors.

A man slipped through the doors into the room,
aking not a sound, and he was one of the guards on
e compound, wearing the regulation fatigues, an
K-47 rifle slung over his shoulder and several clips
ammunition in a wide belt around his waist. He
s big and lanky and looked very strong. He was
earing a close-fitting cap and his head was lowered.
e looked much taller than most of the compound
ards. She didn't immediately recognize him, but she
sn't about to underestimate the danger.

Rafaella felt a moment of terror, then took a deep
eath, cried out, and kicked.

Dominick sat across from Charles Rutledge and
oco, an elegant Waterford crystal glass in his hand.
e was calm, in control of himself and of the situation.
e looked faintly interested as he said to Coco,
"ou've been working with him, haven't you, Coco?"
She nodded, looking toward Charles Rutledge as she
d so. He was smiling at her. She brought her eyes
ck to Dominick. Telling him that she'd been behind

Bathsheba, enjoying the pain on his face at her betray.
seeing his incredulity that an irrational woman cou
plan such a thing—She prayed it would give her fa
some dignity. It was well done of her, and despite h
terror, she knew it was right. She said now, "I on
wish Cavelli had killed you in Miami. But you intin
dated him, did the unexpected, forced him to kill th
poor girl. Then he panicked totally." Coco paused
moment, then continued, her voice low and vibra
and bitter, "Damn Marcus, he should have minded h
own business. Tulp would have had you that first tim
It was so perfectly set up. If only Marcus hadn't—'
"That's right, if only Marcus hadn't," Domini
said. "I also discovered just a short while ago th
Mario Calpas was in on it with you. He wants me o
of the way, the illiterate little fascist. He has visio
of running the show, using DeLorio as his front, h
stooge. I've sent Frank to Miami to take care of him
Charles could only stare at the man who looked lil
an aristocrat to the manor born, a man who seem
to exude gentility and charm until he spoke of murd
as though speaking of eliminating weeds in his garde
It was frightening, the calmness of it, the matter-c
factness of it.
"And those attempts on Rafaella's life? Those we
just efforts to get her off the island, to keep her sa
while you killed me?"
"Yes," Coco said, looking quickly toward Charle
"I never wanted to hurt her. You know that, Charle
I knew Marcus would bring the helicopter down wi
no problem. I was the one who fired at them on th
beach. As for the boa, well, my helper got a bit carri
away. I was sorry that was so close. I wanted her
leave, that was all. I just wanted to keep her safe.
did Marcus. That's why he took her to London."
The three of them fell silent. It was a tense silen
that wasn't broken for a long time. Charles was near

eady to yell when Giovanni said quietly, "Why, Coco? Why?"

She looked at him oddly. Hadn't he believed her before? "What I told you before was the truth. You murdered our child. Because I was pregnant with a girl, you forced me to have an abortion. Then you had that butcher fix me, like I was a cat to be spayed. And you were unfaithful, endlessly unfaithful. You never cared about me; I was just your high-class mistress, your property, your tart, to be what you wanted, to do what you told me to do. And then I discovered what you'd ordered that doctor to do to me. When I met Mr. Rutledge at the resort some seven months ago, we got close and I learned what you'd done to his wife. We ended up sharing things, we ended up planning to kill you, to rid our little part of the planet of you. I was so happy that he'd come to the resort to find me.

"His poor wife had become obsessed with you, and she hated her obsession and how it was weakening her and Charles and destroying what they could be together, and she hated you and she simply couldn't bear it anymore.

"You tried to destroy his wife and me, and so much of it was because of this delusional dream of founding a dynasty of little male clones." Coco laughed suddenly, a deep, rich laugh. "And you ended up with DeLorio, and you succeeded there. He's nearly a perfect copy of you, except for that sadistic streak in him that surfaces now and again. You've learned to control yours. Another thing, DeLorio will never believe that you were innocent of his mother's murder. Never."

To Charles's surprise, Dominick said nothing. He continued to look intently at his mistress, but he said nothing.

Charles rose. "I want to call Pine Hill Hospital. I want to see how my wife is doing."

Dominick looked at him as if surprised that he was

still there, and smiled. "As I recall, Margaret was very
enthusiastic in bed, out of bed, on the ground, in my
convertible, against a wall, wherever. It comes back to
me now, our first time together. It was summer and I
took her virginity in a field of flowers. I'd scouted
out the field earlier, of course. It was vastly romantic
particularly suited to an innocent and vulnerable girl
I taught her so many things. Her mouth was very well-
trained by the time I was through with her. At twenty
she was as accomplished as a woman of Coco's age
Not as talented as Coco, but still, she was good."

Charles wasn't used to violent emotion and the rage
that pulsed through him at Giovanni's words left him
shaken, ready to throw himself at Giovanni and pound
his face to a bloody pulp.

"Ah, yes, her beautiful mouth," Dominick continued, his voice dreamy with memory, yet, at the same
time, mocking. "Of all my women, she had the most
inventive style. Does she still?"

Charles stared at him, striving desperately for control. He was afraid that if he tried to speak, he'd leap
on the man, just as Marcus had done. Or he'd say
something and be struck down as Rafaella had been
so he held himself in check. It was the hardest thing
he'd ever done in his life. He said again, his voice
even and calm, "I would like to call my wife to see
how she's doing."

He saw the flash of annoyance in Giovanni's eyes
The man wasn't used to being ignored, wasn't used to
having his baiting remarks disregarded. Charles waited
now, his expression impassive. It was a bit easier
this time.

Dominick waved toward a phone and his voice was
peevish. "Call. Who cares?"

Charles dialed the number, waited for a good two
minutes until the connection had gone through. Then
he listened and was told that nothing had changed
Margaret was still in a coma, still unresponsive, al-

hough the doctors had done another CAT scan and ad seen some improvement. He told the nurse he vould be detained for a while—no, no, he didn't know ow long—and rang off.

"Thank you," he said to Giovanni, and took his seat gain. He wanted to relieve himself, but not badly nough yet to risk Giovanni's reaction to that. He'd noiced that the silent guard by the door had kept his rifle ointed at him during the entire phone conversation.

"As odd as it may seem to you, Mr. Rutledge,")ominick said now, "I really am sorry to have to kill ou. I understand why you wanted me—*want me*—lead. Some men feel deeply about a woman, very leeply indeed. I don't understand it, but there it is. 3ut you've lost. You're an amateur—of course you vould lose. But that woman you hired the first time—·ulp—she was good, very good. Did Coco help you ind her? And, as Coco said, Marcus did save my life.)f course he didn't do it out of love for me, out of oyalty. Oh, no, as I figure it, Marcus saved me beause he couldn't have me arrested for illegal gun ales unless he caught me doing it. He wanted me in ail, not dead."

"So you've found out about Marcus," Coco said.

"It wasn't difficult. It required just one phone call, ince I had his real name. He was working for the J.S. Customs Service. Were you in on it with him as vell, Coco?"

"No. I wish I had been, though. A pity. I had no dea what his real game was."

"Now, my dear, I would like to take you to bed ne last time. Come, Coco, we'll go upstairs now, this noment. This talk of Margaret and her skills has left ne lamentably horny, as the young people say so inel-·gantly but accurately. Mr. Rutledge can remain here ind contemplate what little future he has left."

To Charles's surprise, Coco rose without hesitation. Ie wondered if she intended to try to kill him in bed.

Would Giovanni have guards watching, even while he
had sex, to protect him from his mistress?

Dominick took Coco's arm, then turned at the door.
"Oh, yes, Mr. Rutledge, after you're gone, I promise
you I'll keep checking on Margaret. And if she comes
out of the coma, who knows? Perhaps I'll go back to
her, see how she's matured, see if you've kept her in
good form." He paused a moment, frowning. "You
know, when I was younger I wasn't as smooth with
women as I am now. I didn't lie to them, tell them
what they wanted to hear, except, of course, when I
still wanted them. It was a game, a pursuit, a chase.
Find the prey—an innocent in those days—and stalk
her. Margaret was too easy. But when it was over it
was over. That was my philosophy then. Perhaps I was
a bit rough with Margaret that last time I saw her.
She was very young. I can't really remember whether
or not I would have done something with her had she
birthed a boy. Who knows? I imagine, though, that I
did her a favor. The next man who tried to get her
into bed probably had a good deal of difficulty. Yes,
I did her a favor. I educated her well."

Charles said nothing. He knew now that to show
rage would only give Giovanni what he wanted. He
pointedly ignored the man, watching his frustration,
watching him leave finally, his hand clutching Coco's
arm. He was going to force her to have sex with him
and then kill her? Charles shook his head. Such a man
was beyond his comprehension. And what he'd said
about Margaret. He remembered her journal so well,
those first words she'd written. *He was a wonderful liar.
The best.* Ah, but only at the beginning. At the end
he'd ripped her apart viciously. And such contempt
he had for women. Jesus, half the human race. Any
other posture that was incomprehensible to Charles.

But then he thought of Claudia, of how he'd used
her and women before her to see to his pleasure; and

'd never questioned his right to use her, because
ter all, he'd paid her well.

Now it was too late. He'd never have the chance to
:al himself, to try to fix what he'd broken, to make
nends. He'd die on this miserable island. He'd never
:e Margaret again. He thought of Rafaella. She
adn't hurt anyone. And she would die too.

At least he'd done one good thing. Both he and
oco had done one very good thing.

Only one. It would have to be enough.

He lowered his face in his hands and wept.

Rafaella went for the intruder's throat. She was
st—fear made her very fast—she was right on target,
er moves sharp, but at the last moment the man
nged to his left, swung his arm out so fast it blurred,
d struck her leg away. Rafaella felt the jarring pain
' she twisted about to regain her balance. She cried
ut as the force of his blow sent her reeling back
ward the bed. She tried to ignore the pain, tried
) concentrate, reach deep inside herself. She whirled
out, her hands in position, presented her side, and
elled even as she leapt at him again.

To her utter surprise, he did a side roll onto the
oor, came up on his knees out of her reach, and said,
Dammit, don't kill me. I'm not here to hurt you—
m trying to be a hero. I'm trying to save you."

She heard his words, each one of them very dis-
nctly, but she'd already set herself into motion and
er forward momentum carried her to her target, and
was again only his fast reaction that saved him from
aving his kidneys kicked. He grabbed her leg, twisted
er, then came up quickly and pulled her against him,
rapping his arms around her chest.

He sounded less like a hero this time as he hissed
gainst her left ear, "Stop it. Believe me, I'm here to
ive you. I'm the bloody cavalry."

Rafaella was breathing hard from pain and fear and

weakness. How she hated the weakness. She coul
barely gasp out the words: "Who are you?"

"I'm John Savage, and you, I imagine, are Rafaell
Holland? The lady Marcus wants to—" He broke of
"Are you all right? You're shaking. Did I hurt yo
that last round?"

"No, I'm all right. I had a miscarriage a couple
days ago. I'm still a little bit weak. Let me go nov
all right? I won't try anything more. I believe you."

Savage turned her around even as he clasped he
under the arms and hauled her to her feet. She wa
frayed around the edges, to put it euphemistically. A
tually there were circles beneath her eyes, her ha
was a ratty mess, there was a purple bruise along he
jaw, and her clothes were wrinkled. And dear heaven
she was so pale. "Sit down," he said abruptly. A mi
carriage—He couldn't believe that Marcus would b
so uncaring, so stupid, as to get a woman pregnan
And here she was trying to take on a man singl-
handed.

Rafaella sat. She drew several deep breaths an
said, "Marcus is in the toolshed, outside in the con
pound. It's used for tools but its main purpose is as
jail for prisoners. What are you doing here? How di
you get up here? You're Marcus's partner, aren't yo
his first cousin?"

"Yes, ma'am. It's a pleasure to meet you." Savag
stuck out his hand and she took it. "We need to tal
now. You need to tell me everything I should kno
to get us out of here whole-hide."

"Mr. Savage, I was trying to figure a way out of th
mess and not doing such a great job of coming u
with ideas. You did say you were the cavalry?"

"Marcus said you were different," Savage sai
slowly. "He also said you were—well, never min
about that. Yes, I'm the cavalry—and my troops ar
just waiting for a signal to move in and try to clea
this mess up."

"Sit down, sir. Let me tell you what's going on. Then we can figure out what to do."

Marcus was sitting in muggy darkness, the smell of earth and manure and sweat strong in his nostrils, thinking so hard his brain was beginning to ache. He, of all people, knew the toolshed was escape-proof. One door, double-locked, a guard outside with a 9-mm Uzi submachine gun ready to blast away at the least provocation. No windows, and thick, thick walls. There were even cuffs fastened to chains embedded in the walls, but Merkel had spared him that.

What to do?

Dominick probably knew everything about him now, everything about everybody. Marcus had realized quickly enough that it was Coco who'd been working on the inside against Dominick. Odd that he hadn't seriously considered her before. He wondered again why, all of a sudden, she'd turned so viciously and so vocally against Dominick, telling him everything. As for Charles Rutledge, Marcus was still surprised that that very well-educated man, that very civilized and law-abiding man, had planned to assassinate another. But the provocation was great. More than great, it was perhaps inevitable, preordained.

It seemed that there was nothing more to be done now except stand in front of Dominick's firing squad and die with some sort of dignity. He shook his head violently. He was just too stupid to accept it, too much a romantic, he supposed, to roll over and let himself tolerate being killed.

He couldn't accept anything. He had somehow to save Rafaella, the woman he loved so much it almost hurt. It occurred to him that he might never see her again, and the pain was so great he nearly cried out. No, it wouldn't, couldn't end like that.

He couldn't get her white face out of his mind, or the ugly bruise that was beginning to darken along

her jaw where Dominick had struck. He knew if i
hadn't been for Merkel that first time, he'd have bee
killed on the spot. And that second time, well—H
rubbed his stomach, his muscles still sore from Domi
nick's blow. No, Dominick had decided he didn't wan
him dead just yet. Why? Marcus shook his head i
the dark.

It came to him then, quite unnecessarily, that Coc
had poisoned the Dutchmen who'd been locked in thi
shed, or maybe she had a henchman among the guards
The Dutchmen couldn't have had the poison on them
they had to have been body-searched. Hadn't it oc
curred to Dominick that someone on the inside ha
killed them? Had worked with Tulp to kill him? O
course it had occurred to Dominick. He was far from
stupid. He was biding his time. For something.

When Marcus heard the gentle thud of booted fee
hit the ground outside the shed, he thought: Anto
Rosch. He finally got here, finally alerted Hurle
Maybe, just maybe, we'll get out of this mess. H
wasn't all that sure, but at least something was hap
pening. He crouched next to the door and waited, no
making a sound.

"I'm not quite that crazy yet," Dominick said, look
ing down at his handiwork. "No, I'm not crazy enoug
to leave you free to stick a knife in me. You loo
quite lovely sprawled out like that with your arms an
legs tied. Very tempting."

He sat down beside Coco and looked at her breasts
He lightly pinched a nipple, forcing it to tighten. H
smiled as he saw her grimace, then slid his palm dow
over her flat belly to the dark pubic hair.

He found her flesh cold, unresponsive, but he didn'
care. He toyed with her a bit, watching her face al
the while. She hated what he was doing, but she wa
helpless.

Dominick rose and stood by the bed, looking dow

at her. She was waiting for him to rape her. He smiled. "Oh, no, Coco, I don't want you, ever again. But I'm gong to leave you here, my dear, all sprawled and open and tied down. My guards will enjoy you. And they'll be by, many of them, and they'll see you and you'll see them. Perhaps you'll even smile at them and try to talk them into freeing you. Who knows?"

He paused a moment, then spoke again, his voice shrill. "Damn you, I gave you everything a woman could want, everything! Except for that baby. And you turned on me just for that. You were getting too old anyway. I did protect you by having the doctor fix you. I didn't want you pregnant again. I didn't want any illegitimate children, and Sylvia was so very much alive." He paused, then suddenly leaned down, kissed her hard on the mouth, and rose again. He said nothing more. He turned and left the bedroom, leaving the door wide open.

Coco stared at the empty doorway. It would all be over in a short time now. She wouldn't have to suffer long. If she was lucky, maybe Hector would be one of the guards to come. He could free her or kill her, whatever her need was when he found her. She didn't cry; she'd fought hard, tried her best. She was sorry for the others, so very sorry.

Dominick was told by Link that DeLorio was waiting for him downstairs. He merely nodded and went to join his son.

Things were getting out of hand; he felt it in his gut. There were just too many chess pieces and he had to finish off the game once and for all. He had to move quickly now, get out of here intact. It was time to draw things to a close. It was time to end it. It was time to move on. He felt a leap of excitement. He wasn't too old to begin again. And he wasn't exactly poor. He thought of the eighty million dollars and change he had in the bank in the Caymans. No problem. He'd just set up elsewhere. He still had all his contacts. He knew now whom he could trust. And there was his son, his millionaire son, who would help his father get back in business. DeLorio would obey him. He was a good boy.

And all his betrayers, all his enemies, would soon be dead.

He did want Merkel with him, he needed Merkel. He found him in the living room, watching Charles Rutledge, just watching him, not saying a word.

"It's time to go, Merkel."

Merkel hesitated, and Dominick felt a frisson of dread. Merkel too? No, it wasn't possible.

"It's time, Merkel," he said again. "Past time. Everything's set. Let's go. Get Link. When Lacy is through with Calpas in Miami, he'll contact us."

Merkel looked at him, his clothes immaculate, his broad ugly face twisted with uncertainty. "All of them, Mr. Giovanni? Marcus? Miss Holland? Coco? Paula?"

"You needn't recite the list! Good God, Merkel, they're all our enemies. Think of them as foes, adversaries, to be gotten rid of, nothing more. It'll be fast, you know. It's not like we're going to line them up and shoot them in cold blood."

Merkel nodded. Dominick went one direction, Merkel the other.

Soon now, Dominick thought, soon it would be over and there would be no traces, nothing left.

Twenty-five

Rafaella found Coco naked on her bed, struggling to free herself. She looked, oddly, more furious than scared. She was muttering to herself, watching her wrists and ankles grow raw as she pulled and wrenched and twisted.

"It's all right, Coco, it's going to be all right. Marcus's friend is here with backup." She kept talking, nonsense now, as she untied Coco, rubbed feeling back into her wrists, and helped her dress.

Coco finally interrupted her, her voice harsh, "I wanted to kill him, but he knew it of course. And he did this. He hoped his guards would come by and finish me off. Thank you, Rafaella. Now, there's something no one knows. I found out by accident a long time ago. There are enough explosives to blow this compound out of existence. And I'll just bet you that's what Dominick plans. Killing all of us in cold blood just isn't his style. No, this way would be cleaner."

"Oh, God," Rafaella said. "He'd kill everyone? Even all his own men?" *Even his illegitimate daughter?* Rafaella wanted to laugh at herself. What did being his daughter matter?

"If I know him, and I do, he's probably in one of the helicopters right this minute. He's hoping, no doubt, to watch us all go up in a beautiful orange explosion. It's impersonal, it's clean. I'll also bet there aren't any more guards left in the house."

"Paula's in her room and she's unconscious. No one

else up here. Savage went to free Marcus in the tool-shed. Where's Charles?"

"Locked in the living room, the last I saw him. No, Dominick has doubtless ordered all the men outside—Jiggs, all the servants—and given them guns with orders to cut us down if we try to escape."

It was almost too much for Rafaella to take in. "Let's get ourselves armed and find Marcus and Savage."

When Rafaella heard the burst of submachine gun-fire coming from outside, she froze. Then absolute silence. How many bullets had been fired? Enough to kill twenty men? Thirty?

"Marcus," Rafaella whispered, shouldered the Ka-lashnikov, and ran outside, forgetting about Dominick's guards. There were four men lying sprawled on the ground, covered with blood. Blood everywhere. Rafaella swallowed. Marcus shouted at her, his voice frantic, "Rafe, get back into the house!"

Coco stepped forward and called out in her clear, now very midwestern voice, "Listen to me, all of you. Both Jiggs and Hector can tell you I'm not lying. Mr. Giovanni is going to blow up the compound. Maybe some of you remember when he had the explosives installed. He doesn't care about any of you. We're all loose ends to him, of no account at all. He just wants to get himself and DeLorio out of here safely. There's no reason for any of us to do any more killing. We've got to get out of here, and now, or we'll all die—and it won't matter who's friend or enemy."

Hector, a thin young man with thick black hair and a hairless face, stepped out of a side door. "She's right, let's get the hell out of here—to the other side of the island, where it's safe."

Silence. Then the low buzz of conversation as the guards argued. Rafaella heard Hector, his voice raised, telling them to stop wasting time, to stop everything, the bombs were ticking away.

And then it was over. The guards, including Hector, just melted away into the jungle.

"It was that easy," Marcus said under his breath as he stepped from behind a frangipani tree. He eyed the dead men who'd tried to kill him and Savage. "I don't believe it."

John Savage said from behind him, "Where are the explosives?"

Coco was already dashing into the house, yelling over her shoulder, "The swimming pool!"

Savage sprinted after her. Marcus grabbed Rafaella, hugged her tightly, and whispered against her temple, "We'll make it, Ms. Holland, I swear we'll make it. Then I plan for us to spend the next fifty years sharing a wonderfully boring life together."

Rafaella started to say that was a fine idea, but obscenely loud gunfire cut her off. "That must be Savage's men. I guess they just got the guards."

"Good. But Giovanni and DeLorio will get away." Marcus pointed. "Look!"

There were two helicopters climbing slowly above the trees. Dominick had obviously had the wrecked helicopter repaired. Marcus wished he had one of the Soviet RPG-7 rocket launchers. It would easily destroy a helicopter. The Czech Skorpion VZ-61 he'd taken off a dead guard was like an Israeli Uzi. It could take down twenty charging men, but no way did it have the range to bring down a helicopter.

Giovanni would get away. Clean. To set up shop somewhere else in the world. Was DeLorio in the other helicopter? Merkel? Link? He'd heard the guards outside the toolshed say that Frank Lacy had already been sent to Miami to take out Mario Calpas.

Marcus had failed, and it stuck raw and deep in his craw. His one and only big assignment, and he'd failed, blown it all to hell, just as they could all be blown to hell at any minute.

He grabbed Rafaella's hand and they ran through

the house, out onto the veranda facing the Olympic swimming pool. Savage was on his knees, ripping up tiles near the diving board, Coco working frantically beside him.

"Marcus, quick! I think the plastic is C-4. You know more about how to deal with the stuff than I do. We haven't got all that long before the whole thing blows. Giovanni's got it on a timer."

Marcus dropped to his knees beside Savage and studied the control unit. The wires—four different colors, all intertwined, as complicated as could be.

Rafaella read the digital red numbers over Marcus's shoulder. There was a goodly number of minutes left, but the controls looked so complex and intricate. She felt Marcus's tension building and wondered if the minutes left really meant anything, if just touching the wrong wire, pulling at the wrong switch, would send them to oblivion.

Marcus began talking. "Yeah, what we've got here is PETN mixed with an oily plasticizer. You see that, Savage? Yeah . . . nitrogen compounds . . . very professional, and I'm not, and those wires—it's got to be the green one, see, it's the one that's attached to the timer. You think that's right? I think that's the timer."

Coco snarled in his ear, "Just do it, Marcus, just do it!"

Savage didn't say a word, didn't move as he watched Marcus grip the wire firmly, wrap it around his fingers, then suddenly jerk it free. The four of them froze, waiting, waiting for the explosion, waiting for death. Nothing happened.

They continued silent, frozen in place. Still nothing. Marcus looked up to see the helicopters still hovering. So Dominick was waiting too. Rage exploded inside him.

Then he saw what Coco was clutching tightly against her chest—a SAM-7. The thing could bring down an airliner taking off. Marcus grabbed it from her, posi-

ioned himself on one knee, and quickly balanced the
antiaircraft missile on his right shoulder. It wasn't par-
icularly heavy or difficult to handle, but it wasn't all
hat accurate either. It required skill or luck to inflict
erious damage. If only the helicopters stayed low, if
only they continued to hover and give him a station-
ary target.

He had only one try; that was it.

He shaded his eyes, staring at the helicopters, and
hesitated. Suddenly there was a burst of automatic
fire and the tiles around the swimming pool exploded,
spewing shards everywhere. Marcus saw Rafaella grab
her arm, saw Coco and Savage hit the ground, saw
flower blossoms explode into bits of wild color. One
of the helicopters was firing on them. Dominick must
have realized that they'd neutralized the explosives.
More fire blasted around them. Then there was answering fire from Hurley's men, now coming out of
the trees surrounding the compound.

Marcus saw Hurley go down. He had no choice
now, not really. They were sitting ducks. Slowly he
balanced the missile again on his right shoulder, aiming carefully. Just one chance to bring them down.

He saw Dominick clearly piloting the lower helicopter, the one spraying them with fire. And just as
clearly he saw DeLorio hanging out the open cabin
window, the automatic in his arms; he mowed down
two men even as Marcus aimed the missile. Both father and son in the same helicopter; he didn't have to
decide which one to take down.

He prayed as he aimed the SAM, prayed that his
luck was in, and he fired.

He saw the disbelief on DeLorio's young face just
before the missile struck the helicopter, saw the automatic rifle fly out of his arms. He couldn't make out
Dominick, just saw the wild jerk of his body as the
missile struck. The helicopter exploded instantly into
ball of orange flame. It was an incredible sight, an

awesome sight, and more terrifying than Marcus could have imagined. It had been years since he'd seen a helicopter explode. Long ago, in western Austria.

The other helicopter was already out of range, veering off over the Caribbean, due west. Marcus thought he saw Merkel and Link in that one.

Coco looked up and said dispassionately, "It's over, Charles. It's all right now. The bastard's dead; DeLorio is dead. It's over for both you and Margaret."

Rafaella turned and saw her stepfather watching the flaming helicopter parts as they hit the water, splashing up thick veils of water that steamed and hissed with the impact. She got to her feet and ran into his arms.

Charles couldn't think of a thing to say. He hugged his stepdaughter. "I'm sorry, Rafaella."

"We're alive," she said, pulling back to look at his face, "and Mother will be all right soon now. I know it—no, it's just a scratch on my arm, don't worry."

Marcus looked over at Hurley, his shoulder being attended by one of his men. He'd have to try to deal with Hurley somehow. He'd failed; he hadn't managed to bring Dominick Giovanni to justice. And that had been the agreement. But God, he'd brought the bastard down, he'd sent him straight to hell, him and that lunatic son of his.

He thought of Uncle Morty. He'd best get to Hurley while he was still weak and thankful that Marcus had brought Giovanni down before Hurley and more of his men had been killed. But not just yet.

He looked at Rafaella and smiled. She walked right into his arms. Whatever happened with Hurley and the feds, she was his life, and life for both of them would be vastly different from now on.

He was kissing her when he heard Anton Rosch say to Ross Hurley, "He's Irish. The Irish always get the girl."

Epilogue

Pine Hill Hospital
Long Island, New York
April 2001

I dreamed he came to me last night. He took my hand and leaned down close to my face and said, "Hello, Margaret."

That was all he said for a very long time.

I wasn't surprised to see him, even though I suppose I should have been. Things are easy to accept in dreams.

I knew he was looking at me, and it seemed very odd that he would just stare without saying anything, until I realized that he hadn't seen me for twenty-six years.

A very long time for a woman. Too long.

But in my eyes he hadn't changed, because I'd watched him over the years, so often studied his photographs, so that the years had come easily, and altered him only gradually. He seemed untouched to me.

And then he started speaking, his voice low and tender, and he told me he'd met our daughter and how lovely she was.

Odd that I didn't wonder how he could have met Rafaella, his daughter. But he had; somehow I knew that was true.

He was silent again, but he didn't release my hand. I wished I could speak to him, perhaps even tell him how very sorry I was, but I realized that I wasn't sorry, no, I'd thought about it all very carefully for a very long time. No, I wasn't sorry. I did wish I could say something to him, but it was the sort of dream that is so very real but whose dreamer can't act, can't participate, can't speak. But I thought about what I'd say to him if I could speak. There were so many things, years upon years of things to say. Then I realized that as soon as I thought of these things; formulated them in my mind, they lessened in their importance until they were nothing at all. It was odd, but it was so.

And then he said, leaning down and kissing my mouth, "I must go, Margaret. I must leave now. Your life is yours again. It's over, finally over. It's time for you to wake up, Margaret. It's time for you to live."

And then, just as suddenly as he'd appeared in the dream, he was gone. In the time it took me to draw a breath, it was over and he had vanished. It was all blackness again, and I breathed slowly and deeply and wondered.

This time I knew he would be gone forever.

The Branches
Long Island, New York
April 2001

Charles Rutledge raised his champagne flute. "To Marcus and Rafaella O'Sullivan. May your lives be long and filled with joy."

"Just when does this joy part begin anyway?" Rafaella asked, poking her husband in the side.

He gave her a look that her stepbrother, Benjie, saw, and Benjie laughed deeply, then whispered something to his wife.

For a moment Marcus buried his face in her hair. "I love you so much it sometimes hurts—deep down inside me. I thank God for you, Rafaella."

"And I for you, Marcus Ryan O'Sullivan."

Marcus thought of their wedding ceremony in the small church in Maplewood on Long Island and how the minister had swelled with pride to see the overflowing pews. He'd beamed until he'd seen Punk, sporting a beautiful deep rose silk suit and matching deep rose stripe through her hair. But Coco, exquisite chic Coco, had smoothed it over, laying her white hand on the minister's black-sleeved arm, and he had nearly melted all over her. Charles had flown up many employees from Porto Bianco for the wedding and it was a raucous group who wished Marcus and his new bride well.

Ownership of the resort, and of the entire island, for that matter, wasn't really in question. Dominick Giovanni was dead, as was his only heir, DeLorio. But DeLorio had had a wife, and Paula would soon be a very wealthy young woman. Wealthy and wiser, Marcus hoped, silently wishing her luck. It was probable she would also eventually inherit all of Dominick's vast wealth as well. Marcus wondered if Paula would keep the resort and manage it herself.

Marcus still wondered where Merkel and Link had ended up. Probably as henchmen for another crook, since they didn't know anything else. Oddly enough, he wished them well, particularly Merkel. As for Lacy, he'd be an efficient assassin for another master.

After the minister had finished the ceremony, Marcus had asked Punk what she thought of Rafaella, and Punk, thoughtful under her deep rose stripe, said judiciously, "We didn't know you had it in you, boss." Then, turning to Marcus's new bride, she'd said, "But you know, Rafaella, I'll just bet *something* could be done with your hair—"

Ross Hurley, his arm in a sling, had also attended the ceremony, but thus far Marcus hadn't managed to cut a deal with him. Hurley would just look at him and say, "It doesn't change anything that you probably saved my life, Marcus; the bastard's dead, not in jail, which is what our deal was. Try again, O'Sullivan." But John Savage held out hope. Hurley would bend and mellow, Marcus would see. Besides, Hurley had just gotten a lead on the woman who'd led Uncle Morty into the paths of illegality. If they caught her, they'd forget all about Uncle Morty. And Charles tried his diplomatic best, plying Hurley with the best champagne from his cellars.

Marcus thought now of all the endless details to be gotten through before he and Rafaella could take off for Montreal—her choice—for their honeymoon. She'd firmly vetoed the Caribbean, England, France, as being too far away from her mother. Always, always, there was Margaret Rutledge, lying in the hospital, breathing calmly and smoothly and not opening her eyes.

Rafaella just wanted the reception to be over. The past week had been frenetic, with little time to just *be*, without the constant demands. She'd suggested to Charles initially that their wedding be small and the reception even smaller because of her mother, but he'd objected. "No, we'll celebrate in style, Rafaella. I've been telling your mother all about our preparations, all about your husband-to-be, all about your friends, and I've told her all about Punk's repertoire of colored hair stripes."

They'd put on the dog, as her Aunt Josie was wont to say. Rafaella turned to watch Al Holbein with Marcus's mother, Molly. The two of them were going at each other in fine style. In Rafaella's opinion, Al, for the first time in his adult life, didn't stand a chance.

Rafaella turned to see John Savage, a man loyal to his toes, a fellow who played Marcus's straight-man well and with such seriousness, except for that twinkle in his eye that Marcus never seemed to notice. A man so unlike Marcus, who charmed without trying. Yet the two of them were so closely attuned they many

mes didn't need to exchange words to share what
ey thought, what they felt. It was a good thing, Rafa-
lla thought, that she was so fond of John. She had a
eling he would be very much a part of her new life.
he turned her attention back to her brand-new hus-
and, listening as he spoke to Charles about the merits
f living in New York versus Boston versus Chicago.

Rafaella held back from their conversation for a few
inutes, then said blandly, "You know, I've decided
d like to try for anther Pulitzer and since it's a fact
at an investigative reporter really doesn't have a
ance working for a big newspaper, I've applied to
e Elk Point *Daily News* in South Dakota. What do
ou think, Marcus?"

Before Charles could stop laughing, the Rutledge
utler was at his side, speaking quietly.

ine Hill Hospital
ong Island, New York
pril 2001

watched Charles come into my room. He looked un-
rtain yet hopeful, so full of life and vibrant, and full
f love for me. I didn't really deserve it but he didn't
gree and I wasn't about to argue with him now.

And there was Rafaella, looking so beautiful in a
ress I'd never seen before, a pale pink knit dress—
nusual for her to wear something so outrageously de-
gner. She was wearing heels and her hair was beauti-
lly arranged—long and curly to her shoulders, not
lled back with two clips. And there was a man beside
r, a handsome man with a mobile face that was used
laughter. I could tell he was nice. And he wasn't so
d to look at either. It was her husband, Marcus.
harles had spoken of him throughout the past week.

Suddenly they were all speaking to me and they were
ughing and talking all at once and Charles was kiss-

ing me and Rafaella was hugging me and the man wa
standing back, silent but looking very pleased.

   And it was then that I realized that this was what lif
had to offer, a simple, straightforward reality, and i
was wonderful. This was where I belonged. I've beer
given another chance. And Dominick Giovanni wa
gone forever. I'd known it when the dream had ended

   He was gone because my dear friend Coco had fol
lowed through and managed to kill him.

   How Coco and I had talked and she'd told me hov
she'd discovered that Dominick had had the doctor ti
her tubes after the abortion. I saw her pain and knev
it was nearly as great as mine. We planned and we'
come to trust each other. I had the money and she ha
the contacts. I knew she'd succeeded. Coco would al
ways succeed in what she determined to do. And be
tween us, we killed him, once and for all, and forever

   I thought about Bathsheba and my absurd serendip
ity. I'd loved that painting so, looking at it every da
since Charles had obtained it for my wedding presen
eleven years ago. And when Coco and I had decide
we would have Dominick assassinated, I wanted to us
Bathsheba as our code, so I would never forget why
wanted Dominick to die. Bathsheba, that poor woma
who'd been desired by a king and whose husband ha
been forced to his death by that king. Only the kin
hadn't betrayed Bathsheba, no, he'd kept her until hi
death. And I'd loved the irony of it. The simplicity of i

   Perhaps Dominick was still a ghost, a phantom, bu
he was no longer of this earth, no longer to be part o
my life. The future was mine alone, free and unfettere
from the bitterness of the past.

   Words from a song in Les Miserables came into m
mind. Something about "loving another person is lik
seeing the face of God." There was something to tha
a lot of something. Even that ridiculous accident n
longer seemed important. I'd been driving near Sylvia'
house—I couldn't seem to stay away from her—afte

*l, she was a part of his life still, even though it was
atred that was their bond, hatred and marriage vows.
nd that night her young lover, Tommy was his name,
as high on coke as he spun out of her drive, and he
as laughing and whooping to the moon and driving
ke a wildman and he hit me and I saw him clearly
hen he hit me and I couldn't believe the irony of it.*

*None of it is important any longer. I smile now at
y husband. Such a beautiful man and he's mine and
yal and steadfast and he will never hurt me.*

*And I will never hurt him, ever again. I know he's
nsed there was another man and he's felt helpless
ecause he also knew this man was deep in my mind.*

*That man is gone and Charles will come to realize
at. I'll make sure of it. And he's proved to me that
m the only woman in his life. He'd broken off with
s mistress, Claudia, many months before.*

And Margaret said, "Hello, Charles. I love you."